C0-AUQ-964

THE VIRGIN GODDESS

STUDIES

IN THE HISTORY OF RELIGIONS

(*NUMEN* BOOKSERIES)

EDITED BY

H.G. KIPPENBERG • E.T. LAWSON

VOLUME LIX

THE VIRGIN GODDESS

STUDIES IN
THE PAGAN AND CHRISTIAN ROOTS OF MARIOLOGY

BY

STEPHEN BENKO

E.J. BRILL
LEIDEN • NEW YORK • KÖLN
1993

The paper in this book meets the guidelines for permanence and durability of the Committee on Production Guidelines for Book Longevity of the Council on Library Resources.

BT
612
.B46
1993

Library of Congress Cataloging-in-Publication Data

Benko, Stephen, 1924-
    The virgin goddess: studies in the pagan and Christian roots of Mariology / by Stephen Benko.
        p.   cm.—(Studies in the history of religions, ISSN 0169-8834; v. 59)
    Includes bibliographical references and index.
    ISBN 9004097473
    1. Mary, Blessed Virgin, Saint—History of doctrines—Early church, ca. 60-300. 2. Goddesses—Rome. 3. Christianity and other religions—Roman. 4. Rome—Religion. I. Title. II. Series: Studies in the history of religions; 59.
BT612.B46   1993
232.91—dc20   92-44596
                                                                                    CIP

ISSN   0169-8834
ISBN   90 04 09747 3

© *Copyright 1993 by E.J. Brill, Leiden, The Netherlands*

All rights reserved. No part of this publication may be reproduced, translated, stored in a retrieval system, or transmitted in any form or by any means, electronic, mechanical, photocopying, recording or otherwise, without prior written permission of the publisher.

Authorization to photocopy items for internal or personal use is granted by E.J. Brill provided that the appropriate fees are paid directly to Copyright Clearance Center, 27 Congress Street, SALEM MA 01970, USA. Fees are subject to change.

PRINTED IN THE NETHERLANDS

CONTENTS

LIST OF ILLUSTRATIONS

1. Königin der Nacht. (The Queen of the Night, surrounded by the starry sky as a robe. Stage design for Mozart's Zauberflöte, Berlin, 1823. Deutsches Theatermuseum, München.)
2. Mary "clothed with the sun with the moon under her feet." Albert Glockendon (Nurnberg, 1545) Gebetbuch des Herzogs Wilhelm IV v. Bayern (Reprinted by permission of the Österreichische Nationalbibliothek, Wien.)
3. Black Madonna of Czestochowa. (Reprinted by permission of the Kunst-verlag Maria Laach.)
4. Dressed statue of the Virgin with crown. Lindenholz, ca. 1150. Benediktiner Priorat, Mariazell. (Reprinted by permission of Foto Kuss, Mariazell.)
5. Cake-mould from the palace of Mari (Mesopotamia) for making cakes in the form of Ishtar. (Reprinted by permission of the Réunion des musées nationaux Paris.)
6. Stamp of a physician with the imprint ΥΓΕΙΑ. (Reprinted by permission of the Historisches Museum, Basel.)
7. Modern roman catholic eucharistic host with the chi-rho motiv.
8. Hungarian roman catholic church Csiksomlyo, Transsylvania; Madonna crowned with twelve stars — on her right S. Peter, left S. Paul, at her feet S. Francis and S. Dominic.

ABBREVIATIONS

AAS	Acta Apostolicae Sedis
ANF	Ante Nicene Fathers. Reprint by Eerdmans, 1951.
ANRW	Aufstieg und Niedergang der römischen Welt. Edited by A. Temporini and W. Haase. Berlin, de Gruyter. (Volumes still being published).
CSEL	Corpus Scriptorum Ecclesiasticorum Latinorum, 1866 ff.
ER	Encyclopedia of Religions.
GCS	Die griechischen christlichen Schriftsteller der ersten drei Jahrhunderte.
LCL	Loeb Classical Library.
MPG	Migne, Patrologia Series Graeca.
MPL	Migne, Patrologia Series Latina.
NPNF	Nicene and Post Nicene Fathers. Reprint by Eerdmans, 1951.
PAULY	Pauly-Wissowa-Kroll, Realencyclopaedie.
RAC	Reallexikon für Antike und Christentum 1941 ff.
RGG	Die Religion in Geschichte und Gegenwart, 3rd edition.
SHA	Scriptores Historiae Augustae.

Theol. Realenc. Theologische Realencyclopaedie.

CHAPTER ONE

THE PAGAN GODDESS AS A CONCERN FOR CHRISTIAN THEOLOGY

During the sixteenth century Reformation, Protestants accused the Roman Catholic Church of harboring ideas and practices which had been taken over from the Greco-Roman world. This was considered to be a serious charge, since the goal of Christianity, so the accusers claimed, was to replace paganism with the *vera religio* (true religion), not to continue it under a different name. The often crude and aggressive attacks by Protestants, especially during the era when polemics was a favorite discipline,[1] were strongly countered by Roman Catholic scholars. No area of Roman Catholic theology has received more attention in this debate than the role accorded and the devotion paid to the Virgin Mary. The literature on this topic is so extensive that it is nearly unmanageable,[2] but even a casual acquaintance with Protestant criticism of Mariology reveals that it is in this particular area that the charge of "paganism" is most often heard. However, according to the learned professor R. J. Zwi Werblowsky, every religion is many religions.[3] Therefore, the discovery of elements

---

[1] One example may be Karl von Hase, *Handbuch der Protestantischen Polemik gegen die Römisch Katholische Kirche*, 6th ed., Leipzig: Breitkopf und Härtel, 1894. This is a very scholarly but quite aggressive and often sarcastic book. For a brief review of Roman Catholic criticism of Protestantism, see Franz J. Leenhard, *Der Protestantismus im Urteil der römisch katholischen Kirche*, Zürich: Zwingli Verlag, 1943. Although written by a Protestant, with an introduction by no less a person than Emil Brunner, this book is still a fair and representative collection of sources. To pursue the literature of polemics any further would be an amusing but outdated exercise.

[2] Those interested may look at the bibliography of Stephen Benko, *Protestants, Catholics and Mary*, Philadelphia: Judson Press, 1969, and S. Benko, "An Intellectual History of Changing Protestant Attitudes Towards Mariology Between 1950 and 1967," *Ephemerides Mariologicae* 24 (1974) 211-226. An excellent bibliography is also given in Walter Delius, *Geschichte der Marienverehrung*, München/Basel: Reinhardt, 1963. The list of publications continues.

[3] R. J. Zwi Werblowsky, "Synkretismus in der Religionsgeschichte," in *Synkretismus in den Religionen Zentralasiens*, Wiesbaden: O. Harrassowitz, 1987, p. 2, with reference to the famous Dutch scholar, the late Gerardus Van Der Leeuw. See also W. K. C. Guthrie, *The Greeks and Their Gods*, Boston: Beacon

of our pagan past in the Christian religion should not surprise us.

In its veneration of the Virgin Mary, not only did Roman Catholic Christianity absorb many elements of the cults of Greek and Roman goddesses, but Mary in effect replaced these deities and continued them in a Christian form. This is the view to which the Jesuit scholar Karl Prümm responded in his book *Der Christliche Glaube und die altheidnische Welt.*[4] Prümm investigated the similarities between the ancient goddesses and Mary and quoted many scholars who asserted that in Mary the ancient "mother of the gods" had returned in new glory. After reviewing these mother goddesses and discussing extensively the philosophy of their cults, he concluded that the Marian dogma cannot be deduced from pagan precedents and, furthermore, it was not even encouraged, promoted, or sidetracked by them for one simple and obvious reason: the fundamental principle of Mariology is the motherhood of Mary and this is the greatest argument supporting the full humanity of Jesus. Consequently, Mary could never have been and could never become a goddess in the pagan sense because this would remove one of the two major pillars upon which all orthodox Christian theology rests.[5] Prümm's logic is impeccable, and his statement that the basic principle of Mariology is the motherhood of Mary is undeniable: all later Mariological dogmas and theses are based on this principle.[6] And yet one wonders why he found it necessary to research the history of the mother goddesses and to refute and deny any connection between them

---

Press, 1955, p. 176: "A living religion is a stone of many facets, any one of which can be turned to face the light while the gleam of the others is dulled by shadow: nor is the possessor necessarily conscious that the stone has turned in his hands."

[4] Karl Prümm, *Der Christliche Glaube und die altheidnische Welt*, 2 vols., Leipzig: Jakob Hegner, 1935. Chap. VII in vol. 1, pp. 285-333, is entitled "Die Muttergottes des Christentums und die Muttergöttinnen des Heidentums."

[5] *Ibid.*, p. 328: "Somit liegt kein Anzeichen dafür vor dass die geradlinige Entwickelung des Marianischen Dogmas durch seitliche Anstösse die von heidnischen Anschauungen ausgegangen waren befördert gescheiwge denn gestört worden sei. Menschlich gesprochen lag die grosse Hemmung gegenüber jeden Abgleiten vom Gedenken an die Person Maria zur Vorstellung heidnischer Göttinnen darin dass eben die Marianische Grundtatsache ihr Mutterverhältnis zu Jesus vorzugsweise zum Erweis der wahren Menschheit des Herrn Auswertung fand; Diese Blickrichtung musste davor bewahren Maria jemals auf die Ebene des Göttlichen zu erheben."

[6] See Benko, *Protestants, Catholics and Mary,* chap. 11.

and Mary so extensively if he did not have reasons to believe that such connections might exist.

A similar view concerning the origin of Mariology was forwarded from an unexpected side. Leonhard Fendt, in his *Gnostische Mysterien. Ein Beitrag zur Geschichte des Christlichen Gottesdienstes,*[7] investigated the Gnostic communion feasts and compared them with Christian developments. In discussing the Gnostic Markos, he analyzed the role of Markos' "Charis," whom Fendt called "a Hellenistic form of the mother of gods."[8] This led him to explore the role of Mary in orthodox Christian theology as contrasted with the female figures in Gnostic systems;[9] he concluded that the cult of Mary grew out of Christianity quite independently. Fendt specifically rejected the possibility that the cult of Mary had anything to do with the syncretistic cult of the Great Mother.[10] But he, too, was faced with problems: the Kollyridians, for example, about whom he could say only that they were an exception and an isolated phenomenon, identified Mary with the Great Mother. He also quoted a number of Ophite hymns from Origen, *Contra Celsum* 6.31, "which could be in a Catholic prayer book if one replaces 'Charis' with 'Mary.'"[11] Fendt's book is so rich in insights that even now, sixty-five years after its publication, it is still widely read. In this book, Fendt concluded that

---

[7] Leonhard Fendt, *Gnostische Mysterien. Ein Beitrag zur Geschichte des Christlichen Gottesdienstes,* München: Kaiser Verlag, 1922.

[8] *Ibid.,* p. 41.

[9] *Ibid.,* pp. 79-83, n. 22.

[10] *Ibid.:* "Der Marienkult ist aus dem Christentum selbstandig erwachsen" (p. 81). "An ein Herauswachsen des Marienkults aus dem Kult der Grossen Mutter ist also nicht zu denken" (p. 80). Similar statements occur occasionally in Roman Catholic Mariologies, e.g., P. G. M. Roschini, *Maria Santissima Nella Storia Della Salvezza,* 4 vols., Isola Del Liri: Editrice M. Pisani, 1969, who compares the veneration of pagan goddesses and that of Mary and concludes that the cult of Mary comes directly from scripture and tradition: "Il culto di Maria deriva unicamente, come da limpida fonte, dall idea grandiosa che di Lei offrono la S. Scrittura e la tradiozione apostolica" (vol. 4, pp. 53-54). Our question is: Where does tradition come from? See also Gregory Alastruey, *The Blessed Virgin Mary,* 2 vols., St. Louis, Mo.: B. Herder, 1964: "Mary's cult differs absolutely from any pagan cult, and it is neither essentially nor accidentally derived from it." The author, however, acknowledges that many superficial similarities exist (vol. 2, pp. 259-269). Further literature on the subject includes J. Danielou, "Le culte Marial et le paganisme," in *Maria,* ed. P. Du Manoir, Paris: Beauchesne, 1949, vol. 1, pp. 159-181.

[11] Fendt, *op . cit .,* p . 80.

while there is nothing new under the sun, new things can come into the world from above and this is exactly what happened in the case of Jesus Christ. Therefore, the cult of the Madonna is also something new and different from the pagan cults because of the Spirit of Jesus.[12] That is the reason, Fendt said, why Catholics refuse to be called the revivers of the cults of the mother of the gods.

Today, however, one would be hard put to find any secular historian or historian of religion who would make the fine distinction proposed by such distinguished scholars as Prümm and Fendt. Almost all authors quoted in the present volume in connection with this particular theme would point to Marian piety as the natural outgrowth of the goddess-cults in the ancient world. But just what is the connection? Is it correct to say that the cult of the Virgin was merely "influenced by pagan practices," or that it simply "absorbed" and "assimilated" some ideas that were current among people who embraced Christianity? To point out similarities, interesting parallels between the cults of fertility goddesses and the cult of Mary, would be a waste of time because it would not demonstrate anything that has not been known in the past. But I hope to show that there were powerful causative influences from Greco-Roman religions that shaped the form of Mariology. The biblical roots of Mariology have been sufficiently analyzed; I intend to inquire into some extra-biblical sources of Marian piety, belief, and doctrine. I propose that there is a direct line, unbroken and clearly discernible, from the goddess-cults of the ancients to the reverence paid and eventually the cult accorded to the Virgin Mary. This cult I shall call "Mariology" (by a slight extension of the term) as distinct from "Mariolatry," the excessive worship of Mary as a supernatural power in her own right. I propose, therefore, that Mariology does not simply resemble pagan customs and ideas, but that it is paganism baptized, pure and simple. I am fully aware that this is a controversial statement and may generate some spirited opposition, so I should like to point out that most of our ancestors in the Christian faith were baptized pagans; from the second century on, Jewish converts seem to have been relatively few.

My studies have brought me to the conclusion that in Mario-

---

[12] *Ibid.*, p. 82.

logy the Christian genius preserved and transformed some of the best and noblest ideas that paganism developed before it. Rather than being a "regression" into paganism, Mariology is a progression toward a clearer and better understanding of the feminine aspect of the divine and the role of the female in the history of salvation. Of course, over the centuries there were many aberrations into Mariolatry, but this does not mean that in its basic principle Mariology is a superstition. On the contrary, I hope to show that Mariology is a necessary part of Christianity. In Marian piety, the Christian Church did not simply adopt the pagan structures and forms of worship of the Mother Goddess. In this sense, Prümm, Fendt, and other defenders of the exclusively Christian origins of Mariology are correct: Mariology is not the same as the worship of Cybele or Isis or Caelestis. If this were indeed the case, then Mariology would be outdated, archaic, and irrelevant: there is no place today for *maenads* or for the celebration of an *orgia*, to mention only two examples. Christianity did not simply adopt pagan ideas and cult practices, but transformed them by merging them with elements peculiar to itself.

The cult of the Mother Goddess entered the Christian Church in typically Christian categories, such as the *Ecclesia*, represented as the spiritual mother of Christians, or as "the Second Eve," whose divine motherhood is responsible for mankind's rebirth. It was through such Christian concepts that the idea of the divine feminine took root in Christianity, and it was a long and often confusing process until Mary was declared to be the Mother of God. But it is the primordial mystery of generation and childbirth, the appearance of life, and the age-old belief that motherhood is part of a cosmic order upon which both the pagan and the Christian versions of the cult of the *theotokos* rest. This reverence for motherhood and childbirth is the basic principle of Mariology, a principle which Christianity inherited from its pagan forerunners.

Veneration of motherhood brings us to the fact of sexual differentiation and the question of the relation of male and female to each other. The universal human experiences of sex, generation, fatherhood, and motherhood, when viewed *sub specie aeternitatis*, become ingredients of the divine order. Here the contribution of Mariology is considerable. Let us look briefly at some of the issues involved.

1. We cannot say "male" without at the same time saying "female." This is obvious, yet in Christian theology, the image of God that emerged from Judaism is of a God solely male. Even in its Trinitarian form (Father, Son and Holy Spirit), it is, at least in Latin Christianity, an exclusively male God, since the Holy Spirit is a "he": the word *spiritus* in Latin is a masculine noun.[13] This

[13] In Greek it is neuter *(pneuma)* and in Hebrew it is feminine *(ruah)*. Recent feminist concerns focused attention on this problem. See, among others, Phyllis Trible, *God and the Rhetoric of Sexuality*, Philadelphia: Fortress, 1978; Leonard Swidler, *Biblical Affirmations of Woman*, Philadelphia: Westminster, 1979. Andrew M. Greely, *The Mary Myth. On the Feminity of God*, New York: Seabury Press, 1917, chap. 3, "The Androgyny of God," pp. 49-72, developed this theme and stated, "God is both masculine and feminine and may well have been thought of as a woman long before she/he was ever thought of as male" (p. 49). Greely proposed that Mary should be regarded as the "symbol of the feminine component of the deity" (p. 13) because she "reveals the tender, gentle, comforting, reassuring, 'feminine' dimension of God" (p. 17). "Mary is the Catholic Christian religion's symbol which reveals to us that the Ultimate is androgynous, that in God there is both male and female ... She reveals to us the feminine dimensions of the Christian God, and at the same time reinforces our perceptions of all things, including ourselves, as androgynous in some fashion" (pp. 216-217). See also p. 87 on his ideas about the androgyny of Jesus. But Greely falls short of acknowledging Mary as a goddess, although he admits that "Mary ... is part of a great tradition of female deities, all of whom reflect the human condition that God has feminine as well as masculine characteristics" (p. 13). "Mary reveals, as do all goddesses, the feminine aspect of the deity" (p. 36). Yet Mary is different (p. 71). Greely was not the first to advance such thoughts. Prior to him, George Koepgen, *Die Gnosis des Christentums*, Salzburg: Verlag Otto Müller, 1939, pp. 318-319, proposed that the church is an androgynous entity, because in Jesus, male and female are united. The celibate priest is a visible symbol of this androgyny, and since the priest is virgin, in his soul, male and female are united. (Cf. J. W. Drijvers, "Virginity," *ER*, vol. 15, pp. 179-281.) This is not an altogether new idea. Wayne A. Meeks, "The Image of the Androgyne: Some Uses of a Symbol in Earliest Christianity," *History of Religions* 13 (1974) 165-208, quotes Maximus the Confessor (580-662): Christ "unified man, mystically abolishing by the Spirit the difference between male and female and, in place of the two with their peculiar passions, constituting one free with respect to nature" (*Questiones ad Thalassium*, vol. 48). See also E. Ann Matter, "The Virgin Mary: A Goddess?" in Carl Olson, ed., *The Book of the Goddess. Past and Present*, New York: Crossroad, 1939, pp. 80-96; Rosemary Redford Ruether, *Mary–The Feminine Face of the Church*, Philadelphia: Westminster, 1977; Merlin Stone, *When God Was a Woman*, New York: Dial Press, 1976 (this book has very good references, but no footnotes, and that diminishes its usefulness). Here should also be mentioned Henri de Lubac, *The Eternal Feminine*, London: Collins, 1970, a study of Pierre Teilhard de Chardin's poem of Love and his views on The Eternal Feminine and Mary. De Chardin is quoted as expressing "the need to correct 'a dreadfully masculinized' conception of the Godhead" (p. 126). I am omitting here books dealing with the typology of Mary and the church; the number of these books and articles is very great. (See n. 2

was not the case in paganism, where the many goddesses gave expression to the feminine aspect of the divine image. From this point of view, Christianity had an obvious shortcoming. Resolution was sought through the elevation of the Virgin Mother of God, Mary, to higher and higher levels in the divine economy. That the divine cannot be conceived of as exclusively male or female was clearly understood by the pagans, who sensed that in the absolute all opposites and contraries are present and reconciled. In paganism such primordial unity was widely discussed as early as Hesiod (ca. 700 B.C.), who explained the existence of the world as a result of a series of separations.[14] In one of his comedies, Aristophanes (ca. 457-ca. 385) developed the same theme,[15] and in many of the Near Eastern cosmogonies, which we will briefly mention later, the image of a primeval unity from which everything else developed is also present. These discussions do not conflict with the biblical creation narratives. Although in Genesis, creation is referred to as the activity of a God who is above the universe and creates not with his body but with the agency of his word, yet the net result — a series of separations and multiplications — is the same. The most famous discussion of the male-female polarity is in Plato's *Symposium*, where he posits the existence of a primeval androgynous man who was split into male and female. According to Plato, the intense desire of man and woman for intercourse is determined not by the urge to procreate but by the desire to become one again: "And the reason is that human nature was originally one and we were a whole, and the desire and pursuit of the whole is called love."[16] Jewish mysticism also represented the first man as androgynous.[17] This

above for bibliography.) Caroline Walker Bynum, *Jesus as Mother. Studies in the Spirituality of the High Middle Ages*, Berkeley, Los Angeles, London: UC Press, 1982, deals with the twelfth and thirteenth centuries. See also Virginia Ramey Mollenkott, *The Divine Feminine*, New York: Crossroad, 1983.

14   Hesiod, *Theogony* 120. But see also Empedocles of Acragas (ca. 450 B.C.) and his "twofold tale," in John Burnett, *Early Greek Philosophy*, New York: Macmillan, 1892. Also, M. L. West, *The Orphic Poems*, Oxford: Clarendon, 1983, especially p. 57.

15   Aristophanes, *The Birds*, in B. B. Rogers, *Five Comedies of Aristophanes*, New York: Doubleday, 1955, p. 34.

16   Plato, *Symposium*, 183E-193D, in *The Dialogues of Plato*, ed. B. Jowett, New York: Scribner, 1889, vol. 1, pp. 483-486.

17   The literature on the subject of the *androgyne* is very large. Indispensible for any reader is Mircea Eliade, *The Two and the One*, London: Harvill Press, 1965, and Wendy Doniger O'Flaherty, *Women, Androgynes, and*

view is reflected in the biblical account of the creation of Eve from
Adam, which, according to the text, is the reason why a man and
a woman have intercourse.[18]

2. For both paganism and Christianity sex is a reality; however, sexual separation is a condition which did not exist "in the
beginning." Originally there was unity and to return to that unity
(which includes the *communio dei et hominis*) is the aim of religion.
Early Christian theology — both orthodox and heterodox — strove
to point out a way toward overcoming such separation in order to
arrive at unity. Indeed, the eucharistic feast may conceal an obscure element of the ancient *hieros gamos*, the sacred intercourse

---

Other Mythical Beasts, Chicago: University of Chicago Press, 1980. O'Flaherty
deals mostly with Hindu mythology; chap. V, "Androgynes," however, has
many useful general remarks, especially on pp. 283-309. Also, the article
"Androgynes" in the *ER*, vol. 1, pp. 276-281, by the same two authors (this
article is based on their books mentioned above). A. W. Watts, *The Two
Hands of God. The Myths of Polarity*, New York: George Braziller, 1963, collected many mythological accounts of "the desire and pursuit of the whole"
from such diverse places as ancient Egypt, Greece, India, and others. He
concluded that "almost invariably our mythologies preserve the hint of a
way back to the lost unity, though the price that has to be paid for it is a form
of death." This may be death in a real sense as in Christianity, or self-
denial, treating oneself as already dead, but "that is the state of paradise
regained" (Watts, p. 201). Ernst Benz, *Adam, Der Mythus vom Urmenschen*,
München-Planegg: Otto-Wilhelm-Barth Verlag, 1955, is a useful collection
of texts relating to the problem of the androgyne. The authors discussed in
this book include Jacob Boehme, F. von Baader, and N. Berdjajew; this book
was used by M. Eliade, who referred to it extensively. Wayne A. Meeks, *art.
cit.*, n. 12, investigated the myth of the androgyne in the areas of Paul's
missionary activity and concluded that in the baptismal liturgy there was a
reunification formula in which the Christian was assured that "he has put
on again the image of the Creator, in whom there is no male and female"
(p. 207). In opposition to Meeks, Dennis Ronald MacDonald, *There Is No
Male and Female. The Fate of a Dominical Saying*, Philadelphia: Fortress, 1987,
argues that Paul's concern was the unification of alienated social groups —
Jews/Greeks, slave/free, men/women — and not a baptismal restoration of
the androgyne. (MacDonald, pp. 126, 128, 130, 132: Paul "envisioned a fully
democratized community.") Further literature on the subject includes the
excellent anthropological study by Hermann Baumann, *Das Doppelte Geschlecht*, Berlin: E. Reimer, 1955; Ernst Ludwig Dieterich, "Der Urmensch
als Androgyn," *Zeitschrift für Kirchengeschichte* 58 (1939) 297-345; and Alfred
Bertholet, *Das Geschlecht der Gottheit*, Tübingen: J. C. B. Mohr (Paul Siebeck),
1934. For Jewish mysticism, see Raphael Patai, *The Hebrew Goddess*, New
York: Ktav Publishing House, 1967.

[18] Gen. 2:21-23: "To become one flesh" is to restore their original unity.
For an analysis of this account, together with those of Plato and Aristophanes, see Baumann, *op cit.*, pp. 175-181.

which reenacts the primeval unity that existed prior to creation.[19] In the New Testament Jesus is reported to have said that in heaven there will be no sexual differentiation because all will be "like angels."[20] This thought also appears outside the canonical gospel narratives. According to the Gospel of Thomas, it was with reference to little children that Jesus told his disciples how they can enter the Kingdom: "When you make the two one, and when you make the inner as the outer and the outer as the inner and the above as the below, and when you make the male and the female into a single one, so that the male will not be male and the female not be female ... then shall you enter (the Kingdom)."[21]

---

[19] Stephen Benko, *Pagan Rome and the Early Christians,* Bloomington: Indiana Univ. Press, 1984, pp. 79-102; idem., "The Libertine Gnostic Sect of the Phibionites According to Epiphanius," *Vigiliae Christianae* 21 (1967) 103-119.

[20] Mark 12:18-25; Matt. 22:23-30; Luke 20:27-36. From here we are to understand also Jesus' words about little children: "To such belongs the kingdom of God," obviously, because they have not yet reached full sexual maturation and, thus, division, and live in a state of paradisiacal innocence. Mark 10:13-16; Matt. 18:3, 19:13-15; Luke 18:16-17 .

[21] Logion 22, A. Guillemont et al., eds., *The Gospel According to Thomas,* Leiden: E. J. Brill; New York: Harper and Brothers, 1959, pp. 17-19. This saying is also used in the early Christian homily called 2 Clement, chap. 12. Here, however, the preacher interprets the saying as a call for moral purity and asceticism. See Rudolf Knopf, *Lehre der zwölf Apostel. Zwei Clemensbriefe,* Tübingen: J. C. B. Mohr (Paul Siebeck), 1920, pp. 170-171 (Handbuch zum Neuen Testament, Ergänzungsband I). An English translation is also available in E. J. Goodspeed, *The Apostolic Fathers,* New York: Harper and Brothers, 1950, p. 90, and C. C. Richardson, *Early Christian Fathers,* Philadelphia: Westminster, 1953, pp. 197-198 . See also the fragments of the *Gospel of the Egyptians,* in E. Hennecke and W. Schneemelcher, *New Testament Apocrypha,* Philadelphia: Westminster, 1963, vol. 1, pp. 166-167. On Thomas, see especially Stevan L. Davies, *Thomas and Christian Wisdom,* New York: Harper & Row, 1983. A commentary on the Gospel of Thomas was published by Robert M. Grant, *The Secret Sayings of Jesus,* Garden City, N.Y.: Doubleday, 1960. See also Dennis Ronald MacDonald, *There Is No Male and Female: The Fate of a Dominical Saying in Paul and Gnosticism,* Philadelphia: Fortress Press, 1987. Useful is Jorunn Jacobsen Buckley, *Female Fault and Fulfillment in Gnosticism,* Chapel Hill and London: Univ. of North Carolina Press, 1986, especially chap. 5, "An Interpretation of Logion114 in The Gospel of Thomas," pp. 84-104. Similar is another saying of Jesus, when the disciples asked him: "When will thou be revealed to us and when will we see Thee?" The answer of Jesus was: "When you take off your clothing without being ashamed, and take your clothes and put them under your feet as the little children and tread on them, then (shall you behold) the Son of the Living (One) and you shall not fear." Finally, the last logion: "Simon Peter said to them: Let Mary go out from among us, because women are not worthy of the Life. Jesus said: See, I shall lead her, so that I will make her male, that she too may become a living spirit, resembling you males. For every woman

According to these canonical and aprocryphal sayings of Jesus, in the kingdom of God sexual differentiation will no longer exist; a condition will prevail that existed before the sexes were separated. This state is the result of redemption, which for many church fathers meant the restoration of God's creation to the condition that existed prior to the destructive consequences of sin.[22] Complete redemption, a perfect restoration of the kingdom of God, cannot take place without the reuniting of female and male. The result is a "new creation" in which the universe undergoes a process of cosmic rebirth.[23] Here Mary has her fundamental role. Her figure, as Desire Hirst has expressed it, "mirrors the Divine Nature itself, especially in its most hidden and profound facet ... that of Motherhood which is the complement of the Fatherhood of God."[24]

3. Mary was impregnated by the creative word of God: this is what we call "virgin birth." The phrase[25] means that Mary "did not know man," i.e., a male, prior to the conception and birth of Jesus. This point is important because her virginal condition means that Mary's unspoiled purity and innocence parallels the

---

who makes herself male will enter the Kingdom of Heaven." Logions 37 and 114, Guillemont et al., supra, pp. 23 and 57. Concerning the practice of undressing and treading upon the clothing, see Jonathan Z. Smith, "The Garment of Shame," *History of Religions* 5 (1966) 217-238, according to whom Logion 37 is an interpretation of an "archaic Christian baptismal rite." Cf. the lament of Isis, which I quote from Bertholet, *op. cit.*, p. 18: "I made myself into a man, although I was a woman, to let your name live on earth."

22   See, e.g., Paul in Rom. 5; 1 Cor. 15; similarly Eph. 1. Also *Adversus Haereses* 5, 1 ff.; Augustine, *In Psalmum* 96.15; Origen, *De principiis* 1.6, 1-2.

23   Rom. 8:22-23: "We know that the whole creation has been groaning in travail together until now; and not only the creation, but we ourselves, who have the first fruits of the Spirit, groan inwardly as we wait for adoption as sons, the redemption of our bodies." See also Gal. 4:19, and numerous passages, such as 1 John 4:7, where Christians are referred to as "born of God."

24   Desire Hirst, "The Catholic Concept of the Feminine,"*Bucknell Review* 24 (1978) 67. According to Hirst, Mary was human, not a goddess. But her relationship with God was such that "leads the creature toward deification, to becoming a god through participation in Divine will ... Mary is one of us who may become gods only if we accept our created position and live it through to the end" (p. 64). This begs the question whether Mary has now been deified and whether we are now permitted to think of her as divine. Hirst, as I see it, leaves the question open.

25   The expression is found in other mythologies, too; thus, it is not unique to Christianity.

unspoiled state of creation when "the Spirit of God was moving over the face of the waters."[26] Accordingly, the gospel of Luke emphasizes that the angel Gabriel was sent to a *virgin* in Nazareth; the *Spirit* of God overshadowed her and entered into her as into pure soil; thus the new creative word of God was sown.[27] The Christian recorder of the prologue to the Gospel of Luke thus established a parallel with Genesis 1 which would be more fully developed by later authors who would draw a parallel between the "virgin earth" and the virgin condition of Mary's body. Neither did it escape their attention that both in Genesis 1 and in the conception of Jesus the "word of God" was the seminal agent.

A virgin, as someone who is not engaged in sexual activity either as male or female, is in a sense "neither male nor female," as the sayings of Jesus describe those entering the kingdom of God. Virgins are thus in that state of paradisaical innocence which existed before sin entered the world and man was separated from God. Not subject to the same limitations of the human condition as others, they are, in a manner of speaking, between humanity and God. A virgin stands "for continuity in its most pure state" because "she remain[s] as she had been first created." Her body is "a clear echo of the virgin earth of Paradise — untouched earth, that bore within itself the promise of undreamed-of abundance."[28] The Virgin Mary was the "virgin earth," and thus a perfect choice for the female counterpart in the process of the "new creation."

What happened in the "Virgin Birth"? Two elements — heaven and earth, spirit and flesh, holy and profane — commingled and a second creation took place: the "second Adam" was caused to appear, he "who has made us both one, and has broken down the dividing wall of hostility ... that he might create in himself one new man in place of the two, so making peace."[29] Without Mary, this could not have happened; here her figure reaches those cosmic proportions that will more fully appear in Revelation

---

[26] Gen. 1:2; see D. A. Leeming, "Virgin Birth," *ER*, vol. 15, pp. 272-276.

[27] Luke 1:26-35. See also our later discussion of Mary as earth, p. 206ff..

[28] See Peter Brown, *The Body and Society. Men, Women and Sexual Renunciation in Early Christianity*, New York: Columbia U. Press, 1988, pp. 271 and 278. Also, Aline Rousselle, *Porneia, On Desire and the Body in Antiquity*, Oxford: Basil Bleckwell, 1988, and Han J. W. Drijver, *loc. cit.*

[29] Eph. 2:14-15.

12. Protestants like to point out that the Virgin Birth is a statement about Jesus and not about Mary. That is only partly true. Those who wrote down the infancy narratives of the Gospels of Matthew and Luke may have had Jesus at the center of their attention,[30] but they could not possibly ignore Mary. In Christian belief the conception and birth of Jesus is a cosmic event and Mary is a necessary part of that event.

The apocryphal *Gospel of Bartholomew* reflects the popular belief in the importance of Mary's motherhood. Here the disciples ask her how she conceived and carried "him who cannot be carried or how she bore so much greatness." At first she refuses to answer and warns the disciples that such a mystery cannot be spoken of without great and dangerous consequences. When the disciples insist, Mary begins the story, but she can go only up to the point where the angel came to her. "As she was saying this, fire came from her mouth, and the world was on the point of being burned up. Then came Jesus quickly and said to Mary: 'Say no more, or today my whole creation will come to an end.'"[31] According to this passage, Mary conceived and bore more than the human side of Jesus; she bore the creator of the world. Her image is that of the divine mother, the female who is part of the cosmic creative process. And this is not far from the image of the "Great Mother of the gods" to whom our ancestors were so deeply devoted.

Christianity did not add a new element to religion when it introduced into its theology such concepts as "virgin" and "mother"; rather, it sharpened and refined images that already existed in numerous forms in pagan mythology. If these images are archetypes, then they belong to the "collective unconscious" of humankind; each generation inherits them; they are permanent parts of the human species, biologically determined. Those who find this Jungian theory unacceptable would say that these images are learned and not inherited, but in either case it cannot be denied that here we are dealing with universal human experiences.[32] Our earliest memories are likely to come from our

---

[30] This, of course, may not be the case, either, since it is not very difficult to find elements of very early Christian devotion to Mary in these narratives.

[31] Hennecke and Schneemelcher, *op. cit.*, vol. 1, p. 494.

[32] The Jungian theory about the mother-archetype is discussed in great detail by Erich Neuman, *The Great Mother. An Analysis of the Archetype*

mothers; our concept of life is inseparable from that of the womb; our concept of nurturance is female, and everybody has some understanding of the mother-child relationship.

Whatever its source, a study of ancient history shows that goddess-worship has been an important aspect of human religion from earliest times. The diversity of pagan divinities must not be denied: Sekhnet was goddess of plague and punishment, Bellona of war, etc. However, what those usually called "fertility goddesses" represented was the same in every age and every place. Thus, it cannot be said that Isis and Cybele were historically identical; obviously they were not; functionally, however, they were in some respects equivalent. The best proof of this fact is the syncretism which was generally accepted by everyone during the early centuries of Christianity; if such functional equivalency had not existed among the goddesses, the later syncretism could never have happened. Already in the fifth century B.C. Herodotus

---

(Bollingen Series XLVII), New York: Pantheon Books, 1955. This massive volume (43 p. introduction, 353 p. text, 380 p. plates and index) is still the definitive treatment of the subject. Ann Belford Ulanov, *The Feminine in Jungian Psychology and in Christian Theology*, Evanston: Northwestern Univ. Press, 1971, analyzed Jung's ideas on the feminine and the implications for Christian theology, and generally the role of the feminine in religion and life. The opposite view would be represented among others by Mircea Eliade, *Patterns in Comparative Religion*, New York: Sheed and Ward, 1958, according to whom it is not necessary to work with archetypes because human experiences are similar everywhere. This could be called a cultural-anthropological line, which has been embraced by many historians of religion. Judith Ochshorn, *The Female Experience and the Nature of the Divine*, Bloomington: Indiana Univ. Press, 1981, for example, found the Jungian approaches unsatisfactory because they "oversimplify and violate the complexity and variety of human experience" (p. xv). See also G. Van Der Leeuw, *Phänomenologie der Religion*, Tübingen: Mohr, 1933, pp. 165, 190; and the criticism of Jung and Neumann by J. J. Preston, ed., *Mother Worship*, Chapel Hill: Univ. North Carolina Press, 1982: "Human behavior cannot be reduced to innate principles, infantile phantasies, or archetypes" (p. 328). "It is not necessary to invoke an innate archetype to explain the widespread ambivalence represented in goddess worship ... Mother worship is more complex than Neumann would have us believe ... goddesses are multifaceted phenomena, integrating a wide range of human experiences and aspirations" (p. 332). For our purpose such differentiation is not necessary, since both Jungians and the cultural-anthropologists ultimately talk about religious experiences which appear to be common to all peoples, as Preston himself admitted: "Even if we do not agree with the Jungian idea of a female archetype, all humans understand the mother-infant bond and recognize the related universal symbol of the womb as mother of life" (J. J. Preston, "Goddess Worship," *ER*, vol. 6, p. 58). See also Preston, *Mother Worship, supra*: "... in each of us is a memory of that time of perfect bonding between mother and child" (p. 340).

identified the Greek gods with those of the Egyptians,[33] and by the second century A.D., Apuleius could assertively make Isis identify herself with most of the major goddesses known at that time. Apuleius was a devotee of Isis. That his claim could have been accepted by those devoted to the other goddesses is unlikely. But at the least he shows us how syncretism could be used to claim for one or another cult far wider validity than it previously had been thought to have. For Apuleius, Isis is "the natural mother of all things, mistress and governess of all the elements." Only the names under which she is worshipped are different.[34] So did Lucius invoke her help "by whatever name or fashion or shape it is lawful to call upon thee"[35] until she came and restored his corrupted shape back to its original unspoiled form; from an ass he became a man again.

If we change the name Isis in the story of Lucius' conversion to Mary, we are already speaking in a Mariological context. Even thouqh the *dramatis personae* clearly belong to the pagan world, the function of Isis is that of the great goddess through whom a "new creation" takes place, the effects of a "curse" are reversed, and Lucius is saved. When Apuleius wrote this tale, Christians were already comparing the Virgin Mary to Eve and were beginning to draw parallels between the woman who was the cause of mankind's fall and the woman who was the cause of redemption. Pagan and Christian concepts of the role of the "woman" here run side by side until the pagan concept converges with the Christian one and Mary emerges supreme.

To demonstrate this development, to show how the pagan "queen of heaven" gradually became the Christian "queen of heaven," we must follow a chronological method of investigation to illustrate our thesis adequately. A topical treatment of Mariology is a legitimate approach;[36] my point in this book, however, is

---

[33] See *Histories* 2.155-156, in A. D. Godley, ed., *LCL*, London: Heinemann, 1960, vol. 1, p. 469. Among others, Demeter is identified with Isis. This is the so-called *interpretatio greca*, which is based on the assumption that all peoples worshipped the same gods.

[34] *The Golden Ass* 11.4, in W. Adlington, ed., *LCL*, rev. by S. Gaselee, London: Heinemann, 1935, p. 545.

[35] *Ibid.* 11.2, p. 541.

[36] Giovanni Miegge, *The Virgin Mary*, Philadelphia: Westminster, 1956, to name one example, did this with excellent results. Very informative also is the great three-volume work by Juniper B. Carol, ed., *Mariology*, Milwau-

to show the continuity of the reverence paid to the female aspect of God. This can best be done by proceeding along chronological lines.

This procedure will also reveal that the goddess-cult of most decisive influence on the emerging Christian Church was that of Magna Mater, that is, Cybele, and therefore, that the geographic center of nascent Mariology was western Asia Minor. This does not mean that other goddesses, such as Isis, did not play a formative role in Christianity. The study of Christian iconography, to mention only one field, has shown how much we inherited from the pious worshippers of Isis. On the level of popular devotion Isis left many marks of the cult of Mary.[37] However, it seems to me that Mariology was more substantially determined by the theology of the Great Mother than by any other fertility goddess. It was the motherhood of Mary which became the point of connection between her figure and the pagan goddess concept, and I should like to recall once more that the basic principle of Mariology, from which everything else flows, is the fact that she was the mother of Jesus. I will, therefore, attempt to show how the early Christian theologians used the motherhood of Mary to connect her with the events described in Genesis 3 and how this then led to the use of such epithets for Mary as "the cause of salvation" which eventually raised her image into a cosmic perspective. The vehicle by which many ideas connected with Magna Mater were transferred into Christianity was the Montanist movement. Obviously, there were other important movements in the second century. One of these in which the feminine element also played a significant role was Gnosticism, which, as has been shown, may also have absorbed ideas from the worship of Cybele. The impact of the Gnostic understanding of the feminine element upon mainstream Christianity, however, would require another study.[38]

---

kee: Bruce, 1955-61.

[37] R. E. Witt, *Isis in the Graeco-Roman World*, Ithaca, N.Y.: Cornell Univ. Press, 1971, describes the spread of the cult of Isis, her eventual assimilation with other goddesses, and her impact on Christianity. The author believes that Paul was especially preoccupied with the popularity of Isis.

[38] See Karen L. King, ed., *Images of the Feminine in Gnosticism*, Philadelphia: Fortress Press, 1988. This book contains papers delivered at a conference at the Institute of Antiquity and Christianity in Claremont, California, in 1985, and has the most recent information on the subject. See also

We shall proceed in the following way.

First, we shall investigate a few characteristic pagan goddesses: their stories, their cults, and their impact upon their worshippers

---

Pheme Perkins, "Sophia and the Mother-Father: The Gnostic Goddess," in Carl Olson, *op. cit.*, pp. 97-109; Jorunn Jacobsen Buckley, *op. cit.*; Charles W. Hedrick and Robert Hodgson, Jr., eds., *Nag Hammadi, Gnosticism and Early Christianity*, Peabody, Mass.: Hendrickson, 1988.

Speaking about the Goddess, or Mother Goddess (in the singular and with a capital G and M) is a convenience but the dispute still goes on whether it is legitimate or not.James J. Preston (op. cit. pp. 325-343) argued spiritedly supporting the "multivariant" and the "polymorphous" character of the goddesses. According to him mother deities may be "1. reflections of sociocultural realities, 2. models to be imitated by humans, 3. opposites inversely related to their human counterparts, 4. idealized extensions of motherhood as conceived and practiced in empirical reality." (p. 337). This may all be true (and it should be remembered that Preston argues against the archetypal feminine principle) but A.H. Armstrong's definition provides an operational basis on which the phenomenon of female deities can be discussed. This is what he says:

"The actual figures in most mystery cults of any spiritual importance are female divinities who can be grouped under the title of Goddess or Mother. What do we mean when we speak of the 'Goddess'? It is, of course, a modern generalization covering a great multiplicity of cults and stories in the Mediterranean area. But they all have something in common that is very difficult to apprehend and perhaps impossible even to understand fully. The feminine aspect of divinity in the world can mean so many things. The nearest approach to a successful statement of what it may be is perhaps what Zuntz says when speaking of an early form of the cult of the mother, that of the great Neolithic Temple of Malta: 'These men of an age from which not one word reaches us perceived and worshipped in their goddess the wonder of life unending, embracing death as a stage and step to its eternity.'" A.H. Armstrong, "The Ancient and Continuing Pieties of the Greek World" in A.H. Armstrong's *Classical Mediterranean Spirituality*, New York: Crossroad, 1986, p. 72. The quotation is from G. Zuntz, *Persephone*. Oxford: Clarendon Press, 1971, p. 53.

Urs Winter, *Frau und Göttin*, Göttingen: Vandenhoeck & Ruprecht, 1983, p. 199, makes this remark concerning female statuettes in the Syrian-Palestinian area: "Selbst wenn sie zu einem bestimmten Zweck ... und in Zusammenhang mit magischen Praktiken verwendet worden sein mochten, immer verkörpern sie einen Aspekt einer 'Idealfrau,' deren Ausstrahlung die syrisch-palastinische Frau verklärte. Wenn diese 'Idealfrau' in ihren zeitlich und lokal verschieden ausgeprägten Aspekten im Mittelpunkt der Diskussion steht, finde es legitim, schlechthin von der 'syrischen Göttin' zu reden." The point is well taken. While not many scholars today would reduce the problem to a simple proposition that the "Mother Goddess" was worshiped in ancient times (E. O. James, *The Cult of the Mother Goddess*, London, 1959, gives this impression), it is true that the "eternal feminine," the female face of God, was the object of those various approaches which we know as a bewildering multiplicity of cults. In this sense we should be able to talk about "the" goddess. (See to this, V. Pestalozza, *Eterno Feminimo Mediterraneo*, Venice: Neri Pozza, 1954).

when they were pagans and after they became Christians. The many goddesses in the Roman Empire varied considerably according to the place of their origin, their initial area of responsibility in life and their position in the divine hierarchy. These details, while important for the historian of religion, are less so for our study which is concerned with the feminine aspect of the divine in general rather than the differences among its various forms. Futhermore, the period of time we are studying was a time of syncretism when the images of many originally independent goddesses had merged and were functionally indistinguishable. While in the day-to-day practice of paganism by ordinary people the many goddesses continued to have their proper functions and peculiar shrines, and therefore, their specific established cults, there was in philosophy an increasing tendency to treat the more important ones as aspects of the one, abstract philosophical divinity. The potentialities of this attitude went well beyond the old syncretism presented by Herodotus, who merely identified the deities of different cultures who had similar functions, conveniently but simplistically supposing that they "must have been" the same being. The new, primarily Stoic, and later neo-Platonic, syncretism was spread among the upper classes by teachers of philosophy and their popular followers, the teachers of rhetoric. When Christian clergy began to come from the educated classes, Mary was brought into the process, with the result we shall describe. We must keep in mind that such rigid definitions of subtle theological nuances as we are used to in Christian dogmatics (e.g., the Trinitarian controversies) were alien to the pagans. They felt considerably freer to express the varieties of their religious experiences than did Christians later on. Therefore, in the following pages I will use the simple, all-inclusive term "Goddess," "Queen of Heaven," or "Mother Goddess" to denote this manifestation of the divine; I believe this is a convenience we can afford and to which the ancients would not object.

We will then turn to a review of the image of the "Queen of Heaven" in the New Testament in order to show how the biblical image corresponds to that of her pagan counterparts. In this chapter I rely heavily upon basic research of many scholars. After reviewing their works, I shall give my own interpretation.

In the fourth chapter I shall discuss the Christian sect of the Montanists who absorbed and diffused in the Christian Church many elements of the cult of Magna Mater, the Great Mother Goddess, Cybele.

After this, we shall investigate the story of the Kollyridians, an obscure Christian sect which actually replaced the pagan goddess with Mary and offered sacrifices to her. How significant were the Kollyridians? Because they quickly disappeared from history, it would be easy to dismiss them as being of no consequence. However, they are a link between paganism and Christianity and that suggests what Christianity could have become had not orthodox Christian theology (whatever "orthodox" may mean) developed its own Mariology. The Kollyridians disappeared only when the veneration of Mary became universally accepted in the church Had Mary not been adopted by the church as an alternative to the goddesses of the pagans, would the Kollyridians have developed a larger following and perhaps a rival Christian church? This is idle speculation, but church history provides us with many examples of how sects developed when the church failed to meet the needs of its members.

Chapter VI will treat the role of popular piety in the growth of Marian devotion through discussion of the *Protoevangelium of James,* the idea of the earth-mother, and the development of the image of the queen of heaven into an established article of faith.

Finally, I shall investigate the development of Mariology in official, orthodox Christian theology. This begins with the Eve-Mary parallelism in which Christian theologians reached back to the old theory of primordial creation to explain their theory of the "new creation." Since they could not use the image of a goddess, they substituted for the female face of God the spiritualized image of *Ecclesia* — the church — which they gradually identified with Mary. All that is very confusing, often contradictory, and not at all clear, but this was the best they could do without falling into paganism.

In this way, Mary was eventually declared to be "Mother of God," which is a wholly pagan term filled with new Christian meaning. Did Mary become a goddess when this declaration was made? The answer of Christians was, and still is, an indignant No! — but in fact Mary assumed the functions of pagan female divinities and for many pious Christian folk she did, and does, everything the ancient goddesses used to do.

Such is the scope of this book. It is less a study in the history of religions than what German theology calls *Dogmengeschichte*, i.e., history of dogma, in this case that of Mariology. Since the topic is obviously close to feminist concerns, many books apparently inspired by the current feminist concerns but dealing with strictly historical or theological problems were very helpful in my work. I list these books at their proper places.

But I should like to emphasize that these essays were not intended to be contributions to feminist sutdies; there are many excellent works on women's experiences in early Christian times to which anyone interested can turn. These essays were written over many years, sometimes independently from each other, but always within the framework of historical theology. Many people read parts of this manuscript and offered their criticism. I am indebted to all of them, but here I should like to mention two who are no longer with us. Dr. David Scheidt, former editor of Fortress Press in Philadelphia, gave me invaluable advice and professional help. Professor Morton Smith of Columbia University read and criticized the manuscript with his usual wit and akribia. He and I disagreed on many things in life, but when the chips were down he was always a friend.

Finally, I should like to mention that the problem with which this book deals is far too complex to be dealt with in a single volume. I am taking up for study one single thread that runs through the fabric of that coat of many colors that is called Christianity. Therefore I ask scholarly readers not to judge my book by their own special fields of expertise; rather, I invite pursuit of our main line of thought. The extensive bibliographies attached to the end of each chapter are meant to enable the reader to fill in whatever information may be missing from the text. These bibliographies contain only titles that I have personally consulted.

I hope that what I present here from its pagan background will contribute to the understanding of certain aspects of Christianity: that is my primary concern.

CHAPTER TWO

GODDESSES IN THE GRECO-ROMAN WORLD

A goddess was an ever-present figure in the society in which the first Christians lived. To familiarize ourselves with the role of a goddess in the religious and social life of the Greeks and Romans and to understand better the heritage Gentile Christians brought with them to the new faith, we will study those goddesses who were particularly influential during the early Christian centuries. Caelestis, Isis, the Syrian Goddess, and Cybele were worshipped in areas which were also home to influential Christian communities. They were also closely linked with many other great goddesses of the ancient world, Greek, Roman, and Near Eastern, and thus they are good representations of what is generally called a "goddess." Because of its close relationship to the cult of Cybele, we will also briefly review the cult of Dionysus.

There were many goddesses in the ancient world, as there were many gods. Different conditions, natural environments, and historical experiences created differences in peoples' perception of the nature of the divine. So we find that the goddess-figure also appeared in numerous forms, that the divine feminine revealed herself in many goddesses, among them, Isis, Athena, and Juno. And yet it is possible to study the problem of "the goddess" in a general way. Religion is the human endeavor to approach, understand, and somehow express that which is divine. But we can do that only by employing images already familiar to us, and the number of these is limited to the phenomena that are available to us through our senses, that is, what we can see and hear and otherwise perceive in the world around us. And the world around us is much the same no matter where we live: regardless of the many differences among cultures and peoples, the sky, the earth, the realities of birth and death are roughly the same for all peoples everywhere. Three of these universal experiences are sex, motherhood, and birth. The mystery surrounding these three generates most religious thought among all peoples whose history is available to us and as far back in history as we can reach. Besides, it would be wrong to assume that the peoples of the Mediterranean — Egyptians, Greeks, Romans, and others with whom we are mostly concerned — had developed their religious ideas independently of each other. To do this they would have to have lived in total isolation from one another, which they did not. In fact, there was substantial interaction among these peoples in ancient times,[1] sometimes as peaceful trade, other times as war and conquest, all of which resulted in an exchange of cultures, customs, and religious ideas. As German Chancellor Bismarck supposedly said, *"Ideen sind zollfrei."*[2] And wherever there is *Kulturkontakt* there is also syncretism. Thus, eventually, the process of influencing and being influenced led to mutual accommodation of various religious ideas. By the time of the Christian centuries, many originally different images of divinities had blended into each other. But each time a goddess was venerated, fundamental to that veneration was recognition of the feminine present in the divine.

To understand this means to become sensitive to the issue of Mariology. Comparing present day Marian devotions with Greek and Roman expressions of piety directed to a goddess shows only how local pagan customs merged into new Christian practices. But it does not answer the question why either pagans or Christians turned to feminine dimensions of God in addition to masculine ones. The study of the history and theology of the goddesses we have chosen as examples will reveal the basic principles that underlie their worship. This in turn should illuminate the basic principle of Christian Mariology.

A. Caelestis

The name *Caelestis* is explained by the title of the goddess, "Queen of Heaven." However, while no one will have difficulty understanding what "queen" means, our concept of "heaven" is rather unclear. Nor was it clearly defined by our Greco-Roman ancestors. The etymology of the Greek word for heaven, οὐρανός, yields nothing. We are a little better off with the Latin *caelum*, which derives from the Greek κοῖλος= hollow. We may therefore

---

[1] See the review of J. Ochshorn, *op. cit.*, pp. 25-31.
[2] "Ideas cannot be kept out by the imposition of tariffs."

surmise that when Romans heard the word *caelum* or heard about something or someone who was *caelestis*, they may have pictured the hollow, star-studded, vessel-like covering that appears above the earth. The concept, therefore, refers to the universe as a whole. Here too, the ancients were free to think of a variety of things, as we will show in our next chapter; but for the time being we will use the term *Caelestis* in the sense of "universal." The word is used both as a noun, referring to a specific goddess, and as an adjective to express the quality of a goddess (*Caelestis,* the goddess; *Juno Caelestis* = Juno the heavenly).

At the beginning of the *Aeneid,* Virgil relates the arrival of Aeneas in Carthage. He describes a magnificent city of many buildings, theaters, and harbors.

> Amid the city ... was a grove, luxuriant in shade, the spot
> where first the Phoenicians, tossed by waves and whirlwind, dug
> up the token which queenly Juno had pointed out, a head of the
> spirited horse, ... Here Sidonian Dido was founding to Juno a
> mighty temple, rich in gifts and the presence of the goddess.[3]

No less impressive was the royal palace in which massive silver and gold works of art stood on the banquet tables covered in purple.[4] Of course, Virgil could not have seen Dido's Carthage;[5] he

---

[3] Virgil, *The Aeneid* 1.441-447, H. Rushton Fairclough, ed., *LCL,* London: Heinemann, 1916, pp. 271-273. Thus also Silius Italicus (26-101A.D.), *Punica.* 1.81-84, *LCL,* J. D. Duff, ed., London: Heinemann, 1934,p. 11: "In the centre of Carthage stood a temple, sacred to the spirit of Elissa (Dido) the foundress, and regarded with hereditary awe by the people. Round it stood yew trees and pines with their melancholy shade, which hid it and kept away the light of heaven."

[4] Virgil, *op. cit.* 1.625-645.

[5] For a brief summary of the history of Carthage, see *Der Kleine Pauly,* Stuttgart: Druckenmüller, 1969, 1.135-138. Also Dimitri Baramki, *Phoenicia and the Phoenicians,* Beirut: Khayats, 1961; Donald Harden, *The Phoenicians,* London: Thames and Hudson, 1962; B. H. Warmington, *Carthage,* New York: Praeger, 1969; Sabatino Moscati, *The World of the Phoenicians* , (Praeger History of World Civilization), New York/Washington: Praeger, 1968; Gerhard Herm, *The Phoenicians,* New York: William Morrow, 1975; Gilbert Charles-Picard, *La Civilization de L'Afrique Romain,* Paris: Plon, 1959; Giblert Charles-Picard, *Carthage,* London: Elek Books, 1956. Some of the older books are still valuable, among them F. C. Movers, *Die Phönizier,* 2 vols. (vol. 2 has three parts), Bonn: Weber, 1841 and Berlin: Dummler, 1849; Otto Meltzer, *Geschichte der Karthager,* 2 vols., Berlin: Weidmann, 1879; N. Davis, *Carthage and Her Remains,* New York: Harper, 1861; R. Bosworth Smith, *Carthage and the Carthaginians,* London: Longmans, Green & Co., 1849; Franz Labarre, *Die römische Kolonie Karthago,* Potsdam: Kraemer-Brandt, 1882; but especially Auguste Audollent, *Carthage Romaine,* Paris: Ancienne Librairie

lived between 70 and 19 B.C., when ancient Carthage was only a faded memory. But in its place stood another city no less glorious than the first, and the temple that Virgil described for the time of Dido was one of the greatest and most influential sanctuaries in the early Roman Empire, the seat of the queen of heaven, *Dea Caelestis*. When Carthage was a Phoenician colony, and later an independent city of Phoenician origin, another goddess had been worshipped there; her name was Tanit.

Who was Tanit? In other words, what did the Carthaginian mind condense in the image of Tanit?[6] She is often referred to as "Tanit Pene Baal," i.e., "the face of Baal" or "the image of Baal,"[7] which may mean "Tanit is the appearance (or manifestation) of Baal." She later became a moon-goddess and in this respect the name Pene-Baal suggests that as the moon reflects the light of the sun, so Tanit reflects Baal. As a moon goddess, Tanit embodied some of the same characteristics as Selene, Artemis, and other lunar divinities. First among these characteristics is an association with the female principle through the mysterious connection between the phases of the moon and the menstrual cycle. But the moon is also the ruler of the night, during which dew is formed.

Thorin et Fils, 1901. Also, Gilbert and Colette Charles-Picard, *Daily Life in Carthage*, London: Allen and Unwin, 1961; Gilbert and Colette Charles-Picard, *The Life and Death of Carthage*, London: Sidgwick & Jackson, 1968; Werner Huss, *Geschichte der Karthager*, München: C. H. Beck, 1985. For the modern excavations see John Griffith Pedley, ed., *New Light on Ancient Carthage*, Ann Arbor: University of Michigan Press, 1980 .

6 See K. Preisendanz, "Tanit", *Pauly's Realencyclopädie der Classischen Altertumswissenschaft*, Stuttgart: Druckenmüller Verlag, 1932. 2. Reihe, S. Halbband (IV/A/2), pp. 2178-2205; Philippe M. Berger, "Tanit Pene Baal," *Journal Asiatique*, Septieme Serie, 9 (1877) 147-160; P. Ronzevalle, "Trace de Cult de Tanit en Pheniicie," *Melanges de la Faculte Orientale Universite Saint Joseph* 5 (1912) 75-83; G. Charles-Picard, *Les Religions De L'Afrique Antique*, Paris: Plon, 1954; Friedrich Ch. Munter, *Die Religion der Karthager*, Kopenhagen: Schubothe, 1821; Carl C. Clemen, *Die Phönikische Religion nach Philo von Byblos*, Leipzig: J. C. Hinrichs, 1939; also the literature quoted above on Phoenicia and Carthage. E. Lipinski, "Syro-Fenicische Wortels Van De Karthaagse Religie," *Phoenix* 28 (1982) 51-84, discusses the latest researches on Tanit and other aspects of Carthaginian religion. Here also, a section on the "sign of Tanit" with illustrations from modern excavations.

7 Cf. Gen. 32.30: "So Jacob called the name of the place Peni'el saying, For I have seen God face to face ... " See also Huss, *op. cit.*, pp. 512-516: The god Baal turns his face to men in Tanit. The hypothesis that Pene-Baal is a reference to an originally androgynous god is mentioned by Dietrich, "Der Urmensch," *op. cit.*, p. 328, with reference to Bertholet, *Götterspaltung, op. cit.*, p. 31, n. 110.

Dew is a form of precipitation quite important in maintaining vegetable life in areas where rainfall is often insufficient. The realm of the moon, the night itself, is also a powerful mystical time which played an important role in ancient magic. "For the light of day is single and simple, and Pindar says that the sun is seen 'through the lovely ether,' whereas the night air is a coalescence and fusion of many illuminations and powers which flow down like seeds to one centre from all the stars."[8] No wonder then that Tanit was worshipped as a goddess of fertility, of that creative moisture in which impregnation takes place and life begins. Tanit's signs included not only the crescent moon, but other symbols of fecundity as well, such as the palm tree, the dove, or the fish.[9] Already here we can sense that the association of sea and

---

[8] Plutarch, *De Iside et Osiride* 80b. ET.: J. Gwyn Griffiths, Cardiff: University of Wales Press, 1970, p. 249; see also *ibid.* 79b, p. 245.

[9] The name of Tanit itself may have a connection with the watery element of the sea, which was such an important part of polytheistic mythologies. This idea was suggested by F. M. Cross, who wrote: "The epithet Tannitu, literally 'the one of the (sea) serpent' or 'the Dragon Lady,' is identical with the Carthaginian goddess Tanit (τιννι τεννειτ), consort of Ba'al Hammon, "Lord of Amanus," epithet of Kronos ... " The word Tannit, Cross says, must be derived from TNN, especially Tannin, which means "dragon" or "serpent" and is strikingly similar "to the oldest epithet of Elat-Asherah: Atiratu Yammi, "Asherah of the Sea (dragon)." (Frank Moore Cross, Jr., "The Origin and Early Evolution of the Alphabet," *Eretz Israel* 8 [1967] 8-24. See also his remarks on the great goddess of Canaan, consort of El, whose epithet is "the Serpent Lady." F. M. Cross, "Yahweh and the God of the Patriarchs," *Harvard Theological Review* 55 [1962] 225-259, esp. 238. Also F. M. Cross, *Canaanite Myth and Hebrew Epic*, Cambridge, Mass.: Harvard, 1973, pp. 28-36. See, however, M. Leglay, *Saturne Africaine*, Paris, 1966, who dismisses the claim.)

If this were the case, Tanit on one hand is a goddess associated with the sea and at the same time associated with the moon, and thus, a celestial figure. That the phases of the moon and the tides of the sea are interdependent is a well-known phenomenon, and so is the fact that the female cycle and the moon's phases resemble each other. We remember at this point that the Greek goddess Aphrodite, too, had associations with both the sea and the sky: according to one tradition, she rose from the foam that gathered around the genitals of Ouranos (sky) when Zeus cut them off and threw them into the sea. (On the birth of Aphrodite, see Hesiod, *Theogony* 188-200.) Thus, she is from Heaven and from the sea, and the girls who sing her praises "by looking upward indicate that she is from Heaven and by slightly moving their upturned hands they show that she has come from the sea, and their smile is an intimation of the sea's calm." (Philostratus, *Imagines [Eikones]*, LCL, Arthur Fairbanks, ed., London: Heinemann, 1960, pp. 130-133.)

For a comparison, see Ed Meyer, "Astarte," in W. H. Roscher, *Ausführliches Lexikon der Griechischen und Römischen Mythologie*, Leipzig: Teubner, 1884-

sky, water and moon, moisture and fertilization, are references to
the great universal realities of life in which the female element
plays so significant a role. In the image of the goddess these are
raised to a cosmic level and divinized. We may suppose that Tanit
evoked these associations in the hearts of her worshippers. Thus
she included in herself characteristics of many other fertility
goddesses. It is very difficult, if not impossible, to distinguish between Tanit and Astarte or Juno, *Magna Mater, Bona Dea,* others in
whom the reproductive powers of the female were venerated. The
epithet "heavenly" was matter-of-factly added to these names, indicating the universal, cosmic role of the goddess.[10]

Devotion to Tanit went so deep, and her presence permeated the
life of Carthage to such a degree that she was called the "daemon

---

1886, vol. 1, pp. 645-655, and A. Furtwängler, "Aphrodite," in W. H.
Roscher, supra, vol. 1, pp. 390-419; Wolf Baudissin, "Atargatis," in A. Hauck,
ed., *Realencyklopädie für Protestantische Theologie und Kirche,* Leipzig: J. C.
Hinrichs, 1896-1913, vol. 2, pp. 171-177. "Ist Atargatis, wie wir annehmen,
ursprünglich identisch mit Astarte und ist diese die Repräsentantin des
befruchtenden Nachthimmels, speziell des Mondes, so wird die Darstellung
jener als einer Wasser–und Fischgottheit mit der im Altertum weit
verbreiteten Anschanuung des Mondes als des Prinzips der befruchtenden
Feuchtigkeit, als des Tauspendenden in Verbindung gebracht worden
sein," Baudissin, supra, p. 177; W. Baudissin, "Astarte and Aschera," *op. cit.,*
vol. 2, pp. 147-161. " ... Die befruchtende Kraft des Himmels eignet im
Orient zumeist dem tauspendenden Nachthimmel, und der vornehmste
Repräsentant des Nachthimmels ist der Mond," Baudissin, "Astarte and
Aschera," p. 149.
    [10] E.g., Herodotus, *Histories* 1.105, *LCL,* A. D. Godley, ed., London: Heine-
mann, 1960, vol. 1, pp. 136-137. See also 3.8: The Arabs honor the Heavenly
Aphrodite whom they call Alilat. They only acknowledge her and Dionysus, whom they call Orotalt, *op. cit.,* vol. 2, pp. 10-11. 4.59: The Scythians
worship the heavenly Aphrodite, *op. cit.,* vol. 2, pp. 256-57. Pausanias says the
following about the beginning of the cult of "Heavenly Aphrodite" in
Greece: "Nearby (i.e., the Kerameikos in Athens) is the Sanctuary of
Heavenly Aphrodite. The Assyrians were the first of the human race to
worship the Heavenly one; the people of Paphos in Cyprus, and of Phoenician Askalon in Palestine, and the people of Kythera, who learned her
worship from the Phoenicians. Aigeus instituted her at Athens ... The statue
there now is Parian marble, and by Pheidias. But in Athmon, an Athenian
country town, they claim that it was Porphyrion, a king even earlier than
Aktaios, who set up their local sanctuary of the Heavenly One," *Guide to Greece*
1.14.7, Peter Levi, ed., Harmondsworth: Penguin, 1971, vol. 1, p. 44. In all
these texts the expression "Heavenly One" or "heavenly" would express the
same idea as "Caelestis," because, as K. Latte observed, "Sie alle erheben den
Anspruch auf universale Galtung ihrer Götter." At the same time when the
cult of Tanit was at its peak in Carthage, the "Queen of Heaven" was soundly
repudiated by the prophet Jeremiah, who was active ca. 626-580 B.C. Jer. 7.18
and 44.15-25. See further comments in our chapter on the Kollyridians.

of Carthage." When at the height of the second Carthaginian war
in 215 B.C. , Hannibal concluded a treaty with the king of Mace-
don, Philip V, the preamble to the oath contained the following
words:

> This oath is taken in the presence of Zeus, Hera and Apollo; in the
> presence of the Δαίμων Καρχηδονίων, Hercules, Iolus, Ares, Triton
> and Poseidon; of the gods that accompany the army, and of the
> sun, moon and earth; of rivers, harbors and water; of all the gods
> who rule Carthage ... [11]

---

[11] Polybius, *Histories* 7.9.2; see Ian Scott-Kilvert, *Polybius, the Rise of the Roman Empire*, New York: Penguin, 1979, p. 358, or Alvin H. Bernstein, ed., *Polybius on Roman Imperialism*, South Bend, Ind.: Regnery/Gateway, 1980, p. 224. Cf. Elias J Bickerman, "An Oath of Hannibal," *Transactions of the American Philological Association* 75 (1944) 87-102. Bickerman argues that the Greek text is a translation from the Punic, which would make the use of the word δαίμων even more significant. See also E. J. Bickerman, "Hannibal's Covenant," *American Journal of Philology* 73 (1952) 1-23. Both articles were reprinted in a collection of essays by Bickerman, *Religions and Politics in the Hellenistic and Roman Periods*, eds. Emilio Gabba and Morton Smith, Como: Edizioni New Press, 1985, pp. 255-272 and 373-397, respectively. When Servius (ca. 4th century A.D.) wrote his commentary on Virgil and wanted to explain the words in *Georgica* 1.498, "Dii Patris Indigetes" (native gods; "gods of our father and our country"), he wrote: "Dii Patris Indigetes. Qui praesunt singulis civitatibus, ut Minerva Athenis, Iuno Karthaginiensibus," *Servii Grammatici Qui Feruntur in Vergilii Carmina Commentarii*, Lipsiae: Teubneri, 1902. Recenserunt Georgius Thilo et Hermannus Hago, vol. III, Fasc. II, p. 277. The *Georgica, LCL,* H. R. Fairclough, ed., Cambridge, Mass.: Harvard Univ. Press, 1953, p. 114. In the case of an *evocation,* this genius of the city was invited to leave. We know something about this from a brief passage of Macrobius. "Now it is well known"–says Macrobius–"that all cities are under the protection of some god, and that it was a secret custom of the Romans unknown to many, that when they were besieging an enemy city and had reached the point when they were confident that it could be taken, they summoned out the tutelary gods by a certain formula." This is why, Macrobius continues, the Romans kept the true name of their city a secret. According to one tradition a secret name of Rome was Ἔρως, which translated into Latin means *Amor,* and this word read backward would spell *Roma.* Heavy penalty was meted out to those who desecrated this name; Pliny, *Naturalis Historia* 3.65, refers to a certain Valerius Soranius who was sentenced to crucifixion by the Senate because he pronounced the secret name. There were other secret names of Rome.) After this, Macrobius quotes a secret formula of evocation *(Carmen quo di evocantur, cum oppugnatione civitas cingitur)* which was supposedly chanted at the capture of Carthage. He found this in the book of Sammonicus Serenus, an otherwise unknown late second/early third-century author: "O thou, whether thou art a god or a goddess, under whose protection the people and the city of Carthage are, and thou, O greatest one, who has taken under thy protection this city and people, I pray and entreat ye, and ask this indulgence of ye, that ye desert the people and the city of Carthage, and abandon the places, temples, sacred

Although the word δαίμων in this sentence certainly means "god," a better translation would be "the genius of Carthage," i.e., the attendant spirit, guardian, and life force of the city.

---

spots and their city, and that ye depart from them. And cast on that people and city fear, terror and forgetfulness, and abandoned by them, come ye to Rome to me and my people. And may all places, temples, sacred spots, city be more acceptable and agreeable to ye. And may ye be propitious to me, the Roman people, and my soldiers, so that we may know and understand. If ye accomplish these things, I vow that temples and games will be established in your honor ... " Macrobius, *Saturnalia* 3.9.7-11, *Ambrosii Theodosii Macrobii Saturnalia*, ed. Iacobus Willis, Leipzig: Teubner, 1970, pp. 185-186. See Naphtali Lewis and Meyer Reinhold, *Roman Civilization*, vol. 1, New York: Harper, 1966, p. 145; also Macrobius, *Saturnalia*, ed. Percival U. Davies, New York and London: Columbia Univ. Press, 1969, pp. 218-219; and Servius to *Aeneid* 12.841. See also Th. H. Hopfner, "Mageia," in Pauly-Wissowa-Krol, *Realencyclopadie der classischen Altertumswissenschaft*, vol. 28, Stuttgart: Druckenmüller Verlag, 1928, pp. 301-394, esp. p. 337. Th. H. Hopfner, *Griechisch-Ägyptischer Offenbarungszauber*, 2 vols., Studien zur Palaeographie und Papyruskunde, 21 and 23, Leipzig: H. Haessel, 1921-1924. Martin P. Nilsson, *Greek Piety*, New York: W. W. Norton, 1969, pp. 170-175; W. Foerster, "Δαίμων" *Theologisches Wörterbuch zum Neuen Testament*, G. Kittel, ed., Stuttgart: Kohlhammer, 1935, vol. 2, pp. 1-21. See also H. H. Scullard, "Caelestis," *The Oxford Classical Dictionary* , Oxford: Clarendon, 1970, pp. 187-188. The one *evocatio* of which we have more information was in connection with the capture of Veii in 396 B.C. Here the *evocation* was uttered by the general, Camillus, as follows: "Pythian Apollo, led by you and inspired by your holy breath, I go forward to the destruction of Veii, and I vow to you a tenth part of the spoils. Queen Juno, to you too I pray, that you may leave this town where now you dwell and follow our victorious arms into our City of Rome, your future home, which will receive you in a temple worthy of your greatness," Livy, *Ab Urbe Condita* 5.21, in Livy, *The Early History of Rome*, ed. A. de Selincourt, Baltimore, Md.: Penguin Books, 1969, p. 348. The vow was fulfilled and in 392 B.C. a temple was dedicated on the Aventine to Juno Regina. (I read with considerable interest and with some surprise that in Roschini's massive Mariology exactly these words of Livy are quoted in support of the thesis of Mary's Queenship. Since Camillus did dedicate the temple to "Juno Regina" the pagan climate was made favorable to the concept of "Maria Regina" and in fact "A Giunone Regina sull' Aventino, succede Maria Regina," says Roschini (Roschini, op. cit., vol. 2, p. 379, with reference to Ildefonso Schuster, "Maria Regina Nell' Arte Paleocristiana in Roma," *La Regalita Di Maria* 5 (1952) 2-4. The roots of the tradition on which the cult of Mary is based, therefore, go back to the time of the capture of Veii and lead directly to the cult of Juno Regina, according to Roschini.) At one time, however, there was a Senate decree concerning Caelestis, as it appears from the *Regulae Iuris* 22.6 of Ulpian: "We cannot appoint any of the gods our heirs, except those whom we are permitted to appoint by a decree of the Senate, or by the Imperial Constitutions; for instance, the Tarpeian Jove, the Didymean Apollo of Miletus, Mars in Gaul, the Trojan Minerva, Hercules of Gades, Diana of Ephesus, the Sipyleian Mother of the gods worshipped at Smyrna, and the Heavenly Goddess Selene of Carthage." See the English translation in *Corpus Iuris Civilis*, ed. S. P. Scott, Cincinnati: The Central Trust Co., 1932; repr. New York: AMS Press, 1973, p. 242.

What happened to Tanit after Carthage was destroyed in 146 B.C.? Perhaps her cult continued in the countryside, since the destruction of Carthage did not mean that Punic civilization was totally annihilated. The Punic language was spoken in North Africa for many more centuries, and so it is possible that her cult also continued. What we know for certain, however, is that the name of the goddess who was worshipped in Roman Carthage was Caelestis, and we have reason to believe that the Romans connected Juno with the original "genius" of the destroyed city. Juno shared many features with Tanit. She was originally also a goddess of menstruation through association with the moon. Most of her functions involved presiding over the experiences of women: as *Juno Interduca* she led the bride to her new home, as *Cinxia* she assisted in the loosening of her girdle, as *Opigenia* she assisted in childbirth, as *Lucina* she caused the child to see the light, and so forth.[12] So close was the resemblance between the two goddesses that Hannibal, at the invasion of Italy, chose the temple of Juno in Lacinium, near Croton, to dedicate "an altar with a long inscription containing a record of his achievements. The inscription was in Punic and Greek."[13]

---

[12] References in Iul. Vogel "Iuno," in W. H. Roscher, *Ausführliches Lexikon der Griechischen und Römischen Mythologie*, Leipzig: Teubner, 1890-1897, vol. 2, pp. 574-611; also W. H. Roscher, "Iuno Caelestis," *op. cit.*, pp. 612-615; H. J. Rose, *Religion in Greece and Rome*, New York: Harper & Row, 1959, pp. 216-219; H. J. Rose, "Juno," in *Oxford Classical Dictionary, op. cit.*, pp. 568-569.

[13] Croton is at the southern shore of the toe of Italy, near the Gulf of Taranto. See Livy, op. cit., 28.46, in Livy, *The War with Hannibal*, A. de Selincourt, ed., Baltimore, Md.: Penguin, 1965, p. 564. Polybious claims that he saw this tablet: see *Histories* 3.33.18, op. cit., p. 115. Obviously, Hannibal assumed Juno to be the Italian equivalent of the Carthaginian Queen of Heaven in whose temple as a nine-year-old boy he may have taken a solemn vow to be an enemy of Rome. (Livy, *op. cit.* 21.1; for English translation, see loc. cit., p. 23. According to Polybius, *Histories* 3.11.5, Bernstein, *op. cit.*, p. 101, the oath was made during a sacrifice to Zeus, i.e., Baal. See E. J. Bickerman, "Hannibal's Covenant," *art. cit.*, n. 22.) Similarly, the Romans viewed the temple of Tanit in Carthage as that of Juno. (Pliny: *Historia Naturalis* 6.36.20; and LCL, H. Rackham, ed., Cambridge, Mass.: Harvard, 1947, vol. 2, p. 487, ct. Virgil, *Aeneid* 1.7: " ... in Carthage alone beyond all other lands had Juno her seat ... Here was her armor, here her chariot." See J. W. MacKail, *Virgil's Works*, New York: Modern Library, 1950, p. 3. Pliny the Elder matter-of-factly relates that Hanno of Carthage found on the islands of the Gorgades native women who "had hair all over their bodies" and "he deposited the skins of the two female natives in the Temple of Juno as a proof of the truth of his story and as curiosities, which were kept on display until Carthage was taken by Rome." Apart from the fact that the

The year 146 B.C. ends the history of Carthage as a Phoenician city and also the worship of the Queen of Heaven under the name of Tanit. The new name of the "genius of Carthage" soon would be Iuno Caelestis, from which the name Juno was dropped and the goddess was called simply "Caelestis." Almost certainly the Gracchan settlement *Iunonia* [14] had a sanctuary of Caelestis, but

---

natives in question were probably chimpanzees, it is interesting that the temple of Tanit was equated by a Roman with that of Juno. The epithet "Queen of Heaven" was also current for Juno, thus could Virgil write about the sufferings of Aeneas: " ... why did the Queen of Heaven urge on a man ... to circle through all those afflictions?" *Aeneid* 1.15. Similarly, Cicero could thunder against Verres: "Hear me Juno, Queen of Heaven; thou whose two sacred and ancient shrines, built by our allies in their two islands of Melita and Samos, this same Verres with an equal wickedness stripped of all their offerings and adornment": *The Verrine Orations* 5.72, in L. H. G. Greenwood, *LCL*, Cambridge, Mass.: Harvard, 1953, vol. 2, p. 673; also 4.103, *op. cit.*, p. 409. See also Ovid, *Fasti* 6.37: *"cur igitur regina vocar princepsque dearum?"* J. G. Frazer, ed., London: Heinemann, 1931, p. 320.) This might give us an indication why the settlement established under Gaius Gracchus was called Iunoia: Carthage was from the beginning a city of the Queen of Heaven and if in 146 B.C. the evocation and the vow to build a temple to her was indeed taken, by the establishment of Iunoia and the building of a temple to Juno that vow would have been fulfilled.

We have some information about the temple of Juno in Lacinium; because of the close resemblance between Juno and Tanit, and the general similarity of the architectural features of ancient sanctuaries, we may have an idea of the appearance of the temple of Tanit. Livy reports: "Six miles from (Croton) was a temple more famous than the city itself, that of Lacinian Juno, revered by all the surrounding peoples. There a sacred grove, which was enclosed by dense woods and tall fir trees, had in its centre luxurious pastures, where cattle of all kinds, being sacred to the goddess, used to pasture without any shepherd" (*Ab urbe condita* 24.3; see the English translation of *LCL*, Frank G. Moore, ed., Cambridge, Mass.: Harvard Univ. Press, 1966, vol . 6, pp. 181-183.) This description compares favorably with Virgil's picture of the temple in Carthage (see n. 3 above). We have already seen that Hannibal visited this temple and this visit was also remembered by Cicero, who wrote that Hannibal wanted to carry off a golden column from the temple of Juno at Lacinium, but the goddess appeared to him in a vision and warned him not to do it. Hannibal obeyed the goddess and made the image of a calf from the gold he had purloined from the column (he bored into it to see whether it was solid gold) and placed it on the top. (*De Divinatione* 1.24.48, *LCL*, William A. Falconer, ed., Cambridge, Mass.: Harvard, 1953, p. 277.) Like all temples, this one housed the image of the goddess, which, again in accordance with the custom of the ancients, was dressed in a robe. The robe was beautiful and admired by all; but more about that later.

14 Plutarch, *Gaius Gracchus* 9.2: "And now Rubrius, one of his colleagues in the tribuneship, brought in a bill for the founding of a colony on the site of Carthage, which had been destroyed by Scipio, and Caius, upon whom the lot fell, sailed off to Africa as superintendent of the foundation." *Plutarch's Lives*, Bernadette Perrin, ed., *LCL*, London: Heinemann, 1959, pp. 218-219.

the real fame and popularity of the goddess came after the time of Octavian Augustus. It was then that the temple of Juno Caelestis became a large and famous complex and that her worship spread over a large part of the Roman Empire.

Who was this Juno Caelestis, and what did she represent?[15] She was for Roman Carthage basically what Tanit was for the Phoenician city, but with important modifications. The syncretism which had already begun in the original city progressed steadily in the Roman colony. First, identification of Juno with other goddesses was easy, and of this we have many examples.[16] But

---

Ibid. 11.1-2: "In Africa, moreover, in connection with the planting of a colony on the site of Carthage, to which Caius gave the name Iunonia, in Greek Heraea, there are said to have been many prohibitory signs from the gods." *Op. cit.*, pp. 220-221. See also Plutarch, *The Lives of the Noble Grecians and Romans*, trans. John Dryden, rev. Arthur H. Clough, New York: Modern Library, n.d., pp. 1013-1014. Iunonia is also mentioned by Iulius Solinus (fl. 200 A.D.), *Collectanea Rerum Memorabilium*, chap. 39, English trans. by Arthur Golding (1587), facsimile repr. by George Kish, Gainsville, Fla.: Scholars' Facsimiles and Reprints, 1955, n.p. Another edition by Theodor Mommsen, *C. Iulii Solini Collectanea Rerum Memorabilium*, Berlin: Weidmann, 1895. See also Th. Mommsen, *The History of Rome*, Cleveland/New York: World,1967, pp. 63, 79 .

[15] One would expect that because of the importance of the topic there would be at least one monograph on Caelestis, but this is not the case. The best book on the subject is still A. Audollent, Carthage Romain, supra, n. 5. He collected much of the epigraphical evidence for the cult of Caelestis, as well as the ancient Greco-Roman and Christian references. Also very useful is F. Cumont, "Caelestis," in *Pauly's Realencyclopadie*, op. cit., vol. 3:1, pp. 1247-1250; Joseph Dölger, "Die Himmelskönigin von Karthago. Ein religionsgeschichtlicher Beitrag zu den Schriften Tertullians," *Antike und Christentum* 1 (1929) 92-106, is more than just what its title says. G. H. Halsberghe's "Le Culte de Dea Caelestis," *Aufstieg und Niedergang der römischen Welt*, Berlin/New York: Walter de Gruyter, 1984, Series II (Prinzipat), vol. 17/4, pp. 2204-2223, is based largely on Dölger. See also Howard H. Scullard, "Caelestis," *The Oxford Classical Dictionary*, 2nd ed., pp. 187-188; W. H. Roscher, "Iuno Caelestis," in Roscher's *Lexikon, op. cit.*, pp. 612-615. Some material is also in works dealing with the history of Carthage and Carthaginian religion, especially those of Movers, *op. cit.*; Davis, *op. cit.*; G. Charles-Picard, *Les Religions de l'Afrique antique*, Paris: Plon,1954. The spread of the cult under the emperor Septimius Severus is dealt with by Alfred von Domaszewski, *Die Religion des römischen Heeres*, Trier: Fr. Lintz, 1895, and *Abhandlungen zur römischen Religion*, Leipzig/Berlin: Teubner, 1909. A reaction to Domaszewski's thesis is Ilsemarie Mundle, "Dea Caelestis in der Religionspolitik des Septimius Severus und der Julia Domna," *Historia* 10 (1960) 228-237. See also Kurt Latte, *Römische Religionsgeschichte*, München: Beck, 1967, pp. 345-347.

[16] Thus, Horace, in *Odes* 2.1, referring to the defeat of the republicans in Africa, says: "Juno quit Africa with all the gods." H. E. Butler, *The Odes of Horace in English Verse*, Latin text with translation, London: G. Bell, 1929,

syncretization went on until it embraced all goddesses of fertility, as we can see from the prayer of Lucius at the end of the *Meta-morphoses:* "Blessed Queen of Heaven, whether you are pleased to be known as Ceres ... or whether as celestial Venus ... Artemis ... Proserpine ... I beseech you, by whatever name, in whatever aspect, in whatever ceremonies you deign to be invoked, have mercy on me ..." After this prayer, the goddess appeared and affirmed that all the different names under which the primordial mistress of all the elements is worshipped, whether that name is Cybele, Artemis, Aphrodite, Juno, or any other, refer to the same, namely Queen Isis.[17] Thus, all divinities representing female functions, including the Near Eastern fertility goddesses, were identified.[18]

Juno Caelestis reflected all these aspects. Tertullian mentions her once along with Cybele, at another time with Astarte, and again with Atargatis.[19] The fourth-century convert to Christianity, Firmicus Maternus (ca. 340 A.D.), a pagan until shortly before he wrote his book, remembered Caelestis as Juno or Venus, i.e., a

---

pp. 94-95. See also R. G. M. Nisbet and Margaret Hubbard, *A Commentary on Horace: Odes, Book II*, Oxford: Clarendon, 1978, pp. 24-25; Cyprian, *Quod idola dii nonsunt* 4: "Mars is a Thracian, and Jupiter a Cretan, and Juno either Argive, or Saurian or Carthaginian." (*Juno vel Argiva, vel Sauria, vel Poena.*) *ANF* 5.466. See also Valerius Maximus, *Factorum et dictorum memorabilium libri novem*, ed. C. Kempf, Lipsiae: Teubner, 1988, 1.1 Ext. 2 (p. 11), where Caelestis is simply called Juno. In the story of Amor and Psyche we read that Psyche came to a beautiful temple of Juno in the valley, in the middle of a sacred grove. There she prayed: "Sister and wife of great Jupiter, I cannot tell where you may be at the moment. You may be residing in one of your ancient temples on Samos ... Or you may be visiting *your happy city of Carthage* on its high hill, where you are adored as a virgin travelling across Heaven in a lion-drawn chariot. Or you may be watching over the famous walls of Argos ... where you are adored as the Queen of Heaven ... Wherever you are, you whom the whole East venerates as Zygia, the Goddess of Marriage, and the whole West as Lucina, Goddess of Childbirth, I appeal to you now as Juno the Protectress ... You see, Goddess, I am very, very tired, and very, very frightened and I know that you are always ready to help ..." Apuleius, *Meta-morphoses* 6.4 ET.: Robert Graves, *The Golden Ass*, New York: Farrar, Straus & Giroux, 1970, p. 128.
   17   11.3-5, *op. cit.*, pp. 262-265.
   18   "Juno autem sine dubitatione ab illis Astarte vocatur." Augustine, *Quaestiones in Heptateuchum* 7.16, MPL, 34.797.
   19   *Apologeticum* 12, *ANF* 3.28; *Apol.* 24: "Every province even, and every city, has its god. Syria has Astarte, Arabia has Dusares, the Norici have Belenus, Africa has Caelestis ... " *ANF* 3.29; *Ad Nationes* 2.8; *Apol.* 24: "How many have either seen or heard of the Syrian Atargatis, the African Caelestis ... " *ANF* 3.136.

goddess of fertility, and in this connection he said that she was the "air." He may have been referring simply to Hera (by that time it was common practice among the Stoics to make ἀήρ out of Ἥρα. It seems more likely, however, that he sensed the pagan concept of the mystery of the air as "an intermediary between sea and sky," that is, the element which filled the space created after the upper and lower regions of the universe were separated in primordial times. This separation, as we shall see in our later discussions, was the cosmogonic event which initiated the creative process. Caelestis, in the mind of the pagans, became a goddess of primordial creative powers.[20]

Considering the many inscriptions that mention the name of Caelestis and the frequent references made to her by Christian and pagan authors, we may assume that she was extremely popular, as one would expect of the patroness and "genius" of "New Carthage." Her temple, if indeed Virgil and Silius Italicus[21] patterned their descriptions after it, must have been very large, situated in a park-like setting and surrounded by many trees. Nothing remains of it. This time the destruction came not from a conquering enemy but from the recently established Christian church. The destruction of the temple was so total that no archaeological reconstruction is possible, but we know that the statue of Caelestis stood within it. Tertullian referred to that statue when he criticized pagan idols;[22] so did Augustine, who saw the image in the sanctuary.[23] This statue had been moved temporarily to Rome by the emperor Elagabalus (218-222 A.D.), who in his desire to further monotheism under the aegis of his sun-god, Elah-Gabal,

---

[20] "The Assyrians and part of the Africans ascribe the primacy among the elements to the air, and worship it in a shape which is the product of their imagination. For exactly this, the air, is what they have consecrated under the name of Juno or Venus the virgin—if virginity ever suited the fancy of Venus! ... Animated by some sort of reverential feelings, they actually have made this element into a woman. For, because air is our intermediary between sea and sky *(quia aer interiectus est inter mare et caelum)*, they honor it through priests who have womanish voices ... " Firmicus Maternus, *De errore profanorum religionum*, 4, Konrat Ziegler, ed., München: Max Hueber Verlag, 1953, p. 45. This translation is from Charles A. Forbes, ed., *Firmicus Maternus. The Error of Pagan Religions*, New York: Newman Press, 1970 (Ancient Christian Writers, vol. 37), p. 50. See also the editor's notes on pp. 150-153, and our chap. 3.

[21] See above, n. 3.

[22] *Apol.*12; ANF 3.28.

[23] *De Civitate Dei* 2.26; NPNF 2 Series, vol. 2, p. 40.

"married" him to Caelestis. First he chose Pallas Athene as a mate for his god, "but then he declared that his god was displeased with such a war-like goddess who was always armed and sent for the statue of Urania, who was worshipped widely among the Carthaginians and others in Libya."[24] Elagabalus then built a temple to Caelestis on the Capitoline near the temple of Juno Moneta.[25] Thus, Elagabalus may have been responsible for offiially introducing the cult of Caelestis into the city,[26] but it is more than likely that private worship of the goddess had begun there long before. After the assassination of Elagabalus, the statue was returned to its original home.

The temple of Caelestis was a place of oracles. We are told that when he was proconsul in Africa, the emperor Pertinax (193 A.D.) suppressed many rebellions "by the aid of prophetic verses which issued from the temple of Caelestis." A similar statement is made in the story of Macrianus (260-261 A.D.): "The priestess of Caelestis at Carthage was wont, when inspired by the goddess, to predict the truth."[27] To some extent the popularity of Caelestis may be attributed to her fame as a source of oracles; the early imperial age was a time when people were greatly worried about the

---

[24] Herodian, *History* 5.6.4-6, *LCL*, C. R. Whittaker, ed., Cambridge, Mass.: Harvard, 1969, pp. 48-51. The rest of Herodian's description is as follows: "Tradition says that Dido the Phoenician set up the statue at the time presumably when she founded the ancient city of Carthage, after cutting up the hide. The name used by the Libyans for the goddess is Urania, by the Phoenicians Astroarche; they would also have it that she is the moon goddess. A marriage between the sun and the moon, Antoninus declared, was very appropriate, and he sent for the statue together with all the gold from her temple. He also issued orders that a very large sum of money should be contributed, supposedly as a dowry. When the statue had been brought, he married it to the god, giving instructions that all the inhabitants of Rome and Italy should celebrate in public and private with all kinds of festivities and banquets, as though this were a real marriage of the gods." The story is also related by Dio, *Roman History* 79.12, LCL, Earnest Cary, ed., London: Heinemann, 1961, vol. 9, p. 461.

[25] Today the church of the *Ara Coeli* stands on the site of the temple of Juno Moneta; no sign of the temple of Caelestis is discernible.

[26] See Mundle, *op. cit.*, pp. 235-236, who argues against the thesis of Domaszewski that it was Septimius Severus (193-211 A.D.) and his second wife, Julia Domna, who popularized the cult. According to Domaszewski, Elagabalus built two temples for Caelestis, one on the Capitoline (this he concludes from the *Scriptores Historiae Augustae Vita Heliogabali* 1.6) and a larger one farther out (which he bases on Herodian 5.6.6).

[27] SHA, Pertinax 4.2, *op. cit.*, vol. 1, p. 321; SHA, Macrianus 3.1, *op. cit.*, vol. 2, p. 53.

salvation of their souls and eagerly looked for answers to questions raised by the facts of life and death.[28] The temple had priests
as well as the priestesses mentioned by Macrianus and various
orders of minor clergy. Augustine refers to "priests and choristers" who took part in the liturgy and to a "vast assemblage of
people" who attended.[29] Indeed, the shrine of Caelestis may have
been the most common place to turn to in time of need. Cyprian,
the aristocratic bishop of Carthage (200-258 A.D.), relates a story
which sounds typical of social conditions in the third century: an
abandoned child was found and was taken "to the idol where the
people flocked *(apud idolum quo populus confluebat)*, and in the
presence of the idol they gave the child bread mingled with
wine, because it was not yet able to eat meat."[30] Although the
name of Caelestis is not directly mentioned here, it is quite likely
that her temple is meant.

The church fathers who were active in North Africa, where
Caelestis was most popular, criticized and attacked her relent-
lessly. Tertullian (160-240 A.D.), a native Carthaginian, was familiar with her cult and referred to it several times in his writings.[31]
When he became a Montanist he tried to introduce the rigorous
practices of that sect among the Christians in Carthage: he wrote a
book *On Fasting*[32] in which he may have borrowed some ideas
from the cult of Caelestis. At least that was the charge raised
against him by Christians who rejected such fasts and considered
them improper innovations.[33] Tertullian advocated so-called "dry

----

[28] Alexander of Abunoteichos is a prime example of how such credulous
people could be taken advantage of by unscrupulous deceivers. See S. Benko,
Pagan Rome and the Early Christians, Bloomington: Indiana Univ. Press, 1986,
pp. 108-113. No such ill fame is attached to the shrine of Caelestis.

[29] *De Civitate Dei* 2.4, *NPNF* Series 1, vol. 2, p. 25.

[30] *De Lapsis* 25, *ANF* 5.444. The rest of the story is informative about the
mentality of some Christians, which may not have been very different from
that of their pagan neighbors. Cyprian, who claims to have been an eyewitness of these events, says that the bread and wine given to this child was
taken from food that was previously dedicated to an idol. When later the
child was given the Eucharist (infant communion!), she began to cry and
vomit, i.e., the elements of the Eucharist and pagan sacrificial food rejected
each other — a case of so-called "antipathetic magic." See Benko, *op. cit.,* p.
125.

[31] See also *Apol.* 12, 23, 24; *Ad Nat.* 2.8.

[32] *De Ieiunio, CSEL* 20.296; *ANF* 4.113.

[33] Hippolytus, *Refutation* 12: "They introduce the novelties of fasts and
feasts, and meals of parched food ... " *ANF* 5.123. See also Jerome, *Epistola*
41.3, *NPNF,* Series 2, vol. 6, p. 56.

fasts" *(Xerophagies)*, i.e., fasts involving abstention from not only solid food but also water. He bitterly attacked other Christians for criticizing this practice and in the process gave us information about Caelestis:

> Whence it is that even they who court their idols by dressing them, and by adorning them in their sanctuary,[34] and by saluting them at each particular hour, are said to do them service. But, more than that, the heathens recognize every form of humiliation (ταπεινοφρόνησις). When the heaven is rigid and they year arid, barefooted processions are enjoined by public proclamation; the magistrates lay aside their purple, reverse the fasces, utter prayer, offer a victim.

In some areas, he continues, people put on sackcloth and sprinkled themselves with ashes, closed their shops and baths, kept only one fire in public on the altars and "no water even in their platters ... " What a magnificent portrait of public penance and a day of prayer dedicated to the *pluviarum pollicitatrix* for the blessings of rain in a time of draught! Tertullian ranked it as an ultimate insult that the "orthodox" Christians put his *xerophagy* on the same level with the cult of the pagan goddesses.[35] Yet his report is testimony to pagan piety.

In spite of the rapid progress of Christianity, the popularity of Caelestis remained. Her temple is mentioned as the most popular public place by the Cathaginian bishop Cyprian (200-258 A.D.).[36] Ambrose, the bishop of Milan (339-397 A.D.), mentions her matter-of-factly in his response to the letter of Symmachus, in which that noble Roman requested the restoration of the Altar of Victory in the Senate.[37] The religion of Caelestis was still alive and well in 363 A.D. when the temple of Apollo at Daphnae burned down. The emperor Julian suspected the Christians as the arsonists, but Ammianus Marcellinus (330-395 A.D.), the last great Roman historian, who accompanied Julian in his campaigns, said that the fire may have been started by the philosopher Asclepiades, who "placed before the lofty feet of the statue a little silver image of the *Dea Caelestis*, which he always carried with

---

[34] Reference to the Robe of Caelestis; more on this in our next chapter.
[35] *Loc. cit.*, n. 32.
[36] See p. 34.
[37] *Letter* 18.30, *Epistola Contra Symmachum, MPL* 16, 980, *NPNF*, Series 2, vol. 10, p. 421.

him wherever he went, and after lighting some wax tapers as usual, went away."[38] Some pagans, it seems, carried an image of the goddess with them much the same way as some Christians today wear around their necks a medallion bearing an image of Mary.

We gain considerable information about Caelestis from Augustine (354-430 A.D.), the great bishop of Hippo. He was born in North Africa at Thagaste,[39] taught at one time in Carthage, and knew the cult from firsthand experience. As a young man he participated in the services in her temple; he listened to the choir and watched the priests. At one time he attended a *ferculum*, i.e., a religious banquet at which actors gave performances before the statue of the goddess which was placed on a couch as if it were to be feasted. In retrospect he judged the words spoken there lewd and the whole performance offensive.[40] He does not say how old he was when he attended this service, but if he was twenty-one, then in the year 375 A.D. "vast crowds" were still coming to the temple of Caelestis from all quarters of the city. Not only women but men, too, came to these services. Augustine says they came

---

[38] *Histories* 22.13.3, LCL, John C. Rolfe, ed., London: Heinemann,1950, pp. 270-271.

[39] Hippo was at the site of modern Bone in what is Algeria today and Thagaste is Souk Ahras, Algeria.

[40] *De civitate dei* 2.4: "I myself, when I was a young man, used sometimes to go to the sacrilegious entertainments and spectacles; I saw the priests raving in religious excitement, and heard the choristers; I took pleasure in the shameful games which were celebrated in honor of gods and goddesses, of the virgin Caelestis, and Berecynthia, the mother of the gods. (*Berecyntus* is a mountain in Phyrgia sacred to Cybele; from this came the expression *Berecynthia mater*, i.e., Cybele, the Great Mother.) And on the holy day consecrated to her purification, there were sung before her couch productions so obscene and filthy for the ear — I do not say of the mother of the gods, but of the mother of any senator or honest man — nay, so impure, that not even the mother of the foul mouthed players themselves could have formed one of the audience. For natural reverence for parents is a bond which the most abandoned cannot ignore. And, accordingly, the lewd actions and filthy words with which these players honored the mother of the gods, in presence of a vast assemblage and audience of both sexes, they could not for very shame have rehearsed at home in presence of their own mother. And the crowds that were gathered from all quarters by curiosity, offended modesty must, I should suppose, have scattered in the confusion of shame. If these are sacred rites, what is sacrilege? If this is purification, what is pollution? This festivity was called the Tables (=*Fercula*) as if a banquet were being given at which unclean devils might find suitable refreshment ... " *NPNF*, Series 1, vol. 2, p. 25. See also *De civ. dei* 4.10, *op. cit.*, p. 70, where he repeats these charges.

out of curiosity. But how does he know that? Perhaps the service of Caelestis touched a responsive chord in the hearts of the worshippers. Unwillingly Augustine paid a compliment to pagan piety: "There are some," he says, "who dismiss God when they hunger in this world and they ask Mercury or Jupiter to grant a boon which may be granted to them, or they may ask the same of her whom they call Caelestis, or some other similar daemon: but their flesh does not thirst after God."[41] Who were these who in time of need abandoned God and turned to Caelestis? Could they have been unstable Christians? Augustine did not say, but he was intrigued enough by the popularity of Caelestis to return to the topic again. Once more he described this pagan ceremony, or perhaps another which he had attended. Again he was offended by the presence of prostitutes and did not understand how they could have a place in the service of a "virgin" goddess. The rites were so obscene that many prudent women turned away from what was going on because they were not able to watch acts so licentious. Even in the privacy of their homes, Augustine says, people could do such things only in secret. Augustine did not close his eyes to what he saw, but carefully watched and observed everything; only in retrospect did he condemn in righteous indignation what he saw.[42] It is interesting to note that Augustine

---

[41] *Enarratio in Psalmum* 62.7, *MPL* 36.752.

[42] *De civitate dei* 2.26: "Where and when those initiated in the mysteries of Caelestis received any good instructions, we know not. What we do know is, that before her shrine, in which her image is set, and amidst a vast crowd gathering from all quarters, and standing closely packed together, we were intensely interested spectators of the games which were going on, and saw, as we pleased to turn the eye, on this side a grand display of harlots, on the other the virgin goddess; we saw this virgin worshipped with prayer and with obscene rites. There we saw no shame-faced mimes, no actress overburdened with modesty; all that the obscene rite demanded was fully complied with. We were plainly shown what was pleasing to the virgin deity, and the matron who witnessed the spectacle returned home from the temple a wise woman. Some indeed, of the more prudent women turned their faces from the immodest movements of the players, and learned the art of wickedness by a furtive regard. For they were restrained, by the modest demeanor due to men, from looking boldly at the immodest gestures; but much more they were restrained from condemning with chaste heart the sacred rites of her whom they adored. And yet this licentiousness — which, if practiced in one's home, could only be done there in secret — was practiced as a public lesson in the temple; and if any modesty remained in men, it was occupied in marvelling that wickedness which men could not unrestrainedly commit should be part of the religious teaching of the gods, and that to omit its exhibition should incur the anger of the

was so terribly upset by sexual inferences in connection with the
"Virgin Caelestis" at a time when Christians were openly discussing sexual matters pertaining to the Virgin Mary. They constantly talked about the virginity of Mary, which they described as
"ante partum, in partu, post partum," i.e., before, during, and after the
birth of Jesus. What could be more indelicate than the detailed
description of the condition of Mary's hymen in the Christian
treatise called the *Protoevangelium of James?*[43] This treatise did not
upset Augustine or the Christian congregations; nonetheless, they
condemned their pagan contemporaries for what they called
their open lewdness.

Another practice for which Augustine criticized the Carthaginians was that of temple prostitution. Speaking about Venus, he
says: "To her also the Phoenicians offered a gift by prostituting
their daughters before they united them to husbands."[44] A similar
custom was also reported by the Roman historian Valerius Maximus, who lived during the reign of Emperor Tiberius (14-37
A.D.):

> In Sicca in fact, there is a temple of Venus, into which respectable
> ladies used to gather, and so after they had gone forth to enrich
> themselves they contracted for their dowries by dishonoring their
> bodies: respectable marriage, then, no wonder (is made) so dis-
> reputable by this obligation of the union.[45]

---

gods. What spirit can that be, which by a hidden inspiration stirs men's
corruption, and goads them to adultery, and feeds on the full fledged iniqui-
ty, unless it be the same that finds pleasure in such religious ceremonies,
sets in the temples images of devils, and loves to see in play the images of
vices; that whisper in secret some righteous sayings to deceive the few who
are good, and scatters in public invitations to profligacy, to gain possession of
the millions who are wicked?" *NPNF*, Series 2, vol. 2, p. 40.

43   Second century A.D.; see chap. VI, p. 196ff.

44   *De civitate dei* 4.10, *op. cit.*, p. 70.

45   *"Siccae enim fanum est Veneri, in quod se matronae conferebant atque dei
procedentes ad questum, dotis corporis iniuria contrahebant honesta nimirum tam
inhonesto vinculo coniugia inuncturae."* Valerius Maximus, *Factorum et Dictorum
memorabilium libri novem* 2.6.15, Lipsiae: Teubner,1988, C. Kempf, ed., p. 81.
Sicca or Sicca Veneria in what is today Tunisia was the center of the cult of
Venus. Modern name of the town is *le Kef.* Action was taken against two
such temples by the emperor Constantine, as reported by Eusebius *Vita
Constantini* 3.55 and 58. This is what he says; 3.55 *NPNF*, Series II, vol. 1, pp.
534-535: Constantine had the temple of the "foul demon" Venus at Aphaka
on Mt. Lebanon destroyed, because in there effeminate priests "forgot the
dignity of their sex" and there was "unlawful commerce of women and
adulterous intercourse." 3.58 *NPNF*, *op. cit.*, pp. 535-536: in the City of

Not noted for the depth of his thought, accuracy, or critical analysis, Valerius Maximus here may have misinterpreted an element in this practice: the women prostituted themselves for the goddess and not to supplement their dowry. This comes out clearly in the report of Herodotus, who says that the obligation was on both rich and poor women, and that after they fulfilled their duty to the goddess "it [would] be impossible to seduce them by any offer."[46] Lucian, in *De Dea Syria* (chap. 6), also mentions something similar and emphasizes that the money thus gained would become an offering to Aphrodite. Prostitution before marriage for the purpose of collecting a dowry did exist in the ancient world, but it was undertaken on one's private initiative.[47] Temple prostitution as a work of piety is difficult for us to understand, but for the ancients fertility and the enjoyment of it was a divine command and blessed by the goddess of love. As sympathetic magic, its practice was believed to enhance agricultural production as well as human fertility in the community. Even more importantly, sacred intercourse represented a sacramental suspension of sexual differentiation and a return to the primordial state of union when the sexes were not yet separated. In a proleptic way, it also points forward to the time of final restoration of the cosmos' perfect state when "there is no male and female." We

Heliopolis in Phoenicia "in which those who dignify licentious pleasure with a distinguishing title of honor, had permitted their wives and daughters to commit shameless fornication." These practices were forbidden and a church was built in this city.

[46] Herodotus, *Histories* 1.199. His report concerns the temple of Aphrodite (=Mylitta) in Babylon. See *LCL*, A. D. Godley, ed., Cambridge: Harvard Univ. Press, 1975, vol. 1, p. 253; or the Penguin edition, A. de Selincourt, ed., Baltimore: Penguin, 1966, pp. 94-95. Karel van der Toorn, "Female Prostitution in Payment of Vows in Ancient Israel." *Journal of Biblical Literature* 108 (1989) 193-205 suggested that Herodotus may have "mistaken the prostitution in payment of a vow for a general, once-in-a-life-time duty p. 204. Already, however, Brigitte Menzel, *Assyrische Tempel*, Rome: Biblical Institute Press, 1981, vol. II, pp. 27-23, stated, that "...'Hierodulie' nichts mit Tempelprostitution zu tun hat ... sondern zunächst nur generell 'Tempelpersonal' bezeichnet ... Herodot (Hist. 1.199) darf nicht als Beleg für Tempelprostitution herangezogen werden." Criticism of cultic prostitution in Mesopotamia was also voiced by D. Arnaud, "La Prostitution sacree en Mesopotamie, un mythe historographique?" *Revue de l'Historie des Religions* 183 (1973) 111-115. See also article "Hieroduloi" in Pauly, op. cit. 8 (1913) 1459 ff. Very instructive is the analysis of the Herodotus passage in Urs Winter, *op. cit.*, pp. 335-337 and his general remarks on sacred prostitution, pp. 334-342.

[47] See, e.g., Herodotus, *Histories* 1.92 about Lydian girls, and van der Toorn, above, about voluntary prostitution in payment of a vow.

will return to this theme when we discuss Cybele, the Phrygian
Great Mother.[48]

The priests of Caelestis were not eunuchs and we do not hear
about "Galli" in Carthage; Roman moderation and sobriety, together with the fusion of Carthaginian Tanit with Roman Juno in
Caelestis, precluded that. This did not prevent Firmicus Maternus
(ca. 340 A.D.) from including the Africans in his diatribe against
effeminate priests who had womanish voices, rubbed their skin
smooth, wore female clothing, flaunted their impure bodies, and
boasted of their depravity. What kind of divinity was it, Firmicus
asks, which delighted in such unnatural human bodies?

> Blush ... you poor wretches; God created you other than this! ...
> Reject this great and calamitous error, and abandon at last
> the inclination of the heathen heart. Do not take your body which
> God created and condemn it by the wicked law of the devil. While
> time still permits, go to the rescue of your disastrous situation.[49]

All this sounds very much like Gibbon's condemnation of early
Christian monasticism.[50]

Without trying to excuse the behavior of the *Galli*, one can
wonder whether Firmicus would similarly criticize the Anchorites and Cenobites of the Egyptian and Syrian deserts or praise
them for torturing their bodies "which God created"? At any rate,
the cult of Caelestis did not include this rite of priestly castration,
and Firmicus' criticism fits only Cybele or the *Dea Syria*.

The worship of Caelestis continued and the temple in Carthage
served its purpose. Filastrius (died ca. 397 A.D.) still referred to it
as a living religion and cult.[51] But when the end came in 399
A.D., the temple was taken over amid loud pagan protests and
converted into a Christian church. Forcible christianization now
went at full speed, and soon Christians demanded total destruction

[48] Chap . 2 , p. 70ff.
[49] Firmicus Maternus, *De errore profanorum religionum* 4.4, *op. cit.*, pp. 50-51.
The repulsive behavior of the eunuch priests is described in the eighth
chapter of Apuleius, *Metamorphoses*.
[50] *Decline and Fall of the Roman Empire*, chap. 37, J. B. Bury, ed., London:
Methuen, 1909, vol. 4, pp. 78-79.
[51] *Liber de haeresibus* 15: "*Alia est haeresis in Judaeis, quae reginam quam et
fortunam coeli nuncupant, quam et coelestem vocant in Africa, eique sacrificia offerre
non dubitabant, ut etiam prophetae Jeremiae Judaei tunc dicerent ex aperto . . .*"
(quotes Jer. 44.27), *MPL* 12.1126-1127; also *CSEL* 38.1898 and *CCL* 9.1957;
Filastrius composed this book between 385 and 391 A.D.

of paganism. In 401 a general council was held in Carthage under the chairmanship of Bishop Aurelius, and the assembled fathers called upon the emperors to destroy pagan sanctuaries, images and relics of the gods, even the parks and gardens in which the sanctuaries and shrines stood. Even today the sanctimonious words fall heavy on the ear:

> Item placuit, ab imperatoribus gloriosissimis peti, ut reliquiae idololatriae non solum in simulacris, sed in quibuscumque locis, vel lucis, vel arboribus omnimode deleantur. Aurelius episcopus ecclesiae Carthaginis, supra comprehensis in nostro concilio statutis subscripsi. Similiter septuaginta duo episcopi suscripserunt.[52]

In 421 A.D., under the supervision of the imperial tribune Ursus, the magnificent temple was demolished and the site became a Christian cemetery. Whether this wanton destruction had to do with the pagans' demand that the church be returned to them, we do not know. We do know that the pagans claimed that they had received an oracle from Caelestis[53] to that effect, and we do know that soon after that, all the buildings of the complex were demolished. Why? If, as Christians claimed, the pagan deities did not exist, why bother to destroy their idols and temples? No answer was ever given.

But the power of Caelestis was broken. Augustine reflects with melancholy upon her past glory: "What were the kingdoms of this earth? The kingdoms of idols, the kingdoms of daemons are broken ... How great was the power of Caelestis which was in Carthage! Where is now the kingdom of Caelestis?"[54] By then, however, more was broken than the kingdom of Caelestis, and Augustine knew it. The empire of Rome was broken, the barbarians were battering at the door of Utica, and the Christian bishop there was desperately trying to exonerate the church from blame for the disaster which befell Rome. Christians were not the cause of Rome's problems, he claimed. Constantinople was the proof because it was founded by a Christian emperor, lost its false gods,

---

[52] Johannes Dominicus Mansi, *Sacrorum conciliorum nova et amplissima collectio*, vol. 3, Florentiae: Expensis Antonii Zatti Veneti, 1795, p. 971. The date of the Fifth General Council was 401, according to Carl J. Hefele, *Conciliengeschichte*, Freiburg: Herder, 1875, vol. 2, pp. 80-81.

[53] See below, n.57.

[54] *Enarratio in psalmum* 94.14, *MPL* 37, 1270.

and still prospered. "Carthage remains now in its possession of the name of Christ, yet once upon a time its goddess Caelestis was overthrown; because celestial she was not, but terrestrial."[55] Carthage, however, did not long survive as a Roman city. In 439 Gaiseric, the Vandal king, captured it and, among others, destroyed "the theatres, the temple 'Memory' with the passage surnamed 'Celestis.'"[56] At the time of the Vandal invasion there was still a street called Celestis in Carthage!

One of Augustine's pupils, Quodvultdeus, became bishop of Carthage in 437 A.D., but was expelled when the city fell. Thereupon he fled to Campania where he wrote a book in which he reminisced about Carthaginian Caelestis. Since he was an eyewitness to some of the events that he described, his report is worth quoting in full:

> In Africa, at Carthage, Caelestis — as they called her — had a vast temple surrounded by sanctuaries of all their gods; its street was decorated with mosaics as well as lavish columns and walls of stone which extended very nearly 2,000 feet. It had been closed for a long time, fenced in and obscured by wild thorny thickets, when the Christian people wanted to appropriate it for the service of the true religion. But the pagan people cried out that there were dragons and serpents to protect the temple. This only further inflamed the Christians with zeal, and they removed all the bushes without coming to any harm; with the same ease they consecrated the temple to their God and Lord. In fact, when they celebrated the solemn rite of Easter, and a great crowd had gathered, coming from far and wide in curiosity, the one we must call the father of a number of priests and a man worthy of our reverance, Bishop Aurelius, now a citizen of the Heavenly Kingdom (City), established his throne there in the house of Caelestis and set siege. I myself was present then, with some friends and companions, and as we turned from side to side in our youthful impatience, examining each detail according to its importance, something marvelous and incredible presented itself to our eyes: an inscription in huge bronze letters on the front of the temple read: *Aurelius Pontifex dedicavit* (Aurelius, the High Priest, has dedicated [this temple]). Upon reading this the people were amazed that the foreseeing God had accomplished this deed, which the prophetic spirit had inspired, by his own sure command. And when a

---

55 *Sermon* 55.12, *NPNF*, Series 1, vol. 6, p. 434.

56 Victor of Vita, *Historia persecutionis africanae provinciae*, 1.3.6, Michael Petschenig, ed., Vienna: C. Gerld, 1881. Also, *CSEL* 7.5. There is an English translation: *The Memorable and Tragical History of the Persecutions in Africke ...* 1605, repr. Menston, Yorkshire: Scholar Press, 1969. Victor wrote around 488-489.

pagan put forth a certain false oracle as if it came from the same Caelestis, which said that the voice and the temples would be returned to their former rites, then God, that true God whose prophetic oracles know nothing of how to lie or how to deceive, commanded through the present emperor, the pious and Christian Valentinian, son of Constantine and Augusta Placida, that through the efforts the tribune Ursus, all the temples should be razed to the ground and, scattering [their stones], he should leave only the fields, evidently as a sepulchre for the dead. Even the voice of Caelestis, destroyed now by the Vandals, was left without memory.[57]

But faith dies hard, and in spite of what Quodvultdeus said, the Carthaginians remained attached to their Queen, even under Vandal rule. Not only were there many pagans who openly confessed their attachment to Caelestis, there were even Christians who secretly paid homage to her. Salvian, a Christian clergyman (400-480 A.D.) living in Marseilles, reflected upon this situation in Africa and complained that many "so-called" Christians went to the service of Caelestis before or after the Christian worship service. It would have been better, he says, if these Christians had not come at all, because then they would be guilty only of negligence, but this way they were guilty of sacrilege.[58] Slowly, however, the memory of Caelestis faded, as did the cults of other divine queens in other parts of what was and what remained of the Roman Empire.

B. Isis

Unlike Caelestis, Isis has been written about so often in recent years that a short summary of her cult will here suffice.[59] Isis

---

[57] *De promissionibus et predictionibus dei*, 3.38.44, MPL 51.835-836. The book is sometimes ascribed to Prosper of Tiro (390-455); on the controversy, see B. Altaner and R. Stuiber, Patrologie, 7th ed., Freiburg: Herder, 1966, p. 449. Also Rene Braun, Quodvultdeus. Livre des promesses et des predictions de dieu, Tome II, Paris: Cerf, 1964, pp. 547-579.

[58] *De Gubernatione Dei* 8.2 ET., *The Writings of Salvian the Presbyter*, Jeremiah F. O'Sullivan, ed. (The Fathers of the Church), New York: Cima Publishing, 1947, pp. 226-227. The book was written around 440 A.D.

[59] Some of the recent literature includes R. E. Witt, *Isis in the Graeco-Roman World*, Ithaca, N.Y.: Cornell Univ. Press, 1971; Ladislaw Vidman, *Isis und Sarapis bei den Griechen und Römern*, Berlin: Walter de Gruyter, 1970; Sharon K. Heyob, *The Cult of Isis Among Women in the Graeco-Roman World*, Leiden: E. J. Brill, 1975; Friedrich Solmsen, *Isis Among Greeks and Romans*, Cambridge: Harvard Univ. Press, 1979; G. Roeder, "Isis," in *Pauly-Wissowa*, 9.2084-2132; Ed Meyer and W. Drexel, "Isis," in *W. H. Roscher, Lexikon*, II/1,

emerged as the most popular goddess in Egypt after a long period of development. It is important to note that this development took place in two distinct periods: that of ancient Egypt and the other of Hellenistic Egypt, when it became the cult that was known to Romans and Christians.

According to ancient Egyptian mythology, Isis came into being at the third level of creation. The wife of Osiris, she was a celestial divinity. However, for the Egyptians the "heavens" were also the primordial ocean, the water from which everything came. As wife of Osiris and mother of the sun-god, Horus, she was deeply connected with the origin of life. In the myth of Osiris, best known to us from the account of Plutarch,[60] it is Isis who resurrects her dead husband, saves her child Horus, and even protects Seth, the murderer of Osiris. Thus viewed as one in possession of powerful magic, the mother of god who could bestow immortality, Isis grew in importance.

As the Greeks began to identify the Egyptian divinities with their own, Isis became Demeter, a nature goddess who also presided over a powerful mystery. Osiris became Dionysus, and Horus, Apollo.[61] The real popularity of Isis in the Greco-Roman world, however, began in Hellenistic times when she became associated with the new god, Sarapis.[62] When and exactly how this happened is a controversial topic. However, at this time a new Isis cult developed and quickly spread into Greece and Italy. In the fourth century B.C. there was already a sanctuary of Isis in Athens, and possibly a hundred years later she was known in Sicily. From there the cult spread northward into other Italian cities, including Pompeii, where excavations yielded evidence that the cult flourished there by the first century A.D.

In Rome the atmosphere was not favorable for foreign, especially oriental, cults. Isis had a stormy history there, sometimes tolerated, sometimes forbidden, depending on the mood of the Senate and later, the emperors. It was only Caligula (37-41 A.D.)

360-548; A. D. Nock, *Conversion*, Oxford: Oxford Univ. Press, 1933; J. Gwynn Griffiths, *Plutarch's De Iside et Osiride*, Univ. of Wales, 1970; J. Gwynn Griffiths, *Apuleius of Madauros. The Isis Book. (Metamorphoses, Book XI)*, Leiden: E. J. Brill, 1975; Tran Tam Tinh, *Isis Lactans*, Leiden: E. J. Brill, 1973.

[60] See J. G. Griffith's analysis quoted above.

[61] Herodotus 2, 42.59.156.

[62] The name may derive from Osiris-Apis, Apis in this connection meaning the soul of Osiris; for references, see Heyob, *op. cit.*, p. 3.

who finally gave official recognition to the cult. Isis became a very popular goddess, even though a great number of oriental mysteries competed for people's loyalties in the early empire. Isis flourished even under the pressure of the growing and increasingly aggressive Christian movement. By the end of the fourth century, pagan cults were deliberately and violently exterminated. As a result of this systematic persecution, Isis, too, slowly disappeared in a process similar to that of Caelestis.

Two great festivals, the *Isia* and the *Navigium Isidis*, belonged to the cult of Isis. The first, a dramatic presentation of the story of Osiris, was celebrated in Rome at the beginning of November. After Osiris was brutally murdered by Seth and his body was cut into pieces, Isis wandered through the land, weeping and looking for the corpse of her husband. All this was reenacted during the festival. When the corpse was found, the participants cried out in joy: "We have found it, let us rejoice together!" Then Osiris was raised from the dead and there was general rejoicing.[63] No doubt this mystery play made as deep an impression on the pagans as the reenactment of the passion of Jesus Christ made upon Christians. People wept and beat their breasts over the death of Osiris; with loud jubilation they rejoiced when the body was found and Osiris was resurrected. Christian and non-initiated Roman authors made fun of this ritual; to them, this grieving and rejoicing made no sense since, to them, nothing was lost and nothing was found. But readers who are familiar with Good Friday and Easter celebrations will understand that for Isiac initiates these were deeply meaningful rites; they dealt with the mysteries of death and resurrection and evoked in the participants a sense of eternal life.

The *Navigium Isidis* (πλοιαφεσία = "Navigation of Isis") was held on March 5, as a festival commemorating either the launching of the ship of Isis to Phoenicia, searching for Osiris, or her arrival from Phoenicia. The celebration marked the beginning of the new season of seafaring and it was a festive and joyful gather-

---

[63] Herodotus, 2.171; Plutarch, *op. cit.*, chap. 27 = Griffiths, op. cit., pp. 388-393, for commentary; Athenagoras, *Supplicatio* 22; Firmicus Maternus, *De errore* ... 2.3, 6, 9, 27; Seneca, *Apocolocyntosis* 13 quotes the words when Claudius arrives in the underworld. (Apostolos Athanassakis, *Apocolocyntosis Divi Claudii*, Lawrence, Kan.: Coronado Press, 1973, p. 12; Minucius Felix, *Octavius* 23. For references from classical Latin authors, see Heyob, *op. cit.*, p. 55, n.9.)

ing. Apuleius (*Metamorphoses* 11.7-17) described such a procession. Soon after sunrise the streets were already full of people. All nature seemed joyful, birds were singing melodiously "making sweet welcome ... to the mother of the stars, the parent of times and mistress of all the world." The trees seemed to rejoice in their fertility, and the sky was fair and clear.People came dressed in the habits of various professions: one came as a warrior, another as a hunter, another as a gladiator, yet another as a fisherman, and so forth. In the midst of the multitude one might see the "saving goddess" triumphantly marching forward. Women, dressed in white and wearing garlands on their heads, spread herbs along her way; others held mirrors in their hands turned toward the goddess; yet others had ivory combs in their hands, indicating that they were trained to adorn the hair of the goddess. Some people dropped balm and precious ointments on the way, and a multitude of men and women held lamps, candles, and torches in their hands in honor of the one who was "born of the celestial stars." Then came a group of singing youths in white vestments, followed by trumpeters and musicians with pipes and flutes. The initiates followed, all in glistening white linen dresses. The women had their hair anointed but the heads of the men were shaven. In their hands they held brass timbrels which gave out a shrill sound. Now came the principal priests, carrying ceremonial objects, and then people dressed as the gods: Anubis wearing the head of a dog, then a cow representing the great and youthful "mother of all." Following them came the officials who carried in precious boxes the secrets of the religion, which nobody could see. And finally came the high priest, holding in his hand a timbrel and a garland of roses. The procession went to the sea coast where the high priest dedicated and launched a beautifully decorated ship that the breeze soon blew far away out of sight. After this the people assembled in the temple, where the holy objects were properly disposed of and prayers were said. The multitude then was dismissed and "all the people gave a great shout," embraced and kissed each other, and took home all kinds of leafy branches, herbs, and flowers.[64]

And now Apuleius describes the initiation of Lucius into the mysteries of Isis as the conclusion of the whole story, for *Meta-*

---

[64] *LCL*, Adlington and S. Gaselee, ed., pp. 550-569 (1935).

morphoses, as the title of the book indicates, is the account of a conversion.[65] The conversion of Lucius was so complete that he rented for himself a place within the temple precinct of Isis and lived there until the time for initiation arrived. Prior to that, he had to go through various rites of purification, and on the great appointed day and in the presence of a multitude of priests (the laity and the uninitiated were dismissed), he was given a new linen robe and taken to the most sacred, secret place of the temple. This is the mystery which he cannot divulge, he says, but to satisfy the curiosity of the reader he indicates so much:

> ... I approached near into hell, even to the gate of Proserpine, and after that I was ravished throughout all the elements, I returned to my proper place: about midnight I saw the sun brightly shine, I saw likewise the gods celestial and the gods internal, before whom I presented myself and worshipped them.[66]

On the second day of the ceremonies he was introduced to all the people as a new priest. Vested in fine linen decorated with symbolic flowers and images of animals, he stood on a pulpit before the image of the goddess. This was a celebration of the "nativity of his holy order," which was followed by a sumptuous banquet. This was repeated on the third day. Then Lucius went to Rome where, in the temple of Isis on the Campus Martius, he was initiated as a priest of Osiris and, with his head shaven, continued to serve as a priest.

The mysteries of Isis had sanctuaries in which the important ceremonies of the cult took place. These contained an open court with altars where the morning sacrifices were conducted, an inner chamber with the image of the goddess, and an underground crypt. This probably represented the underworld, where Lucius, too, underwent his initiation. These crypts contained water and the rite performed on Lucius must have been a symbolic drowning with Osiris and a rising again to new life.[67] While various activities took place in these temples, the most important was the worship of the goddess before her image.

---

[65] See A. D. Nock, *Conversion,* Oxford: Oxford Univ. Press, 1933; James Tatum, *Apuleius and the Golden Ass,* Ithaca and London: Cornell Univ. Press, 1979.

[66] 11.23, *LCL, op. cit.,* p. 581.

[67] Robert A. Wild, *Water in the Cultic Worship of Isis and Sarapis,* Leiden: E. J. Brill, 1981, p. 52.

Sacrifices and prayers offered to Isis are often depicted on frescoes and reliefs.

The services included the singing of hymns and music with several instruments. The nature of the mysteries demanded that some parts of the services were open only to initiates, while in others everybody could participate. People attracted to the Isiac mysteries were thus divided into three groups: priests, initiates, and laymen.

The priesthood had a number of grades and functions. The highest rank was the *chief priest* and *prophet,* after whom came the *stolist,* who was in charge of the goddess's clothing. The *pastophors* were responsible for carrying the statue, while the *neocorus* took care of the temple. There were also *scribes, astrologs,* who observed the hours, and *cantors* who performed the ritual chanting.

The initiates were called by the goddess personally, usually in a dream. As is told of Lucius in the *Metamorphoses,* they went through a series of ceremonies which included fasting, ritual cleansing and baths. These initiatory rites led eventually to a lower order of the priesthood — in the case of Lucius, to admission into the rank of the *pastophor.*

Laymen, if they so desired, could join a cult association, of which there were many. Those who were seriously interested could become members of a unit that was under the direction of a priest. From here they could go into a higher level of organization where they were given certain tasks in the cult. Such cult associations were composed of the *Sarapiastai,* the *Therapeutae,* and the *Melanophors,* who wore black clothing, indicating that they were particularly dedicated to the grieving and mourning Isis. But mention is also made of people who were identified as *Isiacus, Anubiacus,* or *Bubasticus,* referring to the person's particular devotion.

A special feature in the mysteries of Isis was the participation of women. This has been researched by Sharon Kelly Heyob in her book *The Cult of Isis Among Women in the Graeco Roman World.*[68] Many women were among the office holders of the cult.

Although most of the principal priests appear to have been men, women priests became increasingly common from the first century A.D. onward, especially in the Roman sphere. Women

---

[68] Heyob, *loc. cit.*

devotees are frequently mentioned in inscriptions and are also depicted on the wall paintings of Herculaneum. The *Metamorphoses* (Chap. 11) mentions them several times, and there is much epigraphical information to show that they were present in the cult associations.[69]

This was so, Heyob asserts, because Isis was perceived as a goddess who presided over fertility and birth and who was looked upon as the protectress of lovers. From the very beginning she was associated with the generative forces of nature, and so Lucius addressed her as "the original and motherly source of all fruitful things in the earth" and "the celestial Venus, who in the beginning of the world coupled together male and female with an engendered love."[70] As wife she could be looked upon as a prototype of earthly relationships and as mother she was often depicted in statues holding her infant son in her lap. This theme later developed into *Isis lactans*, i.e., Isis nursing her son. In the procession described by Apuleius[71] the goddess who nourishes was represented by a golden vessel shaped as a breast from which milk flowed down. Women thus saw Isis as the divine protectress who on a celestial level already experienced everything that a woman can experience in her life cycle;[72] to all her devotees she was the divine image of the female sex, protectress of all female functions.

Many religions know ablutions and sprinklings as means of spiritual purification, but in the cult of Isis water seems to have played a more important role. An indication of that is hinted at in the story of Lucius, whose first thought after the initial appearance of the goddess was to sprinkle himself with seawater. Then, before his initiation, he had to take an ordinary bath after which he was sprinkled by the priest in the sanctuary.[73] Indeed, ablution facilities found in many sanctuaries of Isis reveal elaborate systems of waterworks built for this purpose. (This aspect of the Isiac mystery was researched and analyzed by Robert A. Wild, who

---

[69] *Op. cit*, pp. 81-110.
[70] *Op. cit.*, 11.2.
[71] *Op. cit.*, 11.10.
[72] Heyob, *op. cit.*, pp. 53-80.
[73] *Metamorphoses* 11.7, 23. But see also 11.1, where Lucius plunged his head seven times in the sea to purify himself even before making his prayer.

collected much archaeological material for his book, quoted above, and enhanced his research with diagrams and pictures to shed light on the subject.) Nile-water was especially valued by her devotees and in many sanctuaries containers for such water were present. The blessings which the flooding of the Nile bestows on the land and people of Egypt is well know; the Egyptians, however, attributed a greater potency to water. As Plutarch says, "They call not only the Nile but all moisture generally the efflux of Osiris, and in honor of the god the water-pitcher always leads the procession of the sacred ceremonies."[74] This mystical connection between the god and water may account for Plutarch's also stating that such purifications were conducive to health: the use of water had a hygienic effect.[75]

The connection of Isis with water goes back to her very origin: as a celestial divinity she was the daughter of Geb, god of earth, and Nut, the heavenly queen, the divinity of the primordial water, heaven, the "mother of all the gods."[76] According to this identification of waters and heaven, therefore, Isis was not only a queen of heaven but a creative, generative principle whose primordial connection with water gave to that element a mysterious purifying and vivifying potency. For the followers of the Isiac mysteries, ablutions and sprinkling with water were a sacramental experience, i.e., a physical action available to the senses in which a spiritual gift was given to the partakers. This can be compared to Christian Baptism, for Christians regard baptismal water as laden with spiritual potency by virtue of that water's union with the Holy Spirit.[77] Similarly, Isis was regarded as a savior goddess.

In the *Metamorphoses* 11.2, Lucius addressed Isis as "Queen of

---

[74] *Op. cit.*, chap. 36; Griffiths, op. cit., p. 173. In his commentary, Griffiths quotes other Egyptian references; see p. 436: "The Nile is the discharge of his body, to nourish the nobility and the commons." "The water belongs to thee, thine inundation belongs to thee, the efflux which has come from the god, the body secretion which has come from Osiris, that thy hands may be washed therewith." See *Metamorphoses* 11.11 for the sacred water container in the procession.

[75] *Op. cit.*, chap. 79; see, however, Griffiths' comments on p. 566. See also Theodor Hopfner, *Plutarch Über Isis and Osiris,* rpt. of 1940 ed., Hildesheim/ New York: George Olms, 1974, pp. 165-169.

[76] References in Hopfner, *op. cit.,* p. 20.

[77] See about this below, especially Tertullian's view on baptism.

Heaven" and "Heavenly Venus."[78] Since the titles are the same as those given to Juno Caelestis in Carthage, Apuleius, whose birthplace of Madaurus was not very far from Carthage, may have been influenced by the overwhelming popularity of Caelestis. If indeed he applied the epithets of Caelestis to Isis, he did something that in the middle of the second century was not surprising, for that creative power which "illumines all city walls with its feminine light ... nourishing the happy seeds ... " cannot vary greatly, regardless of the name or ceremony by which she is invoked.[79]

Since messages from Isis were usually received in the form of a dream, incubation, that is, sleeping in the temple at night, was often practiced. The worshipper rented a room in the temple compound, spent the night there, and waited for the appearance of the goddess or the god. The opportunity for vicious rumors, especially when incubation was practiced by women, was ever present, and sometimes illicit activities may have taken place. Best known is the story reported by Josephus,[80] according to which a Roman knight, by bribing the priests, was able to have an illicit relation with a lady in the temple of Isis. He appeared to the lady disguised as Anubis, and the lady, believing that a great honor was bestowed upon her and that she actually had a union with the god, told of her experiences to everybody, including her husband. The fraud was discovered and exemplary punishments were meted out to all guilty parties. Many other veiled and not so veiled references can be found in Roman literature about the supposed tendency of Isis to encourage sexual misconduct. Heyob made a valiant attempt to prove these charges false and to exonerate Isis.[81] Her arguments seem convincing, but an additional remark needs to be made: nothing pleased adherents of one religion more than to level charges of sexual misbehavior and aberration against another cult. Ancient history is full of such incidents, perhaps because they were so easy to make and many people liked them and did not ask for substantiation. The Romans made such

---

[78] "*Regina Caeli ... sive tu Ceres ... seu tu Caelestis Venus ...*"

[79] *Metamorphoses* 11.2: "*... ista luce feminea collustrans cuncta moenia ... nutriens laeta semina ... quoquo nomine, quoquo ritu, quaqua facie te fas invocare ...*" See Griffiths, *The Isis Book*, pp. 114-117.

[80] *Antiquities* 18.65-80.

[81] *Op. cit.*, pp. 111-127.

charges against Christians, and one has only to read the *Octavius* by Minucius Felix to see how vicious some people could be. But Christians returned the favor, as the examples we quoted concerning Caelestis should suffice to illustrate. If occasional wrongs took place within the religion of Isis, that was not its outstanding characteristic. In fact, the opposite appears to be true.

The similarities between the cult of Isis and certain Christian practices have been pointed out many times. Scholarly commentaries on the books of the New Testament usually contain references to parallel ideas and concepts. Christian iconography also has been compared to that of Isis, especially the representations of the Virgin Mary with the child Jesus, which indeed resemble closely those of Isis nursing her son. The similarities are impressive. When one looks at the illustrations of Isis reprinted by Tran Tam Tinh in *Isis Lactans* it is easy to understand why so many scholars consider Isis to be the prototype of Mary. Most recently, R. E. Witt called Isis the "Great Forerunner," emphasizing Paul's familiarity with Isiac liturgy.[82] But Tran Tam Tinh pointed out the large chronological gap between the statues of *Isis Lactans* and *Maria Lactans*. In the West the first representations of Mary nursing her son date from the twelfth century.[83] The theological roots of Mariology are very probably in Asia Minor rather than in North Africa. And even though, as Witt points out, the cult of Isis was known in Asia Minor, the major female divinity, whose influence overshadowed everything else there, was not Isis but Cybele, the Great Mother. This is not to underestimate the influence of Isis upon the later *praxis pietatis* directed toward Mary. Pious Christians observing their pagan neighbors offering devotion to Isis could not fail to be impressed by the many attractive features of her rituals. But this was also the case at places where a goddess other than Isis was venerated.

Mariology is much too complex a phenomenon to be derived from a single source; there are many "forerunners" of the veneration of Mary. It is not isolated and sometimes superficial similarities that we must look for, but rather, general and broad principles which apply wherever a goddess is worshipped. We find these in the cult of Isis. This was a cosmic religion which

---

[82] *Op. cit.*, pp. 255-281.
[83] *Op. cit.*, p. 47; see also pp. 40-49 for the total background.

held out the hope of personal salvation by an intimate reintegration into a totality. In the mysteries of Isis this totality was represented by the primordial waters. Over and above the chaotic divisions and separations in the world, Isis pointed to an essential order in the universe and offered a way to attain it. In this the cult of Isis came very close to the teachings of Pauline Christianity as expressed in Ephesians 1 and Colossians 1 as well as to the concept of a *"unio mystica"* of man with God which played such an important role in early Christian theology. Of course, other mysteries did the same, and we now turn to review another of these, the rites of the Syrian Goddess.

C. THE SYRIAN GODDESS

At the time when Juno Caelestis was worshipped in Carthage and the cult of Isis was spread over the Mediterranean world, another goddess reigned supreme in Hierapolis. We learn of her from Lucian's essay, *De Dea Syria* (On the Syrian goddess).[84] This essay, we must remember, is a parody; it is uncertain how much of it is true. Nevertheless, this is what Lucian says.

> At the outset, he asserts that Hierapolis is called "Hire" ("holy") in Greek because it is a city holy to the Assyrian deity Hera (Ch. 1).[85] Then he writes of the spread of religious ideas from

---

[84] Hierapolis is in northern Syria (Coelesyria) near the Euphrates river. Much good material is available on *De Dea Syria*. The following represents only a selection directly used by me. Text and translation in the *LCL*, A. M. Harmon, ed., London: Heinemann, 1961, pp. 337-441. Another good translation is *De Dea Syria*, Harold W. Attridge and Robert A. Oden, eds., Missoula, Mont.: Scholars Press, 1976 (Society of Biblical Literature, Texts and Translations 9); Carl Clemen, *Lukian's Schrift über die Syrische Göttin*, Leipzig: J. C. Hinrichs, 1938 (pp. 1-27 provide a German translation); Monika Hörig, "Dea Syria-Atargatis," *ANRW* II. Prinzipat, 17.3, Berlin/ New York: Walter de Gruyter, 1984, pp. 1536-1581; R. A. Oden, *Studies in Lucian's De Dea Syria*, Missoula, Mont.: Scholars Press, 1977; H. J. W. Drijvers, *Cults and Beliefs at Edessa*, Leiden: E. J. Brill, 1980 (Etudes Preliminaries aux Religious Orientales Dans L'empire Romain, vol. 82); H. J. W. Drijvers, "Die Dea Syria und andere syrische Gottheiten im Imperium Romanum," in Maarten J. Vermaseren, *Die orientalische Religionen im Römerreich*, Leiden: E. J. Brill, 1981, pp. 241-263; H. Stocks, "Studien zu Lukian's 'De Dea Syria,'" *Berytus* 4 (1937) 1-40.

[85] The pronunciation of "Hera" and "hire" is, of course, similar, but let us remember that Hera is the Greek Juno. About speculations "Hera" and "aer," see p.32. The modern name of the place is Mambij, which comes from the ancient Mabbug. Pliny, Natural History 5.19.81: "Bambyce which is also named Hierapolis, and by the Syrians Mabog—here the monstrous goddess Atargatis, who is called by the Greeks Derceto, is worshipped." *LCL*, R.

Egypt to Assyria (Chs. 2, 3) and briefly notes that there is also a
sanctuary of the Sidonians in honor of Astarte, which he identifies with the moon goddess Selene (Ch. 4).Lucian refers to
another sanctuary which he did not visit (Ch. 5) and then
describes the great sanctuary of Aphrodite in Byblos, where the
rites of Adonis were performed. Women who, in connection with
these rites, refuse to shave their heads must offer themselves for
sale for one day (Ch. 6). Osiris is believed to be buried in Byblos,
and each year a head comes miraculously from Egypt to Byblos
(Ch. 7). Another miracle in Byblos is that each year the river
Adonis changes its color to red, which some people connected
with the story of the killing of Adonis; others explained the
change in color by saying simply that the winds blew red dust
into the water (Ch. 8). In Ch. 9 Lucian reports that there was a
sanctuary of Aphrodite in Lebanon. He then proceeds to describe
the temple in Hierapolis.

That temple, larger than any mentioned so far, housed many
gifts of gold and silver. Its statues of the gods were believed to
move, perspire, and give oracles (Ch. 10). Many stories were told
about the age of this temple (Ch. 11), but most people believed its
founder was Deucalion, the Noah of Greek mythology. In Ch. 12
Lucian tells the story of Deucalion and the flood. The inhabitants
of Hierapolis believed that the flood-waters receded when a great
chasm (χάσμα) was formed which absorbed all the water. Deucalion built a temple over the chasm and dedicated it to Hera. In
remembrance of this event, priests and laymen alike go twice
each year to the sea to fetch water which they pour out in the
temple and, thus, down into the chasm. (Lucian saw this chasm
under the temple; it was quite small.) This rite recalls the
memory of the disaster and divine favor (Ch. 13). Yet others said
that the temple was founded for the mother of Hera, Derketo. In
Phoenicia Lucian had seen an image of Derketo which was half
woman and half fish; in Hierapolis he had seen one which was
all woman. The people there regarded fish as sacred (Ch. 14).[86]
Yet another story told about the sanctuary is that Attis, having been
castrated by Rhea, established the temple at Hierapolis. As proof

---

Rackham, ed., London: Heinemann, 1947, vol. 2, pp. 282-283. Strabo, *Geography* 16.1.27: "Bambyce which is also called Edessa and Hierapolis, where
the Syrian goddess Atargatis is worshipped." *LCL,* H. L. Jones, ed., London:
Heinemann, 1930, vol. 7, pp. 234-235. Strabo is wrong in including Edessa
in the list; it was about fifteen miles northeast of Hierapolis on the other
side of the Euphrates.

[86] On fish and the cult of Atargatis, see Franz Joseph Dölger, ΙΧΘΥC *Das
Fischsymbol in frühchristlicher Zeit,* München: Aschendorf,1928, pp. 120-142;
also pp. 431-446 about fish in the cult of Tanit. Some material in Hermann
Usener, *Die Sintfluthsagen,* Bonn: Cohen, 1899 (Religionsgeschichtliche
Untersuchungen, dritter theil). See also Oden, op. cit., p. 88, who compares
Atargatis not only with Astarte and Anat, but also with Aserah, the goddess
who has close connections with the fish. Similarly, Hörig, op. cit., p. 1539.

there is an image of Rhea carried by lions and wearing a tower on her head. The Galli[87] in the temple castrated themselves in imitation of Attis (Ch. 15). The tradition that Dionysus founded the temple is supported by the presence in the gateway of two large phalli dedicated by Dionysus himself. A bronze statue of a small man with a large penis reminded Lucian of the Greek custom of honoring Dionysus by putting up phalli on the top of which sat small wooden men with large genitals (Ch. 16). The next two chapters relate the story of Stratonice,[88] whose stepson fell in love with her (Chs. 17, 18) and who promised to build a temple in Hierapolis. Her husband sent her there with a young man named Combabus, who, before he left, castrated himself and left his genitals in a box with the king so that later he could not be accused of seducing the queen (Chs. 19, 20). They built the temple in Hierapolis; nonetheless, Stratonice fell in love with Combabus and tried to seduce him, but he resisted and told her what he had done. Stratonice ceased her efforts at seduction, but she still loved the young man. This sort of love still exists in Hierapolis, Lucian asserts: the Galli lust for the women and the women for the Galli (Chs. 21, 22). When Stratonice and Combabus returned home, she accused him of trying to seduce her, and Combabus was arrested, tried, and sentenced to death. Combabus then asked for the box he had left with the king and showed his severed genitals contained therein, whereupon the king relented and rewarded Combabus for his loyalty (Chs. 23, 24, 25). The temple was completed and a statue of Combabus was placed in it. That is the temple which Lucian saw and which, according to some, is the origin of the practice of castration in the temple (Ch. 26). Even to the present day, men castrate themselves, put on women's clothing, and perform the work usually done by women (Ch. 27). The sanctuary was built on a hill. In the entranceway stood the phalli, which were very tall. Twice a year a man climbed to the top[89] and stayed there for seven days, according to some, in memory of the flood when people fled to high elevations and to the tops of the trees; according to others, this was done in honor of Dionysus. People came and deposited money in a container, spoke their names, and the man on the top spoke a prayer for them.[90]

---

[87] Emasculated priests of Cybele and other divinities. More about this problem in our chapter on Cybele.

[88] She was the Macedonian wife of Seleucus I (358-281 B.C.). She rebuilt the temple around 300 B.C.

[89] Lucian says that the phalli were 1,800 feet; see, however, Harmon, *op. cit.*, comments on chap. 28. He also describes how the man climbed on the top with the help of ropes and wooden steps big enough for the toes.

[90] Did the Christian "pillar-saints" learn something from this practice? It certainly would stand to reason since these anchorites were also from Syria and some form of influence cannot be rejected. Theodoret of Cyprus, *Historia religiosa seu ascetica vivendi ratio* (*MPG* 82, 1283-1496), or *History of the Monks*, in chap. 26 gives an account of the famous Simeon Stylites (395-451),

That man never slept, for fear of falling down (Ch. 29).

At this point, Lucian gives a description of the temple, which could well have been similar to that of Caelestis since most temples of antiquity were built on the same basic plan. This temple faced the rising sun. It stood on a large platform, and a stone ramp led up to it. The doors and the roof were made of gold; inside a pleasant fragrance filled the air, lingering on the visitors' clothing long after they had left (Ch. 30). Inside the temple there was a small chamber which only selected priests might enter: in it were statues of Hera supported by lions, and of Zeus sitting on bulls (Ch. 31). Lucian had no problem with the image of Zeus; it looked in every respect like Zeus. But Hera seemed to have incorporated features of Athena, Aphrodite, Selene, Rhea, Artemis, Nemesis, and the Fates. A tower and rays were on her head, and she wore a girdle with which they decorate only "the heavenly one" (τὴν Οὐρανίην).[91] A gem on her head filled the temple with light at night (Ch. 32). Between the two statues there was a golden image which they called "Sign" (σημήιον); when they brought water from the sea, they take this image with them (Ch. 33). For Helios and Selene there were no statues (Ch. 34), but there was one for Apollo as a mature man (Ch. 35). Apollo gave oracles of his own accord; behind his statue were those of Atlas, Hermes, and Eileithyia (Chs. 36, 37, 38), and many other statues of gods and man (Chs. 39, 40, 41). Wild animals grazed in the courtyard; they were sacred and tame (Ch. 41). There were many priests vested in white robes, but the high priest was vested in purple and wore a golden tiara. Other temple servants included flute players, pipers, Galli, and women (Chs. 42, 43). Sacrifices were performed twice daily (Ch. 44). Sacred fish were raised in a lake nearby. The lake was very deep, and in the middle stood an altar to which people swam in order to bring garlands (Chs. 46, 47). Here a great festival was held, which they called "λύμνην καταβάσις" ("Descent to the Lake"). All sacred objects were taken to the lake where ceremonies were performed (Ch. 47). One of the greatest ceremonies involved bringing water from the sea, and here Lucian mentions again the rite he described in Chapter 13 (Ch. 48). Another great

---

and while the differences between Simeon and the men in Hierapolis are obvious, there are some common elements such as the number of visitors, requests for intercession, lack of sleep, and so forth. A German translation of Theodoret's book is available in the *Bibliothek der Kirchenväter*, München: Kösel Verlag,1926, vol. 50, pp. 156-170, esp. pp. 162-164. Further literature in Johannes Quasten, *Patrology*, Utrecht/Antwerp: Spectrum, 1960, vol. 3, p. 550. See also Hippolyte Delahaye, *Les Saints Stylites*, Bruxelles, Societe des Bollandists, Paris: A. Picard, 1895 (1923).

[91] Translated into Latin, this would mean Caelestis, but in this connection no doubt Aphrodite is meant. The girdle of the goddess had exclusive features, just like that of Caelestis and Isis. On the importance of robes, see below.

festival was the "Fire" or "Lamp" festival. Worshippers chopped down live trees, stood them up in the courtyard, and on them hung live animals along with artifacts of gold and silver. At a given moment everything was burned up. Those who came to the festival brought with them an imitation of the "Sign" (Ch. 49). Next Lucian describes ceremonies during which men became Galli, along with customs relating to these eunuchs (Chs. 50, 51, 52, 53). Sacrificial animals included all kinds except pigs (Ch. 54). The treatise ends with a description of customs pertaining to pilgrims and pilgrimages (Chs. 55, 56) and sacrifices by private individuals (Chs. 57, 58, 59, 60).

The *Dea Syria*, whom Lucian calls Hera, is Atargatis, a fertility goddess.[92] Her cult was very popular and widespread. We are told by the imperial biographer Suetonius that Nero, who "utterly despised all cults," was, for awhile at least, a devoted follower of the "Syrian Goddess."[93] She was also called Derceto, but the two names sound so similar that the suggestion has been made that "Derceto" was a derivation of "Atargatis."[94] The etymology of the name Atargatis points to a connection with "Astarte" (Ishtar), "Ata" (Anath),[95] and this in turn suggests that Atargatis was a syncretistic figure which incorporated elements of many Near Eastern fertility divinities. The picture given us by Lucian is characteristic of the worship not only of Astarte-Ishtar, but also of Aphrodite, Cybele, Ashera, Isis, and Caelestis. The representation of Atargatis as half woman/half fish, the emphasis on water (an essential element in the process of fertilization) and the sea, and their common titles "Urania" ("Heavenly") and "Queen of Heaven," points to a theology which was shared by many cults of fertility goddesses.

Lucian mentions the tradition that the cult originated with Deucalion, who built the temple when the flood had receded. In summary, the people of Hierapolis believed that the great flood ended when the water had receded and disappeared into a great χάσμα (chasm). The temple was built over this chasm, and twice

---

[92] Oden, *Studies*, p. 55; Francis R. Walton, "Atargatis," *Oxford Classical Dictionary*, p. 136; and literature in n. 84, above.

[93] *Nero* 54, ET, *The Lives of the Twelve Caesars by Suetonius*, Joseph Gavorse, ed., New York: Modern Library, 1959, p. 279.

[94] Hörig, *op. cit.*, p. 1539, derives the name from the semitic Darkatu and explains it as "lady" or "queen." See also Oden, *op. cit.*, pp. 71 ff; Clemen, *op. cit.*, p. 41. See also Cross, *Canaanite Myth ...*, *op. cit.*, p. 31.

[95] Hörig, *op. cit.*, p. 1539; Oden, *Studies*, p. 88.

every year this event was liturgically recalled by the worshippers in a ceremony of ὑδροφορία, i.e., the bringing of the water.[96] The cult was based, therefore, on an act of the gods by which they saved the human race from extinction. But more is involved. Agriculture could begin only when the chaos of the flood was replaced by a world order which enabled the fertilization of the ground and the beginning of ordered life. The temple built over that spot, therefore, was a constant reminder of the fact that civilized life depended on the overcoming of chaos and on the beneficient, creative powers of water.[97]

A tradition similar to that preserved in Hierapolis existed in

---

[96] Chap. 13, 48; also chap. 33, where a golden dove is mentioned sitting on the head of Dionysus, recalling the dove that also appears in the flood stories, e.g., Gen. 8.8.

[97] There is a legend in the so-called Pseudo-Melito Apology 44, according to which there was a well in Mabug in which there dwelled an unclean spirit that committed acts of violence against all who passed by. Sivir, the daughter of Hadad, was charged with pouring seawater into the well in order to restrain the spirit. However, the only similarity between this and the rites in Hierapolis is the pouring of seawater into a hole—not enough from which to draw any conclusion. The full text from William Cureton, *Spicilegium Syriacum*, London: Rivingtons, 1855, pp. 41-51: *An Oration of Meliton the Philosopher:* "But touching Nebo, which is in Mabug, why should I write to you; for lo! all the priests which are in Mabug know that it is the image of Orpheus, the Thracian Magus. And Hadran is the image of Zaradusht, a Persian Magus, because both of these Magi practiced Magism to a well which is in a wood in Mabug, in which was an unclean spirit, and it committed violence and attacked the passage of everyone who was passing by in all that place in which now the fortress Mabug is located; and these same Magi charged Simi, the daughter of Hadad,that she should draw water from the sea and cast it into the well, in order that the spirit should not come up and commit injury, according to that which was a mystery in their Magism" (*op. cit.*, pp. 44-55). The "violence" which the spirit committed was, according to Cureton (p. 91), "the exhalation of pestilential vapors"; Stocks, op. cit., p. 24, n. 103, however, discusses the possibility that it was an attack on men's genitals (= cf. Galli). See also Oden, *Studies ...*, pp. 127-128. Here may be mentioned a four-day celebration observed by the Egyptians in commemoration of the recession of the waters of the Nile. On the third day of the festival the Egyptians went down to the sea and performed a rite symbolizing the fertilization of the earth through water: the priests produced a sacred chest in which was a golden container. Into this container they poured potable water (in contrast to the saltwater of the sea), and the people rejoiced with great exultation that Osiris had been found. After this they would knead together soil and water, mix it with spices and expensive incense, and form from the mixture crescent-shaped figures which they adored (Plutarch, *De Iside et Osiride* 39, LCL, *Plutarch's Moralia*, Frank C. Babbit, ed., London: Heinemann, 1936, vol. 5, p. 97).

Judaism.[98] According to this tradition, the waters of chaos were
kept under control by God, who placed a huge rock over them,
preventing them from again rushing forth. According to one
version, the rock was formed from the stones upon which Jacob
rested his head at Bethel (Gen. 28.11). This rock was like a vault
which held up the earth and upon which rested the temple in
Jerusalem.[99] The prophet Jonah saw this rock from below when
the great fish swallowed him and took him under the temple of
God.[100] Were this stone removed for any reason, the primeval
water would rise again, with disastrous consequences. When
King David dug up the foundation of the sanctuary (according to
another rabbinic reference, it was the altar), he reached the level
of the primeval water, with near fatal consequences.[101] The Jewish
tradition states further that the altar in the temple was surrounded
by a gutter by which the blood and wine offerings were gathered
into an underground room. Every seventy years young men of
the priesthood descended into that room and collected the congealed wine and blood, which had the appearance of dried figs;
these were then burned with great solemnity.[102] But this underground room went deeper and eventually reached the abyss
(tehom), so that the sacrificial libations, at least in pious imagination, reached the primeval ocean. Rabbinic mysticism found a
reference to this in the Song of Songs:

---

[98] This was explored first by Gustav Dalman, *Neue Petra Forschungen und
der Heilige Felsen von Jerusalem,* Leipzig: Hinrichs, 1912. All Talmudic
references are collected here. On this important research is based H. Stock's
essay, see n. 1. On Stock's proposal of an Anatolian influence on the cult of
Hierapolis, see Carl Clemen, "Temple and Kult in Hierapolis," *Pisciculi.
Studien zur Religion and Kultur des Altertums* (F. J. Dölger Festschrift), ed.
Theodor Klauser und Adolf Rucker, München: Aschendarff, 1939, pp. 66-69.
Mr. Sheldon Brunswick, the learned librarian and keeper of the Hebrew
material at the Doe Library, U.C. Berkeley, helped me to verify the Talmu-
dic and related Hebrew tests. Does the Hebrew tradition go back to
Babylonian precedents? "Babylon ... had been built upon *bab apsi,* the 'Gate
of Apsu,' *apsu* designating the water of chaos before creation," says M.
Eliade, *Cosmos and History,* New York: Harper, 1959, p. 15, who refers to
Jeremias, *op. cit.,* p. 113.

[99] *Pirke Rabbi Eliezer* 35, Dalman, *op. cit.,* pp. 135-136.

[100] *Pirke Rabbi Eliezer* 10, ET, Gerald Friedlander, London: Kegan Paul,
1916, p. 71. According to the Targum Yerushalmi I to Exodus 28.30, the
name of God was written on this stone, "with which the Master of the
World sealed the Great Depth from the beginning ..."

[101] Dalman, *op. cit.,* p. 144.

[102] Sukkah 49a, Dalman, *op. cit.,* p. 144.

... The Pits i.e., the pits under the altar into which the wine
offerings flowed] have existed since the six days of creation, for
it is said, *"The rounding of thy thighs are like the links of a chain,
the works of the hands of a skilled workman."* *"The rounding of
the thighs"* refers to the Pits; *"like the links of a chain"* implies
that their cavity descends to the abyss; *"the work of the hands
of a skilled workman"* means that they are the skillful handiwork
of the Holy One, blessed be He ... It has been taught, R. Jose
says, that the cavity of the Pits descended to the abyss, for it
is said, *"Let me sing of my beloved, a song of my beloved touching
his vineyard. My well-beloved had a vineyard on a very fruitful
hill. And he digged it, and cleared it of stones, and planted it
with the choicest wine, and built a tower in the midst of it, and
also hewed out a vat therein."* *"And planted it with the choicest
wine"* refers to the temple; *"and built a tower in the midst of it"*
refers to the altar; *"and also hewed out a vat therein"* refers to
the Pits. [103]

The mind of the pious Jew, therefore, envisaged under the altar of
the Jerusalem temple, a rock, and under the rock, the abyss of the
primeval sea. It would mean the end of the world if this plug were
removed. [104]

Another element in Jewish tradition that was similar to the cult
of the *Dea Syria* was the ὑδροφορία (carrying of the water). In
Judaism this was practiced in connection with various purification rites such as those involving uncleanness by contact with
dead bodies. According to Numbers 19:17, the ashes of the red
heifer sacrificed for the occasion had to be mixed with running
water, and we read in the Talmud that children went to Siloam
with stone containers and filled them with water for this rite. [105]
Particularly well known is the water libation ceremony of the
Feast of Tabernacles. On the first day of this seven-day feast, a
procession led by the priests went to Siloam and brought water

---

[103] Sukkah 4.9, Gemara, *The Babylonian Talmud*, ET, I Epstein, London:
Soncino Press, 1938, vol. 6, pp. 229-230.

[104] Dalman, *op. cit.*, p. 145: "Der Fels, ein Grundstein der Weltschöp-
fung, die Höhle ein Schlund, der zum Urmeere hinabführt, das war es, was
man da schaute. Grollend und kulturfeindlich lauert das Chaos under der
Höhle. Wer ihren Boden durchbricht, beschwört den Weltuntergang
herauf. In der Seelenhöhle und dem Seelenbrunnen der moslemischen
Sage lebt das Grauen vor einer unter dem Felsen befindlichen Öffnung zur
Unterwelt noch immer fort und verhindert jede durchgreifende Unter-
sunchung."

[105] *Parah* 3.2-3, *The Babylonian Talmud, op. cit.*, p. 327. See also the *Tosefta*
(i.e., the Supplement) to *Parah* 3.1-3.3, in Jacob Neusner, *The Tosefta*, New
York: Ktav, 1977, vol. 6, pp. 175-176.

through the "water-gate" while the trumpets were sounding. They then went around the altar, which the priest ascended. There he performed the sacrifice, using two silver bowls, one for water and one for wine.[106] The two liquids thus mixed flowed down and were believed to reach the tehom. This means that the ceremony, like the one in Hierapolis, preserved the memory of the flood and the taming of the waters. The Feast of Tabernacles was an agricultural festival and many elements in it, such as the libation ceremony, had fertility motifs.[107] That is the reason behind the eschatological element that Jewish piety added to the concept of the altar: the altar is not only symbolic of the subterranean ocean, it is from there that living waters shall bubble forth: "And it is written about Jerusalem, 'And it shall come to pass in that day that living waters shall go out from Jerusalem' (Zachariah 14.8). This refers to the well which will arise in Jerusalem in the future, and will water all its surroundings."[108]

---

106 *Shekalim* 6, *Mishnah* 3: "... Wherefore was its name called water-gate? Because through it was brought in the flask of water for the libation of the Feast of the Tabernacles. R. Eliezer the son of Jacob says: through it the water trickled forth and in the hereafter they will issue out from under the threshold of the house" (*op. cit.*, vol. 7, p. 23). (See also Herbert Danby, *The Mishnah*, London: Oxford Univ. Press, 1933, p. 158; *Sukkah* 4.9: "How as the water libation (performed)? A golden flagon holding three logs was filled from the Siloam. When they arrived at the water-gate, they sounded a 'tekiah' (long blast), a 'ternah' (tremulous note) and again a 'tekiah' (long blast). (The priest then) went up the ascent (of the altar) and turned to his left where there were two silver bowls. R. Judah said, they were of plaster (but they looked silver) because their surfaces were darkened from the wine. They had each a hole like a slender snout, one (hole) being wide and the other narrow so that both emptied themselves together. The one on the west was for water and the one on the east for wine ... " (*op. cit.*, vol. 6, p. 226). This is the sacrifice that goes into the Pit. See also J. C. Rylaarsdom, "Booths, Feast of," *The Interpreter's Dictionary of the Bible*, New York/ Nashville: Abingdon, 1962, vol. 2, pp. 455-458.
107 See Rylaarsdom, *art. cit.*, p. 457.
108 *Pirke Rabbi Eliezer* 35, ET, Gerald Friedlander, London: Kegan Paul, 1916, p. 263. See also *Yoma* 77b-78a: "R. Eliezer b. Jacob said: (Hence) go forth to the waters which will bubble forth from under the threshold of the Sanctuary," *The Babylonian Talmud*, *op. cit.*, *Seder Mo'ed*, pp. 379-380. The waters of the pool of Siloam from which the libation water was taken were believed to have miraculous qualities and were sometimes compared with the waters of creation: "If a man had an impurity in his hand even if he dipped it in the water of Siloam or the water of creation, he could not purify himself eternally. But if he throws the impurity away he could purify himself immediately," *Talmud Yerushalmi*, *Tannit* 65a, Venice: Daniel Bomberg, 1524. Jesus sent the blind man here to wash off the clay from his eyes, John 9.7; see to this, Gustav Dalman, *Sacred Sites and Ways*, London: SPCK, 1935, pp.

According to Greek mythology, the floodwaters drained off in Athens within the precincts of the temple of Zeus. Here were statues and shrines of deities involved with the establishment of an ordered universe, such as Zeus, Cronos, Rhea, and Ge (Earth). The floor of the temple opened to the width of a cubit and into this opening each year was cast wheat meal mixed with honey, in remembrance of the flood, the waters of which flowed into this opening.[109] This event was celebrated on the Anthesteria, a three-day festival held on the twelfth, thirteenth, and fourteenth days of the month Anthesterion (roughly, our February). The festival included a number of features which are difficult to interpret. The name itself (ἄνθος = flower) indicates that it was a spring festival. Indeed, children were given wreaths of flowers, but the main tone of the festival was the polarity between a dionysiac celebration of life and a somber remembrance of the dead.

The first day, called *Pithoigia* (Opening of the Jars), was dedicated to the opening of large earthenware jars *(pithoi)* in which the juice of the grapes was stored after the harvest. The now fermented juice was taken to the temple of Dionysus "in the Marshes," where libations and prayers were offered and the new wine, properly mixed with water, was first tasted. The rest of the day was spent in drinking. The second day was called *Choes* (wine jugs, cups). The main event of this day was a procession in which Dionysus himself, perhaps personified by a masked actor, was conveyed on a carriage that looked like a ship. The procession was quite uninhibited, but a serious aspect of it was the *Hieros Gamos* (holy marriage) of the King Archon[110] with his wife, whose official title was Basilinna. The third day was *Chytroi* (Pots). All kinds of vegetables were cooked together in one pot and offered to Hermes on behalf of the dead. The doorways of homes were smeared with pitch as a protection against ghosts because this was a day of the dead and ghosts were invited to

---

310-311. This book is the English translation of the author's *Orte und Wege Jesu.*
[109] Pausanias, *Description of Greece* 1.18.7, LCL, W. H. S. Jones, ed., London: Heinemann, 1918, p. 91. About the location of this opening and the possible site of Deukalion's tomb, see Walter Judeich, *Topographie von Athen,* München: Beck, 1931, pp. 385-386.
[110] *Archon Basileus* = a magistrate whose office included mostly the religious duties of the former kings; he had charge over the mysteries.

return to their abode at the end of the day. The explanation of this one-pot meal was that those who survived the flood cooked everything together in one pot on the first day.[111] The traditions

---

[111] Martin P. Nilsson, *Geschichte der Griechischen Religion*, München: Beck, 1955, vol. 1, p. 595: "Das Aition knüpft an die deukalionische Flut an. Die Menschen, welche dieser entronnen waren, kochten am ersten Tag, an dem sie wieder Mut fassten, allerlei in einem Topf zusammen; daher erhielt der Tag und das Fest den Namen χύτροι; der Inhalt der Töpfe wird als Panspermie bezeichnet ... Die Lexicographen erwähnen ein athenisches Trauerfest, die Hydrophorie, die zur Erinnerung an die in der grossen Flut Umgekommenen gefeiert wurde." See also H. J. Rose, *Religion in Greece and Rome*, New York: Haper Row, 1959, pp. 79-82; August Mommsen, *Feste der Stadt Athen*, Leipzig: Teubner, 1898, pp. 384-404; Martin P. Nilsson, "Die Anthesterion und die Aiora," *Eranos* 15 (1915)181-200; Erwin Rohde, *Psyche. Seelencult und Unsterblichbeitsglaube der Griechen*, Tübingen: J. C. B. Mohr, 1925, vol. 1, pp. 237-245; Ludwig Deubner, *Attische Feste*, Berlin: Keller, 1932, pp. 93-123; Willy Borgeaud, "Le Deluge, Delphes, et les Anthesteries," *Museum Helveticum* 4 (1947) 205-250; Carl Kerényi, *Dionysus. Archetypal Image of Indestructable Life* (Bollingen Series, LXV. 2), Princeton: Princeton Univ. Press, 1976, pp. 290-315. Nilsson also mentions an Athenian feast of ύδγο-φορία, which was a mournful occasion in remembrance of the great flood of Deukalion and of those who perished by it.

Other fertility rites of the Athenians included the *Munichia*, which were held on the sixteenth day of the month Munichion (ca. April). On this day a she-goat was sacrificed in place of a young girl, as was the case in pre-classical times when human sacrifice was practiced in connection with the cult of Artemis (cf. *De Dea Syria* 58). Other items offered to the goddess were round cakes with burning candles in the middle, which represented Artemis as a moon-goddess. Another observance worth citing is known to us from Pausanias, *Guide to Greece* 1.27.4, ET, Peter Levi, New York: Penguin, 1971, vol. 1, pp. 76-77: "There was a thing that amazed me which not everyone knows; I shall describe what happens. Two virgin girls live not far from the temple of Athene of the city; the Athenians call them the bearers Arrephoroi,["Carriers of Unspoken Thinqs"]. For a certain time they have their living from the goddess: and when the festival comes they have to perform certain ceremonies during the night. They carry on their heads what Athene's priestess gives them to carry, and neither she who gives it nor they who carry it know what it is she gives them. In the city not far from Aphrodite-in-the-Gardens is an enclosed place with a natural entrance to an underground descent; this is where the virgin girls go down. They leave down there what they were carrying, and take another thing and bring it back covered up. They are then sent away, and other virgin girls are brought to the Acropolis instead of them." These rites were called *Arrephoria* and they may have been held in the last month of the year called *Skirophorion*.

On the twelfth day of *Skirophorion* there was also an obscure rite dedicated either to Athene or Demeter. This observance was a women's festival and included a procession, but we do not know what happened when the procession arrived at its destination near Eleusis, except that it was a kind of fertility rite. On this day women threw live piglets, cakes made in the form of male genitals, and models of snakes into caverns. On the *Thesmophoria*, the great festival of the grain-goddess Demeter, held on the eleventh,

of Greece, Judaism, and Hierapolis meet in these points.

As we have seen, the element of water, as the origin and genesis of life, was central to a religious life focused on the mystery of
fertility. The cult of the *Dea Syria* , like those of Caelestis and Isis,
dealt with ultimate causes and sources. In this pursuit, the story of
the flood served as a vehicle to explain the origins of civilization
on earth, while the general emphasis on water pointed beyond
the flood to the primodial separation of the elements and the
beginning of life *per se.* But what is the significance of the Galli in
the cult of the *Dea Syria* and of the ritual promiscuity in the
Anthesteria? In one practice we see the violent removal of men's
distinguishing sexual characteristics and in the other, a compa-
rably frenzied elimination of sexual diversity by indiscriminate
and chaotic copulation. The same phenomena will reappear in
the cult of Cybele, which will shed more light on this matter. We
now turn our attention to the mysteries of Dionysus as an introduction to an investigation of the cult of the Great Mother, Cybele.

D. The Cult of Dionysus

The cult of Dionysus was closely related to the cult of Cybele, the
Great Mother. It is generally accepted by most scholars today that
his cult spread to Greece from Thrace, but the Thracians were
related to the Phrygians;[112] thus, the religious beliefs of the two
peoples flowed from the same sources. The Dionysiac cult has
been throughly investigated and, fortunately, we have many
classical Greek works that contain information about it.[113] These

---

twelfth, and thirteenth days of *Pyanepsion* (October), the women went down
and brought back the decayed remains, placed them on an altar, and burned
them — a rite reminiscent of the Jewish collection of congealed wine and
blood from the Pit. The Athenian women who carried out this ugly task
were required to keep themselves pure by abstaining from sex for three days
(they chewed garlic to discourage their husbands; see literature at the
beginning of this note for sources), thus suggesting some fertility mystery.
[112] See Johannes Friedrich, "Phrygia," in Pauly, *op. cit.*, 20/1, 883, concerning the migration of the Thracians to Phrygia and the "kulturelle
Gemeinschaft" of the two peoples. Also, Herodotus, *Histories* 7.73, ET, Selincourt, *op. cit.*, p. 441.
[113] The most often quoted classical source is Euripides' *Bacchae*, but Greek
vase painting also provides valuable information. For a commentary on the
Bacchae, see E. R. Dodds, *Euripides' Bacchae*, Oxford: Clarendon 1960. The *LCL*
edition of the *Bacchae* was prepared by Arthur S. Way and published in 1942.
Among scholarly analyses outstanding are the following: Erwin Rohde,

testify to the Greeks' own awareness that the Dionysiac rites, characterized by excessive enthusiasm overflowing into irrational behavior, were essentially the same as those of the Phrygian Mother.[114]

Several festivals were connected with Dionysus. The biennial *orgia* were ecstatic rites held over mountaintops in the darkness of night, flickering torches providing the only light. The worshippers, dressed in long robes made of animal skins, let their hair flow freely in the wind. Some attached horns to their heads; some carried sacred snakes[115] and the *thyrsos*, a spear topped with a pine cone and wreathed with ivory and vine branches. Phrygian flutes, drums, and cymbals filled the air with music, which caused the excited participants to break out in uncontrollable and incoherent cries of joy. They danced and drank intoxicating drinks — above all, wine, which they believed contained the spirit of Dionysus. Thus wine was consumed as a solemn sacramental act, not merely as revelry. Eventually, as they began to hallucinate, they perceived the world of nature as supremely beautiful

---

Psyche, London: Rutledge and Kegan, 1925 (orig. German ed.,1893). This is to be supplemented by E. R. Dodds, *The Greeks and the Irrational*, Boston: Beacon Press, 1957, esp. pp. 64-101, "The Blessings of Madness," and pp. 270-282, "Maenadism." W. Otto, *Dionysus, Myth and Cult*, Bloomington: Indiana Univ. Press, 1965; W. K. C. Guthrie, *The Greeks and Their Gods*, Boston: Beacon Press, 1955, pp. 145-182; M. P. Nilsson, "Dionysus," *Oxford Classical Dictionary*, pp. 352-353. With regard to the relationship between Dionysus, Thrace, and Asia Minor, see the German Ph.D.dissertation by A. Rupp, *Die Beziehungen des Dionysus-Kultes zu Thrakien und zur Kleinasien*, Stuttgart, 1882. Furthermore, M. P. Nilsson, *Geschichte der Griechischen Religion* I/2; M. P. Nilsson, *The Dionysiac Mysteries of the Hellenistic and Roman Age*, Lund: C. W. K. Gleerup, 1957. Farnell, op. cit., 5.85 ff.; and a modern psychological investigation by Károly Kerényi, *Dionysus; Archetypal Image of Indestructible Life*, Princeton: Princeton Univ. Press, 1976. The subject is treated from women's point of view by Ross Shepard Kraemer, *Ecstatics and Ascetics: Studies in the Functions of Religious Activities for Women in the Greco-Roman World*, unpublished Ph.D. dissertation, Princeton Univ., 1976, and "Ecstasy and Possession: The Attraction of Women to the Cult of Dionysus," *Harvard Theological Review* 72 (1979) 55-80. Useful illustrations from Athenian vase paintings in Eva C. Keuls, *The Reign of the Phallus*, New York: Harper & Row, 1985. See also Marcel Detienne, *Dionysos Slain*, Baltimore: Johns Hopkins Univ. Press,1979.

[114] Compare these lines from the *Bacchae:* "From Asian soil, for over the hallowed ridges of Tmolus fleeting ... do I speed" (64-65); " ... the orgies of Cybele mystery-folden, of the Mother-olden, wreathed with ivy sprays ... child of God, o'er the mountain of Phrygia who trod" (79-88), and so forth, *LCL*, pp. 11-13. See, however, Kraemer, *op. cit.*, 29-35, for a summary of other opinions about the origin of the cult.

[115] Mark 16.18: "They will pick up serpents ... "

and sweet, or as Euripides says in the *Bacchae*, for them the ground flowed with milk, wine, and nectar.[116] They felt possessed by the god, filled by the god, and the religion of Dionysus knew such inspired people who, in a state of extreme ecstasy, prophesied.[117]

Both sexes were attracted to this religion, but R. S. Kraemer has argued convincingly that it was more common for women than for men. It is quite possible that women who otherwise had to conduct themselves in a restrained and decorous manner found this temporary liberation from their daily routine an especially welcome change.[118] Sexual license was a part of the Dionysiac *orgia*,[119] and according to Livy,[120] in Rome the promiscuous Bacchic celebrations were occasions for immorality and obscene behavior. The Bacchic rites were suppressed in Rome in 186 B.C. largely for reasons of immorality.

In Athens the Dionysiac festival included the public display of *phalli* and the *Hieros Gamos* which was performed during the second day of *Anthesteria*, the main festival with which Dionysus was connected. In a procession the *Basileus* and his wife, the *Basilinna*,[121] were taken to their official residence, the *Boukoleion*, where they performed the sacred act of intercourse while the

---

[116] *Bacchae, op. cit.*, 146-147; *LCL*, p. 17. More references from classical literature in Rohde, p. 274. This may be compared to what modern drug users experience. I interviewed some students of mine who at one time used drugs, and they unanimously assured me that the effect of the drugs was a state of mind beautiful beyond description. Unfortunately, it was a temporary one, and it was this fact which eventually made them abandon the drug culture. Dionysiac worshippers also became temporarily insensitive to pain, much like the Galli when they emasculated themselves, and some Christian ascetics and martyrs who during the greatest torture behaved as if they were oblivious to pain.

[117] Rohde, *op. cit.*, pp. 260, 275; Herodotus, 7.111, *op. cit.*, p. 451. Euripides, *Bacchae* 298. Livy reports that in Rome, men attached to the Bacchic cult "apparently out of their wits would utter prophecies with frenzied bodily convulsions," op. cit., 39.13, ET, H. Bettenson, Livy, New York: Penguin, 1981, p. 407.

[118] See the discussion of Kraemer, *Ecstatics ...*, pp. 74-85. In summary she believes that "participation in the Dionysiac *orgia* afforded Greek women a means of expressing their hostility and frustration at the male dominated society, by temporarily abandoning their homes and household responsibilities, and engaging in somewhat outrageous activities," p. 85; "Ecstasy and Possession ...," p. 80.

[119] References in Guthrie, p. 149.

[120] *Op. cit.*, 39.8-19, ET, Bettenson, *op. cit.*, pp. 401-415.

[121] See above, p. 63

people spent the evening drinking wine and observing holy silence.[122] Strange as this may be to us, it appears to be quite mild in comparison with what happened during the festival of *Haloa,* held on the twenty-sixth day of the month Poseidon (roughly, our December-January). This was a celebration honoring Dionysus and Demeter, during which women carried models of male and female genital organs, used obscene language, and encouraged each other to take lovers. On the tables were cakes made in the form of phalli and female organs, and the celebration, restricted to women, eventually developed into an all-night orgy where women shed all standards of decency.[123] What does obscenity have to do with religion? In an article, "Some Collective Expressions of Obscenity in Africa," E. E. Evans-Pritchard investigated the use of obscene language, songs, and bodily movements among several African tribes and concluded, among other things, that such behavior, while not normally permitted, was allowed as "an important religious ceremony" (p. 313)[124] — curiously enough, sometimes at funerals. No sense of shame was experienced under these circumstances and the ceremonies seemed to serve an important social function, namely, to direct "human emotions into prescribed channels of expression at periods of human crisis" (p. 331). While this explains the use of obscenity as a means of releasing tension, it leaves unanswered

---

[122] See Ludwig Deubner, *Attische Feste,* Berlin: Akademie Verlag, 1966, pp. 104-117. On sacred marriage generally see Albert Klinz, *Hieros Gamos,* Halle: E. Klinz, 1933. This is a Ph.D. dissertation at the University of Halle, written in Latin. It contains a collection of Greek and Roman sources that refer to divine marriages. On the Sumerian roots of this rite: Samuel N. Kramer, *The Sacred Marriage Rite,* Bloomington: Indiana Univ. Press,1969. Much interesting material is also found in M. H. Pope, *Song of Songs,* Garden City, N.Y.: Doubleday, 1977, and Urs Winter, *op. cit.* pp. 252-260; 311-368.

[123] A somewhat similar behavior was displayed by the women during the second day of the *Thesmorphoria* held on the eleventh day of the month *Pyanepsion* (October-November). It was a day of fast during which the women hurled insults at each other, even hit each other and generally mocked each other. The practice is explained as an imitation of the story of Demeter who, in search for her lost daughter Persephone, once was hosted by Iambe. Iambe, to cheer up Demeter, the sorrowing mother, made all kinds of lascivious jokes. Obscene songs were also used at the Eleusian mysteries of Demeter; see Robert Graves, *The Greek Myths,* vol. 1, pp. 94-95, Baltimore, Md.: Penguin, 1955. Also H. J. Rose, *Religions in Greece and Rome,* New York: Harper, 1959, pp. 77-78.

[124] Journal of the Royal Anthropological Institute of Great Britain and Ireland 49 (1929) 311-331.

the question of why such release was needed in a religious ceremony. In his article, Evans-Pritchard remarks: "In normal times the abnormal is taboo, but in abnormal times the abnormal things are done to restore the normal condition of affairs."[125]

The cults of Dionysus and Cybele, as other fertility rites, included wild, unrestrained acts in which conventional morals and standards of human behavior disappeared. All animal instincts, submerged and suppressed, were released in these orgies, as if the rock holding back the primordial waters in Jewish mythology had been removed and chaos permitted to return.[126] The music of the drums, the clashing of the cymbals, induced a sensation of the "raging of the elements let loose,"[127] and with wild leaps, the intoxicated dancers reintegrated themselves into a mystical, cosmic unity. The Dionysiac *orgia* was an attempt "to restore the normal condition of affairs," so to speak. Because unity is normal, not separation, the devotees of Dionysus reached out for the primordial condition and in a proleptic way experienced the joyful restoration of the cosmos to its undifferentiated state. Here is the key to understanding the *Hieros Gamos*. No doubt it was a fertility rite which was meant to ensure good harvest, but beyond that, it pointed toward the great mystery of the union of Earth and Sky, which was viewed in many myths as the cause of the Earth's fertility. As we shall see in our next chapter, the union of Earth and Sky was the prototype of human intercourse, through which male and female experienced a temporary victory over separation. Lucretius (95-52 B.C.) beautifully describes intercourse as a vain attempt of lovers to melt into each other:

> And when at last with twining limbs they taste the
> flower of youth, when now their bodies feel a foretaste
> of delight, and Venus hath the man in act to sow the
> female soil, even then frame unto frame they wildly
> lock, mingling the moisture of their mouths, and e'en
> draw in each other's breath, as teeth on lips they
> madly press; yet all in vain, since naught can they
> remove there from, nor penetrate body in body, and thus
> merge into one. For this they seem at times to crave,
> and strive to do ...[128]

---

125   *Art. cit.*, p. 323, is a quotation from another work.
126   See above, p. 59.
127   Crawley, *op. cit.*, pp. 247-248.
128   *De rerum natura* 4.1103-11114, ET, Charles E. Bennett, New York: W. J.

This may shed light on ritual promiscuity: it was a religious act because in the act of intercourse male and female, albeit momentarily, became one and in orgasm came as close to divinity as is humanly possible. Dionysiac madness, including the *Hieros Gamos,* was a sacramental *henosis,* the deepest religious experience accessible to men and women, a return to unity with God, being completely filled with and absorbed into the divine.

> The Greek word ὄργια may come from ἔργον, in which case the meaning of ὄργια would be "a work done for the gods." However, there is also a possibility that the word comes from ὀργάς (i.e. = γῆ), which means "any well-watered, fertile spot of land" and so "a tract of land sacred to the gods." A piece of land between Athens and Megara which was dedicated to the corn goddess Demeter was specifically called ἡ ὀργάς. From here comes the word ὀργασμός.[129] If ὄργια indeed comes from ὀργάς, for which I could not find irrefutable evidence, then the Greek *orgia* conceals a subtle reference to an association with *orgasm* as the climax of intercourse. Furthermore, since ὀργάς points to the goddess Demeter and fertile earth, the *orgia* could be understood as an experience of the *Hieros Gamos.* While I cannot prove this hypothesis with classical references, I think it is possible that the similarity of the words may have conjured up these ideas in the Greek mind. The modern English word "orgasm" no longer contains this hint that in the climax of intercourse the divine is present. It was different for ancient Greeks who regarded erotic experience as a "kind of death which is more intense than the life of a normal consciousness and points to the emergence of a new consciousness, however unidentifiable."[130]

Indiscriminate sexual behavior in religion is a temporary suspension of order in human relations and a sacramental demonstration of chaos, i.e. the condition of commingling elements and the absence of divisions and separations. This was mysticism on the most exalted level, similar to the visions of the medieval saints, comparable to the mystical imagery of the New Testament, as well as to the experience of Cybele's initiates, to which we now turn.

Black, 1946, pp. 219-220.

[129] Liddell-Scott, *op. cit.,* pp. 1245-1456.

[130] W. Corrigan, "Body and Soul of Ancient Religious Experience," in A. H. Armstromg, *op. cit.,* p. 364.

E. Cybele, the Great Mother

Cybele is one name under which the mysterious power of bringing forth life was venerated.[131] In Asia Minor reverence paid to such power can be traced back to 6000 B.C., but the most direct ancestor of Cybele seems to have been the Hittite deity Kubaba.[132] The center of Cybele's worship was in Pessinus, where a sacred stone, believed to have fallen from heaven (from *Pesein* 'to fall'), was worshipped as the goddess.[133] She also ruled over Mount Ida near Troy, and for this reason the Romans also called her the Idean Mother. It was from here (or from Pergamum) that the Romans brought her statue to Rome in 204 B.C. to help them to overcome Hannibal.[134] The young Scipio, accompanied by married women, received the goddess at Ostia and gave her to the women who took her to Rome. There "the women passed the goddess from hand to hand, one to another in succession," and eventually brought her to the Palatine, where later a temple was built in her honor, the ruins of which are still visible. The Romans also instituted the festivities called *Megalensia* to be held in her honor in April.

---

[131] Since the literature on this topic is very great, the interested student must make a careful selection. Still a very useful book is Grant Showerman, *The Great Mother of the Gods,* Chicago: Argonaut, 1969 (reprint of 1902 edition). Most up to date is Maarten J. Vermaseren, *Cybele and Attis. The Myth and the Cult,* London: Thames and Hudson, 1977 . Also G. M. Sanders, "Gallos," *RAC* 8, 983-1034; Harold Willoughby, *Pagan Regeneration,* Chicago: Univ. of Chicago Press, 1929; W. Drexel, "Meter," in Roscher, *op. cit.,* 2.2848-2931; A. Momigliano, "Cybele," *ER,* Mircea Eliade, ed., New York: Macmillan, 1984, 4.185-187; Garth Thomas, "Magna Mater and Attis," *ANRW* 2.17.3, pp. 1500-1535. Some texts pertaining to the Great Mother were collected and reprinted by Marion W. Meyer, *The Ancient Mysteries. A Sourcebook,* San Francisco: Harper and Row, 1987. Most books dealing with Montanism also deal with Cybele; these are listed below.

[132] On the meaning of the name, see Vermaseren, *op. cit.,* pp. 21-24.

[133] Sacred stones falling from heaven were probably meteorites. One is mentioned in Acts 19.35, but there were others, such as the black stone of Emesa, the worship of which by the Emperor Elagabalus eventually caused his assassination (Herodian, *Histories* 5.3.5). The "Palladium," which supposedly was brought by Aeneas from Troy to Rome, was worshipped as the image of Pallas Athene sent down from heaven (Pausanias, *Guide to Greece* 2, 23.5). This was guarded by the Vestal Virgins. On the Palladium, see Clarence A. Forbes, *Firmicus Maternus: The Error of the Pagan Religions,* New York: Newman Press, 1970, pp. 74-76, and the editor's critical remarks. Also Cyril Bailey, "Palladium," *The Oxford Classical Dictionary, op. cit.,* pp. 771-772.

[134] Livy, *Ab Urbe Condita* 29.10, 11, 14.

The myths that grew up around Cybele are known in various versions, all of which are further complicated by the figure of Attis, her youthful companion.[135] It is impossible to reconcile these stories with each other, but the main features are these: The goddess loved Attis, but he was unfaithful to her and in sorrow over his infidelity he emasculated himself and died. Cybele mourned him, but in the end, Attis was restored to life and deified. The core of the myth is the typical explanation of the changing seasons by an agriculturally oriented society: Cybele is Mother Earth; Attis is the god of vegetation. In the spring (the youth of Attis) the two of them are in love, but when summer comes the fruits are harvested, the fields are barren, and Attis is dead. Autumn and winter come, the mother grieves, but Attis is revived.[136] The same elements appear in the stories of the grieving mother Demeter in search of Persephone, the myth upon which the Eleusinian mysteries were based, and of the Mesopotamian Ishtar and her young lover Tammuz, whose annual death was mourned with weeping by women.[137] The festivals of Cybele reflected the events told in the myths. According to the Roman festival, which was based upon the Phrygian rites, these were the holy days:[138]

March 15 *Canna intrat* :	"Entry of the reed" *(Canna)*. Worshippers remembered on this day the early life of Attis when he was abandoned among the reeds of the river Gallus and rescued by shepherds.
March 22 *Arbor intrat* :	"Entry of the tree" *(Arbor)*. On this day a pine tree was cut before

---

[135] Vermaseren, *op. cit.*, pp. 76-95, quotes and analyzes them all.

[136] "The earth, they maintain, loves the crops, Attis is the very thing that grows from the crops, and the punishment which he suffered is what a harvester does to the injured crops with his sickle. His death they interpret as the storing away of the collected seed, his resurrection as the sprouting of the scattered seeds in the annual time of the season." Firmicus Maternus, *op. cit.* 3.2, p. 48.

[137] See Ezek. 9.14: "Then he brought me to the entrance of the north gate of the house of the Lord, and behold, there sat women weeping for Tammuz." Ishtar and Tammuz in the Sumerian pantheon are Inanna and Dumuzi.

[138] Vermaseren, *op. cit.*, pp. 113-125; Showerman, *op. cit.*, pp. 49-70; Willoughby, *op. cit.*, pp. 122-129.

sunrise, because Attis died under a pine tree. An image of Attis was attached to the tree, solemnly carried into the temple, and laid out as though it were a dead body. Lamentations followed and continued through the next day, which was a day of mourning accompanied by fasting.

March 23 Day of Mourning:

The *Salii*, dancing priests of Mars, performed their sacred dance, and the mourning and fasting continued.

March 24 *Dies Sanguinis* : "The Day of Blood."

Fanatic worshippers flagellated themselves with leather scourges and sprinkled their blood upon the altars. The music of cymbals, drums, flutes, and horns incited the faithful into frenzied dancing, loud and howling singing, while they inflicted all manner of injury upon their bodies, including biting themselves.[139] This was also the day on which some, driven to unrestrained frenzy, emasculated themselves and thus identified themselves

---

[139] Lucian, *Dialogues of the Gods* 20 (12), M. D. Macleod, *LCL*, London: Heinemann, 1946, vol. 7, p. 333: "She (Rhea) keeps shrieking for Attis, while the Corybantes slash their arms with swords or let down their hair and rush madly over the mountains, or blow on the horn, thunder on the drums, or bang cymbals; it is just chaotic frenzy all over Ida." Compare the description of Apuleius, *Metamorphoses* 8.27-28, ET, W. Adlington, *LCL*, London: Heinemann 1935, p. 391: "They went forth with their arms naked to their shoulder, bearing with them great swords and mighty axes, shouting and dancing like mad persons to the sound of the pipe ... they began to howl all out of tune and hurl themselves hither and thither, as though they were mad. They made a thousand gests with their feet and their heads; they would bend down their necks and spin round so that their hair flew out in a circle; they would bite their own flesh; finally, every one took his two-edged weapon and wounded his arms in diverse places ..." Compare with this the story of the priests of Baal in their confrontation with Elijah: " ... they cried aloud, and cut themselves after their custom with swords and lances until the blood gushed out upon them ... and they raved on until the time of the offering ... " 1 Kings 18 . 28-29.

March 25 *Hilaria* :

with the deity. They believed that by this act they achieved a particularly intimate relationship with Cybele.[140] "Day of Rejoicing."

During the night prior to this day, "Attis" was buried. Early in the morning, however, a priest brought in light, anointed the throats of the mourners, and said: "Be of good cheer, *mystae*, the god was saved. For us, too, there will be salvation from afflictions." Attis was raised, and the day was given over to happy entertainment.

March 26 *Requietio* : "A day of rest."

---

[140] According to Pliny, *Hist. Nat.* 35.46.165, they used a piece of Samian pottery to avoid "dangerous results," P. H. Rackham, *LCL*, Cambridge, Mass.: Harvard Univ. Press, 1947-1963, pp. 382-383. Lucian, *De Dea Syria* 51, describes the emasculation, and Catullus' poem number 63, *Attis*, is a powerful study of the after effects on some men of such a senseless act. Lucretius, *De Rerum Natura*, 597-698, also described the rites of the Great Mother and passed a gentle judgement on the whole matter: it is well meant, but far from reason. For an English translation, see Charles E. Bennett, *On the Nature of Things*, New York: W. J. Black, 1946, p. 86. See also Ovid, *Fasti* 4.179-372, J. G. Frazer, ed., *LCL*, Cambridge, Mass.: Harvard Univ. Press, 1931, pp. 200-215, of which the following lines must suffice: " ... straightaway the Berecynthian (= Phrygian) flute will blow a blast on its bent horn, and the festival of the Idaean Mother will have come. Eunuchs will march and thump their hollow drums, and cymbals clashed on cymbals will give out their tinkling notes; seated on the unmanly necks of her attendants, the goddess herself will be borne with howls through the streets in the city's midst. The stage is clattering, the games are calling. To your places, Quirites! And in the empty law courts let the war of suitors cease ... !" See also Martial, *esp.* 3.81.1-6.

Christians naturally deplored this act in the strongest terms; see, e.g., Minucius Felix, Octavius 24.4 "Would not a man who makes libations of his own blood, and supplicates his god by his own wounds, be better if he were altogether profane, than religious in such a way as this? And he whose shameful parts are cut off, how greatly does he wrong God in seeking to propitiate Him in this manner! Since if God wished for eunuchs, He could bring them as such into existence, and would not make them so afterwards. Who does not perceive that people of unsound mind and of weak and degraded apprehension, are foolish in these things, and that the very multitude of those who err affords to each of them mutual patronage? Here the defense of the general madness is the multitude of the mad people." English translation from *ANF* 4, 187-188.

March 27 *Lavatio* :   "Day of washing."
The statue of the goddess was taken to a river and washed, then, in festal procession, it was returned to the temple. Flowers, singing, and dancing were a part of this procession.

The cult of Cybele must have included several office holders such as the *Cannophori*, those in charge of the proper performance of the first day's solemnities. Women were admitted to this group of functionaries, a fact that distinguished Cybele's from other cults that limited the priesthood to men.[141] The *Dendrophoroi* were responsible for the pine tree, but those who dedicated themselves fully to the service of the goddess by emasculating themselves were called the Galli.[142] Their chief was called the Archigallus. In Rome only Orientals were originally permitted to serve in the hierarchy. Later this restriction was abolished and we hear of several Roman men and women who served as priests and priestesses of Cybele. Her temple, like others, needed many servants to take care of everyday necessities and the sacred objects. Among these were musicians and singers, whose number, according to the testimony of ancient authors, must have been very great.[143]

Cybele was a chaste goddess, "beautiful and kindly,"[144] whose religion was one of salvation. This is vividly illustrated by the rite of the *Taurobolium,* in which the fresh blood of the bull flowed upon the devotees as they stood in a pit under a grate.[145] This ceremony, so reminiscent of a "baptism by blood," elicited criticism from later Christian authors who ridiculed the gory proceedings and contrasted them with the cleansing power of the blood of

---

[141] See Livy, 34.7: "They cannot partake of magistracies, priesthoods, triumphs, badges of office, gifts or spoils of war." Virginia Burrus, *Chastity as Autonomy. Women in the Stories of the Apocryphal Acts.* Lewiston/Queenston: Edwin Mellen Press, 1987, p. 100.

[142] The name comes either from Gallus, which means "cock," which the galli adopted as their symbol, or from the River Gallos near which Attis was abandoned (or near which he emasculated himself), or from a certain King Gallus.

[143] Vermaseren, *op . cit .*, pp.109-110.

[144] Showerman, *op. cit.,* pp. 80,82, emphasizes this point strongly.

[145] In the *taurobolium* a bull was killed; in the *criobolium* it was a ram. See Robert Duthoy, *The Taurobolium: Its Evolution and Terminology*, Leiden: Brill, 1969.

Jesus.[146] Elements which appeared symbolically in Christian baptism were presented very realistically in the rite of the *taurobolium*. Here the devotee actually descended into a pit resembling a tomb and was actually drenched in blood; when he reappeared he was "reborn for eternity."[147] Baptism by immersion, St. Paul explained in Romans 6, symbolized a death and resurrection with Christ "so that we too might walk in newness of life."

Another element in the worship of Cybele which irritated Christians was an otherwise obscure rite of initiation which took place during the night preceding the *Hilaria*. As is usual with mystery religions, little is known about the rite itself, but some elements of it have been preserved by Clement of Alexandria, according to whom the person just initiated uttered these words: "I have eaten out of the drum, I have drunk out of the cymbal, I have carried the Cernos, I have slipped into the bedroom."[148] Some kind of eating and drinking took place in this ceremony which had a sacramental effect, making the person a "mystes" of Attis. The similarity to the Christian eucharist is obvious and one wonders whether St. Paul, who received his education in Asia Minor and must have known about the mysteries of Cybele, was influenced by these ideas when he wrote to the Corinthians: "The cup of blessing which we bless, is it not a participation in the blood of

---

[146] Firmicus Maternus, *De Errore Profanum Religionum* 27.8: "That blood pollutes, it does not redeem ... it destroys a person in death. Unhappy are they who are drenched by the outpouring of sacrilegious blood, that sacrifice of a bull or a ram pours out upon you the stain of wicked blood." English translation, Clarence A. Forbes, *Firmicus Maternus: The Error of Pagan Religions*, New York: Newman Press, 1970, p. 107. The book of Firmicus Maternus was written ca. 350 A.D.. See also Prudentius, *Peristephanon* 10.1006-50. The English translation of parts of the poem of Prudentius in Vermaseren, *op. cit.*, pp. 102-103. For a complete translation, see H. J. Thomson, ed., *Prudentius, LCL*, Cambridge, Mass.: Harvard Univ. Press, 1961, vol. 2, pp. 294-299.

[147] Vermaseren, *op. cit.*, p. 106.

[148] *Protrepticus* 2.15, ANF 2.175. The full report of Clement is as follows: "Such rites the Phrygians perform in honor of Attis and Cybele and the Corybantes. As the story goes, Zeus, having torn away the orchites of a ram, brought them out and cast them at the breasts of Demeter, thus paying a fraudulent penalty for his violent embrace, pretending to have cut out his own. The symbols of initiation in these rites, when set before you in a vacant hour, I know will excite your laughter, although on account of the exposure by no means inclined to laugh. 'I have eaten ... etc.' Are not these tokens of disgrace? Are not the mysteries absurdity?" See to this passage, G. E. Mylonas, *op. cit.*, p. 288 ff. In Firmicus Maternus, *De Errore* ... 18, the sentence is quoted in slightly different form: "I have eaten from the drum, I have drunk from the cymbal, I became an initiate (μύστης) of Attis."

Christ? The bread which we break, is it not a participation in the body of Christ? ... I imply that what pagans sacrifice they offer to demons and not to God ... "[149] Firmicus Maternus also compared the pagan and Christian "communion" and could offer no differentiation except the lame comment that what the devotees of Cybele drink is "the cup of doom," what they eat "brings death and punishment," while Christian communion brings salvation and life.[150] The meaning of going "into the bedrom" is not known. Whether there was a real or symbolic sacred marriage remains unresolved, but it is clear that the devotees believed that they had had an experience of mystical union with the divine.

These, then, were the chief characteristics of the cult of Cybele. It was a religion deeply rooted in the soil of Asia Minor, and even in later times it preserved many ancient elements. The goddess often was pictured riding on a lion or flanked by lions, giving expression to her power over wildlife and nature. Her divine power also controlled the creative forces of the earth and the myths which arose about her were expressions of her great mystery, that of bringing forth life. Thus, the worshippers of Cybele were given answers to the greatest and most ancient concerns of humanity, those of life and death. These concerns were centered in the idea of the earth, for it was a common observation of ancient people that every living thing comes from earth and eventually returns to it.[151] Cybele, the Great Mother, touched sensitive chords in the human soul and the response was highly emotional; to the issues raised by Cybele, rational, sensible answers could not be given and would have been inadequate. Her worship was characterized by communication other than intelligent speech, i.e., the expression of thoughts in articulate sounds. Dancing — uncontrolled movements of the limbs of the body and the head, twisting and whirling — was one of these. In such dancing the worshippers seemed to lose their individual identities and to merge into a divine presence.[152] Music — that is, sounds in melodic, harmonic,

---

[149]   1 Cor. 10.14-22.

[150]   *Op. cit.*, chap. 18; English translation in *op. cit.*, p. 81.

[151]   See on this below, chap. VI, p. 207, in connection with the cult of the earth-goddess.

[152]   "The power of dance in religious practice lies in its multisensory, emotional, and symbolic capacity to communicate. It can create moods and a sense of situation in attention riveting patterns by framing, prolonging, or discontinuing communication. Dance is a vehicle that incorporates inchoate

and rhythmic combination — was another such means of communication; ancient authors mention a multitude of musical instruments which were used in the festival. Whether this music was a planned, organized communication or simply spontaneous noise-making no one knows because no examples of ancient music have survived. But we know the music's effect: it was ecstasy,[153] a supernatural rapture which put devotees into a state of mind in which they became vehicles for the proclamation of the divine will. Prophecy was a part of such frenzy,[154] which overwhelmed men and women alike. This phenomenon is attested to in other Near Eastern cultures[155] as well as in ancient Israel,

---

ideas in visible human form and modifies inner experience as well as social action." " ... Dance is a means of religious concentration as well as of corporeal merging with the infinite God." Judith Lynn Hanna, "Dance," *ER*, 4.203, 205.

[153] Anyone who has seen the effect of "rock music" — loud, shrill, and seemingly disorganized — upon large groups of young people will have no difficulty imagining the ancient "happening." According to newspaper accounts, such "rock" concerts often result in faintings and violence. We see another similarity between the external appearance of the devotees of Cybele and some modern "rock" performers. The *galli* appeared in ostentatious clothing, men "feminized their faces," wore soft garments, and their "scandalous performances" were "accompanied by the moaning of the throng" (Firmicus Maternus, op. cit., 4.2, p. 50). They wore their hair long and used make-up on their faces, according to Augustine, *De civitate dei* 7.26: "These effeminates, no later than yesterday, were going through the streets and places of Carthage, with anointed hair, whitened faces, relaxed bodies, and feminine gait exacting from the people the means of maintaining their ignominious lives." (English translation in *NPNF*, Series 1, vol. 2, p. 137; there is a similar description of the "hideous" eunuch priests in Apuleius, *Metamorphoses* 8.27, *LCL*, op. cit., p. 389.) The same things could be said of some "punk-rock" performers.

[154] Strabo, Geography 11.4.7, describes the custom of the Albanians: "The office of the priest is held by the man who, after the king, is held in the highest honor; he has charge of the sacred lance ... and also of the temple slaves, many of whom are subject to religious frenzy and utter prophecies." Then he relates that some of those who were "violently possessed" wandered alone in the forest; these were arrested, feasted for that year, and then were sacrificed "in honor of the goddess." The sacrificial killing was accomplished with a sacred lance by which the victim was stabbed in the heart. From his fall the Albanians also drew auguries. *LCL*, H. L. Jones, ed., London: Heinemann, 1961, vol. 5, 228-231. See the Taurobolium, where the bull is killed with a sacred lance. Albania was located in the Caucasus, near the Kura river. Its main city was Χαβάλα (E. H. Warmington, "Albania" *The Oxford Classical Dictionary, op. cit.*, p. 34: "Their chief worship was an orgiastic cult of the moon goddess."); see also Pliny, *Naturalis Historia* 6.29: he mentions Cabalaca. Also, Wilhelm Schepelern, *Der Montanismus und die Phrygischen Kulte*, Tübingen: J. C. B. Mohr, 1929, pp. 94-95.

[155] According to William F. Albright, *From Stone Age to Christianity*, New

where it eventually developed into the prophetic movement known from the Old Testament.

Religious frenzy led some followers of Cybele to a quite different conclusion: these unfortunates castrated themselves and many of them afterwards put on female clothing and affected female behavior. Severing of the genitals has been understood primarily as an attempt to conform to the goddess as closely as possible, to assimilate oneself to Cybele, so as to be able to serve the goddess more perfectly.[156] Castration, however, changes a man into a condition which is "neither male nor female," and from this vantage point the religious significance of the act becomes much larger. The castrated devotee received a new identity beyond sexuality; he became an androgynous person and thus returned to the primordial state of undifferentiation. Thus a castrated person is like a virgin. And the reason why so often in ancient religions virginity was a prerequisite for visiting the sanctuaries or serving the divinities[157] is that a virgin or a castrated person, as one in an "in-between" state, was believed to be able to perform a mediating function between God and humanity.

We shall discuss the importance of clothing later;[158] right now let us try to understand what the Galli may have believed when they exchanged male attire for female attire. As described by Apuleius, and as criticized by Augustine, this was a repulsive show, but from the vantage point of the religiously motivated, it was an attempt to merge male and female: the deficiency that arises from the condition of being a "male" was compensated by adding the "female" in the form of dress. Thus, the male was completed and the androgyne restored.[159] The practice of changing clothing belonged to the baptismal ceremonies of the early Christians, too. Since baptism symbolized the "new man" in whom the image of God was restored, this was made visible by

---

York: Doubleday/Anchor, 1957, p. 304, in the Assyrian area most of the "bearers of oracles were females."

[156] A. D. Nock, "Eunuchs in Ancient Religion," *Archiv für Religionswissenschaft* 23 (1952) 25-33.

[157] For references, see Nock, *op. cit.*, and Drijvers, *op. cit.*, p. 280. Celibacy, that is, voluntary virginity of the priest today, has been explained by a Roman Catholic scholar in very much the same categories; see Introduction, n.13.

[158] Chap. 3, "The Robe of the Woman."

[159] See Baumann, *op. cit.*, p. 46, and A. Bertholet, *art. cit.*, p. 19.

the new garment worn by the "reborn" Christian. Paul uses the imagery of dressing and undressing when he speaks about "putting off the old nature" and "putting on the new nature"[160] and when he says that in baptism a person "has put on Christ."[161] Being "dressed in Christ" as in a robe symbolized the merging of Christ's nature with that of the newly baptized person: the result was a new person in whom the primordial division had been reversed. Paul adds immediately in the next sentence: "There is no male or female."[162] In their religious enthusiasm, Cybele's devotees reached for salvation in *henosis* with the divine; that they did this in ways abhorrent and unacceptable to us does not detract from their piety and dedication.

The issues touched upon, however briefly, in this review of the cult of Cybele are so close to many concerns of Christian theology that the question must be faced: what is the relationship of Christianity to the worship of Magna Mater in Asia Minor? This is a complex problem. In the following pages we shall try to find those answers that shed light on the role of Mary in Christian piety and faith. Our study will focus on two Christian phenomena in Asia Minor that were contemporary with the cult of Cybele: the book of Revelation, with its central image of the "woman clothed with the sun," and the Montanist movement, in which women seem to have played a greater part than in other congregations of the early church.

But first, let us summarize what we have thus far discussed. Fertility goddesses were personifications of all those forces in nature which represent reproduction and life. Caelestis was *"pluviarum pollicitatrix,"* as Tertullian said,[163] "the promiser of rain," that gentle mystery that fertilizes land and people, that energy in the sky that rules over and controls the stars and the moon, the night air and all celestial phenomena. Similar statements could

---

160 Eph. 4.22-24; Col. 3.10.
161 Gal. 3.27.
162 Gal. 3.28. Was Paul influenced in his use of such imagery by what he saw in Cybele's mysteries? See below, p. 166. See also Jonathan Z. Smith, "The Garment of Shame," *History of Religions* 5 (1966) 217-238; Wayne A. Meeks, "The Image of the Androgyne: Some Uses of a Symbol in Earliest Christianity," *History of Religions* 13 (1974) 165-208; Dennis R. MacDonald, *There Is No Male and Female. The Fate of a Dominical Saying in Paul*, Philadelphia: Fortress Press, 1987.
163 *Apol.* 23; *ANF* 3.37.

be made about the other goddesses whose chief characteristics we reviewed, and so it may be said that a fertility goddess is the conqueror of aridity and dryness, i.e., conditions that would impede the generation of life. She is, as the great emperor Julian said, "the very goddess whom some call Venus, others Juno, whom still others regard as the natural cause which supplies from moisture the beginnings and seeds of everything, and points out to mankind the source of all blessings."[164]

She is the principle and cause of all generation,[165] the universal mother, mother of gods and man.[166] What did pagans have in mind when they said "Mother of the Gods"? Julian gave this definition:

> She is the source of the intellectual and creative gods, who in
> their turn guide the visible gods: she is both the mother and the
> spouse of mighty Zeus; she came into being next to and together
> with the great creator; she is in control of every form of life
> and the cause of all generation; she easily brings to perfection
> all things that are made; without pain she brings to birth, and
> with the father's aid creates all things that are; she is the mother-
>   less maiden,
> enthroned at the side of Zeus, and in very truth is the Mother of all
>   the Gods.[167]

Thus, for ancient Greeks and Romans a goddess represented everything that femininity meant and stood for. That in physical life this had sexual connotations should be neither surprising nor

---

[164] Plutarch, *Crassus* 17, *Plutarch's Lives*, *LCL*, Bernadette Perrin, ed., London: Heinemann, 1915, pp. 366-367. Andrew Greely, *op. cit.*, pp. 36-55, explores and explains this issue with clarity. One of his statements should be quoted: "The feminine goddesses of antiquity, then, represent the fact that the 'feminine principle' is present in the deity. They are developments for more primitive androgynous deities, in all likelihood, and of course they reflect the human experience of sexuality as sacred. Fertility is a good, indeed, and indispensible thing, and fertility involves sexuality; then surely sexuality must be found in the ultimate and the absolute. But it is difficult to deal with an ultimate that is masculine and feminine at the same time. Therefore, we have gods and goddesses, and underlying the vast systems of ritual and cult we build to those deities, there is still the notion that in whatever is *really* ultimate, the two are combined" (*op. cit.*, p. 55).

[165] Julian, *Oration V*, Hymn to the Mother of the Gods, 166, *LCL*, *The Works of the Emperor Julian*, Wilber C. Wright, ed., London: Heinemann, 1913, pp. 462-463. This oration was written in 362 at Pessinus in Phrygia in honor of Cybele, whose cult Julian explains in Neo-Platonic terms.

[166] Oration V, 179D, *op. cit.*, p. 463.

[167] Julian, *Oration V* 166, op. cit., p. 463.

offensive. It is possible, for example, that in the temple of Caelestis in Carthage the cult included sexually explicit rites similar to those of Hierapolis; at least Valerius Maximus and Augustine[168] definitely mention Carthage when they condemn the "immoral" practices of the pagans. If so, the worshippers of Caelestis did nothing more than recognize an aspect of physical life in which the divine reveals itself.

We can express ourselves only by using images of existing realities,[169] and the image most readily available with respect to the origin of life is the union of sexes. Because we experience in their union the beginning of a process of creation, "male" and "female" are understood to have a primordial origin. Pagan mythologies tell of cosmic unions which led to the creation of the universe. The Bible speaks of God and his word, or God and his spirit, as the primary creative forces. Whether it is pagan or Judeo-Christian tradition that one follows, prior to the coming into being of the universe there was an androgynous energy or force in which "male" and "female," potentially present, were united. Life began when "male" and "female" issued from this force as differentiated powers. A goddess, therefore, is that half of the divine which presides over and represents female functions, just as a god does with respect to male functions.

As we have seen, the image of the divine female is an extremely complex religious phenomenon about which no single comprehensive statement can be made. Many goddesses, for example, represented evil forces and negative elements in the world. These would require a study beyond the scope of this book. Our concern is the relationship between the image of Mary in Christianity and the pagan goddesses of fertility. Already it seems clear that the Mariological principle, i.e., veneration of the motherhood of Mary, is much more indebted to pagan belief and practice than many scholars are willing to admit. As we consider the role of these goddesses in pagan faith and piety, the conclusion seems inevitable that Mary eventually fulfilled the same role and filled the same need in Christian theology and piety.

---

[168] See above p. 36f.

[169] Andrew Greely, *op. cit.*, p. 35 elaborated on this theme which was first presented, as far as I know, by Mircea Eliade in his *Patterns of Comparative Reliqion.*

Fundamental to Christian theology is the idea of a primordial creation which was corrupted by sin and a new creation in which the process of separation will be reversed and the union of divine and human will be restored. Mary is the feminine half of the divine activity which results in a new creation, i.e., the beginning of a process which leads to salvation. Mary is the female aspect of God the Redeemer, just as God's "Word" or Spirit was the cooperating principle in the primordial creation. Without Mary there is no divine conception and birth, no beginning of a new race, no new heaven and earth.

We now turn to chapter 12 of the book of Revelation, to the woman "clothed with the sun." Is she an echo of the pagan goddess?

CHAPTER THREE

THE IMAGE OF THE GODDESS IN
THE NEW TESTAMENT

And a great portent appeared in heaven, a woman clothed with the sun, with the moon under her feet, and on her head a crown of twelve stars; she was with child and she cried out in her pangs of birth, in anguish for delivery. And another portent appeared in heaven; behold, a great red dragon, with seven heads and ten horns, and seven diadems upon his heads. His tail swept down a third of the stars of heaven, and cast them to the earth. And the dragon stood before the woman who was about to bear a child, that he might devour her child when she brought it forth; she brought forth a male child, one who is to rule all the nations with a rod of iron, but her child was caught up to God and to his throne, and the woman fled into the wilderness, where she has a place prepared by God, in which to be nourished for one thousand two hundred and sixty days.

Now war arose in heaven, Michael and his angels fighting against the dragon; and the dragon and his angels fought, but they were defeated and there was no longer any place for them in heaven. And the great dragon was thrown down, that ancient serpent, who is called the Devil and Satan, the deceiver of the whole world — he was thrown down to the earth, and his angels were thrown down with him. And I heard a loud voice in heaven, saying, "Now the salvation and the power and the kingdom of our God and the authority of his Christ have come, for the accuser of our brethren has been thrown down, who accuses them day and night before our God. And they have conquered him by the blood of the Lamb and by the word of their testimony, for they loved not their lives even unto death. Rejoice then, O heaven and you that dwell therein! But woe to you, O earth and sea, for the devil has come down to you in great wrath, because he knows that his time is short!"

And when the dragon saw that he had been thrown down to the earth, he pursued the woman who had born the male child. But the woman was given the two wings of the great eagle that she might fly from the serpent into the wilderness, to the place where she is to be nourished for a time, and times, and half a time. The serpent poured water like a river out of his mouth after the woman, and the earth opened its mouth and swallowed the river which the dragon had poured form his mouth. Then the dragon was angry with the woman, and went off to make war on the rest of her offspring, on those who keep the commandments of God and bear testimony to Jesus. And he stood on the sand of the sea. (Revelation 12:1-16)[1]

To what extent is this "woman" a reflection of the pagan "Queen of Heaven"?[2] To discover this we will investigate the extra-biblical material and mythology that may have shaped the view of the author of the book of Revelation and that may be reflected in this particular vision.[3] The drama itself — the birth of a child and events related to it — are beyond the scope of this study. Our interest will be limited to the figure of the "woman" only and this to the degree that she may be a product of pagan mythological thought patterns.

The entire myth is of pre-Christian origin.[4] It was the so-called

---

[1] The revised Standard Version, New York: Thomas Nelson & Sons, 1952.

[2] Thus, we do not plan to pursue a systematic exegesis of the text. These are plentiful and the resulting interpretations are by and large all variations on the same theme: the woman is either the symbol of the church, the synagogue, or Mary, or a combination of these. These hypotheses are being endlessly repeated, of which the following selections of publications may serve as an example. J. E. Bruns, "The Contrasted Woman of Apocalypse 12 and 17." *Catholic Biblical Quarterly* 26 (1964) 459-463; P.P. James, "Mary and the Great Sign." *American Ecclesiastical Review* 142 (1960) 321-329; J. Ernst, "Die Himmlische Frau im 12 Kapitel der Apokalypse." *Theologie und Glaube* 58 (1968) 39-59; J. Sickenberger, "Die Messiasmutter im 12 Kapitel der Apokalypse." *Theologische Quartalschrift* 126 (1946) 357-427; J. Michl, "Die Deutung der apokalyptischen Frau in der Gegenwart." *Biblische Zeitschrift* N.F. 3 (1959) 301-310; see also the numerous commentaries on the book of Revelation, *ad loc.* Johann Kosnetter, "Die Sonnenfrau (Apok. 12.1-17) in der Neueren Exegese." *Theologische Fragen der Gegenwart.* Festschrift, Kardinal Theodor Innitzer. Wien: Domverlag, 1952, pp. 93-108, demonstrates among others, that any single identification of the *Sonnenfrau* is inadequate and cannot be supported by some verse in chapter 12. The author's final conclusion is that the woman is "ein zusammenfassendes symbol für die menschliche komponente der Heilsgeschichte." (p. 108). A useful summary of present-day research on the subject is in R.E. Brown et al., eds., *Mary in the Church*, Philadelphia: Fortress Press, 1978, pp. 218-239. Adele Yarboro Collins, *Crisis and Catharsis: The Power of the Apocalypse.* Philadelphia: Westminster, 1984 has a good section on authorship, time and place of origin and the social situation at the time of composition.

The Old Testament element in Revelation and the Jewish orientation of the author has been also scrutinized by numerous commentators some of whom find the prototype of the "woman" of Rev. 12 in the many references to "woman" in the Old Testament as symbolizing the synagogue or the people of God. The same course was and is followed by those who compare the Christian church to the symbolic "woman" in the Old Testament.

[3] For Jewish examples see below p.227f., "Eve, Mary and the Church."

[4] See Hans Lietzmann, *Der Weltheiland.* Bonn, 1909. E. Norden, *Die Geburt des Kindes.* Leipzig und Berlin: Teubner, 1924.

"religionsgeschichtliche Schule" in Germany at the end of the nineteenth and at the beginning of the twentieth centuries that called attention to these facts, and it was scholars belonging to this school whose genius and tireless work opened up new horizons in the understanding of the book of Revelation. By refusing to view the book in isolation and by integrating it into the total experience of the Mediterranean world these scholars gave meaning to many of the mysterious references in the book, especially to those pertaining to our problem in Chapter 12.

Eberhard Vischer was the first to suggest that the book of Revelation should be understood from a Jewish background. He used talmudic parallels to prove his point. The name of the great historian Adolf von Harnack in the title of Vischer's book added greater weight to his arguments.[5] Soon after Vischer, Albrecht Dieterich pointed to Greek mythology and suggested that there was a similarity between the pythian dragon, the birth of Apollo from Leto, and the story in Revelation 12.[6] Herman Gunkel then opened up Babylonian mythology for biblical research and showed the interdependency of the world of ideas in Genesis 1 and Revelation 12.[7] It was Gunkel who formulated the position of the *religionsgeschichtliche Schule* with the statement that *"die neutestamentliche Religion bei ihrer Entstehung und Ausbildung in wichtigen, ja in einigen wesentlichen Punkten unter entscheidenden Einfluss fremder Religionen gestanden hat, und dass dieser Einfluss zu den Männern des Neuen Testaments durch das Judentum hindurch gekommen ist."*[8] The publication of Wilhelm Bousset's commentary on the book of Revelation in 1906 was a major event; this book still has not been superseded. For the interpretation of Revelation 12 his major contribution was the investigation of Egyptian mythology, in which he pointed to the figures of Hathor = Isis, the great mother of gods;

---

5 *Die Offenbarung Johannis eine jüdische Apokalypse in Christlicher Bearbeitung, mit einem Vorwort von A. Harnack* (Texte und Untersuchungen II.3) Leipzig: J. C. Hinrichs, 1886; 2nd ed. 1895.

6 Albrecht Dieterich, *Abraxas. Studien zur Religionsgeschichte des späteren Altertums,* Leipzig: Teubner, 1891. The work is available now in the edition of Aachen: Scientia Verlag, 1975, which is a reprint of the 1905 Leipzig edition. See here esp. pp. 111-126 for the Leto-Python parallels.

7 Hermann Gunkel, *Schöpfung und Chaos in Urzeit und Endzeit,* Göttingen: Vandenhoeck and Ruprecht, 1895.

8 *Zum religionsgeschichtlichen Verständnis des Neuen Testaments,* Göttingen: Vandenhoeck and Ruprecht, 1910, p. 1.

Horus, the young sun-god, and the dragon Typhon as parallels to the figures in Revelation 12. "*Solche Herübernahme von Mythen, Erzählungen, Sagen und Symbolen, Lehren und Vorschriften von einer Religion in die andere,*" Bousset said. "*Gehören doch zu den allergewöhnlichsten geschichtlichen Vorgängen. Durch nichts kann wirkungsvoller für eine neue Religion Propaganda gemacht werden, als wenn man sie im Gewand der alten darstellt.*"[9]

Alfred Jeremias[10] compared the Egyptian myth of the struggle between Ra and Apophis with the cosmic battle in Revelation 12. Carl Clemen put the entire New Testament under the magnifying glass of the *religionsgeschichtliche* method, taking into account all previously published scholarly works written on the subject.[11] His book is a mine of information; reading it gives one the impression that all later Ph.D. theses and commentaries on Revelation were based on his researches; nothing essentially new has been added.

Unfortunately for Christian scholarship, one aspect of the study of Revelation 12 is often neglected: the influence of astrology, which was considerable in the early Roman empire. Indeed, so preoccupied were people with the influence of the stars that one major Roman historian called astrology "the religion *par excellence* of the Mediterranean world at this time."[12] Yet in the study of the New Testament this is seldom considered. In this respect Franz Boll has contributed much invaluable material; he was the first to research this problem and to show the frequency with which contemporary readers' minds turned to astral mythology upon reading Revelation 12.[13]

---

[9] *Die Offenbarung Johannis. Kritisich-Exegetischer Kommentar über das Neue Testament,* Begründet von Heinr. Aug. Wilh. Meyer, vol. 16, Göttingen: Vandenhoeck and Ruprecht, 1906. Exegesis of Ch. 12, pp. 335-358; the quote above is on p. 354.

[10] *Das alte Testament im Lichte des alten Orients,* Leipzig: J. C. Hinrich'sche Buchhardlung, 1905; 3rd ed., 1916, p. 145; Die Pambabylonisten, Leipzig; J. C. Hinrichs, 1907, p. 51 ff.

[11] *Religionsgeschichtlichee Erklärung des Neuen Testaments. Die Abhängigkeit des altesten Christentums von den nichtjüdischen Religionen und Philosophischen Systemen,* Giessen: A. Töpelmann, 1909.

[12] Michael Grant, *The World of Rome,* Cleveland and New York: World, 1960, p. 135.

[13] Franz Boll, *Aus der Offenbarung Johannis. Hellenistische Studien zum Weltbild der Apokalypse,* Leipzig/Berlin: Teubner, 1914. See also his *Sphaera,* Leipzig: Teubner, 1903. Also, "Stern der Weisen," *Zeitschrift für Neutestamentliche Wissenschaft,* Giessen: Töpelmann, 1900-; 18 (1917/18), pp. 41-48.

We will now give a brief account of how the material drawn from outside the corpus of biblical literature aids us in understanding the historical background of Revelation 12.

A. The Woman Clothed with the Sun
and Pagan Mythology

Few modern scholars deny the pagan mythological elements in Revelation 12. However, many point out that there are substantial differences between the respective pagan myths and the biblical statements. For this reason J. Kosnetter[14] does not even discuss the *religionsgeschichtliche Deutung*. But without utilizing the results of that research, all attempts of interpreting Revelation 12 on a purely biblical basis fail, as Kosnetter himself must admit. They fail because none of the interpretations of the woman fits perfectly; each one is contradicted by a particular verse of Chapter 12.

Aetiological in nature, myths are prescientific attempts to explain natural phenomena presented as narratives involving supernatural persons and actions. They deal with cosmology, theology, and even soteriology. The mental process that gave rise to and eventually developed the story of the woman in Revelation 12 certainly presupposed basic ideas expressed in pagan mythology, and for this reason alone this perspective should not be ignored in interpreting the text.

The setting of the story provides the framework and background of everything that takes place and defines the nature of the woman who appears there. Some pagan mythological concepts that seem to have had a formative influence on the image of the woman as the author "painted" her are: (1) "heaven" as the place where the whole drama takes place; (2) the robe of the woman; (3) the astral motifs; (4) the battle with the dragon. I will discuss each of these, concluding with a review of the earliest Christian interpretations of Revelation 12.

1. *The Concept of Heaven*

The word "heaven" = οὐρανός, Aristotle says, can be used in three different contexts. First, it can mean "the substance of the outermost circumference of the world ... in which we also believe

---

14   *Op cit* p. 94.

all divinity to have its seat." Secondly, the word can be applied "to that body which occupies the next place to the outermost circumference of the world, in which are the moon and the sun and certain of the stars ... " Thirdly, "it is customary to give the name of *ouranos* to the world as a whole," i.e., to that whole body which is "enclosed by the outermost circumference."[15] Aristotle's first two definitions are similar to modern usage, for which the word "heaven" can refer either to the abode of God and of immortal beings, or to that space appearing as a vault or canopy over the earth, in which the sun, moon, and stars are seen.

The third definition of Aristotle, "heaven" meaning the entire universe, encompassing earth and sky, is no longer in everyday usage. However, this seems to have been the generally accepted view in the ancient world.[16] In his study of *Sumerian Mythology*, Samuel N. Kramer concluded that Sumerian cosmogeny already included the following ideas: Before everything else there was a primeval sea; this begot a cosmic mountain consisting of a united heaven and earth; only later were heaven and earth separated by the air-god Enlil.[17] Similar ideas were present in Egyptian mythologies. These maintain that out of the primeval ocean rose a united world; the goddess Nut lay upon her husband Geb. Then came Shu, god of the air, who forced himself between the two and lifted up Nut; thus, everything in the world found its proper place.[18] The Greco-Roman idea of the origin of heaven was summarized by Diodorus Siculus:

---

[15] *De Caelo* 278 b. W. K. C. Guthrie, *Aristotle on the Heavens, LCL,* London: Heinemann, 1953, pp. 88-89.

[16] Collections of ancient creation myths are available in several convenient editions: Barbara C. Sproul, *Primal Myths. Creating the World,* San Francisco: Harper and Row, 1979; Charles H. Long, *Alpha. The Myths of Creation,* New York: George Braziller, 1963; S. G. F. Brandon, *Creation Legends of the Ancient Near East,* London: Hodder and Stoughton, 1963. For an extensive analysis of the Mesopotamian, Egyptian, Greek, and bibilical cosmogonies, the reader is requested to turn to Brandon.

[17] *Op. cit.*, pp. VII-VIII; 41-42: "The Sumerian expression for 'universe' is *an-ki*, literally 'heaven-earth.'"; 73-75; Brandon, *op. cit.*, p. 71; 100-102.

[18] S. Morenz, *op. cit.*, pp. 182-183. Brandon, *op. cit.*, pp. 27-28. See also Adolf Erman, *Die Religion der Ägypter,* Berlin and Leipzig: De Gruyter, 1934,pp. 61-63; Kurt Sethe, *Urgeschichte und Älteste Religion der Ägypter,* Leipzig:Deutsche Morgenlandische Gesellschaft, 1930, par. 75, p. 62. Also Willibald Staudacher, *Die Trennung von Himmel und Erde,* Darmstadt: Wissenschaftliche Buchgesellschaft, 1968 (reprint of 1942 edition). Staudacher has shown that the idea was widespread in Asia and Africa, too.

When in the beginning, as the account runs, the universe was being formed, both heaven and earth were indistinguishable in appearance, since their elements were intermingled: then, when their bodies separated from one another, the universe took on in all its parts the ordered form in which it is now seen; the air set up a continual motion, and the fiery element in it gathered into the highest regions ... while all that was mud-like and thick and contained an admixture of moisture sank because of its weight into one place ..."[19]

The earliest theogonies (accounts of the birth of the divinities) reflect similar ideas. According to Hesiod, the first power was chaos and then arose "Gaia, broad-bosomed earth"; after her, Eros, Night, and Erebos. "Gaia first gave birth to him who is equal to her, star-studded Ouranos, to cover her everywhere over and be an ever-immovable base for the gods ... "[20]

Ouranos and Gaia had intercourse, giving birth to Okeanos. A rapid succession of events led finally to the violent separation of Ouranos and Gaia by Kronos. While the account of Hesiod is less than crystal clear, it does contain elements which survived. The tradition that heaven and earth were once one and that life arose from their intercourse continued to live in Greece. "The tale is not mine," wrote Euripides. "I learned it from my mother, that heaven and earth were once one (ὡς οὐρανός τε γαῖά τ'ἦν μορφὴ μία). But when they were parted from each other, they brought forth all things and brought them to light, trees, birds, beasts, creatures of brine and the race of men.''[21] We read a similar account in the *Argonautica* where Apollonius of Rhodes makes Orpheus sing "how the earth, the heaven and the sea, once mingled together in one form (μιῇ συναρηρότα μορφῇ), after deadly strife were separated from each other ... "[22]

These myths ascribe the origin of heaven to a primordial, cosmic cataclysm in which heaven was separated from and forced

---

[19] *The Library of History* 1.7, *LCL*, C. H. Oldfather, ed., London: Heinemann, 1960, p. 25.

[20] *Theogony* 116-136; R. M. Frazer, *The Poems of Hesiod*, Norman: University of Oklahoma, 1983, pp. 30-33; Brandon, *op. cit.*, pp. 167-170.

[21] *Fragment* 484, in August Nauck, *Tragicorum Graecorum Fragmenta*, Hildesheim: Georg Olms, 1964 (reprint with additions of Bruno Snell), p. 511. English translation after James G. Frazer, *The Worship of Nature*, New York: Macmillan, 1926, p. 40.

[22] 1.496-499, *LCL*, R. C. Seaton, ed., London: Heinemann, 1930, p. 37. See also Aristophanes, *The Birds*, 693-705.

above earth. For lack of space and light, life on earth would have been impossible without this event. Hesiod speaks of the darkness of night as the time when Ouranos descends upon Gaia, "closely embracing her, stretching everywhere over her."[23] In his view, there is continuous intercourse between heaven and earth, and thus, not only did life begin from that union, it continually renews itself because heaven and earth love each other. Similarly, in Egyptian mythology the sun arises out of a sexual union of heaven and earth, and this process repeats itself every day. At night heaven and earth make love and in the morning the sun rises from the primeval ocean.[24] The fertilizing moisture of rain comes from heaven, and earth loves it, so "when the two are joined in love's embrace, they make all things to grow."[25] Aeschylus calls this a marriage of heaven and earth, and the Homeric Hymn to Earth calls Earth "the wife of starry Ouranos."[26] This is the πρώτιστος γάμος, prototype of all marriage relationships;[27] consequently, in Athens marriages were dedicated to *Ouranos* and *Gaia*.[28] The learned bishop of Hippo, Augustine, knew pagan mythology very well, but he could not, or perhaps refused to, give credit to the pagans for the depth of their thoughts. Instead of praising them for giving expression to a profound idea, he wrote sarcastically:

> Let us assume that Jupiter is now the soul of this material world ... Now let him be Aether, that he may embrace from above Juno, the air spread below, now let him be the whole sky, including the air, and impregnate with the life-giving rain and seed the earth, who is called at the same time his wife and his mother, for this is no disgrace in divine affairs.[29]

The idea that originally there was a unity from which every-

---

[23] *Theogony* 176-178, *op. cit.*, p. 36.

[24] Kurt H. Sethe, *op. cit.*, pars. 70 and 113, pp. 58 and 94.

[25] Euripides, *Fragment* 898, in Nauck, *op. cit.*, p. 648.

[26] Aeschylus, *Fragment* 44, in Nauck, *op. cit.*, p. 16; *Homeric Hymn to Earth* 30.17. Compare with this Lucretius, *De rerum natura* 2.991-1022: "We all came from heavenly seeds, he is father of all, by whom mother earth received the drops of liquid moisture ... etc."

[27] Staudacher, *op. cit.*, p. 88.

[28] Proclus in a comment on Plato's *Republic* (G. Kroll, ed., *Procli Diadochi in Platonis Rem Publicam Commentarii*, Leipzig: Teubner, 1899, p. 134, line 9). See also A. Dieterich, *Mutter Erde*, Leipzig/Berlin: Teubner, 1905, p. 45.

[29] Augustine, *De Civitate Dei* 4.11, *LCL*, Wm. Green, ed., London: Heinemann, 1963, vol. 2, p. 45.

thing came into being was familiar to the Greek philosophers. Beginning with Thales, they struggled with the problem of the material origin of all things, supposing that all things have an origin and that that origin must be one thing. Eventually Greek philosophy developed into a more abstract way of thinking. Plato's *Symposium*, as we have seen, contains an elaborate discussion of the origin of male and female from an androgynous unity. The original unity of heaven and earth is the cosmic aspect of the same thought. Thus, if the divided halves of male and female desire to be united again, to use Plato's terminology, the same must be true of the divided halves of heaven and earth.[30] It was, therefore, not without reason that pagan mythologies assigned gender distinctions to heaven and earth. In most, heaven is male and earth is female. However, Egyptian mythologies reverse this order; there, earth is male, heaven is female. Egyptian illustrations show Shu, the god of the air, pushing up Nut, who is pictured as a naked woman arching her body over Geb and thus covering him like a canopy. While there is a yawning gap between the two, they are parts of the same whole: the universe is one; heaven and earth belong together.[31]

The view of heaven that we find scattered in the pages of the Old and New Testaments is not a consistent one.[32] The New

---

[30] Konrat Ziegler, "Menschen und Weltwerden," *Neue Jahrbücher für das klassische Altertum*, 16 (1913), 529 ff, brought androgyny and the myths about the separation of heaven and earth together in a fascinating essay. For a useful summary of the Greek philosophers' thoughts, see W. K. C. Guthrie, *In the Beginning*, London: Methuen, 1957, and F. M. Cornford, *Principium Sapientiae. The Origins of Greek Philosophical Thought*, Cambridge: University Press, 1952.

[31] The following material contains more useful information: Ernst Wüst, "Uranos," in Pauly, *op. cit.*, Zweite Reihe, 9/1 (17. Halbband) 966-980; E. Oberhummer, "Urania," Pauly, op. cit., Zweite Reihe, 9/1 (17. Halbband) 931- 942; N. J. Girandoot, "Chaos," *ER* 3.213-218; Linda M. Taber and F. Stanley Lusby, "Heaven and Hell," *ER* 6.237-243; Ian Petru Culianu, "Sky. The Heavens as Hierophany," *ER* 13.343-345; Peter Chemerey, "Sky. Myths and Symbolism," *ER* 13.345-353; Charles H. Long, "Cosmogony," *ER* 4.94–100; Kees W. Bolle, "Cosmology: An Overview," ER 4.100-107.

[32] The account of the creation in Gen. 1 shows some similarities with Hesiod's *Theogony:* both mention the elements of chaos, the placing of heaven above the earth, light which makes the day possible, etc. As far as the nature of heaven is concerned, the Old Testament can describe it in various ways: in Gen. 1:6 heaven is a firmament; according to Job 26:11, it is like a house that has pillars; Ps. 104:2 refers to it as a tent stretched out.

Testament even mentions several heavens.[33] But in one point
there seems to be agreement: heaven and earth are parts of the
same creation of God. "In the beginning God created the heavens
and the earth," Genesis1:1 says, and the same belief is reflected
throughout the Bible in spite of the extremely liberal manner in
which the authors employed these terms. This view leads to the
assumption of a cosmic correspondence between heaven and
earth: whatever happens in either sphere affects the other. Events
taking place on earth have their appropriate response in heaven,
and decisions made in heaven will have their effects on earth for
better or for worse. This relationship is well illustrated in the announcement of the birth of Jesus to the shepherds: immediately
after the announcement, a multitude of heavenly hosts appeared,
praising God in the highest (i.e. in *heaven)* and proclaiming peace
on *earth.*[34] It is because of this cosmic correspondence that the
redemption promised in the Bible is also a cosmic event, universal in nature: it is the reunification of all things, "things in
heaven and things on earth."[35]

Despite everything the Bible says about it, however, Christianity has never offered a uniform definition of heaven and so
the Aristotelian views have prevailed. One can think of heaven as
the place where God lives and where the blessed go after death
("Our Father who are in heaven ... " Matt. 6.9; " ... our common-
wealth is in heaven ... " Phil. 3.20); one can also look up to the sky
and say, with Psalm 19.1, "The heavens are telling the glory of
God; and the firmament proclaims his handiwork." To my
knowledge, however, the view of heaven as the natural half of
earth has not been part of Christian piety and even scholars who
discuss it are hard to find. One notable exception is the great
Origen (died 253/254), who in his book *De principiis* discussed at
length the idea of the cosmos and stated that "the universe is
bounded by heaven and earth."[36]

The numerous personifications of heaven found in the Bible as
well as in pagan literature suggest a cult of heavenly bodies, a

---

[33] 2 Cor. 12.2-4; for a biblical view of heaven, see Ulrich Simon, *Heaven in
Christian Tradition*, New York: Harper & Brothers, 1958; S. Morenz,
"Himmel," *RGG*, 328-333.

[34] Luke 2.13-14.

[35] Eph. 1.10; Col. 1.15-17; see also Heb. 9.24.

[36] 2.3.6; ANF 4.273; see also 2.3.7 and 2.11.6.

practice which was of great concern to the Old Testament prophets. We also find in the Bible an underlying sexual differentiation between heaven and earth; things that pertain to the celestial sphere are usually masculine and those representing earthly dimensions are feminine. In the symbolic imagery of the Old Testament, God is the father-figure and also the husband, Israel, the wife. Similarly, in the New Testament Christ is always the groom, never the bride. The eroticism so starkly represented in pagan mythologies of the relationship between Ouranos and Gaia comes to the surface in the *Song of Songs,* which is usually interpreted as an expression of God's love for his people. Just as the pagan mythologies spoke about the natural love of *Ouranos* and *Gaia,* so the gospel of John proclaimed that God loves the world (3:16), and just as *Ouranos* fertilizes *Gaia* by his moisture, so we are told in 1 John 3:9 that those who are born of God have the sperm of God (σπέρμα θεοῦ) in them. Indeed, such cosmic love is a constant theme of the Bible, in which the final restoration of the universe is pictured as a meeting of bridegroom and bride to consummate their marriage.[37]

To those familiar with the pagan myths, and the authors of the books of the New Testament certainly were, the bridal imagery of the Bible does not seem very different from the pagan concept of a union between heaven and earth, personified as Ouranos and Gaia. Such a return to the original condition of the universe was of concern to Christians as well as pagans. Elaborate systems were developed on this theme by Origen, from the Christian side, and by Plotinus, from the pagan, Neoplatonic point of view.[38] Even without lengthy philosophical discussion, the assumption that everything came out of an original unity suggests that everything will again be dissolved into one: ἐξ ἑνὸς τά πάντα γίνεσθαι, κὰι εἰς ταυτὸν ἀναλύεσθαι.[39] Obviously, this has to include the reunification of heaven and earth. The "great portent" of Revelation 12.1 that "appeared in heaven" is without doubt the beginning of an eschatological drama, the end of which, according to Revelation 21, will be the elimination of the distance between heaven and earth and of the separation of God and men.

---

[37] Rev. 21.1-2; 22.17. See also Matt. 25.1-13; Rev. 17.6-9.
[38] See S. Benko, *Pagan Rome,* pp. 90-91.
[39] Diogenes Laertius, *Prologue* 1.3, *LCL,* R. n. Hicks, ed., London: Heinemann, 1950, p. 4.

It seems to me unreasonable to deny that the author of Revelation and the scribe to whom he dictated this vision conceptualized heaven in pagan mythological categories, for they had no other avenue of apprehension. So we will look at the picture desribed in Revelation 12.1 in this way: somewhere in the mythological sphere of heaven, the image of a pregnant woman comes in sight. By whom was she impregnated? The text does not say. How did she reach the heavenly spheres and what is her function there? The more we analyze the picture, the more elusive it becomes. May we then take advantage of the resources offered by Greco-Roman mythology and assume that the mind of the author, permeated with pagan mythological presuppositions, is using such images to express his Christian views? To do so suggests that, in this instance, pagan mythology exerted a causative influence upon a Christian object of faith, namely, the end of the world, which in the faith of the Christians is preceded by the pregnancy of a woman chosen by God and the subsequent birth of a child who begins a new humanity. The conception of Jesus is understood as the result of a union between heaven and earth — the Holy Spirit and the Virgin Mary — just as in pagan mythology it is Ouranos who impregnates Gaia. The figure of the woman in Revelation 12.1, then, was patterned after the image of Earth, Gaia, pregnant as a result of her union with Ouranos, Heaven. We shall see later that the image of Mary as the Earth Mother was well known in Christian piety and to a certain degree even in Christian Mariology. Using the images of Ouranos and Gaia, the Christian author presents here a picture of reestablishment of the primordial unity between heaven and earth.[40]

What the author of Revelation 12 saw in the heavenly spheres was what anybody living in the Mediterranean world at the end of the first century would immediately recognize as the "Queen of Heaven." *"Die Attribute die ihr gegeben sind weisen auf das Bild der Himmelskönigin hin,"* wrote E. Lohmeyer in his definitive commentary on the Apocalypse.[41] Similar statements were made by other

---

[40]   H. Gallinger, op. cit. p. 32, m. 36 quotes C.G. Jung, who "sieht in der Frau die Gestalt, die zum Hellen das Dunkle fügt, so den *hieros gamos* der Gegensätze bildet und die Natur mit dem Geiste versöhnt."

[41]   Ernst Lohmeyer, *Die Offenbarung des Johannes.* 2. ed. Tübingen: J.C.B. Mohr, 1953, p. 98. See also Oskar Holtzmann, *Das Neue Testament.* Giessen: Töpelmann, 1928, p. 928: "Die Mutter des Messias ist nach dem Bild einer

commentators and to these we must add Gunkel's suggestion in
Schöpfung und Chaos [42] that a relationship exists between Revelation
12 and the Genesis narratives. If the pagan mythological foundation of the woman's figure is thus established, then the concept of
the *hieros gamos* that I suggest for this particular vision is not so far
fetched as it may seem. The culminating point of the entire book
is after all a marriage celebration on a cosmic scale, a great consummation which both the pagan and the Judeo-Christian traditions can only hint at by referring to sexual union between male
and female. It was again E. Lohmeyer who pointed out that
certain elements in the book of Revelation, i.e. the birth of a savior
child who after maturing enters a holy marriage, is also reflected
in Virgil's *4. Eclogue:* the child, whose birth Virgil prophesizes,
shares the bed of a goddess at the end of the poem.[43] It is in this
context that we should see the "woman clothed with the sun": she
is a goddess, a Christian goddess, whose role is to play the female
part in the reunification of God with his creatures.

2. *The Robe of the Woman*

In the ancient world, the sky meant one thing to farmer and city-
dweller alike: it was the huge dome that covered the earth, the
immensity of which immediately evoked religious feelings.
Cicero wrote:

> When we gaze upward to the sky and contemplate the heavenly
> bodies, what can be so obvious and so manifest than that there
> must exist some power possessing transcendent intelligence by
> whom these things are ruled? Were it not so, how comes it that
> the words convey conviction to all readers, 'Behold, the dazzling
> vault of heaven, which all mankind as Jove invoke ... "[44]

Later Cicero quoted a passage from Euripides: "Thou seest the
boundless aether's spreading vault, whose soft embrace encompas-

---

heidnischen Himmelskönigin gebildet, wie 1.12-17, 10.1-2 Heidnische
Kultbilder die Vorlage waren." Similarly H. Ringgren, *Das Alte Testament
Deutsch* 16/2, Göttingen, 1958, *ad loc.* and many others quoted by Hildegard
Gillinger, *Das "Grosse Zeichen" von Apokalypse 12.* Würzburg/Stuttgart: Echter
Verlag, 1971, pp. 76-77.

[42] *Op. cit.*

[43] E. Lohmeyer, *op. cit.* p. 155.

[44] *De natura deorum* 2.4; H.R. Rackham, *Cicero, LCL,* London: Heine-mann,
1979, vol. 19, p. 125. The Ennius quotation also appears in 2.65, p. 187.

seth the earth; this deem thou god of gods, the supreme Jove."[45]
And so, the shape of a vault or dome became the ultimate artistic
expression of heaven, the abode of the gods. In the history of
architecture, such designs can be found from very early times on,
including perhaps the Mycenean behive tombs, but without doubt
the elaborate circular burial chambers of the Romans, the ceilings
of which were originally dome-like.[46] While a reminder of heaven in connection with burials is quite natural, the dome-design
was utilized in other areas, too. The most outstanding example is
the Pantheon in Rome, built originally by Marcus Agrippa in 27-
25 B.C. and rebuilt by the emperor Hadrian. Its magnificent dome
measures 43.30 meters. (St. Peter's, another marvel of architecture,
measures only 42.52 meters.) "Pantheon" means "all gods," and
so, as the historian Dio wrote, it was long assumed that "it has this
name, because it received among the images which decorated it
the statues of many gods, including Mars and Venus"; however,
Dio adds, "my own opinion of the name is that, because of its
vaulted roof, it resembles the heavens."[47] Nero's famous Golden
House was also supposed to resemble heaven, and we read that
there were in it "dining rooms, with fretted ceilings of ivory,
whose panels could turn and shower down flowers and were
fitted with pipes for sprinkling the guests with perfumes. The
main banquet hall was circular and constantly revolved day and
night, like the heavens."[48] The examples could be multiplied,[49]

---

[45] Euripides, *Fragment* 386; Cicero, *op. cit.*, 2.65, p. 187.

[46] The visitor to modern Rome can still see some of these, such as
Hadrian's tomb, the mausoleum of Augustus, and some more on the Via
Appia.

[47] Dio, *History* 53.27, *LCL*, F. Carr, ed., London: Heinemann, 1979, vol. 6,
p. 263. Virgil says that in the temple where Dido received Aeneas, she sat
down "beneath the central vaulting of the temple": *Aeneid* 1.505. To this
Servius added the remark: *"Ideo sic fit, ut similari caeli imaginem reddat, quod
constat esse convexum"*: G. Thilo and H. Hager, *Servii Grammatici Qui Feruntur In
Vergilii Carmlna Commentarii*, Leipzig and Berlin: Teubner, 1923, p. 157. Of
course, Servius wrote in the context of the fourth century A.D.

[48] Suetonius, *Nero* 31, J. C. Rolfe, ed., *Suetonius*, *LCL*, London: Heinemann,
1950, p. 137. A reference to this feature of the Golden House is also in Seneca,
Epistula 90.15: " ... one who invents a process for spraying saffron perfumes to
tremendous heights from hidden pipes ... who so cleverly constructs a
dining room with a ceiling of movable panels that it presents one pattern
after another, the roof changing as often as the courses ... " R. P. Gummere,
ed., *Seneca. Epistolae Morales*, vol. 2, p. 405, *LCL*, London: Heinemann, 1920.

[49] Other similar structures were in Hadrian's villa in Tivoli, in several
of the imperial baths, and other buildings. Philostratus, *Life of Apollonius of*

but these are enough to show that when Christian architecture adopted the dome-design, it took over and continued an image of heaven familiar to the pagan world.

This image is continued in the half-dome over the apse of many Christian churches. Among the oldest examples are S. Maria in Trastevere, which some claim is the oldest church in Rome, and S. Pudenziana, for which others make the same claim. High above the apse in the canopy of the half-dome, the image of the exalted Christ is visible in both churches. In the magnificent S. Maria Maggiore, there appears below the half-dome a picture of the Virgin Mary's death with Jesus Christ in attendance; above this, in the half-dome, we see Mary assumed into heaven and crowned by Jesus. The script below it explains: *"Exaltata est Santa Dei Genetrix super choros angelorum ad celestia regna."* Of special interest is Santa Constanza, a circular church, originally built as a mausoleum for the daughters of Constantine the Great. Not only is the church reminiscent of pagan tombs, but its decoration is more pagan that Christian. The exquisite mosaics with their floral designs which ornament the vaulting are a classic example of an architecture in which "the pagan and Christian worlds meet and mingle."[50] All of this supports the claim that there is "an unbroken continuity between antique and Christian monuments of this kind."[51]

Tyana 1.25, says that during his travels, Apollonius saw in Babylon a house, the roof of which was made "in the form of a dome, to resemble in a manner the heavens and that it was roofed with sapphire, a stone that is very blue and like the heavens to the eye, and there were images of the gods, which they worship, fixed aloft and looking like golden figures shining out of the ether": *LCL*, F. C. Conybeare, ed., London: Heinemann, 1948, vol. 1, p. 77.

[50] Georgina Masson, *Rome*, New York: McKay, 1971, p. 295. Magnificent pictures of these domes and many others may be found in Paolo Marton, *Rome, Mirror of the Centuries*, Udine: Magnus 1983.

[51] Karl Lehmann, "The Dome of Heaven," *Art Bulletin* 27 (1945): 1-27; this quotation, p. 9. "If the derivation of the Christian vision of heaven from an unbroken and ever growing stream of pagan tradition is obvious, the connection is further borne out by the persistence and reorganization of specific elements of classical tradition": Lehmann, op. cit., p. 9. Karl Lehman's study of celestial symbolism in Western architectural decorations was continued and expanded to the Asian world by Alexander Coburn Soper, "The 'Dome of Heaven' in Asia," *Art Bulletin* 29 (1947): 225-248. Amanda K. Coomaraswamy, "The Symbolism of the Dome," investigated the idea in Hindu thought. This essay can be found in Roger Lipsey, *Coomaraswamy*, Princeton: University Press, 1977 (Bollingen Series 89). See also Jean Pepin,

In addition to the vaulted shape, the idea of heaven is also expressed with the decoration of the ceiling. Even when the ceiling is not a dome but a flat roof, its color and its decoration with stars, sun, and moon recall a vision of heaven. Such designs were utilized in flat ceilings, tents, and even awnings. Pliny says that "awnings colored as the sky and spangled with stars have been stretched with ropes even in emperor Nero's amphitheater,"[52] to serve as shades from the sun for the spectators. In Euripides' *Ion* there is a description of a tent, the ceiling of which was a "canopy of shawls" decorated with the sun, moon, the Pleiades, and other heavenly bodies.[53] Thus, even temporarily erected canopies symbolized heaven and the shape of a tent could be compared to the sky as it covers the earth. Heaven, then, is being viewed as a cosmic tent. And since a tent is so similar in shape to a robe, it takes only a short stretch of the imagination to think of the cosmic tent as a cosmic robe which surrounds and covers the great mystery that is called God. "Thou art clothed with honor and majesty, who coverest thyself with light as a garment, who hast stretched out the heavens like a tent."[54]

Images of the gods and goddesses were often painted with robes covered with celestial symbols, usually with many stars.[55] This was done, of course, to express their celestial character, their authority, and their rule over the universe. Thus Apuleius described Isis as wearing a black robe embroidered with glittering stars around a full moon.[56] According to Martianus Capella, the

---

"Cosmic Piety" in A. H. Armstrong, op. cit. pp. 408-435, esp. pp. 421-424 "The Temple, the Image of the World."

[52] Pliny, *Naturalis Historia* 19.6, "*Vela colore coeli stellata,*" LCL, H. R. Rackham, ed., London: Heinemann, 1950, pp. 434-437.

[53] *Ion* 1141-1158, Arthur S. Way, ed., *Euripides*, LCL, London: Heinemann, 1964, vol. 4, pp. 110-113.

[54] Ps. 104.2-3; see also Ps. 102.25-27 and Is. 40:22; compare also with Akhenaton's "Hymn to the Aton," in J. B. Pritchard, *Ancient Near Eastern Texts Relating to the Old Testament*, Princeton: University Press, 1950, pp. 370-371.

[55] Robert Eisler, *Weltmantel und Himmelzelt. Religionsgeschichtliche Untersuchungen zur Urgeschichte des antiken Weltbildes*, München: C. H. Beck, 1910, mentions Marduk, Mithra, Attis, Aphrodite, the Ephesian Artemis, among others, pp. 60-68.

[56] *Metamorphoses* 11.3-4. See also Heinrich Schäfer, "Das Gewand der Isis," Festschrift zu C. F. Lehmann-Haupt's sechzigstem Geburtstage, Herausgegeben von K. Regling und H. Reich, Wien and Leipzig: Wilhelm Braumüller, 1921, pp. 194- 206.

tunic of Juno was grass-green and her robe was made of clouds; her shoes were dark, the soles like night.[57] Similarly, ancient statues of divinities were covered with robes that reflected their main characteristics. In Athens a robe for Athene, the Peplos, was woven by the women and given to the goddess during the Great Panathenian Festival in connection with an elaborate procession.

Now we return briefly to Caelestis. As we have mentioned, in Lacinium the statue of Juno was dressed in a robe whose extraordinary beauty was admired by all.[58] The following story is related about it by Athenaeus: A certain Sybarite citizen, Alcisthenes by name, had such a yen for luxury that he had a very expensive robe made for himself. During the festival of Hera (= Juno) in Lacinium, "at which all Greeks of Italy gather," he exhibited the robe and it was much admired. When Dionysus, tyrant of Syracus, "came into possession of it, he sold it to the Carthaginians for one hundred and twenty talents." A certain Polemon, Athenaeus continues, also related this story in a book entitled *On the Robes of Carthage*. Nothing remains of Polemon's work, but we know from Aristotle's description of it that the robe "was of purple, fifteen cubits in size, and on each side it was ornamented with embroidered figures, of Susa above, and of the Persians below; in the center were Zeus, Hera, Themis, Athene, Apollo, and Aphrodite. At one extremity was Alcimenes, and on either side Sybaris."[59]

---

[57] Martianus Capella was of North African origin and wrote between 410-436. He was a pagan, and a contemporary of St. Augustine. Both men observed the death of the Roman Empire, but while the bishop's reaction to this tragedy was almost like a defiant "Good riddance!" Martianus, with uncertain hands, collected and compiled the wisdom of his age as if to salvage something from the coming destruction. His book *De Nuptiis Philologiae et Mercurii* is an allegorical story in which the groom presents his bride with seven wedding gifts--Grammar, Rhetoric, Dialectic, Arithmetic, Geometry, Astronomy, Music. Though poorly written and despite the fact that it was a compilation from previous compilers, this book became a widely accepted textbook during the Middle Ages. The Latin text is available in the following edition: *Martianus Capella, De Nuptiis Philologiae et Mercurii*, A. Dick, ed., Stuttgart: Teubner, 1978 (reprint). An English translation and detailed study of the work in two volumes was prepared by William H. Stahl and Richard Johnson: *Martianus Capella and the Seven Liberal Arts*, New York and London: Columbia University Press, 1971 and 1977. See also Haijo J. Westra, *The Commentary on Martianus Capella's De Nuptiis Philologiae et Mercurii. Attributed to Bernardus Silvestris*, Leiden: E . J . Brill 1986

[58] Chapter II, p. 28ff.

[59] *Deipnosophistae* 12.541, in Charles B. Gulick, ed., *LCL*, Cambridge, Mass.: Harvard, 1943, pp. 447-449. Athenaeus flourished ca. 200 A.D.; the title

According to R. Eisler,[60] however, this customary translation is incorrect. In the Greek text ζωδίος should be translated with "zodiac," "σούσιος," and "πέρσαι" should not be capitalized but left as simple nouns: σοῦσον (lily) and περαία (peach). Accordingly, the robe was decorated with the signs of the zodiac, flowers, and peaches. Juno and Caelestis were universal goddesses and Eisler's interpretation reveals that the decorations on this robe, as we should expect, emphasized their cosmic role. This robe, then, was taken to Carthage where we assume it decorated the statue of Tanit.

What became of the robe? Did it perish in the general destruction of Carthage in 146 B.C. or was it saved? Once again we recall the capture of Veii, after which the statue of "Queen Juno" was moved to Rome "with deepest reverence." Something like this could have happened in 146 B.C., but if so, no mention of it was made by Polybius or Livy, both of whom were impressed chiefly with the ferocity of the city's destruction. This is a pity, because our knowledge of this robe is extremely limited, and robes were important parts of the statue of a goddess; those who made them have woven into them their confession of faith. The robe of Lacinium could tell us much about what the Romans believed about Juno, the Greeks about Hera (the temple was originally built

---

of his book means "The Learned Banquet." This information he took from Aristotle, of which see below. Dionysius the Elder, tyrant of Syracuse, lived between c . 430 and 367 B. C. Croton was captured by Dionysus in 379 B.C., and thus, the event must date from or after this year. It is impossible to establish the modern value of Dionysius' talent because of the difference of wages, prices, and the purchasing power of average people. But if one talent was 6,000 drachmas and one drachma was worth about $20, then one talent was worth $120,000. In this case, 120 talents would be $14,400,000 an amount which only governments can spend. If correct, the robe deserved its fame. In ascertaining these values, I have used the chart in Frank J. Frost, *Greek Society*, Lexington, Mass.: D. C. Heath, 1971, p. 58. See also Gustave Glotz, *Ancient Greece at Work. An Economic History of Greece from the Homeric Period to the Roman Conquest*, New York: Norton, 1967, pp. 231-244. This book was originally published in 1920. Also John Scarborough, *Facets of Hellenic Life*, Boston: Houghton Mifflin, 1976, p. 7. However, Gulick in his edition of the *Deipnosophistae*, p. 123, puts the value of the robe at $130,000–in 1955 values, which is a more realistic figure. See K. Deichgraber, *Pauly's Realencyklopädie, op. cit.*, 21.2, p. 1301-1302. According to Athenaeus, the title of his work in Greek was καρχηδόνι πέπλων. Aristotle's work is called *De Mirabilibus Auscultationibus (On Marvelous Things Heard)* 96, W. S. Hett, ed., *Aristotle, Minor Works, LCL*, London: Heinemann, 1955, p. 279. The work is considered to be spurious and a set of compilations dating from the second to the sixth century A.D.

[60] *Op. cit.*, p. 35.

by the Greeks for Hera), and the Carthaginians about Tanit, who eventually received it. When Carthage became a Roman city and Caelestis took the place of Tanit as the chief goddess, her statue was also covered with a beautiful robe. It was probably to this robe that Tertullian referred when he said that "they who court their idols by dressing them, and by adorning them in their sanctuary, and by saluting them at each particular hour, are said to do them service."[61] Even if this robe was not the same as the one described by Aristotle, it must have been worthy of the honor paid to the goddess. In the *Historia Augusta* we read that during a particularly turbulent period of the empire, "the Africans .... created an emperor, Celsus, dressing him with the robe of the goddess Caelestis *(peplo deae Caelestis ornatum)."* The robe represented authority and Celsus hoped that if he wore it divine sanction would be given to his imperial claim.[62]

Clearly, a robe, even a simple dress, is more than a means to cover the body. "A garment is an expression of personality"; it is "a second skin."[63] It becomes a part of the person who wears it and reveals much about him or her, so much indeed that by simply looking at a dress, one can have a fairly accurate impression of the person. A garment is an extension of the personality and a way of communicating with the world outside oneself. The garment worn by a powerful person may even absorb some of that person's power. Thus when the prophet Elijah was taken up into heaven by the chariot of fire, his successor, Elisha "took hold of

---

[61]   *De ieiunio* 16; *CSEL* 20.296; ET.: *ANF* 4.113.

[62]   *Tyranni Triginta* 29, *The Scriptores Historiae Augustae*, David Magie, ed., London: Heinemann, 1932, vol. 3, pp. 132-133. This Celsus probably never existed, but the so-called Thirty Tyrants were pretenders to the office of emperor during the third century. See B. H. Warmington, "Thirty Tyrants," *Oxford Classical Dictionary, op. cit.,* pp. 1064-1065; and the comments of David Magie, *op. cit.,* p. 65.

[63]   Ernest Crawley, *Dress, Drinks and Drums*, London: Methuen, 1931, pp. 65-64. "Dress, in fact, as a secondary human character, must be treated, as regards its origins, in the same way as human weapons, tools, and machines. Dress increases the static resisting power of the surface of the body, just as tools increase the dynamic capacity of the limbs. It is an extension (and thereby an intension) of the passive area of the person, just as a tool is of the active mechanism of the arm. It is a second skin, as the other is a second hand": p. 4. See also J. C. Flugel, *The Psychology of Clothes*, New York: International Universities Press, 1971 (reprint of the 1930 edition); Marilyn J. Horn and Lois M. Gurel, *The Second Skin. An Interdisciplinary Study of Clothing*, Boston: Houghton Mifflin, 1975, 1981.

his own clothes and rent them into two pieces. And he took up the
mantle of Elijah that had fallen from him." Presently the prophet's power was transferred to him; he could even part the waters
of the Jordan river, and the people who saw him said, "The spirit
of Elijah rests on Elisha."[64] Similarly, we read that miraculous
power was attributed to the garment of Jesus. When a gravely ill
woman came to be healed, she said, "If I touch even his garments, I shall be made well." She did touch his garment and was
immediately healed. "And Jesus, perceiving in himself that
power had gone forth from him, immediately turned about in the
crowd and said,'Who touched my garments?'"[65]

Apuleius tells us that during the process of his initiation Lucius
received twelve robes, indicating his gradual and eventually total
rebirth. Each robe represented a different stage in his transforma-
tion until the last one which, sumptuously decorated, was called
the "Olympian robe." This one showed Lucius in a state of assimilation to Isis and Osiris.[66] In the apocryphal *Acts of Thomas* Jesus
relates that he received a "splendid robe" which he had to take off
when he went to the land of the Egyptians. There he clothed himself "in garments like theirs that they might not suspect that I was
come without." After awhile he took off these "dirty and unclean
garments," and having returned home, he saw his "splendid
robe." Suddenly

> "... when I saw it over against me, the (splendid robe) became like
> me, as my reflection in a mirror; I saw it (wholly) in me, and in
> it I saw myself (quite) apart (from myself), so that we were two in
> distinction, and again one in a single form ..."[67]

The "splendid robe" here means, of course, the heavenly ego of
Jesus.

When someone puts on new garments, he/she must first take
off the old ones. Apuleius, too, was naked momentarily (see Griffiths, p. 309) which did embarrass him. Similarly, in the early

---

[64] 2 Kings 2.9-15.
[65] Mark 5.25-30; Luke 8.43-46.
[66] *Metamorphoses* 11.24, see also J. Gwyn Griffiths, *The Isis Book*, pp. 310-
314.
[67] *Acts of Thomas* 108-113, Hennecke-Schneemelcher, *op. cit.* vol. 2, pp. 498-
504. Compare this with the "garment of ladyship" given to Inanna in
Inanna's Descent to the Nether World, Pritchard, *ANET*, 53, as analyzed by
Judith Ochshorn, *op. cit.* p. 48.

Christian practice of baptism spiritual rebirth was symbolized not only by going under water and re-emerging again, but by the very real act of taking off the old clothing and putting on new ones.[68]

When Revelation 12 says that the woman who appeared in heaven was "clothed with the sun," the significance of the statement cannot be overestimated. She is wearing the sun as her robe, and that robe is the expression of her personality; that is how she is to be regarded by the rest of the world. But how did pagan mythology view the sun? Personified as Helios or Sol, the sun was conceived of by the Greeks and Romans as the ruler of the entire universe and the power that regulates the flow and rhythm of the cosmos. The effect of the sun on life is obvious; everyone can see it. It was not without reason that the "heretic king" Akhenaton promoted the Aton, i.e., the sun-disc, as the "sole god." In his beautiful hymn,[69] he praised Aton as a radiant energy from which all life arose and by which everything was sustained. While his religious reform was doomed to failure, the thought of a sole sun-god continued. By the end of the Hellenistic age, there was a definite tendency toward the development of a sun-cult, i.e., a religion in which the functions of all gods and goddesses would be merged into the one image of the sun.[70] Macrobius, in the early fifth century A.D., said exactly this: all gods are identical with the sun. He also explained that since the planets rule the fate of men and the sun leads the planets, it is clear that the sun is the ultimate reason of everything.[71] He is "pantokrator," the soul of the cosmos, the energy of the cosmos, the light of the cosmos.

---

[68] This issue was treated by Jonathan Z. Smith, "The Garment of Shame." *History of Religions* 5 (1966) 217-238. See also Dennis R. MacDonald, *There is No Male and Female. The Fate of a Dominical Saying in Paul.* Philadelphia: Fortress Press, 1987. Ritual nudity in paganism has been treated by F. Pfister, "Nacktheit." *Pauly-Wissowa, op. cit.* 16/2, 1541-49.

[69] See footnote #11 above. On Akhenaton and his sun-cult, see F. G. Bratton, *The First Heretic. The Life and Times of Ikhnaton the King,* Boston: Beacon Press, 1961; Leslie A. White, "Ikhnaton: The Great Man vs. the Cultural Process," *Journal of the American Oriental Society* 68 (1948): 91-103; F. J. Giles, *Ikhnaton, Legend and History,* London: Hutchinson, 1970.

[70] Martin P. Nilsson, *Geschichte der Griechischen Religion,* München: Beck, 1961 (2nd ed.), vol. 2, pp. 507-519.

[71] *Saturnalia* 1.17.3 ff and 1.19.7 ff. See also the emperor Julian's *Oratio* 4 on the *Dies Natalis Invicti.* For the development of the sun cult in Rome, see Gaston H. Halsberghe, *The Cult of Sol Invictus,* Leiden: Brill, 1977.

This is the garment with which the woman in Revelation 12 was clothed.

Thus clothed, she is revealed in a state of assimilation to the divine principle, as united with God. This is *hieros gamos* on the most exalted level. Under her feet is the moon. While the sun was usually personified as male, with a radiant crown on his head, the moon was female, Selene or Luna, and associated with female functions. Nothing is more natural than that these two heavenly bodies would be associated in mythology and popular religion, which indeed happened very early. Selene was looked upon as the wife of Helios. The conjunction of sun and moon was called in Greek, σύνοδος = coming together; the same word is also used in a sexual sense, i.e., coitus. πρὸς γάμον τινὶ συνελθεῖν means to marry, and as this became a technical term, the word γάμος was often omitted from the phrase.[72] There is a marriage relationship between the sun and the moon, and people regarded the day of the new moon as particularly favorable for a wedding.[73]

This is the vision of Revelation 12.1: the woman has been hypostatically united with the divine, and in her person, standing on the moon, the sun and the moon are brought together in a conjunction which carries elements of a great "coming together," a cosmic *hieros gamos*. This image points toward the eschatological marriage feast at the end of the book. The picture is soon obscured by the following verses, but the image is there and it does have a message.[74]

---

[72] William F. Arndt and F. Wilbur Gingrich, *A Greek-English Lexicon of the New Testament and Other Early Christian Literature*, Chicago: University of Chicago University of Chicago Press, 1957, pp. 795-796; W. H. Roscher, "Mondgöttin" Roscher, op. cit. 2.3119-3200; A. Rapp, "Helios," Roscher, *op. cit.*, pp. 1993-2026. Karl Kerényi, "Vater Helios," *Eranos Jahrbuch* 10 (1943): 81-124; Karl Kerényi, *Tochter der Sonne*, Zürich: Rascher Verlag, 1944.

[73] What Elagabalus did when he "married" his sun-god to Caelestis (see above, Chapter II) was in itself not at all a revolting idea. It was the ceremonies attending the cult and the obvious dementia of Elagabalus that caused his downfall.

[74] The flight of the woman into the wilderness is one argument that scholars opposed to the Marian interpretation of Rev. 12 often use. But as I observed above, there is no interpretation which would be one hundred percent satisfactory. It is in the nature of myths that they have many variants often contradictory to each other, as anybody with an even superficial knowledge of pagan mythology knows. We must accept the fact that this is so in Rev. 12, too, and should resist the temptation to look for a logical, systematic presentation of a thesis in it.

There is another vision of a woman in Revelation whose clothing also expresses her identity. This is

> ... the great whore, enthroned above the ocean. The kings of the earth have committed fornication with her, and on the wine of her fornication men all over the world have made themselves drunk ... I saw a woman mounted on a scarlet beast which was covered with blasphemous names and had seven heads and ten horns. The woman was clothed in purple and scarlet and bedizened with gold and jewels and pearls. In her hand she held a gold cup, full of obscenities and the fondness of her fornication; and written on her forehead was a name with a secret meaning: "Babylon the great, the mother of whores and of every obscenity on earth." The woman I saw was drunk with the blood of God's people and with the blood of those who had borne their testimony to Jesus ... [75]

The following verses offer an explanation of the vision: the woman is "the great city" which most modern interpreters take to be Rome, since Babylon in literal sense is out of the question.[76] But there are certain elements in this vision which conjure up the image of a pagan goddess. The robe of this woman, decorated with jewels and pearls, is similar to those that clothed the statues of goddesses, who were commonly associated with wild beasts, such as lions. Homer called Artemis πότνια θηρῶν, and the image of a goddess as the mistress of wild animals is a familiar one in pagan mythology and art.[77] Among the wild animals the lion is often depicted, sometimes surrounding the throne of the goddess, sometimes bearing the goddess on its back.[78] The lion was part of the retinue of the *Dea Syria* and in a favorite representation of Cybele, she sits in a chariot drawn by lions.[79] The association of this woman with a city is also typical of pagan goddesses. As we have seen above, they were often protective deities of cities and were identified as the "genius" of that particular city. Thus they were sometimes represented with a city wall as a crown on

---

[75] 17.1-6, from the New English Bible.

[76] So Kuhn in the *TWNT* 1.512-514, article "Babylon." An exception seems to be E. Lohmeyer, *op. cit. ad loc.*

[77] *Iliad* 21.470. See to this Chris Winter, *Frau und Göttin.* Göttingen: Vandenhoeck to Ruprecht, 1983, pp. 185-186 and the illustration reprinted at the end of the book.

[78] Winter, *op. cit.* pictures #253, 487-491 and others.

[79] Lucian, *op. cit.*, ch. 15; see to this the comments of Hörig, *op. cit.* pp. 51-128.

their heads, as were Cybele and the Artemis of Ephesus. There is, however, a deeper analogy: a city is like a woman who bears, nurtures, and protects her children. The city *is* a woman in a symbolic sense. In Revelation 17, "the great whore" is associated with a sinful entity, Babylon, which is then contrasted with the new city, Jeruselem "coming down out of heaven from God, made ready like a bride adorned for her husband."[80] The city as the "great whore" represents chaos; the true city, however, is a holy place, in which chaos and chaotic powers are conquered.[81]

Whatever the interpretation of this woman may be, the image is clearly patterned after that of a pagan goddess. I suggest that this goddess was Cybele to whose image Christians in Asia Minor were most often exposed. They were exposed to an image of the goddess wearing a richly decorated robe, with a symbolic wall on her head, and accompanied by lions. They were exposed to orgiastic, chaotic celebrations, promiscuity which Christians associated with the sin of fornication. The words with which she is most identified reminded Christians in Asia Minor of Cybele: "Babylon the great, mother of whores ... " If we leave out the comma, it is not difficult to read in verse 17.5 "ἡ μεγάλη ἡ μήτηρ," i.e. "the great mother." Possibly Christians in Asia Minor could read between the lines. From this sinful mystery they were called away into the mystery of Jesus: "Come out of her, my people, lest you take part in her sins and share in her plagues ... She says in her heart, 'I am a queen on my throne ...' Because of this, her plagues shall strike her in a single day ... no more shall the sound of harps and minstrels, of flute players and trumpeters be heard in you ..."[82] Cybele's orgiastic celebrations which were accompanied by just such music. Cybele, for the author, is the incorporated sum of all demonic powers, she is Babylon, a city which gives birth to, nourishes and protects all those forces and activities that are inimical to the rule of God.

---

[80] 21.2.

[81] Mircea Eliade, *Cosmos and History. The Myth of the Eternal Return.* New York: Harper, 1959 discusses this issue; see also the summaries in Rudolf Halver, *Der Mythos im letzten Buch der Bibel.* Hamburg: H. Reich, 1964, pp. 111-114. See to this also below our discussion of the dragon.

[82] 18. 4-24. Possibly 14.4 also refers to Cybele if the plural γυναικῶν originally read in the singular γυναικός: those who did not defile themselves with the cult of Magna Mater. U. Burch, *Anthropology and the Apocalypse.* London, 1939 quoted by Halver, *op. cit.*, p. 100-102.

The whorish queen is contrasted with the queen of heaven: one is in alliance with chaotic elements, the other opposes them. One is clothed with purple and scarlet, colors associated with destruction,[83] the other with the sun, the divine element itself. The "*hieros gamos*" of one is fornication, of the other it is the consummation of the eschatological union between heaven and earth.

This leads us back to the *heilsgeschichtliche* view of biblical history, characterized by the principle of *Urzeit* and *Endzeit,* and the work of H. Gunkel who pointed to the relationship between Genesis and Revelation. We find that the clothing of the woman in Revelation 12 fits this pattern perfectly. After the Fall, according to Genesis, Adam and Eve lost their original clothing and their bodies were covered with fig leaves (Gen. 3.7) According to Jewish and early Christian interpretations they were orginally clothed in "garments of glory" and "garments of light" which will be restored to them at the end of time. At the eschatological marriage feast such a robe will be a requirement (Rev. 22.14; Mt. 22.11); it is acquired in baptism. Eve lost her robe of glory in the Fall which, according to the *Revelation of Moses,* she lamented with these words: "And in that very hour mine eyes were opened, and I knew that I was stripped of the righteousness with which I had been clothed; and I wept saying, What is this thou hast done to me, because I have been deprived of the glory with which I was clothed?"[84] Now, in Revelation 12, Eve appears restored in her original robe of glory. This is the ultimate message of the "woman clothed with the sun."

We turn now to the astral motifs. But first let us summarize what we have thus far discussed. In the pagan view, heaven was seen as a dome and also as a cosmic robe. A robe is an expression and an extension of its wearer's personality. Thus, if Revelation 12 is indeed based on pagan mythological presuppositions, the woman who appeared to the seer is a celestial figure whose cosmic robe demonstrates her divine authority. The contrast between her

---

[83] See below, The Dragon.

[84] *ANF* 8, 567. My attention was called to this passage by Sebastian Brock, "Clothing Metaphors as a Means of Theological Expression in Syriac Tradition," in *Typus, Symbol, Allegorie bei den östlichen Väter und ihren Parallelen in Mittelalter.* Herangegeben von Margot Schmidt in Zusammenarbeit mit Carl Friedrich Geyer. Regensburg: Verlag Friedrich Pustet, 1981, pp. 11-38. See also E. Peterson, "Theologie des Kleides," *Benediktinische Monatsschrift* 16 (1934), 347-56.

attire and that of the "great whore" in ch. 17.1-6 further enhances the image of the woman in Revelation 12.1 as that of a heavenly figure who is deeply involved in the process of the final consummation.

3. *The Astral Motifs*

Stars and constellations permeate the whole story we are studying. Such celestial images are essential to representations of "heavenly queens." To the ancient Greeks and Romans, stars and constellations were living beings, each with its peculiar personality. Traces of this belief are reflected in the New Testament, as, for example, when, in connection with the resurrection, Paul speaks about "celestial bodies" and "terrestrial bodies" whose "glory" differs from one another. "There is one glory of the sun, and another glory of the moon, and another glory of the stars; for one star differs from another star in glory."[85] This view is based on a system of magic in which the planets figured as intermediary beings possessing various characteristics which the Greeks called πάθος.

Planets were not the only intermediaries, however. Ancient daemonology posited the existence of a host of daemons, that is, mediators, between gods and men. Plato (429-347 B.C.) had distinguished daemons from gods and men, assigning to daemons the role of mediators in creation and generally in leading the world.[86] Eventually the Neoplatonic philosophers[87] developed a hierarchical order, descending from the gods to archangels, angels, and daemons down to men. Depending on their proximity to the gods, the bodies of the daemons may be air, water, or steam; the closer they are to men, the more their bodies will consist of a material substance. All of them, however, belong to the same universal world-soul. Thus by conceiving this system, the philosophers not only preserved the unity of the universe but also assured the possibility of communication between the divine

---

[85]   1 Cor. 15.40-41.

[86]   *Symposium* 202D: "κὰι γὰρ πᾶν τὸ δαιμόνιον μεταξύ ἐστι Θεοῦ τε καὶ θνητοῦ." (The whole of the daimonion is between divine and mortal.) Plato, *Symposium*, W.R. M. Lamb, ed., LCC, Cambridge, Mass: Harvard, 1967, pp. 202-203.

[87]   Especially Porphyry (232-305 A.D.); Iamblichos (250-325 A.D.); and Proclus (410-485 A.D.).

and the human.[88] Through the daemons, the divine penetrates into the lowest regions of the universe; it is present and accessible in the sensible and physical. By contacting or perceiving the "daemon" in a certain physical object, an ascent toward the divine is possible. This linking of the universe from its highest to its lowest parts constitutes the principle of "sympathy" which permeates everything.

Such "sympathy" implies interdependence as well, and since power also descends from the higher to the lower, so does the exertion of influence work from above to below. Thus the heavenly bodies and their movements were understood to affect the lives of men: belief in a mystical cosmic harmony meant that events in heaven were thought to have their reflection on earth. This thought pattern, which can be followed from the epics of Homer down to the book of Revelation, is known to us as astrology, which claims to study the influences of the celestial bodies on human destiny. The seven planets, that is, the stars which appear to have motions of their own,[89] are, in order of their closeness to the earth, the Moon, Mercury, Venus, Sun, Mars, Jupiter, and Saturn. The motions of these planets take place in a sphere called the zodiac.[90] The zodiac is divided into twelve constellations, called Aries, Taurus, Gemini, Cancer, Leo, Virgo, Libra, Scorpio, Sagittarius, Capricorn, Aquarius, and Pisces. Each month the sun passes through one of these "signs", thus enhancing the influence of that constellation on the earth. Ancient astrology and magic also held that the soul is preexistent and descends into a material body by way of the planets and the fixed stars.[91] From each celestial body the soul was understood to absorb a certain $\pi\acute{\alpha}\theta$ος, thus at birth not only the basic character of the person was thought to be determined, but also the basic pattern of his or her earthly destiny. To cast a horoscope, an astrologer finds the exact constellations at the moment of birth and then applies the relevant $\pi\acute{\alpha}\theta\eta$ to the person in question. The author of Revelation gives us every reason to believe that he was familiar with these principles of

---

[88] See Hopfner, *op. cit.*, pp. 327-328; S. Benko, *Pagan Rome* ..., pp. 103.

[89] $\pi\lambda\alpha\nu\acute{\eta}\tau\eta\varsigma$ = wanderer.

[90] $\zeta\tilde{\omega}$ον = animal; $\zeta\tilde{\omega}\delta\iota$ον = sculpture of an animal; $\zeta\omega\delta\iota\alpha\kappa\acute{o}\varsigma$ $\kappa\acute{\nu}\kappa\lambda$ος = the circle containing such figures.

[91] Plato, *Timaeus*, 34B-35A. R. D. Archer-Hind, *The Timaeus of Plato*, London: Macmillan, pp. 104-150.

cosmic harmony and sympathy, and keeping this in mind, we may see his book in a broader dimension.

The vision of Revelation 12 takes place in the sky, and many actors in the celestial drama are those personified constellations that were so familiar to everyone living in the early Roman Empire. Several references seem to call for not merely mythological but also astrological explanations. The following items mentioned in the text may have astral meanings:[92]

The Crown on the woman's head recalls the constellation Στέφανος (Corona) which according to Greek mythology was placed in heaven to commemorate Ariadne, the tragic lover of Theseus (Rev. 12.1).

The Dragon is a constellation called Δράκων in Greek (*Draco* in Latin) and was identified either with the dragon killed by Cadmus or the Python killed by Apollo (Rev. 12.3).

The Hydra ("Υδρα), or Water-Snake, consists of stars forming coils and tails. A similar constellation is *the Snake* ("Οφις) (Rev.12.14).

The Eagle ('Αετός; *Aquila*), also a constellation, was a bird sacred to Zeus (Rev. 12.14).

Aquarius, as such, is not mentioned in Revelation 12, but this is the "Water-Pourer" who was connected with Deucalion, the Noah of Greek mythology. He is represented as a man holding an urn from which water pours out, an image similar to the one presented in Revelation 12.15.

The overwhelming figure in the vision, however, is a woman clothed with the sun, under whose feet is the moon, and who wears a crown of twelve stars. Any Greek or Roman reading such a description would have thought of the constellation Virgo (παρθένος; Virgin), the sixth sign of the zodiac who was repre-

---

92 Thomas L Heath and Otto E. Neugebauer,"Constellations," *Oxford Classical Dictionary, op. cit.,* pp. 282-285; F. Boll and W. Gundel, "Sternbilder." Roscher, *Lexicon* ..., op. cit., vol. 6, pp. 867-1070. Franz Boll: *Aus der Offenbarung Johannis. Hellenistische Studien zum Weltbild der Apokalypse,* Leipzig/Berlin: Teubner, 1914; F. Boll, *Sphaera. Neue griechische Texte und Untersuchungen zur Geschichte der Sternbilder,* Leipzig: Teubner, 1903; F. Boll, *Sternglaube und Sterndeutung. Die Geschichte und Wesen der Astrologie.* Leipzig and Berlin: Teubner, 1931 (lst edition 1919); F. Boll, "Der Stern der Weisen," *Zeitscrift für die neutestamentliche Wissenschaft,* 18 (1917/18), 41-48; Werner Foerster, 'αστήρ, ἄστρον, *TWNT* 1.501-502. Alfred Jeremias, "Sterne (Bei den Babyloniern)" Roscher, *op. cit.,* vol. 4.1427-1500; George Thiele, *Antike Himmelsbilder,* Berlin: Weidmann, 1898, pp. 65-66, 97.

sented as a woman holding an ear of corn and having wings. A Hellenistic work described this sign as follows:

> The Virgin. Hesiod in his Theogony has called her the daughter of Zeus and Themis, and she is called "Justice" (Δίκη).[93] But after mortals had changed their ways and no longer cared for just behavior, she no longer dwelled among them but departed into the mountains. Afterwards, when strife and war had become endemic among men due to their savage injustice, she ascended into heaven. There are also the most numerous accounts concerning her: Some say she is *Demeter* because she holds an ear of corn. Others say she is *Isis*. Still others call her, *Atargatis,* others, *Fate (Tyche)* because they give her a headless form. She has one dim star on top of her head, one on top of each shoulder, and two on each wing. The star on the right wing, between the shoulder and the top of the wing, is called *Protrugeter.*[94] There is one star upon each elbow, and one upon each tip of the hands, the bright star of the left hand is called *Stachus.*[95] Upon the edge of her garment there are six dim stars ... one upon each foot. The sum total of all are twenty.[96]

Thus the image of a woman standing in the sky was one with which people were familiar and to which they could relate. Apuleius also pictured Isis as a celestial figure.[97] On her forehead she wore a shining round disc like the moon, held up by snakes rising from the earth; behind her head appeared ears of corn. She

---

[93] Hesiod, *Theogony* 901-902; See Works and Days 256, Aratus, *Phaenomena* 99- 136, in Maass, Ernestus, *Arati Phaenomena*, Berlin: Weidmann, 1955, pp. 9-11. See also Ovid, *Fasti* 1.248-250. Justice was put to flight by the sin of mortals; she was the last of celestials to forsake the earth. *Metamorphoses* 1.149-150: "*Victa jacet pietas et Virgo caede madentes, Ultima caelestum, terras Astraea reliquit.*" (Piety was over-thrown and the Virgin, Astraea, the last of the celestials, left the blood-sweating earth.) Also, Juvenal, *Satire* 6.1-20: "In older days when Saturn ruled the earth, and men were housed in cold caves, chastity stayed on earth, ... Justice, however, left earth for heaven and took her sister, Chastity, along." After these, the Christian Lactantius, *Divinae Institutiones* 5.5 (*ANF* 7.140).

[94] Literally translated, this means "before the vintage." It is also the name of a star in the constellation of Virgo which the Romans called *Vindemiatrix*, or *Vindemiator.*

[95] "Ear of corn, " in Latin *spica.*

[96] Psuedo-Eratosthenes, *Catasterismi* 9. The Greek text is in Alexander Olivieri, *Psuedo-Eratosthenis Catasterismi*, Lipsiae: Teubner, 1897, (*Mythographi Graeci*, III.1), pp. 11-12. The word καταστερισμός comes from κατά and ἀστήρ, thus the meaning is "placing among the stars." There is a break in the text which probably indicated where the twentieth star should be; as it is we only have the positions of nineteen.

[97] *Metamorphoses* 11.3-5. See also J. Gwyn Griffiths, *Apuleius of Madauros. The Isis Book (Metamorphoses, Book XI)*, Leiden: E. J. Brill, 1975, pp. 114- 117.

identified herself with the great fertility goddesses, among them Juno. Indeed, Martianus Capella described Juno in a similar way. In his story, Juno, seated upon a throne next to Jupiter, wore on her head a mantilla on which was a diadem set with precious stones.[98] Other gods and goddesses came before them, among them Saturn, holding a fire-breathing dragon, then Sol (= Sun) and Luna (= Moon). Jupiter addressed them in this fashion: "People of the stars ... "[99] Here, then, we find again the familiar actors in the cosmic drama of Revelation 12: the sun, the moon, the dragon, and the stars. Martianus referred to Juno as "*regina coeli*" queen of heaven, a common epithet, but for us it is interesting that he described Juno's jewelry and appearance in association with the stars in such a way that immediately calls to mind the woman clothed with the sun, who wore on her head a crown of twelve stars.[100]

In this connection must be mentioned the so-called Carvoran inscription. This inscription, left behind by a Roman soldier, Donatianus, in the wall of Hadrian in Northumberland around the third century, reads as follows:

> Imminet Leoni Virgo caelesti situ
> Spicifera, iusti inventrix, urbium conditrix,
> Ex quis muneribus nosse contigit deos,
> Ergo eadem mater divum, pax, virtus, Ceres,
> Dea Syria, lance vitam et iura pensitans.
> In caelo visum Syria sidus edidit
> Libyae colendum. Inde cuncti didicimus.
> Ita intellexit numine inductus tuo
> Marcus Caecilius Donatianus militans
> Tribunus in praefecto dono principis.

> The Virgo stands by Leo in the heavenly place
> the bearer of ears of corn, the inventor of justice,
> the founder of cities,
> out of whose munificence one can know the gods,
> the same is, therefore, the mother of the gods, Peace,

---

[98] "Cui gemmis insitum diadema pretiosis," Ch. 67. A. Dick, *op. cit.*, p. 31. In Ch. 75 the Sun *(Sol)* is said to have worn a crown with twelve burning stones: *"Erat illi in circulum ducta fulgens corona, quae duodecim flammis ignitorum lapidum fulgorabat"*: A. Dick, *op. cit.*, p. 34.

[99] W. Stahl, *op. cit.*, p. 31.

[100] See to this Carl Clemen, *Religionsgeschichtliche Erklärung des Neuen Testaments*, Giessen: Töpelmann, 1909, pp. 78-79, for a review of the authors who bring the twelve stars in connection with the zodiac.

Virtue, Ceres,
the Syrian goddess, weighing with a scale life and right.
Syria handed on the constellation seen on the sky
to Lybia to cultivate. Thence we all learned (the cult).
Induced (or moved) by your divinity thus understood
Marcus Caecilius Donatianus serving as a soldier
tribune, by the grace of the emperor, a prefect.[101]

This inscription was first applied to Revelation 12 by A. Dieterich in 1891.[102] After him many others referred to it, and for our own investigation it is an important reference because it reflects popular piety around the second century A.D., at which time the great fertility goddesses from Syria to Lybia and Rome were considered to be "the same." They were all viewed as images of the *Virgo*, a celestial divinity who was also the mother of the gods. The Roman soldier and the Christian visionary both see a woman appearing in the sky, and for both she is a divine and royal figure. This is not just a coincidence. The concept of the constellation Virgo was destined to play an unusual role in Christian theology just about the time when the inscription of Donatianus was written. Around the middle of the second century, Christians began to return to their pagan intellectual origins, referring to and quoting Greek and Roman authors.[103] Soon they rediscovered Virgil, especially his *Fourth Eclogue* in which the poet sings about the return of the "golden age," the rule of Saturn. This beautiful and mysterious poem written in 40 B.C. centers around the birth of a child whose coming will usher in a new age, free of every sort of wickedness which thus far has hung over mankind as an evil curse. *"Iam redit et Virgo, redeunt Saturnia regna."* "Now returns the *Virgo*, returns Saturn's rule,"[104] Virgil says, and from the context it is clear that he was referring to the

---

[101] *CIL* 7, #759, p. 137; Franciscus Buecheler, *Carmina Latina Epigraphica.* Leipzig: Teubner, 1895, #24, p. 15.

[102] *Abraxas*, p. 111. For later references see, among others, J. Dölger, "Die Himmelskönigin ...," *op. cit.* A von Domaszewszki, "Virgo Caelestis" in *Orientalische Studien.* (Theodor Noldke zum siebzigten Geburtstag.) Carl Bezold, editor. Gieszen: Töpelmann, 1906, vol. 2, pp. 861-863 connected the Carvoran inscription with Virgil, *Aeneis* 4.58 and Caelestis of Carthage.

[103] The first Christian to quote directly from a Greek pagan was Justin Martyr (d. 165 A.D.), while Minucius Felix (d. 240 A.D.) was the first Christian to use a direct quotation from a Latin pagan author. See to this problem W. Krause, *Die Stellung der frühchristlichen Autoren zur heidnischen Literatur,* Wien: Herder, 1958.

[104] Line 6.

constellation *Virgo,* whose return from heaven to earth meant that the conditions which forced her departure from earth, i.e., the proliferation of sin and evil, have been eliminated. It was, of course, not difficult for Christians to put the emphasis upon the meaning of the word *Virgo,* Virgin. While this was legitimate for pagans as well, the Virgin *par excellence* for Christians was the mother of Jesus. And so in Christian interpretation Virgil's poetic line became a reference to Mary. The first Christian work to make this positive identification was the *Oratio ad Coetum Sanctorum,* a good Friday sermon ascribed to Constantine the Great (285-337) and composed around A.D. 323.[105] The rest of Virgil's poem underwent a similar allegorization and eventually Virgil himself was regarded as a prophet who foretold the birth of Christ. But παρθένος, or *Virgo,* in Greco-Roman religious usage can also mean any one of the "virgin" goddesses — Demeter, Juno, Isis, Atargatis, Caelestis, and Aphrodite, to name a few. The question is, then, could Christians interpret Virgil's poem as a reference to Mary if some form of mental association between the image of a virgin goddess and Mary had not already taken place? Whatever the answer to this question may be, the fact remains that in this case there is a direct overlapping of the pagan *Virgo* and the Christian Mary. In other words, it was in the interpretation of the *Fourth Eclogue* that Christians openly identified Mary with the celestial virgin goddess of paganism.

Once again, the astral motifs in Revelation 12 are very close to those used in pagan mythologies to describe and characterize goddesses: the association with sun and moon, the use of the stars as decorations, jewels in a crown, or on a robe are all devices to illustrate the high position of the goddess. In Revelation 12 all this is present and one thing more: the image of the constellation *Virgo* is strongly implied in the text, and this places the image once again into a cosmological context. The *Virgo* left the world when the present conditions arose and will return at the end, when the "golden age" is reestablished. According to Greco-Roman mythology, the return of the Virgin is a sign that "the end is near," and this is what Revelation 12 indicates. The sign of the *Virgo* appeared

---

[105] Before him Cyprian (200-258) and Lactantius (240-320) already utilized the Fourth Eclogue in other contexts. See S. Benko, "Virgil's Fourth Eclogue ...," *op. cit.*

in the sky; this can mean only one thing, namely, that the damage done "in the beginning" has been repaired and the Kingdom of God, to use now Christian terminology, is near.

4. The Cosmic Battle

Immediately after the woman, a second portent appears in heaven: a great red dragon who in a desperate struggle tries to destroy the woman, eventually by pouring water after her. Thus begins the great battle which introduces the visions of the end-time, a motif first discussed by H. Gunkel and later explored by many scholars.[106] Two elements relate directly to our understanding of the woman's role in the drama: first, the figure of the dragon, and second, the significance of water in the cosmic scheme.

a. The Dragon

The dragon is a familiar figure in the mythologies of many peoples. In the Old Testament it appears under the names of "Leviathan," "Monster," "Serpent," and "Rahab" (= "Rager"). Because these monsters are usually associated with the sea, often the sea itself is named as the personification of evil. Whatever their name,

---

[106] Hermann Gunkel, *Schöpfung und Chaos in Urzeit und Endzeit. Eine religionsgeschichtliche Untersuchung über Gen. 1 and Ap. Joh. 12*, Göttingen: Vandenhoeck and Reprecht, 1895. Otto Kaiser, *Die Mythische Bedeutung des Meeres in Ägypten, Ugarit und Israel*, Berlin: Töpelmann, 1962, esp. pp. 140–159. Robert Graves and Raphael Patai, *Hebrew Myths: The Book of Genesis*, New York: McGraw-Hill, 1964, pp. 21-54. R. Merkelbach, "Drache," *Reallexikon für Antike und Christentum*, Stuttgart: Anton Hiersemann, 1954, vol. 4, pp. 226- 250. Theodor H. Gaster, "Cosmogony," *The Interpreter's Dictionary of the Bible*, Nashville: Abingdon, 1962, vol. 3, p. 316. Howard Wallace, "Leviathan and the Beast in Revelation," *The Biblical Archeologist* (1948): 61-68; Marvin H. Pope, *Job* (The Anchor Bible, vol. 15), Garden City, N.Y. Doubleday, 1965, pp. 265-279 (comments on "Behemoth" and "Leviathan"). Biblical commentaries: Hermann Gunkel, *Genesis*, Göttingen: Vandenhoeck & Ruprecht, 1922; John Skinner, *A Critical and Exegetical Commentary on Genesis*, New York: Charles Scribner's Sons, 1925; Cuthbert A. Simpson, *The Book of Genesis*, The Interpreter's Bible, vol. 1, New York/Nashville: Abingdon Cokesbury Press, 1952, pp. 437 ff. A new addition to this literature is John Day, *God's Conflict with the Dragon and the Sea in the Old Testament*, New York: Cambridge University Press, 1985; Susan Niditch, *Chaos to Cosmos: Studies in Biblical Patterns of Creation*, Chico, Calif.: Scholar's Press, 1985. Carola Kloos, *YHWH's Combat with the Sea. A Canaanite Tradition in the Religion of Ancient Israel*. Leiden: E. J. Brill, 1986 analyzes Psalm 29 and the Red Sea Story. The dragon's image in Rev. 12 was investigated by A. Y. Collins, *The Combat Myth in the Book of Revelation*. Missoula, Montana: Scholar's Press, 1976.

they are always enemies of God; thus we have in the Old Testament the familiar juxtaposition of God versus the "serpent."[107] In Sumerian and Babylonian mythology, the sea monster is called Tiamat and her husband is Apsu. Their chaotic unions issued in dragon-like monsters, whose eventual fight set the stage for the creation of mankind.[108] In Canaanite mythology, the chief actors are Baal, who represents fertility and life; Anath, his female counterpart; and Mot, god of sterility and death. Baal's first conflict was with the waters, whose unruliness and tyranny had to be subdued before life could begin. Baal achieved this victory in a successful battle with Yam, i.e., the dragon, the Lord of the Sea.

---

[107] Some relevant texts are: Job 3.18, 7.12, 9.13, 26.12, 41.1-11; Ps. 74.13- 14, 89.10, 104.26, 148.7; Isa. 14.29, 27.1, 30.6, 51.9; Ezek. 29.3, 32.2; Dan. 7.7; Amos 9.3; Habakkuk 3.13, 15. To these texts we may add from early Christian literature Hermas, *Pastor*, Vision 4: Hermas went out on the Campanian way and from a cloud of dust a large beast, "something like a semi- monster," appeared to him; it was about a hundred feet long, and its head was like a wine-jar. It came upon Hermas with a great rush, but it was subdued by the faith of Hermas and stretched out on the ground. Presently, a girl came about whom Hermas immediately recognized as the church. She explained to him that the beast means great affliction, but those who have faith will be saved. E. J. Goodspeed, *The Apostolic Fathers*, New York: Harper, 1950, p. 120. Also, the *Pistis Sophia* 66: The emanations pursued Pistis Sophia, and one of them transformed itself into the form of a basilisk with seven heads, the other into the form of a dragon (δράκων). They threatened Pistis Sophia and led her back into the chaos. Carl Schmidt, *Koptisch Gnostische Schriften*, Berlin: Akademie Verlag, 1959, pp. 88-89. In the newly published English translation of the Greek magical papyri occurs the following sentence: " ... in the parts toward the west you have the shape of a crocodile, with the tail of a snake, from which you send out rains and snows; in the parts toward the east you have (the form of) a winged dragon, a diadem fashioned of air, with which you quell all discords beneath the heaven and on earth ... " The incantation is addressed to God whose name is given in numerous forms. Investigating the Apocalypse from the point of view of the magical papyri is still to be made; it is a fascinating assumption, however, that the author was not only familiar with pagan mythological concepts, but with magical formulas, too. See Hans Dieter Betz, *The Greek Magical Papyri in Translation*, Chicago: University of Chicago Press, 1986, p. 16; *PGM* II, 110-114.

[108] "Enuma Elish," in James B. Pritchard, *Ancient Near Eastern Texts Relating to the Old Testament*, Princeton, N.J.: Princeton University Press, 1955, pp. 60-72. Alfred Jeremias, *Das Alte Testament in Lichte des Alten Orients*, Leipzig: J.C. Hinrichs'sche Buchhandlung, 1916, pp. 6-34. Samuel Noah Kramer, *History Begins at Sumer*, New York: Doubleday, 1958, pp. 170-181. "Tiamat" is philologically the same as "tehom" in Hebrew, i.e., the "deep," in Gen. 1.2 "Rahab" means "Rager" and "Leviathan" is a linguistic relative of the word "tannin," i.e., "monster." See also Pritchard, op. cit., pp. 125-126; Samuel Noah Kramer, ed., *Mythologies of the Ancient World*, Garden City, N.Y.: Doubleday, 1961, pp. 151, 174.

The waters could now be distributed advantageously and Baal was worshipped as the god of rainfall who rode upon the clouds.[109] In later developments the myth assumed the character of dying and rising gods, i.e., the agricultural cycles: Mot caused the death of Baal until through the energetic intervention of Anath he was restored to life and the rains returned.[110]

Greek mythology, although somewhat remote from its Near Eastern counterparts, shows some similarities to it.[111] In these myths the destructive force appears as a dragon, a serpent, or a monster, sometimes with the names of "Hydra," "Typhon" or "Typhaon," or "Pytho," who are eventually killed by a god or a hero. These stories, then, exist in many versions, expressing the same thought in several variations and in different frameworks.[112]

---

[109]   E.O. James, *The Ancient Gods*, New York: Putnam, 1960, pp. 87-90; J. Ray, "Baal," *The Interpreter's Dictionary of the Bible*, 1.328-329; Cyrus H. Gordon, "Canaanite Mythology," *Mythologies of the Ancient World*, S. N. Kramer, ed., pp. 184-201; Theodor H. Gaster, *Thespis. Ritual, Myth and Drama in the Ancient Near East*. New York: Henry Schuman, 1950.

[110]   Anath remained a popular goddess in the Ancient Near East and was one of the few absorbed into Egyptian mythology. She appears in the Old Testament under the name of the father of Shamgar, one of the Judges, and in the name of the city of Anathoth (i.e., "House of the Great Anath", which may have been a Canaanite shrine to the goddess and after the conquest by the Hebrews it became a sacred city of the Israelites. It is best known as the birthplace of Jeremiah, Judg. 3.31, 5.6.

[111]   In addition to the works quoted below, see for the following W. H. Roscher, *Ausführliches Lexicon der Griechischen und Römischen Mythologie*, 6 vols., Leipzig: Teubner, 1984-1937.

[112]   These are some of the best known Greek myths involving dragons or serpents: The dragon killed by Cadmus (Thomas Bulfinch, *Mythology*, New York: Dell, 1979, pp. 80-82 and 108-110. H. J. Rose et al., "Cadmus," in *The Oxford Classical Dictionary*,2 Oxford: Clarendon Press, 1970, pp. 186-187.)

The sea-monster in the myth of Andromeda. (Michael Grant, *The myths of the Greeks and Romans*, New York: New American Library, 1962, p. 346; H. J. Rose, "Andromeda," *The Oxford Classical Dictionary*, 2 pp. 63-64.)

The myth of Typhon (or Typhaon, or Typhoeus) is known in two variants, one recorded in the *Homeric Hymns*, the other by Hesiod in the *Theogony*. (Both are available in the Loeb edition: Hesiod, *The Homeric Hymns and Homerica*, ET by Hugh G. Evelyn-White, *LCL*, Cambridge, Mass." Harvard University Press, 1954.) One is in the *Homeric Hymn to Apollo* 3.300-373, the other in the *Theogony* 820-868. Other variants of the Typhon story are summarized by Robert Graves, *op. cit.*, vol. 1, p. 56; M. Grant, *op. cit.*, pp. 118-126. Joseph Fontenrose, *Python. A Study of Delphic Myth and Its origins*, Berkeley and Los Angeles: University of California Press, 1959, p. 21, lists five versions of Apollo's combat with the dragon.

Closely related to these stories is that of Python. According to this myth, Zeus fell in love with Leto, a female Titan, but Hera sent the serpent Python to pursue her and prevent her from being delivered of her children. Finally

They all contain the same element that is also prominent in the Near Eastern myths, that is, water monsters as enemies of ordered life. When Zeus kills Typhoeous or Apollo kills Typhon or Python, the forces of disorder are eliminated so that civilized life may begin. In Greek cosmogony it is the victory of Zeus over the Titans which expresses the triumph of order "over the monstrous wildness of age-old elemental disorder."[113]

In Egyptian mythology[114] the concept that comes closest to that of a dragon is Apopis (or Apophis, or Apep), the snake.[115] Apopis is an elusive figure, not a god that can be worshipped, but simply a phenomenon that can be experienced as chaos and as an evil

she gave birth to Artemis on the island of Ortygia and soon after that to Apollo on the island of Delos. This is the myth many scholars compare to the story in Rev. 12.

The son of Python and Echidne was the water monster, Hydra (= ὕδωρ, water). (Pausanias *Guide to Greece*, ET by Peter Levi, Harmondsworth, England: Penguin, 1971, vol. 1, pp. 219-221; Bulfinch, *op. cit.*, p. 119; R. Graves, *op. cit.*, vol . 1, pp. 107-110.) R. Graves quotes Servius, the commentator of Virgil, who gave his views on the puzzle of the hydra in his remarks on the *Aeneid* 6 .287, where among many other monsters such as the Gorgons, the harpies, "the flame throwing Chimaera," Virgil also mentions "the Lernaean Hydra that hisses terribly." (R. Graves, *op. cit.*, p. 109.)

Scylla, who was changed into a sea monster with six heads, twelve feet, a voice like a puppy-dog's barking. She captured sailors and slowly devoured them. Odysseus lost six of his best men to the Scylla. (Homer, *Odyssey*, 12.73-259; Graves, *op. cit.*, vol. 1, pp. 59-62; vol. 2, pp. 361-362.)

[113]　Hesiod, *Theogony*, 485 ff. M. Grant, *op. cit.*, p. 111.

[114]　Seigfried Morenz, *Ägyptische Religion*, Stuttgart: Kohlhammer, Verlag, 1960; Henri Frankfort, *Ancient Egyptian Religion*, New York: Columbia University Press, 1948, reprinted as a Harper Torchbook, 1961; Adolf Erman, *Die Religion der Ägypter*, Berlin and Leipzig: Walter de Gruyter, 1934; Hans Bonnett, *Reallexikon der Ägyptischen Religionsgeschicte*, Berlin: Walter de Gruyter, 1952; G. Roeder, *Urkunden zur Religion des Alten Aegyptens*, Jena: E. Diederichs, 1923; H. Te Velde, *Seth, God of Confusion*, Leiden: E. J. Brill, 1977; J. Gwyn Griffiths, *The Origin of Osiris and His Cult*, Leiden: E. J. Brill, 1980; J. Gwyn Griffiths, *The Conflict of Horus and Seth*, Liverpool: Liverpool University Press, 1960; Rudolf Anthes, "Mythology in Ancient Egypt," in *Mythologies of the Ancient World*, Samuel Noah Kramer, ed., New York: Doubleday, 1961, pp. 15-92; Hermann Kees, "Seth," *Pauly's Realencyclopadie der Classischen Altertumswissenschaft*, ed. G. Wissowa, W. Kroll, K. Witte, Stuttgart: Alfred Druckenmüller, 1923, vol. II, Al. 2, pp. 1896-1922; E. A. Wallis Budge, *From Fetish to God in Ancient Egypt*, New York: Benjamin Blom, 1972 (reprint of the 1934 edition).

[115]　*The Instruction for King Meri-Ka-Re* (end of the 22nd century B.C.) contains the following sentence: "Well directed are men, the cattle of the god. He made heaven and earth according to their desire, and he repelled the water-monster." This is very similar to the story of the Babylonian Tiamat and points to an early belief of the Egyptians in the defeat of a monster at creation. See Pritchard, *op. cit.*, pp. 414-418, and footnote 49 on p. 417.

force.[116] According to Egyptian mythology, Apopis' origin goes back to the time of the primordial waters where the mother of Re, Neith, resided. From a spittle of Neith, a snake developed which was one hundred twenty yards long. This snake revolted against Re but was defeated and driven back into his cavern; according to the myth, since then there has been a never-ending struggle against the powers of chaos.[117] The sun and light are constantly exposed to the attacks of darkness, and so the rising of the sun is represented as the victory of Re over Apopis. This rising is a daily occurrence, for Apopis never dies. He is only repelled, overthrown, or conquered in the same way as, in Mesopotamian mythology, Marduk conquers Tiamat at each celebration of the New Year's festival. The possibility of chaos is ever-present and it is Re, with the uraeus-snake on his forehead, who overcomes this danger. Consequently, the pharaoh functions as the incarnation of Re, because he, the king, also conquers disorder and safeguards order in the land.[118]

The Egyptian idea of the god Seth is so closely related to Near Eastern and Greek concepts that eventually he was identified with Baal, Anath, and Typhon.[119] Unlike Apopis, Seth was thought of as a god who came into being at the third level of the development of creation, which, according to the Heliopolitan Ennead, included

---

[116] See to this problem Erich Hornung, "Chaotische Bereiche in der geordneten Welt," *Zeitschrift für Aegyptische Sprache und Altertumskunde* 81 (1956): 23- 32.

[117] The main source is the Papyrus Bremner-Rhind XXII.1, the general title of which is *The Book of Overthrowing Apophis the Enemy of Re ...* Portions are translated in James B. Pritchard, op. cit., pp. 6-7. See also Te Velde, *op. cit.*, pp. 99-107. Many passages mentioning Apopis in ancient literature were collected by Theodor Hopfner, *Plutarch über Isis and Osiris*, Hildesheim: Georg Olms, 1974, vol. 1, pp. 169-172 (This is a reprint of the edition of 1940/41, the two volumes bound in one); H. Bonnett, *op. cit.*, pp. 51-64.

[118] Texts in Morenz, *op. cit.*, p. 177. According to R. Anthes, *op. cit.*, p. 88, the Eye is the Uraeus viper at the forehead of the king. As long as the king lived the Uraeus was guarded, but when the king died, it would escape and leave disturbance and chaos behind in Egypt. Maat, law and order, would not return until the Uraeus would rest again at the forehead of the new king.

[119] See Plutarch, *De Iside et Osiride* (or: *Moralia*, 351-384) in Frank Cole Babbit, *Plutarch's Moralia, LCL*, vol. 5, London: Heinemann, 1957, pp. 7-101; Theodor Hopfner, *Plutarch über Isis and Osiris*; G. Gwyn Griffiths, *Plutarch's De Iside et Osiride*, Cardiff: University of Wales Press, 1970; E. Meyer, *Seth-Typhon. Eine religionsgeschictliche Studie*, Leipzig: W. Englemann, 1875; H. Bonnett, *op. cit.*, pp. 702-714.

nine gods.[120] In the character of Seth, the slayer of Osiris, the Egyptians conceived a hostile god, an enemy of order, a promoter of confusion, a disturber of harmony, who nevertheless is an integral part of total reality. Afraid of Seth, Isis fled to the marshes of Khemnis and gave birth to Horus.[121] After the battle between Horus and Seth, however, Isis did not permit Seth to be killed but rather released him. Plutarch's interpretation of this story is that opposing influences make the world go around and that evil cannot be completely eradicated. If Osiris represents "the whole source and faculty of creative moisture," and Seth (i.e., Typon) "all that is dry, fiery and arid in general, and antagonistic to moisture,"[122] then it follows that the fiery element cannot completely disappear from the world; only the nature opposed to moisture must be relaxed and moderated, but "its tempering potency should persist."[123] Thus, it is out of discordant elements that concord is created in the universe, and destructive forces are curbed, but not eliminated.[124]

The dragon, therefore, is a figure which is connected with the principle of chaos. Chaos is the opposite of order; it is out of chaos

---

[120] The oldest traditions are in the Pyramid texts, i.e., the writings in the pyramids for the funeral of the pharaohs of the Old Kindgom. These were published by Kurt Heinrich Sethe, *Die Altägyptischen Pyramidentexte*, Leipzig: J. C. Hinrichs, 1908, and K.H. Sethe, *Übersetzung und Kommentar zu den altägyptischen Pyramidentexten*, Gluckstadt, Hamburg: J.J. Augustin, 1936-62.

[121] For the flight of Isis before Seth, see Te Velde, *op. cit.*, 28, 32. According to Plutarch, *op. cit.*, 358D, Thueris, concubine of Typhon, was also pursued by a serpent. Fontenrose, *op. cit.*, p. 190, mentions other pursuits: in the Egyptian *Tale of Two Brothers*, the sea pursued Bata's wife; in Ovid, *Metamorphoses* 5.325 ff, Typhoeus pursued Venus, who saved herself by turning into a fish.

[122] Comparable, therefore, to the figure of Satan in the Old Testament, cf. Job 1.6; Zech. 3.1. Also see Plutarch's remarks on the dualistic nature of the Zoroastrian religion, *op. cit.*, 369E-370.

[123] *Op. cit.*, 364B; 371A and B. ET: Babbit, *op. cit.*, p. 81.

[124] *Op. cit.*, 367A. Plutarch presses the point by quoting Homer, *Iliad* 18.107 (Strife may vanish away from the ranks of the gods and mortals), and says that this would be a curse, since all things originate from strife and antagonism This leads him to mention Empedocles' fragments on "Love" and "Strife" (370D-E) and two lines from Euripides, *Aeolus:* "The good and bad cannot be kept apart, but there is some commingling, which is well" (369B). Plutarch then states that "nature brings, in this life of ours, many experiences in which both evil and good are commingled" (369C, ET. Babbit, *op. cit.*, p. 111). In Rev. 12 we observe that the dragon is "thrown down," "defeated," but not killed and even after a victory hymn was sung over him he was still able to pursue the woman and eventually return to his element, the sea.

that the gods created order and made civilized life possible. Chaos was identified with the elemental power of water. Thus, Genesis 1.1-3 speaks of God separating "the waters which were under the firmament from the waters which were above the firmament." The waters under the heavens were restricted to their place so that dry land could appear and vegetation could begin. This unruly, destructive commingling of water and elemental forces was anthropomorphized in the figure of a raging monster, a cosmic opponent of God, conquered by him at the time of creation, and restrained and controlled by him now.[125] In Revelation 12 the dragon is on the loose again, using the element of water in his attempt to destroy the events taking place in heaven. Chaos, once conquered by God, is threatening again to undo God's plans, which are portrayed in the figure of the woman clothed with the sun: she represents cosmic unity, she brings together "things in heaven and things on earth," and thus she is a proleptic realization of the final, eschatological consummation.

b. Water

Ancient mythologies reveal the double nature of the element of water. Unrestrained water represents chaos and is experienced as a destructive force; under control, however, water is absolutely necessary to life. According to one line of thought, all life originated from Oceanus, i.e., water, the primeval cosmic power

---

[125] 373-D. Seth was consequently associated, among others, with the dangerous animals of the Nile: the hippopotamus and the crocodile. [*Op. cit.*, 371C-D-E; see also J. G. Griffiths, *The Conflict of Horus and Seth*, pp. 103, 112-115. For Seth as a serpent, Hermann Kees, *Horus und Seth als Götterpaar*. (Vorderasiatisch-Aegyptische Gesellschaft, Mitteilungen, vols. 28 and 29), Leipzig: J. C. Hinrichs'sche Buchhandlung, 1923-1924, p. 46, and H. Kees, "Seth," in Pauly's *Realencyclopädie*, II.A.2, p. 1902.] According to Plutarch, there was a statue of Seth in the form of a hippopotamus. Plutarch also related that according to the Egyptians, Seth escaped Horus by turning into a crocodile. We would expect, then, that Seth would be identified with Apopis, as indeed seemed to be the case at a certain period of Egypt's history. But this is not the case, for in a characteristically inconsistent way, Seth appears to be fighting Apopis and protecting Re. Te Velde, *op. cit.*, p. 141, 99-108.
Theodore H. Gaster suggested that the idea of such a primordial disorder developed in Mesopotamia as a retrojection of the annual crisis caused by the snow melting on the mountains and welling up in underground springs. The rushing of the waters that had to be dealt with at the beginning of each year was thought of as something similar to what had to be done at the beginning of the world. [Theodore H. Gaster, "Cosmogony," p. 706.]

which is the source of all life. Homer says that the θεῶν γένεσις was Oceanus.[126] This reference lived on in some versions of the Greek Orphic tradition, whose cosmogony also began with Oceanus[127] as well as in the work of the "father of philosophy," Thales of Miletus, who, according to Aristotle, said that everything in the world originates from one substance and that substance is water.[128] Now, it may or may not be true that Thales was influenced in the formation of his ideas by the Egyptians, as W. K. C. Guthrie suggested.[129] The fact is, however, that Egyptian mythology contains many references to the primordial water, Nun, as the source of life.[130] Sumerian mythology, too, refers to the primeval sea as "the mother who gave birth to all the gods," personified in the goddess Nammu. Thus possibly the earliest cosmogonies posited the existence of an eternal and uncreated substance, the sea, from which everything came to be.[131] How-

[126] *Iliad* 14.210, 246, 302. See also Virgil, *The Georgics* 4.382: "Herself therewithal offers prayer to Oceanus father of all things (*patrem rerum*) ...." E.T.: J.W. Mackail, *Virgil's Works*, New York: Modern Library, 1950, p. 347. More references in Fontenrose, *op. cit.*, p. 226.

[127] See M. L. West, *The Orphic Poems*, Oxford: Clarendon Press, 1983, especially pp. 57, 119, 184-190; W. Staudacher, *op. cit.*, pp. 77-121: "Rekonstrucktion der Orphischer Kosmogonien." Also, Konrat Ziegler, "Orphische Dichtung," *Pauly, op. cit.*, 17/2 (34. Halbband), 2308-2349, especially 2315-2316, where he deals with the expression of *theon genesis*.

[128] G. E. R. Lloyd, *Early Greek Science: Thales to Aristotle*, New York: Norton, 1970, pp. 18-23; G. S. Kirk and J. E. Raven, *The Presocratic Philosophers*, Cambridge: University Press, 1957, esp. pp. 8-37. Werner Jaeger, *Paideia*, New York: Oxford University Press, 1965, vol. 1, p. 151. It might be of interest to note here how Ovid in a poetic form retold the traditional myth about the earliest beginning of the world: Before anything came to be there was an uncoordinated mass, Chaos. The elements of land, air, and sea were there, but without lasting shape and "everything got in the way of everything else." Everything fought its opposite, cold-hot, moist-dry, soft-hard. An unnamed god put an end to this confusion by separating the elements and assigning them their proper place and function, "forming a harmonious union." Ovid, *Metamorphoses* 1.1-66, E.T.: Mary M. Innes, *The Metamorphoses of Ovid*, New York: Penguin, 1982, pp. 29-31; Frank Justin Miller, *Ovid. Metamorphoses, LCL,* London: Heinemann, 1929, pp. 2-7.

[129] *In the Beginning. Some Greek Views on the Origins of Life and the State of Man,* London: Methuen, 1957, pp. 17-18.

[130] Siegfried Morenz, *Ägyptische Religion*, Stuttgart: Kohlhammer Verlag, 1960, especially pp. 180-186; E. A. Wallis Budge, *From Fetish to God in Ancient Egypt*, New York: Benjamin Bloom, 1972 (reprint; 1st edition 1934), pp. 141-142, 171, 199; Ochsham, *op. cit.*, p. 33; K. Sethe, *Urgeschichte ...*, paragraphs 70, 113, 163, 164, 167, 222; pp. 57, 94, 133-134, 136, 183.

[131] Samuel Noah Kramer, *Sumerian Mythology. A Study of Spiritual and Literary Achievement in the Third Millenium B.C.*, Philadelphia: University of

ever, even subdued, water is not always a blessing; even then it can be a destructive power and a source of much evil. This negative view of water can be found everywhere in ancient texts, including the Bible[132] and Greek and Roman literature.[133]

Pennsylvania Press, 1972, pp. 68-75.

[132] In the book of Psalms a "time of distress" can be referred to as "the rash of bad waters" [Ps. 32.6] and a time of affliction is described with the following words: "The waters have come up to my neck, I sink in deep mire, where there is no foothold; I have come into deep waters, and the flood sweeps over me" [69.1-2; see also 42.7; 46.1-3]. Similarly, the promise of Yahweh to protect those who believe him is expressed with these words: "When you pass through the water I will be with you; and through the river they shall not overwhelm you" [Isa. 43.2a]. The danger that water represented was so keenly felt that it could be compared with that of fire [Isa. 43.2b; Ps. 66.12]. Often the ocean is a symbol of death, as in the song of Jonah which came "out of the belly of Sheol," out of the belly of the fish: "Thou didst cast me into the deep, into the heart of the seas, and the flood was round about me; all thy waves and thy billows passed over me" [Jon. 2.2-3]. Here Sheol, the deep, and the ocean are nearly synonymous, as in Ps. 88: "Thou hast put me in the depths of the Pit, in the regions dark and deep. Thy wrath lies heavy upon me, and thou dost overwhelm me with all thy waves" [v. 6-7]. More examples could be cited, but these should suffice to enable us to see that in the Old Testament the negative character of water includes the ideas that water can cause death (obviously by drowning) and that the ocean can be described as the realm of death.

[133] See Hesiod's warning concerning seafaring and his ominous remark: "It is fearful to die among the waves" [*Works and Days*, 618-694; Hugh Evelyn White, *Hesiod, op. cit.*, pp. 49-53; see also 236-237: the peaceful and just do not travel on ships, because the earth bears them fruit]. Lucretius wrote that at one time men were harder, ate what Nature provided, and did not know "the wicked way to navigation." Ships and sailors were not killed on the rocks by the "turbulent billows of the sea" and it did not matter whether the sea rose and stormed and nobody could be "enticed to his ruin by the treacherous witchery of a quiet sea with laughing waves" [*De Rerum Natura*, 1000-1006, W. H. D. Rouse and M. F. Smith, *Lucretius, De Rerum Natura, LCL*, London: Heinemann, 1975, pp. 456-457]. According to Virgil, seafaring means "to tempt Thetis with rafts," but in the coming golden age even the "trader himself will forsake the sea and the nautical pine (i.e., ships) will not exchange merchandise" [S. Benko, "Virgil's Fourth Eclogue in Christian Interpretation," *Aufstieg und Niedergang der römischen Welt*, Hildegard Temporini und Wolfgang Haase, eds., Berlin: Walter de Gruyter, 1980, II.311, p. 657. See *Oracula Sibyllina* 3.777 ff: "And all the paths of the plain and the sheer banks and the lofty mountains and the wild sea waves shall become easy to travel over by foot or sail in those days."] Ovid, fearful of Corinna's safety on the sea, wished that sea-going ships were unknown [*Amores* 2.11; Guy Lee, *Ovid's Amores* New York: Viking, 1968, pp. 89-93; Peter Green, *Ovid. The Erotic Poems*, Harmondsworth, England: Penguin, 1982, pp. 125-126]. Horace addressed a poem to his good friend Virgil when he sailed to Greece. In this poem Horace prayed to Venus, and then to Castor and Pollux (i.e., the constellation Gemini, who were invoked in time of peril at sea), that Virgil might be safe on his perilous journey. God in his wisdom

The Egyptians emphasized the beneficent aspect of water more than their Near Eastern neighbors because of the strong connection of this element with Isis and Osiris. In one story, Osiris was drowned in water by Seth;[134] in another, he was tricked into lying in a coffin, the lid of which was nailed down; the coffin, enclosing the body of Osiris, was thrown into a river and carried into the sea.[135] Therefore, the Egyptians could even look upon drowning as an apotheosis because this manner of death assured that the person would immediately become one with Osiris.[136] Yet there are many references in Egyptian literature to water as a "symbol of death and chaos."[137] According to Plutarch, the Egyptians considered the sea as a "corrupt and pestilential residuum of a foreign nature."[138] Sometimes the sea was identified with Typhon[139] and salt with the spume of Typhon.[140] Nor is the fear of water alien to

---

separated the lands from the waters and for men waters are *non tangenda*. To sail ships is a sacrilege; man's audacity in sailing will lead him to ruin. [H. E. Butler, *The Odes of Horace*, London: G. Bell, 1929, pp. 10-15; Helen R. Henze, *The Odes of Horace*, Norman: University of Oklahoma Press, 1961, pp. 22-23. This poem of Horace and also the one by Ovid, is a *Propemptikon*, i.e., a "sending off" poem, and eventually this genre became popular in Greco-Roman literature. Even the Christian author Paulinus of Nola (354/5-431) wrote a *Propemptikon* on the occasion of the departure of his friend Nicetas. In this case, of course, Nicetas' safety from the dangers of the deep is assured by the sign of the cross. See F. Jäger, *Das Antike Propemptikon und das 17. Gedicht des Paulinus von Nola, Rosenheim*, 1913. Also R. G. M. Nisbet and Margaret Hubbard, *A Commentary on Horace: Odes, Book 1*, Oxford: Clarendon Press, 1970, pp. 40-58.] Water carries with it the potentiality of death and destruction.

[134]   H. Bonnet, *op. cit.*, pp. 568-710. See Te Velde, *op. cit.*, pp. 81-86.

[135]   Plutarch, *op. cit.*, p. 356. See the comments of Hopfner, *op. cit.*, pp. 16, 39-40.

[136]   F. J. Dölger, "Esietus. Der Ertrunkene oder zu einem Osiris Gewordene," *Antike und Christentum* 5 (1939): 153-182; Hermann Kees, "Aptheosis by Drowning," *Studies Presented to F. L. E. Griffith*, Egypt Exploration Society, London: Oxford University Press, 1932, pp. 402-405. (Osiris means "die befruchtende Überschwemmung, sein Wassertod gibt also neues Leben, so wie auch das Korn, wenn es bei der Ernte fällt, Nährung und Leben spendet." Yet, Kees warns, this is a late Egyptian view, and drowning was not always viewed as a blessed event.) A Hermann, "Ertrinken," *Reallexikon für Antike und Christentum*, Stuttgart: Anton Hiersman, 1966, vol. 6, pp. 370-410; F. L. E. Griffith, "Herodotus II.90–Apotheosis by Drowning," *Zeitschrift für Ägyptische Sprache und Altertumskunde*, 46 (1910): 132-134. Herodotus, *The Persian Wars* 2.90, reports that the bodies of those who were killed by a crocodile or who drowned in the Nile were embalmed and laid to rest with honors.

[137]   Te Velde, *op. cit.*, pp. 85-86.

[138]   *Op. cit.*, 353E.

[139]   = Seth, Plutarch, *op. cit.*, 363E.

[140]   *Op. cit.*, 363E.

the world of the New Testament. It is in just such a light that the story of Jesus' stilling of the storm-tossed sea must be understood: "Peace, be still!" — Jesus said, and when calm returned, his disciples said to one another: "Who is this, that even wind and sea obey him?"[141] Similarly, Jesus' walking on the sea may be a demonstration both of his power to raise himself above the laws of nature and of his authority over the primordial power of the waters, which would be an added proof of his divinity:[142] as God had subdued the primordial waters, so Jesus now rules over them. In the apocalyptic distress according to Luke, the sea again will be a fearsome threat: "And there will be signs in sun and moon and stars, and upon the earth distress of nations in perplexity at the roaring of the sea and the waves, men fainting with fear and with foreboding of what is coming on the world ... "[143] The meaning is clear: Chaos has been tamed only temporarily and is being kept under control by God. But water is still a potentially deadly element, and at the end of time the power of chaos will again threaten to destroy ordered life. This is what we read about in Revelation 12.

> The phenomenon of the water so fascinated the North African Christian lawyer Tertullian (d. 220) that he based a good part of his encomium of baptism on the excellent character of this element. Here, of course, he emphasized the beneficent qualities of water. His little treatise begins with the statement that heretics (i.e. the Caininites) who wish to deny the importance of baptism are vipers, asps and basilisks who by nature prefer arid and waterless places ... "But we," he says, "little fishes, after the example of our ΙΧΘΥC Jesus Christ, are born in water, nor have we safety in any other way than permanently abiding in water" (Ch. 1). Taking baptism away from Christians is the same as taking little fishes out of water. Why does a material substance have such a great dignity? The answer is this: "Water is one of those things which, before all of the world, were quiescent with God in a yet unshapen state." He makes references to Genesis 1.1-2 and then continues with these words: "The first thing, O man, which you

---

141   Mark 4.35-41, and parallels.
142   Mark 6.48-51, and parallels. Compare with Job 26.312: "By his power he stilled the sea ..." John Paul Heil, *Jesus Walking on the Sea: Meaning and Gospel Functions of Matt. 14.22-33, Mark 6.45-52 and John 6.15b-21*, Rome: Biblical Institute, 1981. Elizabeth Struthers Malbon, "The Jesus of Mark and the Sea of Galilee," *Journal of Biblical Literature* 103 (1984): 363-377.
143   Luke 21.25-26 See also the *Apocalypse of Baruch* (or *2. Baruch*) 29.33-8 and *2.Esdras* 6.49-54: At the end of time Leviathan will again temporarily break loose and then will be finally defeated.

have to venerate, is the age of the waters in that their substance is ancient; the second, their dignity, in that they were the seat of the Divine Spirit, more pleasing to Him, no doubt, than all the other then existing elements." The primeval darkness was without shape, the abyss was gloomy, and the earth unfurnished. "Water alone — always a perfect, gladsome, simple material substance, pure in itself — supplied a worthy vehicle to God." Waters were the regulating powers by which God constituted the world: by dividing the waters, he made dry land. After this the water received the order to bring forth life (Gen. 1.1-2, 6.8). It is in this that Tertullian finds the basis for the mystery of baptism: "That the material substance which governs terrestrial life acts as agent likewise in the celestial" (Ch. 3). Water became holy because the Spirit of God hovered over it, thus bestowing the quality of holiness upon it. "All waters, therefore, in virtue of the pristine privilege of their origin, do, after invocation of God, attain the sacramental power of sanctification" (Ch. 4). Tertullian then deals with the difficult question of why the pagans, such as initiates of the Eleusinian mysteries, also use water for ablutions. Are these also baptisms? He answers that in pagan ceremonies demons are active, whereas Christian baptism is the work of the holy angel of God (Ch. 5). He cites many references to water in the Old Testament, such as the Red Sea, the bitter waters of Marah made sweet by God, the water that came from the rock of Horeb, and others (Ex. 14:12-29, 23-25, 17.6). Then, as if drawing a parallel between the first creation out of chaos and the new creation by Christ, he declares, "Never is Christ without water!" He lists the gospel passages in which water is mentioned in connection with Jesus: he was baptized in water, changed water into wine, invited people to come to him and drink "His own sempiternal water," and so on. Even Pilate's washing of his hands in water and the water that came out Christ's side on the cross carry a mysterious significance (Matt. 3.13-17; John 2.1-11, 7.37; Matt. 10.42; John 4.6; Matt.14.25; Mark 4.36-41; John 13.1-11; Matt. 27.24; John 19.34). In discussing the story of Jesus' quieting the storm on the sea, Tertullian remarks (Ch. 11) that in this storm the disciples were "baptized" in a manner of speaking. The "sea" in this story, he says, is an allegory of the world (saeculum) and the little boat is the church; when Jesus checked the waters, he checked the world. The rest of Tertullian's treatise is of little interest to us; it contains practical instructions concerning baptism. His perception of the element of water, however, based upon the first few verses of Genesis, is as full of mythological elements as his understanding of baptism is full of Christian applications of Greco-Roman magical principles.[144]

Mircea Eliade said: "In all ancient mythologies, "the waters" symbolize: The universal sum of virtualities; they are *"fons et*

---

[144] Tertullian, *De Baptismo*, ET: *ANF* 3.669-679.

origo, " "spring and origin," the reservoir of all the possibilities of existence; they precede every form and support every creation ... Immersion in water signifies repression to the formal, re-incorporation into the undifferentiated mode of preexistence. Emersion repeats the cosmogonic act of formal manifestation; immersion is equivalent to a dissolution of forms ... In whatever religious complex we find them, the waters invariably retain their function; they disintegrate, abolish forms, "wash away sins"; they are at once purifying and regenerating. Their destiny is to precede the Creation and to reabsorb it ..." [145]

Consequently, waters were sometimes looked upon as the primordial androgynous substance, in which everything was mixed and undifferentiated. Creation came from water by a process of separations and divisions.[146]

Revelation 12, however, emphasizes the aspect of water which is represented by the image of the dragon, i.e., the destructive, inimical force, chaos, the primeval water that, according to Jewish mythology, is restrained in the *tehom* under the rock in Jerusalem, the floodwaters of Deucalion that were remembered in the temple at Hierapolis and in the Athenian *Anthesteria.* The intent of the author is to describe a cosmic drama, in which the opponent of the destructive forces is the woman clothed with the sun. In a proleptic way her heavenly marriage is consummated here in a *hieros gamos* that will eventually overcome all separations and reestablish the union of heaven and earth, of God and man. This

---

145 Mircea Eliade, *The Sacred and the Profane,* New York: Harcourt, Brace & World, 1958, pp. 130, 131.

146 See Dietrich, "Der Urmensch ...," p. 308; also Irenaeus, *Adv. Haer.* 1.30.1, *ANF* 1.354; J. Doresse, *The Secret Books of the Egyptian Gnostics,* New York: Viking, 1958, pp. 37, 66-67; R. M. Grant, *Gnosticism,* p. 53. Water has no gender. Some recent feminist writers pointed to the fact that, according to Charles Darwin's theory of evolution, life began in the sea, and they conclude that, therefore, the sea was feminine. "In the beginning ... was a very female sea." So begins a massive feminist book, the thrust of which is to show the primacy and superiority of the female gender. Monica Sjoo and Barbara Mar, *The Great Cosmic Mother,* San Francisco: Harper and Row, 1987, compare, among others, the water of the sea with the amniotic fluid of the womb, the lunar tidal rhythms with the menstrual cycle, and so forth, and then make this statement: "in the beginning ... there were no specialized sex organs; rather a generalized female existence reproduced itself within the female body of the sea" (*op. cit.,* p. 1). This, in many respects inadequately researched, book misses the very obvious point that one cannot say female without saying male at the same time. The words of Alfred Bertholet should be remembered: "Das Geschlecht gehört ursprünglich nicht zur Gottheit .... Am Anfang war die 'Kraft' oder 'Macht' die als solche geschlechtslos ist" (*Das Geschlecht der Gottheit.* Tübingen: J. C. B. Mohr, 1934, p. 22).

is the grand theme of Revelation and thus it is with good reason that chapter 12 has been called the center of the entire book.[147]

5. *Conclusions*

We have analyzed the "woman clothed with the sun" from four different viewpoints because Revelation 12 is, as W. K. C. Guthrie said of all living religions, "a stone of many facets, any one of which can be turned to face the light ... "[148] We exposed four different aspects of Revelation 12 to the light of pagan mythology in search of a better understanding of the text. It would be relatively easy to conclude from our investigations that Christianity is a syncretistic religion that arose as a result of the intermingling of many Jewish and pagan myths. Such a statement would not be original. Already at the end of the second century, Celsus, the great scholarly critic of Christianity, had stated that Christianity is "not a venerable or a new branch of instruction."[149] But Christianity is more than the sum total of many pagan myths and customs. We have seen in the foregoing pages that to all of these myths and beliefs Christianity added its own peculiar interpretation and viewpoint, thus creating something new out of what was old. The fact, therefore, that elements of contemporary myths and beliefs abound in Christianity, and particularly, for our concern, in Revelation 12, means only that Revelation 12 cannot be thoroughly understood unless it is accepted as an integral part of a historical process in which our religious ideas and images were formed.[150] What we read in Revelation 12 is not the free invention of its author, who worked with already existing material available to him in literature, poetry, art, mythology, tales and legends.[151] Therefore, on the basis of what we have seen

---

[147]   P. Prigent, *op. cit.* p. 1.

[148]   See Introduction, footnote 1.

[149]   *The True Word*, in Origen, *Against Celsus* 1.4, *ANF* 4.398.

[150]   " ... Vieles, was man als christlich in Anspruch nehmen möchte, nur zufällig in der ältesten Literatur nicht vertreten ist." Paul Wendland, *Die hellenistisch-römische Kultur in ihren Beziehungen zu Judentum und Christentum*, Tübingen: J. C. B. Mohr, 1907, p. 53.

[151]   The alternative must be, even for a fundamentalist Christian, frightening, since it would mean a "revelation" without points of connection in human history, and that would ultimately mean that the word, after all, did not "become flesh." It is no accident that as a theological school, *"Religionsgeschichte"* led directly to the rediscovery of *"Heilsgeschichte,"* a study of the history of salvation, as an activity of God in and with man in the world.

in this study, I should like to make the following proposals:

1. In Revelation 12, for the first time in Christian literature, mention is made of a goddess-like figure who resembles in many details the great fertility goddesses of paganism at that time. This means that the concept of a goddess was alive in Christianity and began to resurface at the end of the first century. It is not without significance that this happened in Revelation, for this book is a product of the eastern Mediterranean, close to the world of Asia Minor, which was the center of the worship of Cybele, the Great Mother. We will study this question in greater detail in our next chapter, but already we can see that the reemergence of the "Queen of Heaven" concept in Christianity was very probably due to pagan influences. The *Aition* is clearly pregnancy, motherhood, which is the foundation of all later Mariological investigations.

2. This drama is of cosmic proportions and involves fundamental issues of universal significance. We are presented with images of the beginning and the end, the separation of heaven and earth and of male and female, and their eventual reintegration and unification. The woman, therefore, represents here everything that Caelestis meant for the Carthagenians, the *Dea Syria* for the worshippers at Hierapolis, and the Great Mother of the Gods for Julian the Apostate: she is the female aspect of that great mystery which is called God. She is what pagans worshipped under various names and forms as the goddess, who reemerges here in all her glory as a component of Christian religious imagination as well.

3. When ancient Greeks, Romans, and other peoples anthropomorphized their gods and goddesses, they thought of them as real, personal beings who can have crowns on their heads and robes on their shoulders. They can also be pregnant and have children. Thus, it would be contrary to accepted contemporary usage to see in the figure of the woman something other than a woman, such as the allegory of another concept like the synagogue or the church. Regardless of how strong the Old Testament background of Revelation is, this woman is in the distinguished company of other heavenly queens; her position, her robe, her jewelry, her whole appearance identifies her as such. She should be interpreted as the Queen of Heaven of Christianity, Mary, who is soon to be called "Mother of God."

4. Nor can the image of the woman in Revelation 12 be connected with the numerous references to symbolic women in the Old Testament, even though the author used the Old Testament extensively. The crucial fact is that this message was first addressed to Christians, in particular those Christians who lived in an area of Asia Minor that was the center of the cult of *Magna Mater* and where other "Queens of Heaven" such as Isis were also widely venerated. When somebody in Asia Minor at the end of the first century A.D. was told that a woman clothed with the sun appeared in heaven, with a crown of stars on her head and the moon under her feet, it is unlikely that he or she would immediately think of the "daughter of Zion" in the Old Testament. Minimizing the pagan environment of the author and of the intended readership would mean lifting the vision out of its social and religious context; that is why it is not sufficient to interpret the text on the basis of the Old Testament only. Even if it is argued that the Old Testament itself absorbed many non-Jewish ideas and thus pagan elements in Revelation 12 may have come to the author *via* the Old Testament, the fact remains that the author lived in a pagan world. We will see in our investigations of the cult of Cybele and of the Montanist movement how much the world of Revelation was a part of the spiritual and intellectual world of Asia Minor and how deeply immersed in that culture the author of Revelation 12 must have been. Thus, while drawing on Old Testament elements in the interpretation of Revelation 12 is certainly valid, recognition of the pagan components in the image of the "woman" is not only legitimate but essential.

Our objective, as stated at the beginning of this chapter, has been to investigate whether the woman who appeared to the author of Revelation12 was a reflection of the pagan "Queen of Heaven," and if so, to what extent. Our answer is that she is the Queen of Heaven adopted into Christianity.

B. EARLY CHRISTIAN INTERPRETATIONS OF THE WOMAN CLOTHED WITH THE SUN

For the sake of perspective, let us now review briefly how the earliest Christian interpreters of Revelation 12 saw the figure of the woman.[152]

---

[152] The list is not complete, and those who desire more information

1. *The Greek Fathers*

Hippolytus (d. 235), the bishop of Rome, was the first Christian author to deal with this question in his *Treatise on Christ and Antichrist*, Chapter 61.[153] He interpreted the woman as a figure of the church which possesses the Word of God whose brightness is above the sun. The moon under her feet means that she is adorned with heavenly glory. The crown of twelve stars refers to the twelve apostles. The statement that the woman cries in travail of birth means that the church always brings forth the Word, which is persecuted by the world. The male child born of the woman refers to Christ, who is always being brought forth by the church. Christ is heavenly and earthly; this is the meaning of the words that the child was "caught up" to heaven. The two wings of the eagle given to the woman are the faith of Jesus Christ.

Origen (d. 253 or 254) wrote a commentary on Revelation. This was found and published in 1911.[154] Unfortunately, this commentary is incomplete. From Revelation 12, only verses 9 and 13 are briefly mentioned, then again in verse 17. After this the commentary of Origen abruptly ends and what follows is the long section from Irenaeus' *Adversus Haereses*.

The martyr bishop of Tyre in Phoenicia, Methodius (d. 312), dealt with this problem in his book *Symposium*.[155] The woman is the church, he wrote, and the child born of her means the Christians who are being brought forth in baptism. The moon refers to baptism, and thus, the woman standing on the moon represents the church which stands upon the faith of the Christians.

---

may wish to consult the folloiwng works. Pierre Prigent, *Apocalypse 12. Histoire De L'Exegese*, Tübingen: J. C. B. Mohr, 1959. (Beitrage zur Geschichte der Biblischen Exegese, #2); Bernard T. LeFrois, *The Woman Clothed With the Sun (Ap. 12): Individual or Collective?*, Rome: Orbis Catholicus, 1954; D. Unger, "Did St. John See the Virgin Mary in Glory? (Apoc. 12.1)," *Catholic Biblical Quarterly* 11 (1949): 248-262, 392-405; 12 (1950): 74-83, 155-161, 292-300, 405-415.

[153] *GCS* 1 (*Hippolytus Werke*, ed. by H. Achelis, Leipzig: J. C. Hinrich's, 1897- 1929), Zwiter Halbband, p. 41. ET: *ANF* 5.217. According to S. Jerome, *De Viris Illustribus* 61 (*MPL* 23, 671), Hippolytus also wrote a complete commentary on Revelation which is lost. Certain parts of it are thought to be found in some Arabic fragments; see Achelis, *op. cit.*, pp. 321 ff.

[154] Constantin Diobouniotis and Adolf Harnack, *Der Scholien-Kommentar des Origenes zur Apokalypse Johannis* (Texte und Untersuchungen zur Geschichte der Christlichen Literatur, vol. 38.3), Leipzig: J. C. Hinrich's, 1911.

[155] 8.4 ff, *GCS* (by G. Bonwetsch). ET: *The Banquet of the Ten Virgins, ANF*, 6.335-336.

Methodius rejected the interpretation of the "male child" as Christ, because S. John spoke in the book of Revelation about present and future things, but the incarnation took place long before Revelation was written. Neither was Jesus "caught up" to heaven after his birth, but he stayed on to subdue the dragon which is the devil. The church flees into the wilderness, a place unproductive of evils, the place of Virtue. She flies on the heavenly wings of virginity, called the "wings of the great eagle." Christians should imitate the church in the wilderness overcoming the Devil.

Epiphanius of Salamis (d. 403) referred to Revelation 12.4 in his discussion of the sect of the Antidikomarionites.[156] He wrote that this passage may have been fulfilled in Mary, but he was not certain that his interpretation was correct. Nevertheless, Epiphanius was probably the first author to identify the "woman clothed with the sun" with Mary.

The first real commentary on the book of Revelation written in the Eastern Church comes from an otherwise unknown author, Oecumenius.[157] Writing in the first half of the sixth century, he was also the first Greek father to propose a definitely Mariological exegesis of this chapter. For him it was not a future-apocalyptical but a retrospective-historical vision. The woman is Mary, and she is pregnant with Christ, the sun. That is the reason why the Greek text says γυνή περιβεβλημένη τὸν ἥλιον and not τῷ ἡλίῳ περιβεβλῆσθαι τὴν γυναῖκα. In reference to verse 2 he cited Isaiah 66:7 ("Before she was in labor she gave birth, before her pain came upon her she was delivered of a son") and asserted that Mary escaped the pains of labor. Why, then, does verse 2 say that she was in pain and cried? By this we must understand the sorrow and grief which must have overwhelmed Mary, thinking that Joseph suspected her of adultery. When Moses was in distress God asked him, "Why do you *cry* to me?" (Ex. 14:15); similarly,

---

[156] *Panarion* 78.11, *Kata Antidikomarianiton*, GCS 37.452-475 (ed. by Karl Holl, Leipzig: J. C. Hinrich'sche Buchhandlung, 1933). See p. 170 note 1 for information on an English translation. The chapter is available in German in the *Bibliothek der Kirchenväter*, vol. 38, pp. 233-26 3 (ed. by J. Hormann, *Der Heiligen Epiphanius von Salamis ... Ausgewählte Schriften*, Kampten and München: Kösel Verlag, 1919).

[157] The complete text was found at the end of the last century and published later by H. C. Hoskier, *The Complete Commentary of Oecumenius on the Apocalypse*. Ann Arbor: University of Michigan Press, 1928.

Revelation calls the sorrow of Mary *"cry."* In like manner, Oecumenius referred verse 4 to the persecution by Herod and verse 6 to the flight into Egypt; the two wings he explained as the wings of the angel who warned Joseph to flee, and verse 15, allegorically with reference to Jon. 2.5 ("The waters closed in over me").

The archbishop of Caesarea in Cappadocia, Andreas (563-613) wrote his *Commentary* [158] in the second half of the sixth century. It is based on Hippolytus, but in the exegesis of Chapter 12 he followed Methodius. He knew that some interpreted the woman as the Virgin Mary, but he referred to Methodius and quoted his work: the woman is the church, the moon refers to baptism, the church is in travail until Christ be born in the believers. The persecution is upon the church through which Christ Himself is persecuted; he asked Saul on the road to Damascus, "Why do you persecute *me?"* when Saul actually was persecuting the church.

2. *The Latin Fathers*

The first to be mentioned here is Victorinus (d. 304), bishop of Poetovio, which today is in Yugoslavia (formerly Pettau, Steiermark in Austria). Victorinus died as a martyr during the great persecution of emperor Diocletian, and among others, he is remembered as the first Christian exegete to write in Latin. The original text of his commentary on the book of Revelation was found in 1916; until then it was known only in the form of an edition by S. Jerome.[159] For Victorinus also, the woman represented the church which is clothed with the sun, i.e., the hope of resurrection. The moon refers to the death of the saints. "Caught up" to heaven is reference to the Ascension of Jesus; the male child is apparently thought of as Jesus. The eagle's wings were given to the church; these are the prophet Elijah and the "prophet who will be with him." The flight of the church did not yet take place.

The next to advocate an allegorical interpretation of Revelation 12 was Tyconius, a Donatist Christian. His book, written around 380, is lost, but it can be reconstructed from works of others who used his book and wrote their commentaries on the basis of his ideas. Such authors are Primasius; Cassidorus, whose works we

---

[158]   *Commentarius in Apocalypsis, MPG* 106.319 ff.

[159]   *CSEL* 49.104 ff. ET: *Commentary on the Apocalypse of the Blessed John, ANF* 7.355 ff.

will discuss later; and during the Middle Ages, Beda and Beatus. According to a manuscript of his *Commentary* [160] published in 1897, he also interpreted the woman as the church. S. Jerome (d. 419) edited the Commentary of Victorinus,[161] in which, as we have discussed, the woman is understood as a figure of the church. S. Augustine (d. 430) gave an exposition of Revelation 20 and 21 in *De Civitate Dei* 20, 7-17, but not of Chapter 12. This question is touched on by him very briefly in *Enar. in Ps.* 142 where he identifies the woman as the *"Civitas Dei."* [162]

Among the works of S. Augustine were published the sermons *De Symbolo ad Catechumenos II-IV.* These are now generally attributed to Quodvultdeus (d. 455), Augustine's disciple.[163] He identified the woman as Mary, but in the sense that she represented "the figure of the holy church."[164]

Caesarius of Arles (d. 542) wrote in the spirit of authors before Tyconius: the woman is the church, the twelve stars in her crown the twelve apostles. The woman bore a male child, i. e., Christ, and therefore the body of Christ, the church, always bears the members of Christ. The child is called a male because it conquers the devil. The wilderness is the world where the church suffers *omnen virtutem Satanae.*[165]

The commentary of Apringius, bishop of Beja in Portugal, written around 551, is incomplete; it consists of Chapters 1-5.7 and 18.6 to the end. Between these sections is S. Jerome's edition of Victorinus. Otherwise Apringius follows Tyconius in his exegesis.[166]

---

[160]   Tyconii Afri Fragmenta. Commentarii in Apocalypsim. Spicilegium Casiense. III. 1. Montecassino, 1897, pp. 261-331: *MPL Supplementum* 1, 621-652. See also Francesco Lo Bue, *The Turin Fragments of Tyconius' Commentary on Revelation,* Cambridge: University Press, 1963, p. 178: *"In muliere ecclesiam designat* ..., " and pp . 180 -181: *"Draco ... id est diabolus."*

[161]   *CSEL* 49.104 ff. presents both the edition of Victorinus and the recensions of S. Jerome.

[162]   *MPL* 37 .1846.

[163]   *MPL* 40 . 637-668.

[164]   *MPL* 40.667. This is clear from his statement: *Non habebit Deum patrem, qui ecclesiam noluerit habere matrem.* (He who will not have the church as mother will not have God as father.) *MPL* 40.668. See, however, Le Frois, op. cit., p. 51, and Hilda Graef, *Mary. A History of Doctrine and Devotion,* New York: Sheed and Ward, 1963, vol. 1, p. 132, for a different opinion.

[165]   Caesarius Commentary is found among the works of S. Augustine under the title *Expositio in Apocalypsin B. Ioannis.* The exegesis of Ch. 12 starts with *Homilia IX. (MPL* 35.2433 ff.)

[166]   The edition by P. A. C. Vega, *Apringii Pacensis Episcopi Tractatus in Apocalypsin,* Escurial, 1940, has an excerpt from Victorinus on the place of Ch.12.

Primasius (d. after 554), bishop of Hadrumetum in North Africa, was also greatly influenced by Tyconius, and in the exegesis of Chapter 12 he followed the earlier way:[167] the woman is the church, the twelve stars the twelve apostles. He likens her cry of travail because she bears the Christians to that of S. Paul in Galatians 4.19. The dragon, which is the devil, tries to destroy what the woman has borne, as the devil tries to extinguish in us that *novum hominem qui secundum Deum creatus est* (the new man which is created after God). Justly is the child which is born by the woman called a "male" because Christ is the head of the church and He is born in the Christians who are members of His body, and again, as S. Paul says in Galatians 3.27, those who are baptized into Christ have put on Christ. The child was taken up to God as Christ ascended to heaven (Phil. 3.20). The woman fled into the wilderness: the church lives in this world, suffering as the Jews did in the wilderness, yet always being under the care of God.

Cassiodorus (d. 538), "the savior of ancient literature,"[168] comments only on verse 7 in Chapter 12, stating that in this text the mother of Christ is remembered: *Fit iterum commemoratio matris et Domino Christi ...* [169] (It is fitting to remember the mother and Christ the Lord.)

We stop here because our investigation of the "Queen of Heaven" does not extend into the Middle Ages. We have seen, however, that the Mariological interpretation of Revelation 12 is not very old in the Christian Church. Although Epiphanius of Salamis (d. 403) made a vague reference to Mary in connection with Chapter 12, the first author who definitely identified the woman as Mary was Oecumenius in the sixth century. The next to do so will be medieval scholars, Ambrose Autpert (eighth century) and Alcuin (d. 804). Most others see in the figure of the woman the church. But since the early church also saw Mary as the figure of the church, indirectly there appears to be a certain connection between Mary and the "woman." This idea surfaced, for example, in the exegesis of Quodvultdeus (d. 455). Neverthe-

---

167 *Commentarius Super Apocalypsim B. Ioannis Liber III, MPL* 68.872 ff. The book was written around 550.

168 Because in the monastery Vivarium, which he founded, his monks copied ancient manuscripts.

169 *Complexiones in Epistolas et Acta Apostolorum et Apocalypsin, MPL* 70.1411.

less, the fact remains that almost four hundred years passed before the "woman clothed with the sun" was identified with Mary. In view of the fathers' otherwise high opinions of Mary, this is hard to understand. But there is an explanation: up to about 400 A.D. paganism and Christianity were still competitors and in this struggle Christianity could not afford to adopt pagan terminology. No matter how different the Christian interpretations of the "Queen of Heaven" may have been, the pagan connotations of the title were too strong and the woman of Revelation 12 could not be called Mary; she was called the church, and the church was associated with Mary. With the victory of Christianity over paganism all restraint on this aspect of doctrinal development was overcome, and in 431 the Council of Ephesus officially formulated and approved the use of the word *theotokos* ("God bearer") as an appellative of the mother of Jesus Christ. Marian interpretations of the "woman" will not lag much behind and will fully flourish in the Middle Ages and in our own day.

CHAPTER IV

THE GREAT MOTHER AND MONTANISM

A. THE HISTORY AND THEOLOGY OF MONTANISM

Most scholars agree that the Montanist movement[1] started around 156-7 when Montanus began to prophesy.[2] According to Eusebius,

[1] All studies of Montanism begin with the patristic sources which were collected by D. Nathanael Bonwetch, *Texte zur Geschichte des Montanismus.* Bonn: A. Marcus und E. Weber's Verlag, 1914. (Kleine Texte, #129.) G. Nathanael Bonwetch, *Geschichte des Montanismus.* Erlangen: Andreas Deichert, 1881. Other useful literature: Kurt Aland, *Kirchengeschichtliche Entwürfe.* Gütersloh: Gütersloher Verlagshaus, 1960. In this volume two major articles of interest: "Bemerkungen zum Montanismus und zur frühchistlichen Eschatologie." pg. 105-148, and "Augustin und der Montanismus." pg. 149-164; Wilhelm Schepelern, *Der Montanismus und die Phrygischen Kulte.* Tübingen: J. C. B. Mohr, 1929; on this important research William B. Goree, Jr. based his *The Cultural Bases of Montanism.* Ph.D. Thesis, Baylor University, 1980. Still very useful are P. de Labriolle, *Les Sources de L'Histoire du Montanisme.* Fribourg, Switzerland: Universite de Fribourg 1913, P. De Labriolle, *La Crise Montanist,* Paris: E. Leroux 1913; Waldemar Belck, *Geschichte des Montanismus.* Leipzig: Dörffling und Franke, 1883. Furthermore, K. Aland, "Montanus" and "Montanism." *The Encyclopedia of Religion.* 10.81-83; Douglass Powell, "Tertullianists and Cataphrygians." *Vigiliae Christianae* 29 (1975) 33-54; Heinrich Kraft, "Die altkirchliche Prophetie und die Entstehung des Montanismus." *Theologische Zeitschrift* 11 (1955) 249-271; Stephen Gero, "Montanus and Montanism according to a Medieval Syriac Source." *Journal of Theological Studies.* N.S. 28 (1977) 520-524; J. Messingberd Ford, "Was Montanism a Jewish Christian Heresy?" *Journal of Ecclesiastical History.* 17 (1966) 145-158; Timothy D. Barnes, "The Chronology of Montanism." *Journal of Theological Studies* N. S. 20 (1970). Gerhard Ficker, "Wiederlegung eines Montanisten." *Zeitschrift für Kirchengeschichte* 26 (1905) 447-463; Adolf Jülicher, "Ein Gallisches Bischofsschreiben des 6. Jahrhunderts als Zeuge fur die Verfassung der Montanistenkirche," *Zeitschrift für Kirchengeschichte* 16 (1896) 664-671; W. M. Calder, "Philadelphia and Montanism." *Bulletin of the John Rylands Library* 7 (1922-23) 309-354. Useful summaries in W. H. C. Frend, *Martyrdom and Persecution in the Early Church.* New York: University Press, 1967 pp. 217-222; W. H. C. Frend, *Saints and Sinners in the Early Church.* London: Darton, Longman and Todd 1985, pp. 69-72; W. H. C. Frend, *The Rise of Christianity.* Philadelphia. Fortress, 1984, pp. 253-257; Carl Andresen, *Die Kirchen der Alten Christenheit.* Stuttgart: Kohlhammer, 1971, pp. 110-115; R. Seeberg, *Lehrbuch der Dogmengeschichte.* Graz: Akademische Druck und Verlagsanstalt, 1953. Band 1, pp. 321-329; A. Harnack, *History of Dogma.* New York: Dover, 1961 (reprint of the 1900 edition), vol. 2, pp. 95-108.

[2] We arrive at this date by following Epiphanius, however, Eusebius

Montanus was a "recent convert."³ Jerome thought he was formerly a priest of Cybele who had emasculated himself.⁴ According to Didymus of Alexandria, Montanus was the priest of an idol,⁵ and yet another source makes him a priest of Apollo.⁶ Clearly there is no reliable information about Montanus' previous life, but we do know that at one time "he fell into frenzy and convulsions," became ecstatic, spoke in a strange way, and uttered prophecies that were contrary to accepted traditions in the church.⁷ Soon female associates appeared beside him; Priscilla and Maximilla claimed to have seen visions and also uttered prophecies. As is customary with eschatological and charismatic movements, many people responded with faith in the "new prophecy," which became the name of the movement. Individual Christians and eventually whole congregations followed Montanus. In time, however, the church turned against the "new prophecy" and the movement was branded a heresy. What happened to Montanus is uncertain because later references to him came from hostile sources, one of which asserted that he committed suicide.⁸ After his death the prophetesses continued his work, but, as in most eschatological movements, when the prophecies failed to materialize, the movement settled down into a more or less routine church life. The best known convert to Montanism was the great Tertullian of Carthage, many of whose books reflect the theology and ethics of later Montanism.

The "new prophecy" was a vigorous movement. Not only were Montanist preachers powerful speakers but they had fertile minds and produced many books. According to Hippolytus they produced an "infinite number of books,"⁹ none of which has survived, however; only a few sentences from them can be recon-

---

suggests a date around 172; for the controversy on dating see Powell, *op. cit.* and D. Barnes, *op.cit.*, among others.

³ *H. E.* 5.16.7.

⁴ *Epistola* 41.4: *"abscisum et semivirum habuisse."* — "mutilated and emasculated," *NPNF*, Series 2, vol. 6, 55-56.

⁵ *De Trinitate* 3.41.3; *MPG* 39, 449.

⁶ See the "Dialogue," in G. Ficker, *op.cit.* p. 445: καὶ ὁ Μοντανὸς ὁ τοῦ Ἀπόλλωνος ἱερεὺς ἀληθή.

⁷ *H.E.* 5.16.7; ET: *LCL* Kirsopp Lake, editor. London: Heinemann, 1949, vol. 1, 477-475.

⁸ Eusebius, *H.E.* 5.16.13.

⁹ *Refutation* 8.12, *ANF* 5.123, see also Epiphanius, *Haer.* 48.12.

structed.[10] A few of the original prophetic utterances of Montanus, Maximilla, and Priscilla are quoted by Eusebius and Epiphanius, but nothing in them shows any doctrinal deviation from the standards of the rest of the church; in matters concerning the rules of faith (*regula fidei*) the early Montanists were quite orthodox. They differed in practical matters and in their emphasis of certain ethical values, all of which would have been considered quite acceptable to every Christian a generation or two earlier. The Montanists believed in prophecy as a gift of the Holy Spirit; they accepted and practiced glossolalia and believed that a Christian must live up to the highest moral standards. These things were integral parts of early Christian life as it is reflected in the writings of the New Testament and earliest Christian literature. But the church of the middle of the second century was no longer the charismatic church of the apostles, and things that had been looked upon as signs of the activity of the Spirit a hundred years before had come to be viewed as strange and eccentric.

An eschatological movement, the Montanists claimed that through a revelation they were warned that the new Jerusalem would soon descend from heaven.[11] Even the place where this was to happen was revealed to them: the village of Pepuza, and it was here that the faithful were to gather to await for the great event.[12] Montanus even called Pepuza "Jerusalem" and wanted to hold his church meetings there because it was the holy place. So strong was this faith in the immediate coming of God's kingdom that even Tertullian (died c. 220), who was a second generation Montanist, believed in it, although without any reference to the village of Pepuza. It was Tertullian who preserved for us a story, perhaps stemming from the Parthian campaign (197-199) of Emperor Septimius Severus (193-211). According to Tertullian's account, a city was seen in the sky suspended from heaven. This sight could be viewed by everyone, even pagans confessed to having seen it, and it appeared every morning for forty days. For Tertullian this vision was the fulfillment of a Montanist prophecy "which is a part of our belief" that there will be a picture of the

---

[10] W. M. Calder, *op.cit.* p. 322.

[11] See Rev. 21.2: "and I saw the holy city, new Jerusalem, coming down out of heaven from God..."

[12] Epiphanius, *Haer.* 49.1.2-3; Eusebius, *H.E.* 5.18.2; 5.18.13.

heavenly city as a manifestation of the truth of the prophecy.[13]
The vision appeared in Judea, not in Pepuza, and Tertullian did
not investigate whether it was a mirage, an optical illusion often
experienced by visitors in hot sand deserts.

In this respect, the Montanists returned to an early Christian
concept of eschatology, i.e. a very realistic eschatology which
found expression in statements such as Matthew 24.24, "... this
generation will not pass away till all these things take place," and
the early letters of Paul, particularly 1. Thessalonians.[14] The very
realistic view of the "heavenly Jerusalem" in Montanism also
reminds us of a similar view held by Papias, a pupil of bishop
Polycarp, who may have known the apostle John.[15] He believed
that the kingdom of Christ "will be set up in material form on this
earth,"[16] and that in those days each vine will have ten thousand
branches, each branch ten thousand twigs, each twig ten thousand shoots, each shoot ten thousand clusters and each cluster ten
thousand grapes and each grape will produce twenty five metretes
of wine. It will be similar with grain production.[17] This vision of
Papias brings to mind the experience of the worshippers of Dionysus, who, as we have seen above, thought of the world as flowing
with milk, wine and nectar. Now Papias was also a Phrygian and
it is difficult not to sense a certain spiritual affinity between his
material vision of Paradise and the experience of the Bacchantes.
But Eusebius says that Papias must have gotten these ideas from a
"perverse reading" of the Bible, and besides, "he was a man of
very little intelligence."[18] Not so Eusebius, and generally the
church after the post- apostolic period; they no longer nurtured
such material visions of the new Jerusalem. As a matter of fact,
they kept delaying the time of Christ's coming farther and farther
into the future until they no longer had any vision of it at all;
because it was now so far away from them, it did not cause any

---

[13] *Adv. Marc.* 3.24; ET : *ANF* 3,342.
[14] See e.g. Paul's strong convictions that he and many others will still be
alive when the Jesus returns, l.Thess. 4.15.
[15] Eusebius, *H.E.* 3.39.1-17, *op.cit.* pp. 291-299.
[16] *Op.cit.* p. 295.
[17] This story from Papias is quoted in *Irenaeus Adv. Haer.* 5.33.3-4; ET.:
ANF 1.562-563. Irenaeus, Papias and Tertullian were millenialists; i.e. they
believed that prior to the final consummation there will be a thousand year
long rule of Christ on earth.
[18] *H.E.* 3.39.12, *op.cit.* p. 297.

change in their everyday lives. For them it was no longer realistic to talk about the new Jerusalem except in homilies and in hypothetical terms, but for the Montanists eschatology was something immediate and the effect of this belief was a different ethic.

Montanist prophecy was, consequently, directed toward everyday Christian behavior. No new "revelations" concerning the way of salvation were received, as in many Gnostic movements. That the utterances of the three original founders of the movement, Montanus, Priscilla, and Maximilla, were real prophecies, spoken under inspiration, not even the critics denied. What they questioned, however, was whether this inspiration was from the Holy Spirit of God. Their answer was that Montanist prophecies were uttered under the possession of demons; that demons existed, no one doubted. Montanus, we read in Eusebius "became obsessed, and suddenly fell into frenzy and convulsions."[19] He was not the only one of his age subject to such phenomena. One of his contemporaries, who lived not very far from him, Alexander of Abonuteichus,[20] behaved in a similar manner: in religious frenzy, he tossed his long locks and, foaming at the mouth (he produced foam by chewing soapwart plant, Lucian asserts), he screamed at the top of his lungs a volley of unintelligible words; he ran about chanting and praying so that eventually a great number of people believed that he was the chosen prophet of the healing god Asklepios. He then spoke a number of oracles which he developed into a prosperous business. As in the case of Montanus, Alexander's oracles were mostly bits of pious advice on the everyday vicissitudes of life. Lucian indicated in one of his essays that several such people were healed by an exorcist in Palestine. The persons obsessed by the demon, he says, "fall down in the light of the moon and roll their eyes and fill their mouths with foam." For a fee, they were restored to health by an exorcist. The exorcist could talk to the demons who answered him in the

---

[19] H.E. 5.16.7, op.cit. p. 475.

[20] Abonuteichus, or Ionopolis was in Pontus on the northern region of Asia Minor, close to Sinope. Pepuza was in western Asia Minor, in Phrygia. The air distance between the two cities is ca. 300 miles. See F. van der Meer, *Atlas of the Early Christian World.* New York: Nelson, 1958, p. 7. It seems that the lives of Montanus and Alexander overlapped. The story of Alexander is in Lucian of Samosata, (115-200 A.D.) *Alexander the False Prophet LCL.* A.M. Harmon, editor. London: Heinemann, 1961, vol. 4. For a review and evaluation, see Stephen Benko, *Pagan Rome... op.cit.* pp. 103-139.

language of the country from which they came. At the command of the exorcist, they left the body of the one possessed. Lucian says that he himself saw one of these demons coming out "black and smokey in color."[21] The eloquent and scholarly critic, Celsus, who wrote around 180 A.D. and thus was a contemporary of both Montanus and Alexander, confirmed that prophecy of this sort indeed was widely practiced. He wrote: "There are many, who, although of no name, with the greatest facility and on the slightest occasion, whether within or without temples, assume the motions and gestures of inspired persons; while others do it in cities or among armies, for the purpose of attracting attention and exciting surprise. These are accustomed to say, each for himself, 'I am God; I am the Son of God; or, I am the Divine Spirit; I have come because the world is perishing ... And those who know not the punishments which await them will repent and grieve in vain; while those who are faithful to me I will preserve eternally ... ' To these promises are added strange, fanatical, and quite unintelligible words, of which no rational person can find the meaning; they are so dark, as to have no meaning at all; but they give occasion to every fool or impostor to apply them to suit his own purposes." Celsus also claimed to have interviewed such prophets who, when pressed by him, admitted that their incoherent words meant nothing.[22] The testimony of Lucian may be criticized as that of a satirist who emphasized things he disliked. But Celsus was a scholar and his statements must be taken with the same scholarly respect with which he wrote them. Montanus' own prophecies seem to confirm that he considered himself the mouthpiece of the Paraclete,[23] although he did not necessarily

---

[21] *Philopseudes - The Lover of Lies.* 16. *LCL,* A. M. Harmon editor, *op.cit.* vol. 3.345. Compare this story with the exorcism of the Gadarene demoniac by Jesus in Mark 5.1-19.

[22] *The True Word,* in Origen, *Against Celsus* 7.9 and 11; *ANF* 4.614-615. See also R. Joseph Hoffmann, *Celsus on the True Doctrine.* New York and Oxford: Oxford U . Press, 1987, pp. 106-107.

[23] Eusebius, *H.E.* 5.14.11 "Of these (i.e. the enemies of the church) some like poisonous reptiles crawled over Asia and Phrygia, and boasted that Montanus was the Paraclete and that the women of the sect, Priscilla and Maximilla, were the prophetesses of Montanus." *op.cit.* p. 471; Epiphanius, *Panarion* 48.11: Montanus said "It is I, The Lord God the Almighty who am present in man." Again, Montanus said: "I am neither an angel nor an envoy, but I, the Lord, God the Father, have come." Bonwetsch, *Texte, op.cit.* p. 19. Hippolytus, *Refutation* 8.12: "And they assert that into (Priscilla, Maximilla and Montanus) the Paraclete Spirit had departed." *ANF* 5.123;

identify himself with God or with Jesus Christ. Schepelern has convincingly argued that such use of the first person singular meant the god who spoke in the medium, not the medium himself.[24] This is the case with Apollo, who was originally a god of Asia Minor. His mouthpiece, the Pythia in Delphi, always spoke in the first person when she uttered her oracles and it was obvious to all that these were Apollo's words and not those of the Pythia. The Pythia spoke when she was "*entheos*" "filled with God." We have a vivid description of this condition by Virgil who tells us how Aeneas went to inquire of the Sybil at Cumae: when he arrived at the cave the prophetess was "raging fiercely," trying to "shake the mighty goddess from her breast."[25] Similarly, Ovid says that the Sibyl is inspired by "the presence of the god within her," which means that she is "*entheos,*" "*plena deo,*" "filled with god."[26] We also learn from Ovid that the Sybil was a virgin who resisted the advances of Phoebus (Apollo) when she was still an innocent young girl, which recalls the insistence of the Montanists that their prophetesses lived in a celibate state[27] and that Priscilla was a virgin. According to Epiphanius,[28] in Montanist services of worship virgins displayed a certain "enthusiasm," that is, they showed signs of being *entheos*, "filled with God", the condition of prophetic madness well known from ancient literature.[29]

---

according to Didymus, *De trinitate* 3.41 Montanus said: "I am the Father, and the Son and the Paraclete." Bonwetsch, *Texte*, p. 22. The Parclete is, of course, the "counselor" or "advocate" of John 14.16; 15.26; 16.7, see W. F. Arndt and F. W. Gingrich, *A Greek-English Lexicon of the New Testament*. Cambridge: University Press, 1957, pp. 623-624.

[24] *Op. cit.* pp. 145-159.

[25] *Aeneid* 6.77; ET: J.W. Mackail, *Virgil's Works*. New York: Modern Library, 1950, p. 106.

[26] Mary M. Innes, *The Metamorphoses of Ovid* 14.101-137. New York: Penguin, 1982, p. 314. See also E. Norden, "Vergilstudien." *Hermes* 28 (1893) 501-521 and compare R. G. Austin, *P. Vergili Maronis Aeneidos Liber Sixtus With a Commentary*. Oxford: Clarendon Press, 1977, p. 60: "The phrase *plena deo ...* occurs nowhere in Virgil. Obviously it would fit the Sibyl either in this context ... or in that of 77f. It is generally taken to be a remnant of an early draft ..." Austin quotes examples of similar phrases from Ovid, Lucian and other authors. The relevant line from the *Aeneid* in Latin are as follows. 6.50: "*adflata est numine quando iam propiore dei.*" 6.78: "*Bacchatur uates, magnum si pectore possit excussisse deum.*" See Austin, *op.cit. ad.loc.*

[27] Eusebius, *H.E.* 5.18.2.

[28] See below, p. 149.

[29] The problem has been researched by many scholars, for an excellent summary see E. R. Dodds, *The Greeks and the Irrational.* Berkeley, California: U.C. Press, 1957, chapter III: "The Blessing of Madness."

The Montanist prophets and other "ecstatics" mentioned by ancient authors seem to belong to the same group of people, those who spoke under the influence of a superior spiritual power whose voice their sayings were believed to be. This manner of speaking starts out as a coherent message, but as the frenzy grows it develops into an incoherent, ecstatic gibberish. By the second century this was a fairly common phenomenon. In the time of the New Testament it was called *glossolalia*, speaking in tongues, and may have originated with the pentecostal experience of the apostles, who under the influence of the Holy Spirit "spoke in other tongues" and gave the impression to others that they were drunk."[30] Paul is our witness that such *glossolalia* appeared to outsiders as madness[31] and indeed, if we draw upon some examples from gnostic practices we can understand why. Here are two sentences quoted by Irenaeus: *"Basema Chamosse Baoenaora Mistadia Ruada Kousta Babaphor Kalachthei." – "Messia Uphareg Namenpsoemam Chaldoeaur Mosomedoea Acphranoe Psaua Jesus Nazaria."* [32] Another from a gnostic gospel: *"Aeeou iao aoi oia psinother thernops nopsiter zagoure pagoure netmomaoth nepsiomaoth marachachtha thobarrabau tharnachachan zorokothora ieou sabaoth."*[33] Lucian quotes similar gibberish concerning Alexander.[34] The frenzied speech of the Montanists must have been similar to that practiced by other emotionally supercharged people in Asia Minor and the surrounding areas, perhaps similar also to some Pentecostal charismatic speaking of modern times.

The purpose of such behavior is to convey to the group messages from God. We have already seen that the Montanist prophecy consisted of counsels concerning practical, not theological, matters. Apart from the promise of the "new Jerusalem" and its speedy coming[35] the Montanist prophecies appear to have been didactic and homiletic. "Do not listen to me, but listen to

---

[30] Acts 2.4 and 13.
[31] 1 Cor. 14.23 "μαίνεσθε"; all three chapters — 12, 13, 14 — are quite instructive in this matter.
[32] *Adv. Haer* 1.21.23; *ANF* 1.346.
[33] Hennecke-Schneemelcher, *op.cit.* vol. 1, p. 258. Many more examples could be found in *The Greek Magical Papyri in Translation*, H. D. Betz, editor.Chicago: Univ. of Chicago Press, 1986.
[34] See Stephen Benko, *Pagan Rome*, p. 111.
[35] Maximilla said that after her there would be no more prophets but that the end would come. Epiphanius, *Panarion* 48.2; Bonwetsch, *Texte*, p. 16.

Christ!" said Maximilla.[36] Tertullian quoted a "counsel of the Spirit": being defamed by the public is for the believer's own good "for he who is not exposed to dishonor among men is sure to be so before the Lord ... Seek not to die on bridal beds nor in miscarriages, nor in soft fevers, but to die in the martyr's death, that he may be glorified who has suffered for you."[37] In the Montanism represented by Tertullian such practical issues dominate, for, Tertullian said, "the Paraclete's administrative office is the direction of discipline, the revelation of Scriptures, the reformation of the intellect and the advancement toward the better things."[38] The rule of faith needs no improvement and no change, but righteousness develops in stages: first, a rudimentary stage, then, the Law, the prophets, and the gospel. And now finally "through the Paraclete it is settling into maturity. The Paraclete will be after Christ, the only one to be called and revered as Master; for He speaks not from Himself, but what is commanded by Christ."[39] And what does the Paraclete command? – that virgins be veiled, that fasts be observed, that none should marry a second time, that martyrdom not be avoided, and similar matters that do not affect the rule of faith. [40]

The morality of the Montanists was influenced by these "prophecies" and by their acute sense of the impending descent of the heavenly Jerusalem. So it was with Christians generally in apostolic times, but as their eschatological hopes faded so their moral outlook changed. Faith in the unique cleansing power of baptism which should have been effective until the second coming of Jesus was slowly abandoned, and the church developed a penitential system to accommodate repentant sinners. By the time of Tertullian even adultery and fornication were forgiven,[41]

---

[36] Epiphanius, *op.cit.* 48.8.

[37] *De fuga in persecutione* 9; Bonwetsch, *Texte* p. 31; *ANF* 4.121; compare with *De anima* 55; "If you lay down your life for God, as the Paraclete counsels, it is not in gentle fevers and on soft beds, but in the sharp pains of martyrdom." *ANF* 3.231.

[38] Hebrews 11.40; 12.24.

[39] *De virginibus velandis* 1. *ANF* 4.27-28.

[40] Tertullian's treatises dealing with these matters are *De virginibus velandis, De monogamia, De jejunio, De pudicitia, De fuga in persecutione*. All are translated in *ANF* 3 and 4.

[41] So it was stated by Callistus, bishop of Rome (217-222) in his famous edict, which caused Tertullian to write his venomous reply in *De pudicitia*, Hippolytus in his *Philosophumena* 9.12 also attacked the lax standards of the

and it was against such "laxity" that the Montanists maintained high and rigorous standards for their daily lives. They were known for their strict fast which bordered on asceticism. Montanus himself had given laws concerning fasts[42] which Hippolytus called "novel and strange."[43] They appear in the writings of Tertullian, who boasted of the strict practices of the Montanists and scolded the "Psychics" (the main church) whom he called "gluttons" because they "hated fasts."[44] "It is these which raise controversy with the Paraclete; it is on this account that the New Prophecies are rejected; not that Montanus and Priscilla and Maximilla preach another God, nor that they disjoin Jesus Christ (from God), nor that they overturn any particular rule of faith or hope, but that they plainly teach more frequent fasting than marrying..." In addition to more fast days, Tertullian also mentions the Montanist practices of lengthening the fast periods which were observed by all Christians and *xerophagies*, i.e. dry fasts in which they abstained from water and even juicy fruits. The followers of Montanus are, therefore, constantly reproached with "novelty," complains Tertullian, who then lashes into a vigorous defense of the Montanist standards accompanied by an equally vigorous denunciation of the "psychics'" laxity.[45] Abstinence from water included abstinence from bathing, boasted Tertullian, which conjures up images of certain ascetic monastics concerning whom Anatole France said that "the odor of their virtues rose up to heaven."[46]

Montanist morality was equally strict in sexual matters. So rigorous were they in this respect that Apollonius, a writer whose works Eusebius used, believed that Montanus "taught the annulment of marriage ... "[47] Later Apollonius and Eusebius stated that both Priscilla and Maximilla left their husbands as soon as "they were filled with the Spirit"; the Montanists, therefore, lie when

church of Rome.

[42] Eusebius, *H.E.* 5.18.2, *op.cit.* p. 487.

[43] *Philosophumena* 10.22; *ANF* 5.147. See also Epiphanius, *op.cit.* 48.8. Bonwetsch, *Texte* p. 18.

[44] *De jejunio* 1. *ANF* 4.102.

[45] Loc. cit. Tertullian was probably influenced in this matter by cult-practices of the followers of Caelestis, see p. 34 of this manuscript.

[46] *Thais.* Chicago: The U. of Chicago Press, 1976, p. 28 Basil Gulati, translator.

[47] *H.E.* 5.18.2; *op.cit.* p. 487.

they call Priscilla virgin.[48] Of course, marriage, divorce, and virginity should be mutually exclusive, except perhaps under some extremely unusual circumstances, but these references to early Montanism at least show that sex was viewed as a grave matter. These Montanists may have followed strictly Paul's counsels in 1 Corinthians 7, where the apostle only grudgingly approves of marriage and sex because "the appointed time has grown very short,"[49] i.e. the end of the world was near. As an eschatological movement, the Montanists probably wanted to preserve themselves from the involvements of sex and marriage and to achieve perfection by the time the "heavenly Jerusalem" descended.

In this matter, too, Tertullian formulated the Montanist views for his time, devoting an entire treatise to their discussion. He refers to their eschatological views in other writings, too. In his *Exhortation to Chastity*, Tertullian contrasts the desires of the flesh to our sanctification, God's will that His image be restored in us so that we may become holy.[50] He distinguished three kinds of "sanctification": the first is "virginity from one's birth"; the second, "virginity from one's second birth," i.e. baptism. (If married, that means the renunciation of marital sex and for a widowed woman, perseverance in her widowhood.) The third grade of virginity is monogamy, that is, not marrying again after the first marriage is ended by the death of a partner. The first grade Tertullian calls "happiness, total ignorance of that from which you will afterwards wish to be freed"; the second is "virtue," and the third, in addition to virtue, is also "moderation."[51] In this treatise Tertullian quoted Priscilla, "the holy prophetess": "The holy minister knows how to minister sanctity. For purity is harmonious, and they see visions; and turning their faces downward, they even hear manifest voices, as salutary as they are withal secret."[52] Carnality, "the filthy concupiscences of the flesh," averts the Holy Spirit, while "purity" is a precondition for an ecstatic experience.

Tertullian wrote in a similar vein his treatise *On Monogamy*,

---

[48] *H. E.* 5.18.3, *loc. cit.*
[49] 1. Cor. 7.29.
[50] He may have had 1.Thess. 4.3; 1.Cor.11.7; 1.Pet. 1.16 in mind when he wrote this sentence.
[51] *De exhortatione castitatis* 1. *ANF* 4.50.
[52] *Op.cit.* ch. 10, p. 56.

which he begins with a tirade against heretics who do away with marriages and Psychics, who multiply them. "Among us, however, whom the recognition of spiritual gifts entitles to be deservedly called Spirituals," there is only one marriage. The Psychics claim that this teaching of the Paraclete is a novelty, yet it is in harmony with apostolic teaching and tradition.[53] In a letter to his wife, Tertullian advised her not to marry after his death and assured her that in heaven the "voluptuous disgrace" which existed between them, "such frivolities, such impurities," will not exist.[54] What she thought of such a valuation of their married life is not recorded, but fortunately for her, she preceded her husband in death. Tertullian was not the only one to hold such views of coitus and sex. With him we are already in that period of history when the church became preoccupied with the problem of sex in the way of salvation.[55] For the Montanists sexual continence was in the class of fasting, i.e., it was a means in the service of a higher, spiritual experience.

The asexual view of heaven which Tertullian so greatly desired may have contributed to the position of women in Montanism. Since in Christ there is "no male and female"[56] and in the resurrection all will be "like angels in heaven,"[57] the Montanists disregarded sexual differences and, in a proleptic way, created in their church life the new Jerusalem in this respect. The two prophetesses were just as important as Montanus himself; indeed, they may have been regarded even more highly than Montanus himself if we are to accept at face value an account of Hippolytus.[58] Hippolytus says that the Montanists "magnify these wretched

---

[53] *De Monogamia* 1. ET.: *ANF* 4.59-72.

[54] *Ad uxorem* 1. *ANF* 4 39.

[55] D. S. Bailey, *Sexual Relations in Christian Thought.* New York: Harper and Brothers, 1959 is a good introduction to the problem. For more, see Peter Brown, *The Body and Society. Men, Women and Sexual Renunciation in Early Christianity.* New York: Columbia University Press, 1988, and K. Carrigan, "Body and Soul in Ancient Religious Experience" in A. H. Armstrong, editor, *Classical Mediterranean Spirituality.* New York: Crossroad, 1986, pp. 360-383.

[56] Gal. 3.28.

[57] Matthew 22.30.

[58] Refutation 8.12: "These have been rendered victims of error from being previously captivated by two wretched women, called a certain Priscilla and Maximilla, whom they supposed to be prophetesses. And they assert that into these the Paraclete Spirit had departed; and antecedently to them, they in like manner consider Montanus as a prophet." *ANF* 4, 123. Note, that the two women are mentioned first.

women above the Apostles and every gift of grace, so that some of them presume to assert that there is in them something superior to Christ." Even the "novelties of fasts and feasts and meals of parched food" were introduced by them because "they have been instructed by women."[59] Epiphanius wrote that the revelation concerning the holiness of Pepuza and the promise that Jerusalem would descend there was given to one of these women[60] and that in later Montanism the prophetic role of women in the church lived on. He writes: "Often seven white clad virgins come into their church. They carry torches and come before the congregation to prophesy, they demonstrate a certain enthusiasm (ἐνθουσιασμός), they deceive the people and make them all cry. They shed tears as if they would be in mourning of penitence and by their behavior they mourn the fate of men."[61] Tertullian reports about a "sister" in his own congregation who had the spiritual gift of receiving revelation "which she experiences in the Spirit of ecstatic vision amidst the sacred rites of the Lord's day in the church: she converses with angels, and sometimes even with the Lord; she both sees and hears mysterious communications ... "[62]

It is well known that prophecy was one of those ministries that the early church accorded to women without hesitation,[63] but in

---

[59] Hippolytus, *loc.cit.*
[60] *Panarion* 49.1, *loc cit.*
[61] *Panarion* 49.2, *loc.cit.*
[62] *De anima* 9. ANF 3.188.
[63] See Acts 21.9 (Philip's daughters); 1 Cor. 11.4-5 (women must cover their head when prophesying); see also *Didache* 10.7; 11.3. A brief discussion by Jean Danielou, *The Ministry of Women in the Early Church.* London: The Faith Press, 1961. Also Rosemary Reuther and Eleaner McLaughlin, *Women of Spirit. Female Leadership in the Jewish and Christian Tradition.* New York: Simon and Schuster, 1979. The growing number of books dealing with women's place in early Christianity is discussed and analyzed by Susanne Heine, *Women and Early Christianity. A Reappraisal.* Minneapolis: Augsburg Publishing House, 1988. From among the many books that were recently published about women's place in the early Christian church, I have consulted the following, in addition to the others quoted above: Dautzenberg, Gerhard, *et al.* (editors), *Die Frau im Urchristentum.* Freiburg: Herder, 1983; Susanne Heine, *Frauen der Frühen Christenheit.* Göttingen: Vandenhoeck and Ruprecht, 1986, English translation: *Women and Early Christianity.* Minneapolis: Augsburg Press, 1987; Roger Gryson, *Le Ministere des Femmes Dans L'Église Ancienne.* Genbloux: Duculot, 1972; Otto Bangerter *Frauen in Aufbruch,* Neukirchen: Neukirchener Verlag, 1971. Ben Wetherington, *Women in the Earliest Churches.* Cambridge, Cambridge University Press, 1988; Jean La Porte, *The Role of Women in Early Christianity.* New York and Toronto: Edwin Mellen Press, 1982; Bonnie Bowman Thurston, *The Widows. A Woman's*

the Montanist church women were also bishops and presbyters. This practice was justified on the basis of Galatians 3.28: " ... there is no male and female; for you are all one in Christ Jesus." In his pre-Montanist days, Tertullian criticized the "heretics' who accorded women too many rights in the church: "The very women of these heretics, how wanton they are! For they are bold enough to teach, to dispute, to enact exorcisms, to undertake cures — it may be even to baptize," i.e., administer the sacraments.[64] Yet this is what happened in Montanism. Firmilian, bishop of Cappadocia, wrote a letter to Cyprian, probably in 256 A.D., in which he related the story of a woman "who in a state of ecstasy announced herself as a prophetess, and acted as if filled with the Holy Ghost." She deceived many with her marvels: she walked barefooted in the snow without being harmed, predicted earth-quakes, and professed an ability to see the future. She also "sancti-fied bread and celebrated the Eucharist, and offered sacrifice to the Lord, not without the sacrament of the accustomed utterance; and also baptized many, making use of the usual and lawful words of interrogation, that nothing might seem to be different from the ecclesiastical rule."[65] Firmilian's problem was whether these baptisms were valid, seeing that a "most wicked demon baptized through means of a woman."[66] We note that the woman administered the sacraments strictly according to ecclesiastical rules and regulations; the only problem was her sex. Augustine (died 430), who called the Montanists *Pepuziani* or *Quintilliani* , similarly reported that they gave preferential status to women, including the priesthood.[67] Finally, a sixth-century letter from bishops of Gaul forbids the practice, followed in some congrega-tions, of women assisting at the administration of the eucharist, just as in the *"horrenda secta"*— which is more than likely a reference to the Montanists.[68]

Ministry in the Early Church. Minneapolis: Fortress Press, 1989.

[64] *De praescriptione haereticorum* 41. *ANF* 3.263. See also *De virginibus velandis* 9.1, *ANF* 4.3; *De baptismo* 17.4, *ANF* 3.677. He may have been inconsistent in this matter, but Tertullian had a strong bias against women in higher church offices.

[65] This is among the letters of Cyprian, number 74.10; *ANF* 5, 393.

[66] *Ep.* 74.11.

[67] *De haeresibus* 27, *MPL* 42.30-31: "*...tantum dantes mulieribus principatum, ut sacerdotio quoque apud eos honorentur.*"

[68] Adolf Jülicher, "Ein Gallisches Bischofsschreiben des 6. Jahrhunderts

B. Montanism, the Great Mother and the Virgin Mary

Thus there appeared in Asia Minor in the middle of the second century a Christian movement characteristized by intense apocalypticism, ecstasy, morals bordering on asceticism, and emphasis on the role of women. Where did the Montanists get these ideas and what possible formative forces played a role in their development?

Except for the apocalyptic hope for the descent of the new Jerusalem, all major distinctive marks of the pagan cult of Cybele reappear in Montanism. Both were highly emotional religions built on faith, not reason. Tertullian made the famous statement that human wisdom corrupts and the Christian needs no further inquiry after enjoying the gospel. "Away with all attempts to produce a mottled Christianity of Stoic, Platonic, and dialectic composition! ... With our faith we desire no further belief!"[69] Such blind faith, expressing itself in total dedication to the respective objects of faith, was characteristic of the followers of Magna Mater as well. They, too, were very pious, devoted people who could undergo much physical inconvenience, such as fasting, in the fulfillment of their religious obligations, they observed the decorated tree in their sanctuary and sincerely mourned the death of their god and just as sincerely rejoiced in his resurrection. The Montanists' fasts and xerophagies and their rejection of bodily comforts suggest a joyless people. If they followed Tertullian's advice to abstain from all forms of secular entertainment and to concentrate always on their religion,[70] they must have been a

---

als Zeuge für die Verfassung der Montanistenkirche." *Zeitschrift für Kirchengeschicte* 16 (1896) 664-671.

[69] *De praescriptione haereticorum* 7, ANF 3.246. See also *De anima* 2: "Wide are men's inquiries into uncertainties; wider still are their disputes about conjecture ... To the Christian, however, but few words are necessary for the clear understanding of the whole subject. But in the few words there always arises certainty to him, nor is he permitted to give his inquiries a wider range than is compatible with their solution ...." This he bases on 1 Tim. 1.4 (no "speculations" but "divine training") and then adds that all solutions must be learned from God; this statement may conceal a touch of his Montanism, if indeed he meant instruction coming from God by inspired prophets. *ANF* 3 .183 .

[70] He even forbade attendance at shows as one of the earthly pleasures which are "not consistent with true religion. Instead, Christians should think of the second coming of Jesus and the descent of the New Jerusalem. That will be a spectacle to behold!" *De spectaculis* 1 and 30. *ANF* 3.80-91.

dark and sinister looking group. In Cybele's worship, such total dedication and highly pitched emotion, induced by music, dance and mass frenzy, drove some to the ultimate dedication, that is, self-emasculation. This does not seem to have been practiced by the Montanists, although Montanus himself may have been an emasculated man. We know of a few eunuchs who were highly regarded members of the Christian community. One was Melito, the bishop of Sardis, whom Eusebius called a "eunuch"[71] and who was revered in his day as a prophet. Melito lived in Sardis, i.e., near the epicenter of Cybele's worship, and it is possible that at one time he was under the influence of the Great Mother. He was buried there "waiting for the visitation from heaven when he will rise from the dead," a statement which has a strange Montanist ring to it. Also well known is the case of the great Alexandrian teacher, Origen (died 253/254), who in an "immature and youthful mind" castrated himself, following Matthew 19.12, which he took "in too literal and extreme a sense."[72] But Christianity did not develop a group of "Galli." Rather, there developed within Christianity a sexual asceticism which voluntarily renounced sexual relations even within marriage and promoted virginity as a higher way of life. In an extreme form of this self-denial, called *syneisaktism,* a man and a woman lived together and shared the same bed but refused to make love. Which group inflicted greater injury on their bodies must be left unanswered, but such sexual asceticism suggests a form of the "emasculation" that Cybele's cult evoked.

At this point we should recall the night preceding the *Hilaria* when mysteries took place concerning which we have very little information.[73] Clement's reference to some kind of "bedroom" experience indicates a possible mystical union with the divine consummated in a *Hieros Gamos* or sacred intercourse such as we discussed in connection with the cult of Dionysus.[74] In this light, consider the report by Epiphanius of a Montanist vision: "These Quintillians or Priscillans say that in Pepuza either Quintilla or Priscilla, I cannot say exactly which, one of them, as I said, lay down to sleep and Christ came to her and slept with her in this

---

[71] *H.E.* 5 24 5 *op.cit.* p 50.
[72] Eusebius, *H.E.* 6.8.1.
[73] Page 67.
[74] See Stephen Benko, *Pagan Rome ...* pp. 79-98.

way, as this misled woman said, 'in the shape of a woman (ἐν ἰδέα γυναικός) Christ came to me dressed in a shining robe he put wisdom into my heart and revealed to me that this place is holy and that Jerusalem will descend from heaven here!'"[75] Did this prophetess have an experience of "sacred marriage" with Christ? Do we have here a Montanist vestige of the "bedroom" mystery about which Clement wrote? To connect that mysterious event with the New Testament image of Christ as a bridegroom would be an easy step to take.[76] Indeed, Tertullian admonished virgins with these words: "You are wedded to Christ, to Him you have surrendered your flesh, to him you have espoused your maturity."[77] Again he said: "You are wedded to Christ: to Him you have surrendered your body; act as becomes your Husband's discipline."[78] Christ as the husband of the virgin who dedicated her life to him became a popular image during the Middle Ages, which also left many testimonies of ascetic women who had mystic visions involving Christ. Many of these visions were announced and received by those who heard them as messages from God. Hildegard of Bingen (1090-1179), for example, began to relate her messages with these words, *Lux vivens dicit.* — "The living light says." Although these practices are reminiscent of those of the Montanist prophetesses, the medieval ascetic women did not launch sectarian movements. But, as H. O. Taylor says, "Their burning faith tended to melt into ecstatic experiences. They had renounced the passionate love of man in order to devote themselves to the love of Christ; and as their thought leapt toward

---

[75] *Panarion* 49 . 2-3.

[76] See Matthew 9.15; 25.1 ff.; Rev. 19.7; 21.2, 9; 22.17.

[77] *De virginibus velandis* 16, *ANF* 4.37. Therefore, virgins walk around in veils like married women.

[78] *De oratione* 22, *ANF* 3.689. See also Cyprian, *De Habitu Virginum:* Virgins who are corrupted by the world are "widows before they are married, adulterous, not to their husband, but to Christ." *ANF* 4.435; Athanasius, *Apologia ad Constantium* 33: Virgins are called "the brides of Christ." Even "the limbs of the virgins are in an especial manner the Saviour's own." *NPNF* Series 2, vol. 4, 252; Athenagoras, *A Plea* 33: "You would find many among us, both men and women, growing old unmarried, in hope of living in closer communion with God " *ANF* 2.146. Unmarried women who had taken a vow of chastity were often called *ancillae Christi* or *ancillae dei* = slaves of Christ or God. On this see Joseph Vogt, "Ecce Ancilla Domini: the Social Aspects of the Portrayal of the Virgin Mary in Antiquity," in *Ancient Slavery and the Ideal of Man.* Cambridge, Mass., Harvard U. Press, 1975, pp. 146-169.

the Bridegroom, the Church's Spouse and Lord, their visions sometimes kept at least the colour of the love for knight or husband which they had abjured."[79]

The report of Epiphanius does not make clear whether there were two, or only one such appearance of Christ. If there were two, then he first came and "slept with" the prophetess in a holy marriage and later gave a prophecy. If there was only one appearance, then, according to Epiphanius' report, Jesus "slept with" the prophetess "in the shape of a woman." In any case, it seems clear that the revelation about Pepuza was given by a female figure. Now, about the same time this vision is alleged to have taken place, another was reported by Hermas in Cumae. He saw in sleep the vision of a lady who gave him a revelation and he naturally associated this woman with the Sybil of Cumae,[80] who was venerated at that place. If the dream of the Montanist prophetess was similar to that of Hermas, then the ἰδέα γυναικός that the prophetess in Pepuza saw may have also been a local goddess who was worshipped at that place[81] and was known to give oracles just like the Sybil. In the mind of the prophetess, permeated with the love of Christ, this goddess was transformed into Christ, just as the Sybil of Cumae became the symbol of the "church" for Hermas. The goddess who was the most popular dispenser of oracles and visions in and around Pepuza was Cybele. Thus we assume that the hallucination of the prophetess represented a "partial and passing phase" of her personality,[82] in other words, her dream was moulded and shaped by her pagan past. Is it possible that something similar happened to the visionary of Revelation 12?

We find a parallel to this prophecy in the teaching of the Gnostic heretic, Marcus, as preserved by his adversary, Irenaeus: "He declared that the infinitely exalted Tetrad descended upon him from the invisible and indescribable places in the form of a woman (for the world could not have borne it coming in its male form) and expounded to him alone its own nature and the origin

---

[79] Henry Osborn Taylor, *The Medieval Mind*, Cambridge, Mass.: Harvard U. Press, 1951. vol. 1, p. 476. The whole chapter, pp. 458-486 is very interesting for our topic here.

[80] Hermas, *Shepherd* Vis. 2.3.4. See ch. VII, p. 229f.

[81] Epiphanius, *loc. cit.* footnote 4.

[82] Taylor, *op.cit.* p. 458.

of all things..."[83] In the next section we are told that the Tetrad said: "I wish to show you Aletheia (=Truth) herself, for I have brought her down from the dwellings above..."[84] Marcus, who was also active about the middle of the second century, used here concepts and even words similar to those of the Montanist prophetess: the "Tetrad" descended upon him in the form of a woman and revealed Truth (i.e. Wisdom). Now, the curious thing is that Marcus was active in the Rhone valley, which had a large population of Greek speaking people from the Near East. Irenaeus was their bishop. Among these Christians we can detect certain Montanist traits such as eagerness for martyrdom and chiliastic tendencies.[85] We also learn from Irenaeus that Marcus accorded an unusually important role to women in his ministry. Irenaeus speaks of this in very much the same way that "ortho-dox" critics, such as Eusebius and Epiphanius, speak about the Montanists: these women were "deluded" by Marcus, they are wretched women driven to madness, and Marcus even imparted to them his demon of prophecy.

> Behold, my Charis has descended upon thee; open thy mouth and prophesy. On the women replaying "I have never at any time prophesied, nor do I know how to prophesy", then, engaging, for the second time, in certain invocations, so as to astound his deluded victim, he says to her Open thy mouth, speak whatsoever occurs to thee, and thou shalt prophesy. She then, vainly puffed up and elated by these words, and greatly excited in soul by the expectation that it is herself who is to prophesy, her heart beating violently (from emotion), reaches the requisite pitch of audacity, and idly as well as impudently utters some nonsense as it happens to occur to her, such as might be expected from one heated by an empty spirit... Henceforth she reckons herself a prophetess ...[86]

The gift of prophecy was not conferred by Marcus upon men. Thus, some Montanist elements may have found their way into Gnostic thinking and it is an intriguing thought that the emphatic part given to women in the process of salvation by many later

---

[83]   *Adv. Haer.* 1.14.1 *ANF* 1.336.
[84]   *Op.cit.* 1.14.2, p. 337.
[85]   Irenaeus was a chiliast and believed in a thousand year reign of Christ before the final consummation.
[86]   *Adv. haer.* 1.13.1-3 Irenaeus adds that these women then are so grateful to Marcus that they become his mistresses "desiring in every way to be united to him."

Gnostic systems[87] may have had some Montanist roots. But since Marcus and the Montanist prophetesses were contemporaries, an influence of one on the other is not certain. The possibility must be left open that they drank from the same fountain and inasmuch as their ecstatic experiences resemble each other so closely, that common fountain may have been in Asia Minor.

Epiphanius' reference to the bedroom experience of the prophetess may become clearer if we compare it with similar experiences of pagans. Classical literature offers several examples of persons being "filled with god" through an act of intercourse in which the divine was believed to enter the human. Herodotus indicated that this was the case in Babylon, in Thebes, and in Patara: before giving oracles the women in these temples slept with the god.[88] This was the popular belief concerning the Pythia in Delphi; Origen and Chrysostom report that the traditional explanation of her prophetic frenzy was that Apollo entered her through her private parts as she sat on the tripod.[89] In the temple of Larisa in Corinth, says Pausanias, Apollo speakes through a woman, "who is kept from the beds of men"; once in each month "a ewe-lamb is slaughtered at night, she tastes its blood, and the god possesses her."[90] Like early Christian virgins and medieval nuns, this woman was forbidden sexual relations with a man because she was married to Apollo. So we conclude that Montanist and pagan shared a similar experience, in which enthusiasm and prophecy were often the result of "sleeping with the god." This συνουσία is the proleptic realization of the eschatological

---

[87] The Gospel of Philip, Pistis Sophia, Gospel of Mary may serve as some examples. See E. Pagels, *op. cit.*

[88] 1.182.

[89] Origen, *Against Celsus* 7.3: "It is said of the Pythian priestess, whose oracle seems to have been the most celebrated, that when she sat down at the mouth of the Castalian cave, the prophetic spirit of Apollo entered her private parts; and when she was filled with it, she gave utterances to responses ... but as often as she was believed to receive inspiration from Apollo." *ANF* 4.612. Chrysostom, *Homily 20*, On 1. Cor. 12.1-2: "... this same Pythia, then is said, being a female, to sit at times upon the tripod of Apollo astride, and thus the evil spirit ascending from beneath and entering the lower part of her body, filles the woman with madness, and she with disheveled hair begins to play the bacchanal and to foam at the mouth, and thus being in a frenzy to utter the words of her madness." *NPNF* First Series, 12.170.

[90] *Op. cit.* 2.24.1; Peter Levi, op.cit. vol. 1, p. 186. More references in Eugen Fehrle, *Die Kultische Keuschheit im Altertum.* Gieszen: Töpelmann, 1910.

henosis: a mortal body is being entered and filled by the immortal divine spirit.

Montanists were radical Christians who took their faith seriously. This led them to the acceptance of martyrdom even more eagerly than other Christians. An example of this eagerness is Polycarp, bishop of Smyrna, who died a martyr's death in 155 or 156. We take note again of the location of Smyrna, not far from the center of Montanism, and of the year of the bishop's martyrdom, which may coincide with the appearance of Montanus. Whether Polycarp was in any way under the influence of the emerging "new prophecy" — which may be older than Montanus himself — our sources do not say, but the written account of his execution, the "Martydom of Polycarp," contains a reference to Quintus, "a Phyrgian" who encouraged others, in addition to himself, to give themselves up voluntarily. "Phrygian" usually refers to adherents of Montanus and thus Quintus may have been a Christian enthusiast who sought martyrdom.[91] In the same report we read that along with Polycarp "twelve others from Philadelphia" also died; again, the location of Philadelphia brings us into the neighborhood where the "new prophecy" flourished.[92] We also read in Eusebius[93] that the Christians of Lyons and Vienne made a record of their sufferings and sent it to "the brethren in Asia Minor and Phrygia." From this document we gather that some of the martyrs may have come from the Montanist area of influence since some have Greek names. Such was Alexander, "a Phrygian by race and a physician by profession, who had lived in Gaul for many years and was known to almost everyone for his love toward God and boldness of speech, (for he was not without a share of the apostolic gift)..."[94] This "apostolic gift" must have been the gift of the Holy Spirit, for Alexander, too, was *entheos* and his image, as it appears in the report of Eusebius, strongly resembles that of a Montanist. The enthusiasm of the Montanists led them into extreme actions such as rigoristic fasting and ascetic morals. As the ultimate sacrifice they sought martyrdom, the final and complete renunciation of the world

---

[91] *Martydom of Polycarp* 4.1. *LCC* 1.150.
[92] See to this problem W. M. Calder, "Philadelphia and Montanism." *Bulletin of the John Rylands Library* 7 (1922-23) 309-354.
[93] *Op. cit.* 5.1, 1-4, *LCL* p. 407.
[94] *Op. cit.* 5.1.48, *LCL* p. 431.

which they believed would unite them immediately with Christ. How different is this from the self- mutilation and bloody castration of Cybele's priests? Both were driven by frenzy, and what the Galli did in their supreme sacrifice in order to be united with their goddess, the Montanists did through martyrdom. The abuse of their bodies, especially their sexual continence, was a bloodless castration; in martyrdom the element of blood was not missing.[95] It is no surprise, then, to learn that Asia Minor was the place where the word "martyr," which originally meant simply someone who testified or witnessed, received the coloring it later had in Christian usage. Asia Minor was the place where the traditional Christian concept of martyrdom first developed.[96]

In Montanism many elements which appeared in the cults of Magna Mater or Cybele and of Dionysus were adapted and accommodated. In all three, religious experiences shared several characteristic manifestations which distinguished them from other cults. One of these was enthusiasm, that is, the feeling of being *entheos,* filled with god, and the desire to be absorbed into god in a mystical union. Enthusiasm led to hallucinations and prophecy, ecstatic experience of the divine. All three cults were open to both men and women and a "bedroom-experience" may have been a part of each of them. In addition, all three demonstrate masochistic tendencies, ranging from the extreme of self-mutilation to that of sexual abstention. Of course, the worship of Magna Mater was very much alive when Montanism flourished and the two religions existed side by side for a long time. This is not a unique phenomenon, for there are many examples of such influences being absorbed by one religion from another. This happened, and is still happening today to Christianity in the South American countries; it happened to nineteenth century Judaism in Germany. It also happened to "orthodox" Christianity during the second and third centuries when it attempted to present itself to the Roman world in Greco-Roman categories. And so we find that the religious inclination and mentality of the peoples of Asia Minor that created and nurtured the cult of Cybele also

---

[95] According to Tertullian, *De baptismo* 16 martyrdom may replace baptism "when that has not been received, and restored it when lost." – i.e. if a grievous sin would separate someone from Christ, martyrdom restores that relationship. *ANF* 3 . 677 .

[96] H. Strathmann, *THWNT* 4.512.

created in Montanism a form of Christianity that reflected that Cybelene spirit. Our scant references indicate that even the worship services of the Montanists showed the influence of the pagan cult. As we have seen, Epiphanius reported that the Montanists carried torches in their services, prophesied, shed tears, and made everyone weep "as if they were in penitential mourning and by their behavior were mourning the fate of men." Is this not similar to the pagan service of *The Arbor Intrat* on March 22? When the pagans wept for Attis, they indeed bemoaned the "fate of men"; they struggled with the same problem of life and death and they, too, found their answer in salvation by divine intervention. To say to this, as the Christian critics of Magna Mater said, "Yes, but the pagans are motivated by evil demons and Christians are not," is not a very convincing argument. We must accept the probability that in Montanism Christianity absorbed significant elements from the pagan cult of Magna Mater.[97]

But it would be incorrect to classify Montanism as a pagan religion, as if it were an offshoot of the cult of Magna Mater. That was not at all the case. Montanism was a Christian movement, although perhaps a deviant one, which absorbed not only pagan customs. J. Messingberd Ford, in a well researched article[98] attempted to show that the decisive influence on Montanism, in its original Phrygian and later North African form, came from

---

[97] Such influence on Christianity has been demonstrated recently by an interesting anthropological study of an Italian religious sect, the *Fujenti*, devotees of the Virgin Mary. (Tullio Tentori, "An Italian Religious Feast: The *Fujenti* Rites of the Madonna dell'Arco, Naples." J. J. Preston, *op. cit.* pp. 95-122) In summary, these are the main characteristics of their celebration: Monday after Easter they come from their villages running or skipping (fujenti=fujjenti="those who flee"), dressed in white shirts and trousers and go to the sanctuary of the Madonna dell'Arco and there fall into a trance, they cry aloud, groan, offer prayers, some fling themselves to the ground. Some faint, others are seized by convulsion and have to be removed to a first aid tent. As many as twenty five thousand may take part, observed by many more. When they return to their villages, they have dances on the streets for a week and these dances "express themes of violent aggressiveness with strong sexual overtones." (*op. cit.* p. 104) Music is provided by tambourines and castanets which "evoke the music that accompanied the ancient cults of Cybele." And, indeed, the cult of the Great Mother was very popular around Mt. Vesuvius and the peasents, who are descendants of Roman slaves still continue the tradition at the same time in the spring when the mysteries of Attis were celebrated.

[98] "Was Montanism a Jewish Christian Heresy?" *Journal of Ecclesiastical History* 17 (1966) 145-158.

Judaism. Inclusion of women in the clergy, weeping at worship services, and many other elements that we find peculiar to Montanism could be found in Judaism. "The rather heterodox Jewish background of Asia Minor, especially of Phrygia, provided material and practices which Montanism could adopt," Professor Ford claims.[99] This is certainly true, but it does not explain why other heterodox forms of Judaism, such as that in Alexandria, to take one example, did not influence Christianity and bring about a Montanist movement. It seems that Montanism, with its distinguishing characteristics, could arise only in Asia Minor. Nevertheless, Montanism did not grow out of the cult of Cybele; had that been the case, it would have been simply another pagan cult.

Montanism was a Christian movement which developed from the same Christianity in Asia Minor which produced the book of Revelation. Many scholars now regard Revelation as the most immediate basis of Montanism.[100] Revelation is a "mighty prophecy"[101] in which prophets and prophetic word and work are emphasized[102]; ecstatic visions abound[103]; the second coming of Jesus is presented as an immediate and urgent message[104]; the descent of the heavenly Jerusalem is predicted.[105] Steadfastness in the faith is commanded,[106] martyrdom is elevated to the highest honor,[107] and a thousand year rule of Christ (millenarianism) is predicted.[108] In Revelation 14.4 we even have a reference to a hundred and forty four thousand men "who have not defiled themselves with women, for they are chaste; ... and in their mouth no lie was found, for they are spotless." And of course it is in Revelation 12 that we find that exalted figure of a woman "clothed with the sun." Since Revelation was written during the last decade of the first century, our conclusion is that as early as that time elements appeared in the Christian churches of Asia

---

[99] *Op.cit.* p. 152.
[100] See Schepelern, *op.cit.* pp. 159-164.
[101] 1.3.
[102] 19.10; 22.7, 10, 18, 19; 10.11; 11.3, 11.6; False prophets: 16.13; 19.20; 20.10; Prophets: 10.7; 11.10, 18; 16.6; 18.20, 24; 22.6,9.
[103] 1.10, 17; 2.7; 4.2; 17.7; 21.10; etc.
[104] 1.7; 3.10, 11; 16.15; 22.7, 12, 20.
[105] 3.12;21.2, 10.
[106] Chapters 2 and 3.
[107] 7.9-17; 6.9-11; 15.2-4; 20.4-6.
[108] 20.2-8.

Minor which were later recognizable in Montanism. We remember also, that all seven churches to which the letters were addressed in chapters 2-3: Ephesus, Smyrna, Pergamum, Thyatira, Sardis, Philadelphia, Laodicea, were all in the neighborhood of Phyrgia where Montanism originated. Not much later, somewhere around 110-117 A.D, Ignatius, the bishop of Antioch, was transported through Asia Minor as a prisoner, to be executed in Rome. On his journey he wrote letters to the congregations in Ephesus, Philadelphia, Smyrna, Magnesia, Tralles, Rome, and to Polycarp. These cities, with the exception of Rome, are also in the same region, and in these letters, words, expressions and paraphrases can be found which turn up also in Montanist literature.[109] It was Christianity in Asia Minor that produced Montanism. That Christianity, however, was already permeated with the spirit characteristic of that region. In the earliest form of Christianity, as reflected in the book of Revelation, the letters of Ignatius, and similar documents, we can feel the heartbeat of the peoples who came to the church via the mysteries of the Great Mother. These Christians or their parents may have been at one time devotees of the pagan mysteries; if not, they were certainly exposed to their influence, and they brought these ideas with them when they were converted.

The mainstream church later accused the Montanists of various crimes. Apollonius, whose anti-Montanist book was used extensively by Eusebius,[110] accused them of covetousness and robbery, and described the prophets as appearing like the "galli" of Cybele: "If they deny that their prophets have taken gifts, let them admit this, that if they have been convicted, they are not true prophets, and we will give countless proofs of this. But it is necessary to test all the fruits of a prophet. Tell me, does a prophet dye his hair? Does he pencil his eyelids? Does he love ornaments? Does he gamble and dice? Does he lend money? Let them state whether these things are right or not, and I will show that they have been done among them."[111] Cyril of Jerusalem (died

---

[109] These were examined by W. M. Calder, "Philadelphia and Montanism." *Bulletin of the John Ryland Library* 7 (1922/23) 309-354.

[110] *H. E.* 5.17-18.

[111] *Op.cit.* 5.17.11, pp. 491-493. If Montanist prophets in fact made themselves look as Apollonius claimed, then they could only adopt these customs from Cybele's "galli" and not from any Christian practice. In which case

386) said that Montanus "cut the throats of wretched little children, and chopped them up into unholy food, for the purpose of their so-called mysteries,"[112] thus repeating an old charge against the Christians generally.[113] Eusebius, who certainly cannot be accused of covering up the Montanists' shortcomings, mentions nothing about this charge, which can be safely classified as slander. Of more interest is a short and often neglected remark of Epiphanius who says that the Montanists are also called "*Artotyritai* because in their mysteries they offer bread (ἄρτος) and cheese (τύρος) ..."[114] In an agricultural society these are essential staples of life-sustaining food. If the Montanists indeed used these elements in their Eucharist, they again paid reverence to the Great Mother who was the protectress of both plant and animal fertility.

Perhaps as the Montanists were driven out of the "orthodox" fold they reverted more to their pagan roots and adopted more ideas associated with Cybele. Thus they may have put more emphasis on the feminine character of God, leading Epiphanius to report that "they give thanks to Eve, because she first ate from the tree of knowledge."[115] In the same breath Epiphanius also says that they honored the sister of Moses[116] as a prophetess, as they did the four daughters of Philip the evangelist[117] who were unmarried and prophesied. Thus it is conceivable that the Montanists eventually elevated Mary to a position of prominence in their faith. But our sources about this are late and unreliable. Under the name of the Syrian bishop Maruta of Maipherkat (died ca. 420) a catalog of

---

their pagan roots are even more obvious.

[112] *Catechetical Lecture* 16.8, *NPNF* 7, 117. The charge also appears in Epiphanius, Panarion 48.14. and Augustine, *De haeresibus* 26 (*MPL* 42.30) who claim that the Montanists mixed the blood of infants in the Eucharist. On this see Schepelern, *op.cit.* pp. 122-130. A. Rousselle and P. Brown, in Ch. 1, footnote 28.

[113] See Stephen Benko, *op. cit.* pp. 54-78.

[114] Epiphanius *Panarion* 49.1.1 and 49.2.6, K. Hall, *op.cit.* p. 243. N. Bonwetsch, in his *Texte ... op.cit.* p. 20 omitted this sentence. See also Augustine, *De haeresibus* 28. "*Artotyritae sunt, quibus oblatio eorum hoc nomen dedit: offerunt enim panem et caseum, dicentes a primus hominibus oblationes de fructibus terrae et ovium fuisse celebratos. Hos Pepuzianis jungit Epiphanius.*" *MPL* 42.31. For a fuller treatment see P. de Labriolle: "Artotyritae" *RAC*, vol. 1, 718-720.

[115] *Op.cit.* 49.2.2.

[116] Miriam, according to Numbers 12.2. They claimed that God spoke through her also.

[117] Acts 21.9.

heresies was preserved[118] which lists the Montanists, who introduced "unbecoming speech" *(indecora dicta)*, falsified the Scriptures, observed four fasts per year, each lasting forty days, and
"they call the blessed Mary divine *(Divam)*"; they say that an
archon united himself with her and so was the Son of God born of
her. The report of the Syrian bishop is certainly not correct as far
as original Montanism is concerned; they were, as we have seen,
doctrinally quite orthodox. If they had been guilty of any such
deviation, Eusebius and Epiphanius would have been delighted to
report it. But whether later Montanism developed along these
lines is a different question. Here, since we have no information,
we must work with hypotheses. First, we remember that Eve and
Mary were brought into relationship with each other as early as
the second century by many "orthodox" authors,[119] so a Montanist reference to Eve could just as naturally lead to Mary. But they
arrived at this parallelism in a different way: for the "orthodox"
Eve and Mary were in a direct line of the "history of salvation",
for the Montanists their association would have reflected an
emphasis on the role of women in religion. The deepest roots of
that emphasis reached back to the worship of the Great Mother,
i.e., the religious life of Asia Minor which was centered around a
feminine divinity. It is entirely possible that as Montanists became estranged from the mainstream church, uninstructed and
simple believers in some remote Anatolian villages began to
accord to Mary honors similar to those which their ancestors
accorded to Cybele. This, of course, is only a hypothesis, but we
do know that a Christian sect called the *Philomarianites* (Those who
love Mary) did exist, and that in this sect priestesses celebrated the
Eucharist and offered bread as sacrifice to Mary. Possibly they
had Montanist roots. In any case, in that sect, too, the worship of
the Mother Goddess resurfaced in Christianity. In our next chapter we shall investigate that sect, the Kollyridians.

Montanism faded out of Christian history but not without
leaving its pronounced mark. This movement carried into Christian thinking a dependence upon the inexhaustible power of the
feminine aspect of God. Even today, without noticing it, every

---

[118] See for the following Dölger, "Die eigenartige Marienverehrung ..."
op.cit. pp. 112-118. Also Labriolle, *Les Sources ... op.cit.* p. 194.
[119] See chapter V below.

Christian is exposed to expressions of faith which would have seemed quite natural to followers of Cybele. Our Good Friday and Easter celebrations are held at the same time in the spring when pagan mourners lamented the death of Attis and rejoiced at his resurrection. The festival day of the Annunciation, when the angel Gabriel announced to Mary that she would conceive Jesus, is March 25, the day of the pagan *Hilaria*. This is exactly nine months before December 25, when Christians celebrate the birth of Jesus. March 25 is the spring equinox, when the days begin to grow longer than the nights and what the pagans celebrated in their spring festival, Christians celebrate by remembering the growth of the body of Jesus in the womb of Mary.[120]

No wonder then, that many pagan temples, originally dedicated to Cybele or some other fertility goddess, became Christian churches. In Rome alone several churches now stand which replaced former pagan sanctuaries, among them Santa Maria Maggiore which was built on the Esquiline hill by Pope Sixtus III (432-440). Tradition has it that he built this church because Roman women were still going there to a temple of Juno Lucina, the great mother goddess who assisted women in childbirth.[121] The building of this church was probably inspired by the Council of Ephesus in 431 when Mary was officially declared "Mother of God," but whatever the case may be the new doctrine is amply illustrated by the church's mosaics. Another church, the Santa Maria Sopra Minerva, was built in 1280 among the ruins of the temple of Minerva. Santa Maria Ara Coeli stands on the site of Juno Moneta. According to Christian legend, Emperor Augustus saw a vision of the Virgin Mary, clothed in light and carrying the baby Jesus in her arms, at this site and decided to build an altar, which he called *Ara Coeli*, the Altar of Heaven. The church is still the home of the Santo Bambino, the miracle working statue of the baby Jesus. Santa Maria in Trastevere and perhaps even the Pantheon may claim such distinguished heritage. The list could go on, but we must finish with the most important one, the center of Roman Catholic Christianity, St. Peter's in the Vatican: on this site stood a sanctuary of Cybele and Attis, which was called the

---

[120] See Karl Kerényi, *Apollon und Niobe*. Wien: Albert Langen, 1980, pp. 420-426.

[121] Lucina = from *lux*, light; Juno helps to bring the child to light.

Phrygianum. Around it *taurobolia* were held and these were commemorated by altars. The Vatican hill seemed to be favored by pagans for this purpose, in spite of the fact that the older temple of Cybele was on the Palatine hill.[122] The temple on the Vatican probably dates from the second century A.D., i.e., prior to the Constantinian church erected there; the pagan temple was probably build by the Emperor Antoninus Pius.

But the story does not end here. In the thirteenth century A.D., a Muslim family, fleeing the Mongol invasion of Afghanistan, settled in Rum, the name given to Anatolia by the Arabs because it was a Roman province. Here one of the greatest mystics of the Muslims, Rumi Jalal Al-din (1207-1273), son of the Afghan refugee, lived and taught. He presented his teachings in poetry and is revered now not only for the beauty of his poems but also for the depth of his thought.[123] Love was the basis of Rumi's theology. He taught that the experience of love leads to unity with the divine, which can be approached through dance. The first music was God's creative word "which caused creation to dance out of not-being and to unfold in flowers, trees and stars. Everything created participates in the eternal dance," of which the dance of the mystic is only a branch.[124] This was the beginning of a mystical Muslim fraternity, the Whirling Dervishes[125] who, in their long, white robes turn around in rhythmic circles with their eyes closed and appear to be in a trance. This is well known, but few people realize that Rumi was living in Konya, the ancient city of Iconium, which is right in the middle of the area where both Montanism and the cult of Cybele were centered. Thus, the fertile soil of Asia Minor gave us not only the cults of Cybele and Dionysus, but also Christian Montanism, and this highly refined, spiritualized *orgia*, the mystic dance of the Muslim dervishes.

Asia Minor, more than any other area of the Mediterranean,

---

[122] See Vermaseren, op.cit. pp. 45-54; Showerman, *op.cit.* pp. 92-93 and 109; E. Stauffer, "Antike Madonnenreligionen." *ANRW* 2.17.3./ p. 1488. Also Giovanni Miegge, *The Virgin Mary* . Philadelphia: Westminster Press, 1956, p. 76.

[123] See for the following Annemarie Schimmel, "Rumi, Jalal Al-din" *ER* 12, 482- 486, and John L. Esposito, *Islam. The Straight Path*. New York: Oxford U. Press, 1988, pp. 103-112.

[124] Schimmel, *op. cit.* p. 484.

[125] They could be seen in a recent (1987) television presentation of the Smithsonian institution on Suleyman the Magnificent.

was subject to such "outpouring of the Spirit" which filled the hearts of those who then became *entheoi*, "filled with god." So it is not surprising to recall that Apollo, the great god of prophecy, was also of Anatolian origin,[126] and that Paul, who himself spoke in tongues, saw visions and knew a man who was "caught up into the third heaven,"[127] was also born and educated in a city of Asia Minor, Tarsus. Did he know Cybele? It would have been impossible for him not to, since no person in a city where a festival of the Great Mother was held could avoid noticing it. And when in 1 Corinthians 13 he hailed love as superior to "tongues of men and angels," noisy gong and clanging cymbal, prophetic power and torture of the body, did he borrow these images from the services of Cybele, which he must have witnessed many times?[128] Many scholars believe that the man he "knew" and whose experiences he describes in 1 Corinthians 12.1-4 was actually himself,[129] and if this is so, then his exposure to the influence of Cybele may have been more than just casual. He had experiences that were very similar to those enjoyed by the followers of Cybele and Dionysus: he was in ecstasy, he did not know whether he was "in the body or out of the body" and he was unaware of his physical existence. He had a temporary vision of Paradise and heard "things that cannot be told." It is even possible that the spirit of *enthusiasmos* that permeated the people of Asia Minor may have left its mark in Paul's theology, too. For if it is true, as I have suggested, that the cults of Cybele and Dionysus can only be understood in the context of the pattern of the primordial and the eschatological, the beginning and the end, then the many references of Paul to

---

[126] E . R. Dodds, *The Greeks*, pp . 86-87, footnotes 32 and 33.

[127] 1 Cor. 14.18; Acts 9.1-9; 22.6-11; 2 Cor. 12.1-41.

[128] E. Witt, *op. cit.* p. 266 argues for an influence of the mysteries of Isis on Paul. See also Walter W. Hyde, *Paganism to Christianity.* New York: Octagon Books, 1970 (originally published 1946) p. 53-55. I should like to stress, however, that Paul was much closer in every respect to Cybele's cult, not only because the place of his birth and education but also because during his missionary journeys he was more likely to encounter devotees of the Great Mother. Michael P. Carroll, *op. cit.* pp. 111-112 also argues, although from a different perspective, against the origin of the Mary cult from the cult of Isis. But of course, religious syncretism was by now so advanced that it is impossible to make clear distinctions, and in Ephesus, for example, it was "Great Artemis" whose followers caused substantial problems for the apostle. Acts 19.23-41.

[129] This argument is based on verse 7: "And to keep me from being too elated by the abundance of revelations..."

henosis, unification, becoming one, and his emphasis on a return, in Christ, to the primordial condition, in which there is no male and female, begin to sound like a Christian expression of what the pagans also hoped for and imitated in their services.[130] E. R. Dodds[131] pointed out that ecstatic prophecy was practised in Asia Minor already at a very early time, as early perhaps as the fourteenth century B. C. in the Hittite kingdom. This type of prophecy, like Apollo's, which was communicated through the Pythia, was the result of enthusiasm, i.e., being filled with God. In 1 Corinthians 14, Paul praises prophesy and ecstatic speech as one of the supreme gifts of the Spirit: "Make love your aim and earnestly desire the spiritual gifts, especially that you may prophesy. For one who speaks in tongues speaks not to men but to God; for no one understands him, but he utters mysteries in the Spirit ..." Thus, to the degree that certain Christians still follow Paul's example in *glossolalia* and other charismatic manifestations of the Spirit, they are indebted to Cybele and Dionysus to a greater degree than many of them care to admit.[132]

---

[130] A detailed analysis of Paul's ideas can be found in the excellent study of Wayne A. Meeks "The Image of the Androgyne: Some Uses of a Symbol in Earliest Christianity." *History of Religions* 13 (1974) 165-208. Meeks also discusses the idea of the *Hieros Gamos* in Paul's theology and suggests that in the Asian congregations of Paul "a ritual of *hieros gamos*, of which baptism was only the preliminary justification was actually enacted" but he adds that this question "can hardly be answered by the evidence at hand." (p. 206) See also Richard A. Batey, *New Testament Nuptial Imagery*. Leiden: E. J. Brill, 1971. Add to this also the fascinating comparison by Kraemer, *op. cit.* pp. 161-167, of the myth of Dionysus and the apocryphal stories about Paul and Thecla as related in the *Acts of Paul and Thecla*. Kraemer "would not want to argue any direct connection between the Bacchic traditions and those of the Acts" but such a conclusion is difficult to avoid especially if we add to Kraemer's analysis the facts that Thecla was from Iconium too where the Dionysiac-Cybelene influence was strong and that in the *Acts* some sort of *Hieros Gamos* between Paul and Thecla is hinted at, see Kraemer, p. 164. At this point it should be mentioned that according to Herodotus 1.182, *op. cit.* p. 86-87, in "The Lycian Town of Patara," oracles were given by a priestess after she was locked in the temple for one night. That this alludes to a *Hieros Gamos* is clear from the preceeding references to a Chaldean god who sleeps with a woman and a similar story of the temple of Zeus at Thebes. The gift of prophecy in these stories is linked to *Hieros Gamos*, which is how the prophetess became *entheos*, filled with God. Kraemer also rightly points out the strong erotic element in the apocryphal stories and the allusion to "madness" of the converted women, which she compares to the "madness" of the maenads, pp. 175-184.

[131] *Op. cit.* pp. 69-70.

[132] For a continued presence of pneumatic movements in the Christian

C. SUMMARY

The cult of the Great Mother, Cybele, left many distinguishing marks on the early church in Asia Minor. Very probably this influence is found in the book of Revelation, in which case the "woman clothed with the sun" is even more likely to be the vision of a goddess. The influence can also be seen in the Montanist movement, which eventually spread into the Western Mediterranean, notably Gaul and North Africa. The Christian perception of the divine never completely lacked a feminine aspect. It seems that the basic principle of Mariology, the motherhood of Mary, owes much to the figure of the Great Mother in Asia Minor.

It is wrong to say that "the Mary cult was absent in the first few centuries of the Christian era, only to appear relatively suddenly in the fifth."[133] The contrary is true: Mary was in the mind, soul and spirit of Christianity from the beginning and to this we find literary proof beginning with the gospel narratives.[134] The Montanist form of Christian piety, under the powerful inspiration of the cult of Cybele and the book of Revelation (which was already influenced by Cybele), absorbed an even deeper appreciation of the divine feminine and spread this sensitivity to other parts of the Christian world. When the pagan population came into the church in great numbers, they already found in it the image of the divine mother to whom they could easily transfer the devotion which they formerly offered to the Great Mother, Isis, Bona Dea or some other goddess.

It is not without significance that the earliest Christian theological speculations about the motherhood of Mary, in the form of the biblical parallelism "*Eva-Maria*," came from two theologians whose roots were in the Eastern Mediterranean and were exposed

---

church see R. A. Knox, *Enthusiasm. A Chapter in the History of Religion*. Oxford: Clarendon Press, 1950. For a psychological analysis of glossolalia see George Banton Cutten, *Speaking with Tongues*. New York: Yale University Press, 1927. Also, Morton T. Kelsey, *Tongue Speaking. The History and Meaning of Charismatic Experience*. New York: Crossroad, 1981.

[133] Michael P. Carrol, *The Cult of the Virgin Mary*. Princeton: Princeton University Press, 1986, p. XIII. The learned author, whose book we will mention again, ignores the very early development of Mariology within Christianity.

[134] See to this among others Joan Chamberlain Engelsman, *The Feminine Dimension of the Divine*. Philadelphia: Westminister, 1979, p. 122.

to Montanism. Justin Martyr (died 165), the son of Greek-pagan parents, was born in Flavia Neapolis (Nablus) in Palestine. His theology shows strong eschatological motifs[135] which at that time were emphasized primarily by the Montanists. Eventually, he willingly suffered martyrdom for his faith. Irenaeus (c. 130-c. 202) was directly exposed to Montanism and shows certain sympathies with some Montanist principles. He came from Asia Minor and was a disciple of Polycarp, bishop of Smyrna. He became bishop of Lyon in Gaul, where Montanism was already known and became a cause of dissension. On this matter "the brethren in Gaul" sent a letter to bishop Eleutherus in Rome and the ambassador was Irenaeus.[136] These two men are our first literary witnesses to the conjunction of Eve and Mary. Was it Montanist devotion to Eve[137] that guided their attention toward this parallelism? That is certainly possible and thus Montanism may have been been the spark that triggered Orthodox Christian Mariology, culminating eventually in the declaration of the Council of Ephesus (431) that Mary is the "Mother of God."

Before we discuss this subject, however, we will investigate an extreme form of Marian peity, which may have been similarly fostered, perhaps even engendered, by the Montanist movement: The Kollyridians.

---

[135] *Dialogue* 80, 110, 120.
[136] Eusebius, *op. cit.* 5.3.4-5.4.1.
[137] See Epiphanius, *op. cit.* 49.2.2.

CHAPTER FIVE

THE WOMEN WHO SACRIFICED TO MARY:
THE KOLLYRIDIANS

A strange phenomenon of early Christianity flourished for a while in some eastern areas of the Roman empire, notably Thrace and Arabia. We might call this phenomenon a sect, for its chief characteristic was that its adherents sacrificed bread to Mary and in their worship services only women took part. Attention was called to the existence of this group by the pious monk Epiphanius, bishop of Salamis (315-403) whose book *Panarion*, the *Medicine Chest*, discusses eighty heresies, among them this one. Epiphanius' work was composed between 374-77 and although the book is a verbose, intolerant, impatient, and often uncritical work, it is still valuable because it preserves for us much basic information from the life of the early Christians.

Our study begins with a translation of selected passages from the 79th chapter of the *Panarion*.[1] Our analysis of the text begins with a discussion of cereal and bread offerings in the ancient world. We will explore the idea of the "divine bread" in Greco-Roman and Jewish Christian traditions. We will then turn to a discussion of Jewish sacrifices to the "queen of heaven" as related in the Old Testament. This will lead us to a comparison of such

---

[1] This translation, originally prepared in 1968, was revised by Professor Glenn A. Koch from Eastern Baptist Seminary, Philadelphia, Pa. The translation is based on the Greek text of K. Holl in *Die Griechischen- Christlichen Schriftsteller der ersten Jahrhunderte*. Akademie der Wissenschaften, Berlin. Leipzig: J. C. Hinrichs, 1933, vol. 37, pp. 475-484. The numbers before the paragraphs correspond to the numbers found in this edition. Prior to this thorough rebuttal, Epiphanius briefly mentioned this sect in his *Panarion* 73.23 and in his *Ancoratus* 13.8. If the *Anakephalaiosis* is his work, which is doubtful, then a brief reference here should also be counted. I omitted the complete text because while I wrote this book E.J. Brill announced the publication of an English translation of the complete *Panarion*, by F. Williams, as part of the Nag Hammadi Studies Series. The first volume appeared under the following title: Frank Williams, *The Panarion of Epiphanius of Salamis*, Book I (Sects. 1-46). Nag Hammadi Studies 35. Leiden: E.J. Brill, 1987. There is also a translation in Ross S. Kraemer (ed), *Meanads, Martyrs, Matrons Monastics: A Source book on Women's Religions in the Greco Roman World*. Philadelphia: Fortress Press, 1988, pp. 51-58.

sacrifice with the practices of the Kollyridians, the women who offered sacrifice to the Virgin Mary.

A. The Kollyridians according to Epiphanius
Against the Kollyridians
who offer sacrifice to Mary, Heresy LIX of LXXIX in the sequence

I.1 After this, \<another\> famous heresy has appeared, concerning which we already made brief mention in the previous chapter concerning the letter written to/in Arabia about the Virgin Mary.

I.2 And this heresy in turn appeared in Arabia from Thrace and the upper regions of Scythia, and came unto our ears; it appears to be both quite ridiculous and deserving of mockery in the eyes of the prudent man.

I.3 Nevertheless let us begin to expose it, and try to explain what this heresy professes. I have no doubt that it will be found to contain more foolishness than any wisdom at all, just as do other heresies which were similar to it.

I.4 Indeed, just as the above mentioned people, who adopted that sect, sow from human inventions slanderous opinions concerning the Blessed Virgin, so also these, leaning to the opposite side, fall also in extreme harm and danger, in such a manner that the famous saying of pagan philosophers may be confirmed: "The extremes are equals."

I.5 For equal is the mischief inherent in both these heresies: The one disparaging the Holy Virgin, but the other praising her more than they ought.

I.6 For who are those who teach this other than women? For women are by nature unstable, both faltering and low in intelligence.

I.7 Therefore, the devil apparently vomited out that error through them, just as he did in the chapter above in the very ridiculous teaching from Quintilla, Maximilla, and Priscilla, he also did in this heresy. For some women decorate a carriage or a square chair by covering it with fine linen, and on a certain definite day of the year [on certain days] they set forth bread and offer it as sacrifice in the name of Mary. Then all partake from that bread. Certain details of this thing we discussed in the same letter written in Arabia. But now we shall speak accurately about it, and by asking God's help we shall produce to the best of our ability the arguments opposed to it, so that by cutting away the very roots of this idolatrous heresy we may be able with God to tear out such a great madness from some.

> The madness of these women shows once more the disease of the deceived Eve (II.1). This doctrine is an undertaking of demons (II.-6) since women never acted as priests, not even Eve herself. Both old and New Testaments show that only men offered sacrifices and no matter how greatly honored Mary was, she was not given the power of the priesthood (III.1). Women were prophets (II.5) and deaconesses (III.6) but not priests. What the Kollyridian women do is foolish, crazy, idolatry and a work of the devil. (IV.2,3,4) Mary's body was holy (IV.6) but she was not a goddess, and she always remained of the same nature as other women. (V.2) The Old Testament prophets foretold the birth of Jesus from a Virgin (VI.1-6) and "God recreated himself out of the Virgin" and still she was not worshipped, "neither so that she be made into a god, so that we offer sacrifices in her name, nor so that women be instituted as priests after so many generations". (VII.2) Neither Salome, nor Mary nor any of the holy women named in the New Testament were given such honors.   (VII.3-4)

VII.5 Then from whence did this coiled serpent turn up? From where are renewed his crooked plans? Yes, let Mary be honored, but let the Father, Son, and Holy Spirit be worshipped; let no one worship Mary! Because that mystery and cult of adoration is not due to women, nor even for man either, but to the one God: nor do the angels seem worthy enough for such an honor.

VII.6 Let what is written perversely in the hearts of those who are deceived be blotted out; let the lust of the tree be dimmed from the eyes [allusion to Gen. 3]. Let the work itself, the creature, return to God the creator. Let Eve along with Adam be shamed into honoring only God; neither let her be deceived by the voice of the serpent, but persist in God's command: "Do not eat of that tree" [Gen. 2.17]! Though there was no error in the tree itself, still the disobedience of error (sic) crept in through the agency of the tree. Let no one taste that error concerning the Holy Mary: for even if "the tree is in season" [Gen. 2.9], it was not given for food. Similarly, even if Mary may be the most beautiful, holy and has been honored, still she must not be worshipped.

VIII.1 Furthermore, these women of this sect "renew the drink offering to Fortune and set the table for a demon" [Isa. 65.11], not to God, as it is written, and they feast on the food of impiety, as the divine word testifies: "Women knead dough and their sons collect wood to make cakes for the army of heaven" [Jer. 7.18].

VIII.2 Let such women be muzzled by Jeremias, and let them not disturb the world any longer. Let them not say, "We honor the queen of heaven" [Jer. 44.25 (LXX 51.17)]. Taphnes knows well how much they are to be punished. The region of Magdala knows well how to receive their corpses thrown to rotting. Do not, Oh Israel, be persuaded by women! Turn away from the council of wicked women! "For the woman snares the precious souls of men" [Prov. 6.26]! "Her feet guide those who deal with death into Hades" [Prov. 5.5].

> Evil women should be resisted (VII1.3; reference to Prov. 5.3-4) just as the chaste Joseph did not let himself be tricked by the Egyptian seductress (IX.2).

IX.3 How much more can be argued against this heresy? In fact, either these idle women adore Mary and offer her a "collyris" (a small cake), or they offer this ridiculous and absurd oblation in her behalf. The entire matter is folly, and alien, and is instigated by demons; it contains nothing but insolence and fraud.

IX.4 But lest we prolong the discussion, what has been said until now should be enough. Mary is held in honor, but let the Lord be worshipped. Just men practice error for no one, for "God can not be tempted by evil and he tempts no one" [Jas. 1.13], not even are his servants disposed toward evil. "Each one is tempted, enticed, and allured by his own desire. Then desire begets sin and sin, when completed, generates death" [Jas. 1.14f].

IX.5 Therefore, since we believe that we have discussed all these matters sufficiently, beloved, since we crushed with the word of truth this beetle, so to speak, golden colored, winged, and buzzing about, at the same time very venomous and full of poison, let us go to another heresy, the only one that remains, asking God once more that He may give us His help to follow the paths of truth, and to engineer a final overthrow of the opposition.

B. Bread as an Element of Sacrifices

The concern of Epiphanius which prompted this treatise was well founded: There was a Christian sect in Arabia which elevated the Virgin Mary to the status of a goddess and worshipped her with regular sacrifices. Who gave the name "Kollyridians" to this sect is subject to debate.[2] Occasionally the name "Philomarianites," as opposed to "Antidikomarianites," is also used to describe them, but it is highly unlikely that these people would have used any other name than "Christian." They doubtless believed, as members of most sects and heresies did, that theirs was a legitimate form of Christian worship.[3] The name "Kollyridians" comes from the Greek word denoting the bread which the women sacrificed to Mary, "κολλύρις." This is to be distinguished from κολλύριον, a medical expression referring to various drugs and salves that were often marked with the seal of the physician who made them.[4] κολλύρις usually refers to a small loaf of bread, a cake, or a pan-cake[5] which, in addition to secular usage, often figures in sacrifices.

Bread, or cereal offering, is as old as western civilization. The roots of such offering may go back to the dawn of history when man first discovered the mystery of grain production. This pro-cess, which so closely resembles creation as an activity of God, and the result of it, which was so essential for the maintenance of life, was early associated with divine power. The Greeks believed that Demeter discovered grain; accordingly they called it the "καρποὶ Δημητριακοί."[6] The solemn and awesome Eleusinian

[2] Franz Joseph Dölger, "Die eigenartige Marienverehrung der Philo-marianiten oder Kollyridianer in Arabia." *Antike und Christentum* 1(1929) pp. 107-140; S. M. Jackson, "Collyridians." *The New Schaff-Herzog Encyclopedia of Religious Knowledge.* Grand Rapids, Mich.: Baker, 1950, vol. 3, p. 162. Most church histories bypass the Kollyridians and the histories of dogma men-tion them only in passing, see e.g. A. von Harnack, *History of Dogma.* New York: Dover (reprint) 1961, vol. 4, p. 316; Reinhold Seeberg, *Lehrbuch der Dogmengeschichte.* Graz: Akademische Verlagsanstalt, 1953, v. 2, p. 212.

[3] It was often difficult to make a distinction between traditional Christia-nity and fringe groups because "all are called Christian," Justin Martyr complained in his *Apology* 1.7,26. In these passages he was referring to gnostic heretics.

[4] Such as the eye-salve mentioned in Revelation 3.18. The word is also spelled κολλούριον, see Willliam F. Arndt and F. Wilbur Gingrich, *A Greek English Lexicon of the New Testament.* Chicago, Ill.: Univ. of Chicago, 1957, p. 442, and Kind, article κολλύριον in Pauly-Wissowa-Kroll, *op. cit.* XI.1, pp. 1100-1106; also F. W. Bayer, "Augensalbe" *RAC* 1.972-975.

[5] E.A. Sophocles, *Greek Lexicon of the Roman and Byzantine Periods.* New York: F. Unger, 1957, vol. 2, p. 675; G.W.H. Lampe, *A Patristic Greek Lexicon.* Oxford: Clarendon Press, 1961, p. 675.

[6] Diodorus Siculus, *World History (Bibliotheca)* 2.36.2: "In addition to the grain of Demeter (δημητριακῶν καρπῶν) there grows throughout India much millet..." ET.: C. H. Oldfather, *LCL.* Cambridge, Mass.: Harvard U.

mysteries centered around Demeter and partaking of her food may have been the climax of the ritual, recalling the barley drink that refreshed her during her journey.[7] Μεγαλάρτια, i.e., "feast of the great loaves" was a festival of Delos in honor of Demeter. In Boeotia an epithet of her was Μεγαλάρτος. Μεγαλάρτιος was the name of the month of Halos in Thessaly and in Athens Haloa was the festival of Demeter during which the first bread made from the new harvest was dedicated to her.[8] The great festival of Thesmophoria, during the month Pyanepsion, was also dedicated to Demeter. This celebration was restricted to women, and here again, cakes were the cultic sacrificial offerings.[9] But it was not only Demeter who appreciated cakes as offerings; so did Artemis and other divinities. Theocritus tells us that even at the Adonis festival the women presented cakes of all kinds.[10]

It was no different in Rome. In The Golden Ass, Apuleius describes the interior of a temple of Ceres (Demeter) in which Psyche hoped to find temporary refuge. In the temple she saw

---

Press, 1961, vol. 2, pp. 6-7; Th. Klauser, J. Hauszleiter, A. Stuiber, "Brot." *Reallexikon für Antike und Christentum* (ed. Theodor Klauser). Stuttgart: A. Hiersemann, 1954, pp. 611-619; Johannes Behm, "ἄρτος" *Theologisches Wörterbuch zum Neuen Testament.* Stuttgart: Kolhammer, 1933, vol. 1, pp. 475- 476; A. Man, "Bäckerei" Pauly-Wissowa-Kroll, *op. cit.* II.2, pp. 2734-2743. Compare Hippolytus, *Refutation of all Heresies* 5.3: "The Phrygians, however, assert, that (God) is likewise 'a green ear of corn reaped.'" Then Hippolytus discusses the Eleusian mysteries. ET.: *ANF* vol. 5, p. 55.

7 *Homeric Hymn to Demeter* 208; ET.: R. Gordon Wassou, *et al. The Road to Eleusis.* New York and London: Harcourt, Brace, Jovanovich, 1978, p. 64. Ovid, *Metamorphoses* 5.450 mentions a "sweet drink" into which "toasted barley" was sprinkled. Mary M. Innes, *The Metamorphoses of Ovid.* New York: Penguin, 1982, p. 128. H. R. Willoughby, *Pagan Regeneration.* Chicago, Ill.: Univ. of Chicago, 1929, pp. 36-67; G. E. Mylonas, *Eleusis and the Eleusinian Mysteries.* Princeton: Princeton University Press, 1961.

8 See H. G. Liddel and Robert Scott, *A Greek English Lexicon.* Oxford: Clarendon Press, 1953, p. 1086; also the articles Μεγαλάρτια, Μεγαλάρτος in Pauly-Wissowa-Kroll, *op. cit.* vol. 29, p. 140.

9 Lewis R. Farnell, *The Cults of the Greek States.* Oxford: Clarendon Press, 1907, vol. 3, pp.74-106; H. J. Rose, *Religion in Greece and Rome.* New York: Harper & Row, 1959, p. 77; August Mommsen, *Feste de Stadt Athen im Altertum.* Leipzig: Teubner, 1898, pp. 318-319. See Aristophanes *Thesmophoriazusae* 284-285: "Set down the basket Thratta; give me out the sacred cake to offer to the Twain (= Demeter and Persephone)." ET.: B. B. Rogers, *LCL* Cambridge, Mass.: Harvard U. Press, 1946, pp. 156-157.

10 ... "O there is every cake, That every woman kneaded of meal so fair with blossoms bent of every scent of oil or honey rare, Here's all outlaid in semblance made of every bird and beast." Theocritus 15.117-118 "The Women at the Adonis Festival." *The Greek Bucolic Poets.* J. M. Edmonds, editor. *LCL* Cambridge, Mass.: Harvard U. Press, 1938, pp. 190-191.

"sheaves of corn lying on a heap, blades twisted into garlands, and reeds of barley; moreover she saw hooks, scythes, sickles, and other instruments to reap ... "[11] — all items essential to the cult of Demeter-Ceres. Cakes were offered on many occasions, such as the Liberalia, on March 17, in honor of Liber Pater. Ovid is our witness that selling such cakes was an opportunity for old women to make some money. Even the words "offering" (*libamen*) and "cake" (*libum*) he says, are derived from the name of the god: "Libations derive their names from their author, and so do cakes, because part of them is offered on the hallowed hearths. Cakes are made for the god, because he delights in sweet juices ... "[12] Another festival was Parilia, observed on April 21, in honor of the Pales, the ancient god and goddess who were protectors of stock breeding. Ovid reports that on their festival baskets of millet accompanied cakes of millet, for "the rural goddess particularly delights in that food."[13] On the Matralia, the annual celebration of the *Mater Matuta* observed on June 11, Ovid urged the women: "Go, good mothers, (the Matralia is your festival) and offer to the Theban goddess the yellow cakes that are her due ... why she calls for toasted cakes, do thou O Bacchus ... explain ..."[14] In the festival of the October Horse (*Ecus October*), the severed head of a horse was decorated with loaves of bread[15] in the hope of securing a good harvest. This festival was observed in honor of Mars, but Minerva was also fond of cakes[16] and so was Juno,[17] who had a sacred cave in Lanuvium in which serpents lived. On an appointed day each year, girls went down the sacred path bearing barley cakes in their hands. When they found the nest of snakes

---

[11] Metamorphoses 6.1. ET.: S. Gaselee, *Apuleius. The Golden Ass.* London: Heinemann, 1935, p. 251.

[12] *Fasti* 3.725-736, *LCL* James G. Frazer, editor, London: Heinemann, 1931, pp. 174-175.

[13] *Fasti* 4.743, *op. cit.* pp. 244-245.

[14] *Fasti* 6.475-484, *op. cit.* pp. 354-357.

[15] J. H. Rose, *op. cit.* p. 215-216; Laing, *op. cit.* p. 57.

[16] M. Iuniani Iustini Epitoma Historiarum Philippicarum Pompeii Trogi. Otto Seel, editor. Stuttgart, Teubner, 1985, p. 169 (Chapter XX.7): "Itaque cum statuas invenibus iustae magnitudinis et in primis inervae fabricare coepissent, et Metapontini oraculo cognito deorum occupandam manium et deae pacem rati, iuvenibus modica et lapidea simulacra ponunt et deam panificiis placant."

[17] Sexti Pompei Festi, *De Verborum Significatu quae supersunt cum Pauli Epitome.* Wallace M. Lindsay, editor. Leipzig: Teubner, 1913, p. 56, line 21: "Curiales mensae, in quibus immolabatur Iunoni, quae Curis appellata est."

they fed the cakes to them. Popular tradition claimed that if the girls were virgins the snakes accepted the cakes, if not, they were disgraced. If everything went well and the girls returned safely, everyone rejoiced that the year would be a fertile one. Here the cakes, in association with a fertility goddess (Juno), the emphasis on virginity, and the role of the serpent clearly imply a mysterious fertility rite, the exact meaning of which is lost, if indeed such a rite ever was clearly defined and understood.[18]

The list of such festivals could go on: the Fornicalia, Lupercalia, Terminalia and several other festivals included the offering of cakes, which must have had a deep mystical meaning for the Romans. Just how deeply these feelings went we can sense from the custom of *confarreatio,* the most solemn form of marriage ceremony in which *panis farreus,* a bread made of *far* or spelt, a coarse wheat, was used. After prayers and sacrifices the bride formally renounced her maiden name and assumed that of her husband, after which they both ate from the bread. The symbolism of eating from the one bread is quite apparent, but the bread had to be of *far,* the grain sacred to the goddess Demeter-Ceres. That gave to the *confarreatio* a quasi sacramental character, for by partaking of the bread the bride and groom were united not only with each other, but also with the goddess.[19]

---

[18] Propertius, *Elegies* 4.8: "Lanuvium is from of old under the guard of an ancient serpent; thou shalt not count it wasted time if thou give an hour to so wondrous a visit. Here down a dark chasm plunges a sacred path, where penetrates the offering to the hungry snake — beware, O maid, of all such paths as this! — when he demands his yearly tribute of food and sends forth loud hisses from the depths of earth. Maids that are sent down to rites such as this turn pale when their hand is rashly thrusted in the serpent's mouth. He seizes the morsels that the virgin holds toward him: even the baskets tremble in the virgin's hands. If they have been chaste, they return to embrace their parents, and farmers cry: 'Twill be a fertile year!'" *Propertius.* A. E. Butler, ed. *LCL.* Cambridge, Mass.: Harvard, 1939, pp. 314-315. The same story is related also in Aelian, *De Natura Animalum.* 11.16, see Aelian, *On the Characteristics of Animals.* A. F. Scholfield, ed. *LCL.* London: Heinemann, 1959, pp. 380-381. The ritual is somewhat reminiscent of the Thesmophoria when cakes were thrown into the sacred chasm, see Frazer, *op. cit.* Part V., v. II. P. 17. The snake is an ancient fertility symbol; see E. 0. James, *The Ancient Gods.* New York: Putnam, 1960, pp. 54-100.

[19] See Gordon J. Laing, *Survivals of Roman Religion.* New York: Cooper Square, 1963, p. 164. *The Institutes of Gaius* 1.112. "Women are placed in the hand of their husbands by confarreation, through a kind of sacrifice made to Jupiter Farreus, in which a cake is employed, from whence the ceremony obtains its name; and in addition to this, for the purpose of performing the ceremony, many other things are done and take place, accompanied with

It seems immediately clear that by sacrificing a cake the Kollyridians were following an age-old custom. If we knew more about their cake, in particular about its shape, we would know more about the object of their faith. Sacrificial cakes, as well as those used at secular occasions, were made in different shapes and forms, sometimes indicating a religious significance. According to Herodotus, cakes in animal forms were substituted for real animals which poor people could not afford to sacrifice.[20] The Egyptians had long followed this practice, which later became common in Greece and Rome. An image made of dough might also substitute if the proper animal was not available. This was the case once in Cyzicus, when "the festival of Persephone was at hand, and the people, lacking a black heifer for the sacrifice, fashioned one of dough and brought it to the altar."[21] Athenaeus, in his *Deipnosophistae,* has a considerable section dealing only with cakes, in which he describes their shapes, their names, and, where appropriate, their religious use: "Amphiphon" was a flat cake, dedicated to Artemis, with lighted candles around it. "Elophos," a cake moulded in the image of a deer and made of speltdough, honey, and sesame, was dedicated to Artemis also, on the festival of Elaphebolia.[22]

Sometimes the cakes were made in the shape of male and/or female genital organs. In Syracuse, at the end of the Thesmophoria, sesame and honey cakes moulded in the shape of female organs were carried about in honor of Demeter; these cakes were called "Mylloi." The origin of that custom might go back to the myth, related in the Orphic version of the rape of Kore, according to which the grieving Mother Demeter, in search of her lost daughter Persephone, was made to laugh when her host Baubo

---

certain solemn words, in the presence of ten witnesses ... " S. P. Scott, *The Civil Law.* Cincinnati: The Central Trust Co., 1932. vol. 1, p. 97.

[20] "People of slender means make models of pigs out of dough, which they bake and offer in sacrifice instead of real ones." Herodotus, *The Histories* 2.47, ET.: Aubrey de Selincourt, Baltimore, Md.: Penguin, 1966, p. 21.

[21] Plutarch, *Lucullus 10.1 Plutarch's Lives.* B. Perrin, Editor. *LCL.* London: Heinemann, 1914 vol. 11, pp. 500-501.

[22] Athanaeus, *Deipnosophistae* 14.645; 546; but see 642-653 for a description of many kinds of cakes, their ingredients and possible ritual use. ET.: *LCL* Ch. Burton, ed. London: Heinemann, 1959, vol. 5, pp. 470-528. Also, Orth, "Kuchen" Pauly-Wissowa-Kroll, *op. cit.* 11/2, pp. 2088-2099 who gives a complete list of Greek and Roman cakes in a variety of shapes sacrificed to the appropriate divinities.

raised her skirt.[23] Similar cakes, together with phalluses made of cakes, were also exhibited at the Haloa in Eleusis.[24] Clement of Alexandria (died 215 A.D.) said that sexual symbolism was part of the Eleusinian mysteries. Although speaking about these rites was strictly forbidden, Clement scornfully revealed what was in the "mystic chests" of the mysteries: " ... sesame cakes, and pyramidal cakes, and globular and flat cakes, embossed with lumps of salt, and with a serpent, the symbol of Dionysus Bassareus. And besides these, are they not pomegranates, and branches, and rods, and ivy leaves? And besides, round cakes and poppy seeds? And further, there are the unmentionable symbols of Themis: marjoram, a lamp, a sword, a woman's comb, which is a euphemism and expression for the *muliebra*."[25] In Rome such cakes are mentioned especially in connection with Priapus, a god of fertility, who was represented by an oversized phallus.[26] Petronius says that at the banquet of Trimalchio there was a table, in the center of which stood a statuette of Priapus made of pastry. Its erect phallus propped up an apron which was filled with fruits.[27] Martial, in his usual crude style, refers to a Priapus-cake, but the religious

---

[23] Clement of Alexandria, *Protreptikus* 2.21 (ET.: *ANF* 2.176-177) gives the story in the following words: "These are the secret mysteries of the Athenians; these Orpheus records. I shall produce the very words of Orpheus, that you may have the great authority on the mysteries himself, as evidence for this piece of turpitude: –'Having thus spoken, she drew aside her garments, and showed all that shape of the body which it is improper to name, and with her own hand Baubo stripped herself under the breasts. Blandly then the goddess laughed and laughed in her mind, and received the glancing cup in which was the draught." A slightly different version of the story is given by Arnobius, *Contra Gentes* 5.25-26 (ANF 6.499-4500)see also Eusebius, *Praeparatio Evangelica* 2.3; and Kern, "Baubo" in Pauly-Wissowa-Kroll, *op. cit.* 3/1, pp. 150-152; W. Fauth, "Baubo," *Der kleine Pauly*. Stuttgart: Druckenmüller, 1964, 1.843-85. *The Oxford Classical Dictionary, op. cit.* p. 163: Baubo may have been an ancient personification of the "pudendum muliebre"; for the origin of Baubo see Mylonas, *op. cit.* pp. 291-303. Women lifting up their skirts and exposing themelves as part of a religious rite is also reported by Herodotus, 2.59-60 and Diodorus Siculus, 1.85; Athenaeus, *Deipnosophistae* 14.647, *op. cit.* p. 492-493; see also R. Graves, *The Greek Myths*. Baltimore, Md.: Penguin, 1955, vol. 1, p. 90, and Lewis R. Farnell, *The Cults of the Greek States*. Oxford: Clarendon, 1907, vol. 3, p. 99.

[24] James G. Frazer, *The Golden Bough*. Part V. "Spirits of the Corn and of the Wild." London: Macmillan, 1955, p. 62.

[25] Op. cit. p. 177.

[26] H. Rose, "Priapus" *Oxford Classical Dictionary, op. cit.* p. 875; Herter, "Priapus," Pauly-Wissowa-Kroll, *op. cit.* 20.1.2 (24 Halbband) pp. 1914-1942.

[27] William Arrowsmith, *Petronius. The Satyricon*. 60. New York: New American Library, 1959, p. 67.

connotation is missing.[28] He also mentions wheat cakes in the shape of female genital organs, but no religious significance is mentioned.[29]

Epiphanius does not elaborate on the cakes offered by the Kollyridians, but a comparison of their service with that of some Hellenistic women offering sacrifices may shed some light on the subject. This is the subject matter of the fourth Miniambus of Herodas,[30] who describes the visit of two poor women, Kynno and Kokkale, to the temple of Asklepios at Cos.[31] They bring a rooster to the god who, by the "laying on of his gentle hands" (v. 18), wiped away certain sicknesses. After the initial prayer, the women admire the statues in the temple; before they leave, they offer a sacred cake to the snake of Asklepios, which lived in a den.[32] After this, the women place ψαιστά (i.e., "round, cakelike loaves made of pearl barley")[33] on the altar, but they do not leave the temple until they take a piece of the ὑγίεια,[34] for to forget these, says Kynno, would be a greater loss than to leave behind a portion

---

[28] *Epigram* 14.69: "Si vis esse satur, nostrum potes esse Priapum; ipsa licet rodas inguina, purus eris." If you want to be satisfied, you may eat our Priapus, you may gnaw on its *inguen* (=genital) and you remain undefiled. (Probably a reference to fellatio.) See *Martial, Epigrams.* Walter C. A. Kerr, ed. *LCL* London: Heinemann, 1927, vol. 2, pp. 464-465.

[29] "Pauper amicitiae cum sis Lupe, non es amicae/et queritur de te mentula sola nihil./Illa siligeneis (=made of wheat) pinguescit adultera cunnis (=female genital),/Convivuam pascit nigra farina tuum." Although you are a poor man to your friends, Lupus you are not so to your mistress, and only your virility has no grievance against you. She, the adulteress, fattens on " siligeneis cunnis"; black meal feeds your guests. Epigram 9.2, *op. cit.* pp. 70-71.

[30] The name is sometimes spelled Herondas and even Herodes; he was active around 250-260 B.C. The best edition of these poems is I.C. Cunningham, *Herodas. Miniambi.* Oxford: Clarendon, 1971. See also A. D. Knox, *Herodes, Cercidas and the Greek Choliambic Poets. LCL.* London: Heinemann, 1929 (in the same volume with *The Characters of Theophrastus*). Analysis of the fourth Miniambus: Richard Wünsch, "Ein Dankopfer an Asklepios." *Archiv für Religionswissenschaft* 7(1904) 95-116.

[31] On the names of the women see Knox, *op. cit.* p. 127.

[32] Concerning the sacred snakes of Asklepios see Pausanias, *Guide to Greece* 2.23. ET.: Peter Levi, S. J., New York: Penguin, 1971, p. 196; W.K.C. Guthrie, *The Greeks and Their Gods.* Boston: Beacon Press, 1955, pp. 227-228.

[33] Wünsch, *op. cit.* p. 114, "round, cake-like breads made of pearl-barley."

[34] "Health offering" "Es ist langst erkannt, dass ὑγιία hier nichts anderes ist als 'die dargebrachte Opferspeise,' von der ein Teil von den Opferern mit fortgenommen und gegessen wurde." F. J. Dölger "Heidnische und Christliche Brotstempel mit religiösen Zeichen." *Antike und Christentum.* Münster: Aeschendorffsche Verlagsbuchhandlung, 1929. vol. 1, pp. 1-45; the quote is from p. 5.

of the sacrifice (in this case the fowl). Then they may go home and eat what they have taken from the altar: the sacrificial meat and the ὑγίεια. Ὑγίεια is usually associated with Asklepios, although it is also a title of Athena, who eventually became "Health," personified as the daughter of Asklepios. A piece of the bread sacrificed to Asklepios, placed on his altar and then eaten, was regarded as being charged with the healing energy of the god. Here again we are in the realm of magic, which is based on the universal law of sympathy and antipathy. This universal law of nature guarantees that "lower" material objects will absorb "higher" qualities by virtue of physical contact if all the external conditions are met. The bread which Kynno and Kokkale ate was believed to contain a spark of the "daimon" of Asklepios, and when they ate the bread, it was this they believed they were absorbing.[35]

The ancients were familiar with the idea of the divine bread which had healing and restorative powers. The Greek word for such a bread was ἄμυλος ἄρτος; and we know that such bread was widely used in medicine.[36] Its basic ingredient was unmilled wheat, a practice which was also adopted by the Romans. Such a bread was believed to be effective against many illnesses and thus to possess both healing and prophylactic powers.[37] We have

---

[35] This explains the reluctance of Paul to permit the Corinthian Christians to eat what was offered in sacrifice and then sold in the meat markets: he believed in the existence of demons and the possible pollution of Christians by eating sacrificial meat. 1.Cor. 10.14-32. The same principle is behind the "gentle hand of Asklepios" performing healing: by touching the beneficent energy is transmitted, cf. Luke 8.46: "Jesus said, 'Someone touched me; for I perceive that power has gone forth from me.'" The connection with the "laying on of hands" in Greco-Roman and Judeo-Christian traditions is obvious.

[36] R. Wünsch, "Amuletum" Glotta 2(1910) 219-230, Liddell-Scott, op. cit. p. 87: "ἄμυλος finest meal." Sophocles, op. cit. p. 129; Olck "Ἄμυλον Pauly-Wissowa-Kroll, op. cit. 1/2, pp. 2001-2002.

[37] Pliny, Naturalis Historia 22.68.138. "Panis hic ipse quid vivitur innumeros paene continet medicinas." "The very bread which forms our staple diet, has almost innumerable medicinal properties." Among others Pliny lists the following: it softens abscesses; is good against violent fluxes of phlegm, bruises, sprains, callosities of the feet, looseness of the bowels, catarrhs, improvement of voice, scaly eruptions on the face, swollen eyes, palsy. Of course, bread is to be properly prepared for a specific effect. Pliny, Natural History W.H.S. Jones, editor, LCL. London: Heinemann, 1961, vol. 5, pp. 392-395; Amylon cures many diseases, op. cit. p. 22.67.137 (LCL. vol. i,, pp. 392-393) – Oatmeal boiled in vinegar (avenacea farina) removes moles (loc. cit. p. 392-393) – On the Roman use of barley and wheat, op. cit. 18.13.78 -

already noted the association of bread with Demeter. From this association we can form an idea of the feelings and emotions with which the ancients partook in bread which, by virtue of having been placed on the altar of a god, had undergone some mystical transubstantiation.

It is perfectly natural that such beliefs would be continued in Christian communities of Gentile origin. Indeed, as early as the time of Ignatius of Antioch (died ca. 110 A.D.), the Eucharist was regarded as a "medicine of immortality (φάρμακον ἀθανασίας) and an antidote that wards off death."[38] In the Eucharist, Ignatius says, the flesh (σάρξ) of the resurrected Jesus is active and works immortality. According to Irenaeus (died ca. 202 A.D.) of Lyon, the divine Logos is present in the eucharistic bread and wine and effects immortality. Later Christian theologians gave more precise definitions of the holy elements. Ambrose (died 397 A.D.), bishop of Milan, lays down in his treatise De Mysteriis [39] the foundations of the doctrine of the Eucharist: it is not corporeal food but spiritual; the nature of the elements in it having been changed,[40] it is no longer an earthly but a divine food.[41] "Whoever receives it (the sacrament) shall not die the death of a sinner, because this bread is the forgiveness of sins."[42] St. Augustine (died 430 A.D.) completed this process by declaring that the Eucharist is "the daily medicine of the Lord's body."[43] These examples demonstrate the continuity between the Greco-Roman and Christian views of the holy bread,[44] but the similarity does not stop here. The early Christians believed the Eucharist to be a powerful prophylactic, the mere presence of which would be noticed by hostile demons. Early Christian literature is full of miracles involving the Eucharist and showing either "sympathetic" (i.e., blessing) or "anti-

18.28.108 (vol. 5, pp. 240-259.)

[38] Ephesians 20.2. Lothar Wehr, Arznei der Unsterblichkeit. München: Aeschendorf, 1987 analyzes Ignatius' references to the Eucharist and compares them with the Gospel of John and other early Christian literature.

[39] I regard these as genuine works af Ambrose.

[40] 9.50, 52,58.

[41] 8.4.

[42] De benedictione patr. 9.39.

[43] Epistola 54.3.

[44] Lampe, A Patristic Greek Lexicon p. 1472 has many more references illustrating the sacramental use of φάρμακον. See also J.N.D. Kelly, Early Christian Doctrines. New York: Harper, 1958, pp. 440-455; S. Benko, The Meaning of Sanctorum Communio. London: SCM Press, 1964, pp. 34-56.

pathetic" (cursing) effects of the holy bread.[45] In such cases, the Christians used the holy bread almost like an amulet, i.e., an object believed to be charged with divine energy and thus effective in warding off evil and attracting blessing. If indeed the Latin word *amuletum* comes from the Greek ἄμυλος,[46] the medicine against all ills, then there must be a link between these Greco-Roman and Christian religious practices.

In Jewish tradition, bread and cereal play an equally important role. Jewish history properly begins with the Exodus, a joyful occasion celebrated with festive baking of breads which the Israelites were commanded to do forever in remembrance of God's activities.[47] This association of God with bread was intensified when, in the wilderness, manna (i.e., bread from heaven) was given to the Israelites[48] to sustain their lives. Subsequently the offering of the first fruits of cereals became a law.[49] The climax of this development was reached with the ordinance of the "show bread": Moses was commanded to "take fine flour and bake twelve cakes of it; two tenths of an ephah shall be in each cake. And you shall set them in two rows, six in a row, upon the table of pure gold. And you shall put pure frankincense with each row, that it may go with the bread as a memorial portion to be offered by fire to the Lord."[50] Those portions which were not burnt were to be eaten by Aaron, the high priest, and his sons, who were to "eat it in a holy place." Josephus, the first century A.D. Jewish historian, explained that the twelve loaves "denoted the year, as distinguished into so many months." Then Josephus continues and says that the seven handled lampstand[51] "secretly intimated the *Decani*, or seventy divisions of the planets; and as to the seven lamps upon the candlesticks, they referred to the course of the

---

[45] S. Benko, *Pagan Rome...op. cit.* pp. 123-125. Add to this Augustine, *Opus imperfectum contra Iulianum* 3.162: A child was born with its eyelids grown together. The doctors wanted to cut it with metal instruments but its mother refused and instead she placed eucharistic bread on the eyelids, which immediately opened up. *MPL* 45, 1315, quoted by Dölger. "Heidnische und Christliche Brotstempel ..." *op. cit.* p. 15.

[46] Wünsch, "Amuletum" *op. cit.* 230.

[47] Exodus 12.15-21. See article "Bread" in the *Encyclopedia Judaica* 4 1333-1335.

[48] Ex. 16.15; Nehemiah 9.15; Psalms 73.24-25; 105.40.

[49] Leviticus 23.9-14.

[50] Lev. 24.5-9.

[51] Ex. 37.17-24.

planets, of which that is the number."[52] Thus Josephus accorded to these breads cosmic significance; they represented for him the presence of God.[53]

Bread is also prominently mentioned in the curious story of the rape of Tamar by Amnon.[54] Amnon pretended to be ill and Tamar, sent by King David to prepare food for him, "took dough and kneaded it, and made cakes in his sight, and baked the cakes. And she took the pan and emptied it before him, but he refused to eat." The supposed illness of Amnon suggests a healing quality of the bread. Alfred Jeremias[55] has identified this story as belonging to a group of similar Near-Eastern narratives and the bread as the "mythical bread of Istar." According to A. Jeremias, bread was an offering to the mother of the gods and its offering was a joyful occasion; when mourning or in grief, eating of bread was forbidden.[56]

Thus elements typical of Greco-Roman religions, namely the reverential treatment of bread, its association with the sustenance of life, its place in temple worship, and the healing quality accorded to it, also appear in Jewish tradition.

But there is much more. In at least one book of the Old Testament, the offering of cakes to the Near-Eastern fertility goddess appears as a widespread practice among women who refused to stop sacrificing to the mother of the gods even under pressure:

> The children gather wood, the fathers kindle fire, and the women knead their dough, to make cakes for the queen of heaven; and they pour out drink offerings to other gods, to provoke me to anger. (Jeremiah 7.18)[57]

Strong ties bound the women to the queen of heaven, as is clear from Jeremiah 44.15-25:

[52] *Antiquities* 3.7.7. ET.: W. Whiston, *The Life and Works of Falvius Josephus.* Philadelphia: J. 5. Winston Co., 1957, p. 101.
[53] Numbers 4.7; Matthew 12.3-4; for complete OT references see H. F. Beck "Bread of the Presence," *Interpreter's Dictionary of the Bible,* vol. 1. p. 464.
[54] 2.Samuel 13.1-14.
[55] *Das Alte Testament im Lichte des Alten Orients.* Leipzig: J. C. Hinrichs'sche Buchhandlung, 1916, pp. 327-329.
[56] *Op. cit.* p. 611; cf. Psalm 102:9. "For I eat ashes like bread, and mingle tears with my drink."
[57] Concerning the worship of Astarte among the Jews see also 1.Kings 11.5; 33 2.Kings 23.13.

Then all the men who knew that their wives had offered incense to other gods, and all the women who stood by, a great assembly, all the people who dwelt in Pathros in the land of Egypt, answered Jeremiah: 'As for the word which you have spoken to us in the name of the Lord, we will not listen to you. But we will do every-thing that we have vowed, burn incense to the queen of heaven and pour out libations to her, as we did, both we and our fathers, our kings and our princes, in the cities of Judah and in the streets of Jerusalem; for then we had plenty of food, and prospered, and saw no evil. But since we left off burning incense to the queen of heaven and pouring out libations to her, we have lacked every-thing and have been consumed by the sword and by famine.' And the women said, 'When we burned incense to the queen of heaven and poured out libations to her, was it without our hus-bands' approval that we made cakes for her bearing her image and poured out libations to her?'

Then Jeremiah said to all the people, men and women, all the people who had given him this answer: 'As for the incense that you burned in the cities of Judah and in the streets of Jerusalem, you and your fathers, your kings and your princes, and the people of the land, did not the Lord remember it? Did it not come into his mind? The Lord could no longer bear your evil doings and the abominations which you committed, therefore your land has become a desolation and a waste and a curse, without inhabitant, as it is this day. It is because you burned incense, and because you sinned against the Lord and did not obey the voice of the Lord or walk in his law and in his statutes and in his testimonies, that this evil has befallen you, as at this day.'

Jeremiah said to all the people and all the women, 'Hear the word of the Lord, all you of Judah who are in the land of Egypt, Thus says the Lord of hosts, the God of Israel: You and your wives have declared with your mouths, and have fulfilled it with your hands, saying, 'We will surely perform our vows that we have made, to burn incense to the queen of heaven and to pour out libations to her.' Then confirm your vows and perform your vows!

The practice of these Jewish women was not restricted to their sojourn in Egypt, i.e., they did not simply assimilate local cus-toms. They worshipped the queen of heaven already "in the cities of Judah and in the streets of Jerusalem." Moreover, in their reply to Jeremiah they stressed that this was a time honored custom among them, that the royal house was involved in it, and that they offered their sacrifices with the full approval of their hus-bands. The cakes that they made have the "image" of Ishtar—but what was the image? Was it the impression of a female head on a flat cake? Was it the "sign of Tanit" as was known in Carthage?

Was it a flat cake shaped in the form of a female figure? Or was it perhaps a cake resembling the female *muliebra*? If Marvin H. Pope is correct, the present day Jewish custom of baking and eating the "Hamantaschen" at the Purim festival may give some indication of what these cakes looked like. The "Hamantaschen" are triangular pastries filled with ground poppy seeds (sometimes with prunes); the common belief is that their shape resembles the three cornered hat of Haman, villain of the book of Esther, hence the name "Haman's pockets." Now, Purim is celebrated in remembrance of the vindication of Esther, and Esther is the Persian version of Ishtar, i.e., the queen of heaven. Very likely, therefore, "Hamantaschen" have nothing to do with Haman; the name may be a corruption of the German "Mohntaschen" (poppy-seed pockets). What these cakes with their triangle-shape and poppy seed filling indicated was the pubic mound of Ishtar.[58] Purim is a joyful festival and as we have seen above, eating "the food of Ishtar" was reserved for happy occasions. Since the baking of cakes was also characteristic of the Ishtar festivals,[59] we may conclude that the Jewish women's cakes, either by shape or form or impressions, indicated the fertility-character of the festival.[60]

---

[58] Marvin H. Pope, *Song of Songs*. Garden City, N. Y.: Doubleday, 1977, pp. 222; 378-379. Pope also connects this custom with the raisin cakes mentioned in Song of Songs 2.5. "Sustain me with raisins, refresh me with apples; for I am sick with love."

[59] A. Jeremias. *op. cit.* p. 611. Friedrich Blome, *Die Opfermaterie in Babylonien und Israel* (Sacra Srriptura Antiquitatibus Orientalibus Illustrata, Rome: Pontifical Biblical Institute, 1934 investigated the question of the material of sacrifices in Mesopotamia and in Israel during the Old Testament period. Baked bread offerings do not seem to have been particularlv significant. See especially pp. 220-269. See also Winter, *op. cit.*, pp. 570-571.

[60] Most scholars, of course, postulate that the book of Esther has little to do with history and that it was written to justify the celebration of Purim. See W. L. Humphrey "Esther" in *Harper's Bible Dictionary*. San Francisco: Harper & Row, 1985, pp. 280-282; R. H. Pfeiffer, *Introduction to the Old Testament*. New York: Harper, 1948, pp. 732-747; Otto Eissfeldt, *Einleitung in das Alte Testament*. Tübingen: J. C. B. Mohr, 1956, pp. 624-631. Winter, *op. cit.*, pp. 561-576 analyzed the Jeremiah passages and concluded that the "Queen of Heaven" to whom the Jewish women sacrificed cannot be identified. He says that there were so many naked goddess figures found on Palestinian soil that the conclusion is inevitable that not only at the time of Jeremiah but already during the early history of Israel women turned to the goddess with their private concerns. "Weniger die Erhabenheit und Ferne JHWHs, sondern aber wohl sein 'männliches Image' war es, das die Frauen hinderte, sich stärker mit ihm zu identifizieren." p. 575.

C. The Power of Consecrated Bread

Whether Jewish, Greek, or Roman such religious practices are determined by the belief that the divine is accessible to humans because a δαίμων is in everything: plants, rocks, metals, and not only in material substances, but in immaterial ones as well. Such an immaterial element laden with power is, for example, a name. According to ancient belief, the name has a deep, mystic relationship to the *numen* of the person who bears it. Not only are the true names of gods and goddesses holy and unutterable, they must sometimes be replaced by figures and symbols that hide the true name, which only the initiates, and perhaps not even they, can know.[61] The *numen* can thus be indicated by numbers, signs, formulas, charms and images, the use of which was believed to establish a relationship between men and the desired spiritual power. The expected result was a blessing or, if malevolent powers were invoked with bad intentions, a curse. Thus shaping sacrificial bread in forms indicative of the character of a god or goddess, or marking it with such symbols, was a way of calling upon those powers to become effective.

Christians began early to mark their eucharistic bread, a practice that is definitely reported in the *Acts of Thomas*, which was probably composed in the first half of the third century. Here we read: "And the apostle commanded his servant to set a table before them; and he set out a stool which they found there, and spreading a linen cloth upon it set on the bread of blessing." Whereupon the apostle addresses a prayer to Jesus in which a mysterious "hidden Mother" is also invoked: "And when he had said this, he marked the cross upon the bread and broke it and began to distribute it."[62] The sign of the cross was used by the early Christians as a powerful "φυλακτήριον," a device that kept the devil at a distance and made evil demons take flight. Crossing oneself on the forehead assured protection against the myriads of demons with which Christians felt themselves surrounded day and night; the sign of the cross summoned the superior power of

---

[61] See Revelation 19.12: "He has a name inscribed which no one knows but himself."

[62] Ch. 49-50; E. Hennecke–W. Schneemelcher, *New Testament Apocrypha*. Philadelphia: Westminster, 1974, pp. 470-471.

Christ against the powers of darkness.[63] Thus when we read that Christians crossed the bread they ate[64] we may think of an invocation of blessing similar to a grace before meal in a Christian household today. But why cross the eucharistic bread? Was it necessary to increase its potency by the addition of the sign of the cross? Perhaps the Christians simply used this sign to distinguish bread for sacred use, since there was no difference between the bread eaten at home and that used in the Eucharist.[65] Or perhaps this is another area in which pagan and Christian practices overlap. We have seen that in Greco-Roman paganism bread could be specifically marked in two cases: either when the bread was used as a medicine, in which case the physician stamped it, or when it was a sacrificial bread, in which case the shape of the bread or its decoration indicated to whom it was dedicated. I suggest that both of these practices may have played a role in the development of Christian worship. The eucharistic bread was both an "offering" or a "sacrifice" and a spiritual medicine, one that was effective against bodily ills as well.[66]

The ritual described in the *Acts of Thomas* is very similar to the Kollyridian service as Epiphanius describes it: here too, a wooden table is converted to holy use by being covered with a linen cloth, bread alone is used, and all eat from it. The use of the table reflects a Roman pagan custom: any table "which has been dedicated can serve the purpose of an altar."[67] Roman literature provides many

---

[63] See S. Benko, *Pagan Rome ... op. cit.* pp. 118-119 and 135.

[64] Cyril of Jerusalem, *Catechetical Lectures* 13.36, *MPG* 33.816. Because of the explicit statement of Jeremiah, that the cakes have the image of the "Queen of Heaven" we cannot speculate that the Jewish woman may have used such a symbol or something similar to it. Concerning the use of the mark X in Near Eastern religions Urs Winter, *op. cit.*, p. 301 quotes 0. Keel who discovered that the X on the forehead of certain Near-Eastern statuettes is a sign which identified the woman as belonging to the goddess. The X which in the old Canaanite alphabet is the same as the letter Taw meant "Holy for the goddess." So were cakes and breads also marked that were dedicated to the goddess. From the Old Testament Keel refers to Ex. 28.36 and Ezekiel 9.4-6 where such signs were used meaning a dedication for JHWH. See also Winter, *op. cit.* p. 569 concerning remarks on terra- cotta figures which may represent baked goods with the sign of an X.

[65] F. J. Dölger, "Heidnische und Christliche Brotstempel mit religiösen Zeichen." *Antike und Christentum* 1 (1929) 1-46: Here also pictures of several pagan and Christian stamped pieces of bread.

[66] See footnote 45.

[67] Macrobius, Saturnalia 3.11.3-6: "...it is clearly declared in the Papirian legal code, that a table which has been dedicated can serve the purpose of an

examples of tables, rather than regular altars, being used in divine services. Best known is the *lectisternium* (in Greek θεοξένια), when tables were set up as though for a banquet with images of the gods placed around them as if they were eating. Such a "feasting of the gods" was celebrated in Rome as early as 399 B.C. The food placed on the tables was consumed by the priests and the people: first by the priests, whose eating was regarded as the gods' own eating of it. When the people received their share, it was already holy food, sanctified by the fact of having lain on the table of the gods, and so bearing a particle of the divine in it. Similar practices were observed in private homes. Tertullian sarcastically tells us that at the birth of a child the Romans "invoke the aid of Lucina (Juno) and Diana; for a whole week a table is spread in honor of Juno."[68] This table at the birth of a child is probably what Vergil referred to when in his "Messianic Eclogue" he wrote: "Begin little boy: those who do not smile on their parents neither god will honor with his table, nor a goddess with her bed."[69] A cult, therefore, could be established whenever a table was set up and an offering was dedicated; when the table was removed, the cult was finished.

This must have been the custom which was followed in the *Acts of Thomas* as well as by the Kollyridians. Indeed, Christians did not use permanent altars for at least two hundred years. The passage from Epiphanius is the first reference to a Christian altar; at least Epiphanius considered it as such.[70] But there is one great

---

altar. The words are as follows: 'As, for example, in the temple of Juno Populonia there is a sacred table ...'" Then Macrobius explains that in temples there are two kinds of furnishings, some are called "implements" the other "ornaments." Ornaments are shields, crowns, etc. but the implements are things that are always used in sacrifices "and of these a table on which are placed the meat, drink and gifts for the gods is reckoned to be most important. ... The table ... and the small altars are usually dedicated on the same day as the temple itself; so that a table dedicated at this rite may be used in a temple as an altar and has the same sanctity as, for example a sacred couch." ET.: P. V. Davies, *Macrobius. The Saturnalia.* New York and London: Columbia University Press, 1969, p. 223.

[68] *De anima* 39. ET.: *ANF* 3.219. See for this problem Herbert Mischkowski, *Die heiligen Tische im Götterkultus der Griechen und Römer.* Königsberg: Otto Kümmel, 1917 (Diss. Königsberg.) Also H. J. Rose "Lectisterium" *Oxford Classical Dictionary, op. cit.* p. 590.

[69] *Fourth Eclogue* lines 62-63; See S. Benko "Virgil's Fourth Eclogue in Christian Interpretation." *Aufstieg und Niedergang der römischen Welt.* H. Temporini and W. Haase, ed. Berlin: de Gruyter, 1980. II/1, pp. 646-i05.

[70] F. Wieland, *Altar und Altagrab der christlichen Kirchen im 4. Jahrhundert.*

difference between the service described in the *Acts of Thomas* and the Kollyridian service: Thomas clearly dedicated the bread to Jesus, and thus his service was a Christian Eucharist, while the Kollyridian women offered the bread "in sacrifice in the name of Mary" (I.7). Epiphanius does not think that this is a Eucharist, but rather, quoting Isaiah 65.11, calls it a "table for a demon," and what the women ate, "impious food." He then quotes Jeremiah 7.18: "Women knead dough and their sons collect wood to make cakes for the army of heaven" (VIII.l). Epiphanius, therefore, equated the Kollyridian service with a sacrifice to the queen of heaven and thus regarded the cult as a revival of paganism in a Christian garb. Whether the Kollyridians' bread was similar to the bread sacrified by the Jewish women we do not know, but one thing we may assume with a fair degree of certainty: these cakes were not in erotic shapes nor were they stamped with obscene symbols. Had they been, Epiphanius would have made a great issue of it, for he uses every example he can think of to fulminate against women. But he does not even mention it. So the women used simple bread — but bread it was, the "fruit of Demeter," sacred to Artemis, Minerva, Juno and all the great fertility goddesses of the ancient world. For bread has an awesome relationship to Gaia (earth), in whose "womb" the seed is planted in order that it may die and thus multiply, grow, and become a life-giving element. In the sacred mystery of bread, every woman could view herself as possessing a portion of the creative power of the gods, for in every act of intercourse, conception and birth, the sowing of the seed, the miracle of death and life, is repeated. When the Kollyridian women performed their solemn rites, they did so as women in the most exalted sense. Just as at the Thesmophoria or the Roman mysteries of *Bona Dea*, men were excluded: nothing should interfere with this deep feminine experience. It was part of Greco-Roman magical practice to require silence, often solitude, and sometimes even the protective cover of night to assure effectiveness, for any profane sound might break the spell. Strict regulations were established to exclude anything that might interfere with the solemn character of the rites.[71] The

Leipzig: J.C. Hinrichs, 1912. See also the article "Altar" by various authors in *Die Religion in Geschichte and Gegenwart*. Tübingen: Mohr, 1957, pp. 251-266; J. P. Kirsch and Th. Klauser, "Altar" *RAC* 1, 310-354.

[71] S. Benko, *Pagan Rome and the Early Christians*. Bloomington: Indiana U.

Kollyridian sacrifice was celebrated in such a holy manner in order to establish an *unio mystica* with the divine.

D. Who Were the Kollyridians?

It has been correctly pointed out[72] that Epiphanius traced the origin of the Kollyridians to Thrace and Scythia where the goddesses Bendis and Diana were particularly popular. Bendis, the fertility goddess of Thrace, was identified by the Greeks with Artemis, Persephone, and Hecate; Diana was the protectress of women, whose origin may also go back to Artemis.[73] It is entirely possible that these goddesses in the lower Danube area had influenced Christian piety there, but we need not resort to this solution in our case. In Arabia the worship of "heavenly Aphrodite" was already known to Herodotus,[74] indeed the worship of the great goddess under various names and forms was so universally widespread in the whole Mediterranean area that it did not have to be imported from Thrace or anywhere else. What the Kollyridians did came quite naturally to women in the ancient world, and thus, if Epiphanius is right that it was a revival of paganism, it could have started anywhere. But more needs to be considered. Thrace was, as we have seen, the birthplace of the Dionysiac cult, which had strong connections with the cult of Cybele in Asia Minor. Now, if I am correct that Cybele's cult powerfully influenced Montanism, then it is no surprise to read in Eusebius[75] that Priscilla, the Montanist prophetess, was also active in Thrace. For the Montanists to go to Thrace in search of converts would have been as natural as for the first Hellenist Christians in Jerusalem to go to Samaria and preach the gospel to

---

Press, 1986, p. 125; see also Th. Hopfner "Mageia" In Pauly-Wissowa-Knoll, *op. cit.* pp. 305, 321, 373 and Pliny, *Naturalis Historia* 23.3.11.

[72] F. J. Dölger, "Die Eigenartige Marienverehrung..." *op. cit.* p. 112.

[73] H. J. Rose, *The Oxford Classical Dictionary*, *op. cit.* p. 337-338; H. J. Rose, *Religion in Greece and Rome*, *op. cit.* p. 238.

[74] *Histories* 1.105; 3.8; 4.59.

[75] 5.19.3, quotation from a letter of Serapion, bishop of Antioch; who complained that "the working of the so-called new prophecy of this false order is abominated in the whole of Christendom." In this letter of Serapion was a note of Aelius Publius Julius, bishop of Debeltum in Thrace, which said: "As God lives in the heavens the blessed Sotas in Anchialus wished to drive the devil out of Priscilla and the hypocrites would not let him." *op cit.* pp.492-95.

Jews there who had rejected the temple and broken the law, as
Stephen and his kindred souls had done.[76] In Thrace Priscilla
found a predisposition to those qualities which were central for the
Montanists, such as ecstasy, a tendency to see visions, prophecy,
and full participation of women in the cult.

If that indeed is the case, as it seems to be, then Epiphanius
offers the solution for the puzzle of the origin of the Kollyridians.
As he says, they originated in Thrace. I am proposing (this is no
longer Epiphanius) that they were first a local branch of the
Montanists. In the religious climate of Thrace, they absorbed a
number of pagan practices and eventually integrated into their
faith the universally popular mother-goddess idea, which for
them was represented by Mary, the mother of Jesus. This is how
Epiphanius described them. How they got into Arabia is not
known. Perhaps at one time more such congregations were
spreading from Thrace and Epiphanius found one of the last
groups remaining there. However that may be, they give us a
brief but fascinating glance into the development of Mariology by
revealing how the feminine aspect of the divine was carried over
from one generation to the other.[77]

When did the Kollyridian sect come into being? In a popular
book, the British author Geoffrey Ashe[78] suggests that after the
death and resurrection of Jesus there was, alongside the church in
Jerusalem which was under the leadership of the apostles,
another movement under the leadership of Mary. This group,
with Mary at its center, left Jerusalem and withdrew into the
wilderness as a religious community. When she was in her six-
ties, Mary went on a pilgrimage. Her followers never saw her
again, and consequently believed that she was taken up to heaven
like Elijah. Luke and John visited this community and received
from it traditions which were incorporated in their gospel
narratives. This Marian community, according to Ashe, was the

---

[76] Acts 8.1.

[77] Michael P. Carroll, *The Cult of the Virgin Mary*. Princeton: Princeton
University Press, 1986, p. 46 suggested that they were the *Pepuzians*, as the
Montanists were sometimes called. I did not run across any statement in
my research which would indicate that the *Pepuzians* were not "orthodox"
Christians. Nevertheless, Carroll is certainly correct when he says that
there is a similarity between Montanists and Kollyridians.

[78] *The Virgin*. London: Routledge and Kegan Paul, 1976, pp. 149-171.

beginning of the Kollyridian sect. In fairness to Ashe, we must add that he himself calls this story "historical fiction"[79] which it is, and thus we will not pursue his arguments any further. There is no historical reference to a "Marian religion" that existed simultaneously with "orthodox" Christianity. But we do know that the Montanist movement carried in itself the seeds of what, under favorable conditions, could develop into the cult that Epiphanius called the Kollyridians. These conditions were present in Thrace and that is how and when the sect started. For a long time they were simply known by whatever name the followers of Montanus were called, and that may be why no particular attention was paid to them other than the notice given to Montanists in general.

However, by the fourth century, when Eusebius lived, they must have fully developed their distinctive characteristics, because by that time they appear to have become an embarrassment for the mainline church. If we can believe the Patriarch Eutychius, certain Marianites were condemned as early as the Council of Nicea (325) for teaching that besides the supreme God there were two other gods, Christ and his mother, Mary.[80] Eutychius was a patriarch between 933-944, so his report is open to some doubt. Nevertheless, it was adopted by the medieval author, Ibn Kibr, who died about 1363 and who included in a list of heresies the sect of Marianites who believed that Christ and Mary are two gods besides God.[81] The last definite reference to the Kollyridians is a brief remark by Leontius of Byzantium (died 543/44) who refers to the "bread which the Philomarianites offer in the name of Mary."[82] This remark gives the impression that Leontius was referring to practices current in his day, so the sect probably still

---

[79] *Op. cit.* 161; "But it is strictly functional," he claims, p. 170.

[80] *Annales* 440: "Erant ex illis qui affirmaverunt Christum et Matrem ipsius duos esse deos praeter Deum summum: erant hi Barbari, et Marianitae audierunt. *MPG* 111.1006. See Felix Haase, *Altchristliche Kirchengeschichte nach Orientalischen Quellen.* Leipzig: Otto Harrassowitz, 1925, p. 369; Dölger, "Die eigenartige Marienverehrung ... " *op. cit.* p. 116.

[81] F. Haase, *op. cit.* p. 316: "In der Encyklopädie des Schamsch-e Ri'asah Abu l'Barakat ibn Kibr (wird) folgender Ketzerkatalog gegeben: ... die Sekte welche Muntas (Montanus) heisst, oder auch die Mariensekte, weil sie Maria zum Gott machen...die barbarische Sekte...Sie gleichen der Mariensekte, indem sie glauben, dass Christus und Maria zwei Götter neben Gott sind."

[82] *Contra Nestorianos et Eutychianos* 3.6 *MPG* 86.1.

existed then. There is also a reference in the Koran which is sometimes taken as an allusion to the Philomarianites: "And behold, God will say: 'O Jesus, the Son of Mary! Didst thou say unto men, 'Worship me and my mother, As gods in derogation of God?' He will say: "Glory to thee! Never could I say what I had no right to say. Had I said such a thing, thou wouldst indeed have known it.'"[83] If this is indeed a reference to the Kollyridians, the sect must have survived up to the middle of the seventh century and been known to Mohammed, who died in 632. Since Mohammed was active in Arabia, where the original Kollyridians were supposedly centered, such survival is not impossible; however, given Mohammed's strict monotheism, this passage may simply refer to the Marian piety of his time.[84] Thus the Kollyridians fade from the history of Christianity. They no longer filled a need, because by the middle of the seventh century the church's Mariology could comfortably accommodate any piety directed to the Queen of Heaven.

We have pursued the pagan influence in the development of the Christian concept of the divine female, examining how pagan images and concepts were carried over into the Christian community and found expression in such various ways as the image of the "woman clothed with the sun" and the practices of the Montanists and the Kollyridians. We will now to look at this issue from within the Christian church and see how the Christian genius out, of its own resources, began to restore the image of the feminine aspect of God. The Kollyridians were Christians, but they were an extremist fringe and their story soon leads the historian into a blind alley. The further development of Mariology came not from them but from Christian theologians who

---

[83] *Sura* 5.119. *The Holy Qur-an*. Text, Translation and Commentary by Abdullah Yusaf Ali. Beirut: Dar Al Arabia, 1968, p. 20.

[84] Some other references in the Koran which mention Mary are definitely antitrinitarian, but are not strictly anti-Marian. *Sura* 4.171: "O People of the Book! Commit no excess in your religion: nor say of God aught but the truth. Christ Jesus the son of Mary was (no more than) an apostle of God and His Word, which He bestowed on Mary ... Say not Trinity: desist: it will be better for you: For God is one God." *Sura* 5.75-76: "They do blaspheme who say 'God is Christ the son of Mary.' ...Whoever joins other gods with God — God will forbid him the Garden ... They do blaspheme who say: 'God is one of three in a Trinity: for there is no God except one God." *op. cit.* p. 234 and 266.

began to compare Eve with Mary. The significance of Eve was discovered by the Montanists. Two orthodox theologians who were familiar with Montanism first developed the crucial role of the two women in the history of salvation and established a relationship between them. We turn now to this development.

CHAPTER SIX

FROM DEVOTION TO DOCTRINE

Christianity emerged from obscurity during the second century. The correspondence between the governor of Bythinia-Pontus, Pliny the Younger (61-112), and emperor Trajan (98-117) reveals a noticeable group of Christians in Asia Minor who conducted their religious life in a certain set way. Not long after Pliny's tenure as governor of Bythinia-Pontus, the letter of the martyr bishop Ignatius of Antioch testifies to similar conditions in his area. It was at this time that Christians began to identify the beliefs which would distinguish theirs from other religions, first of all from Judaism in which their immediate religious roots lay, but also from the religions of Greece and Rome, where their cultural roots lay and, for an increasing number of them, their national origins as well. That in their period of self- identification they drank simultaneously from the wellsprings of Judaism and paganism should not come as a surprise.

A. Mary as Virgin Mother

It is precisely this mixture which is reflected in a little treatise known as the *Protoevangelium of James*. As the title indicates, the treatise deals with history prior to the nativity of Jesus as recorded in the gospels of Matthew and Luke. The name of James points to the brother of Jesus[1] as the author, but it is improbable that he indeed wrote the book. Rather was his name used to lend authority to the writing, which is usually dated around the middle of the second century. Of course, it is possible that some of the ideas incorporated by the unknown author into his work had been circulating earlier, but just how much earlier no one can say. Here is a brief summary of the contents of the book.

> Joachim belonged to one of the twelve tribes of Israel. He was a very rich man and he used to offer twofold sacrifices: one for the people and one for himself. On the "great day of the Lord" he was

---

[1] Mark 6.3; Gal. 1.19.

on his way to offer a sacrifice when a man named Reuben went
to him and told him that he should not be the first to offer sacrifice
because he had no children. Joachim was greatly offended by this
remark and when he searched the records of the twelve tribes of
Israel he found that all the righteous in Israel had children. He
recalled the story of Abraham and Sara and became depressed.
Joachim did not go back to his wife, but went instead into the wilderness where he fasted for forty days and forty nights. At home
his wife, Anna, was being insulted by her servant because of her
childlessness. In a tree, she caught sight of a nest of sparrows
which reminded her of her childless condition and she broke out
in a lamentation. After her lamentation the angel of the Lord
appeared to her and announced that she would conceive and bear
and a child that would be spoken of in the whole world. Thereupon Anna vowed that, regardless of the child's sex, she would
consecrate her child as a sacrifice to the Lord. At the same time an
angel appeared to Joachim and urged him to return home because
his wife had conceived a child. Joachim offered a sacrifice
consisting of 122 animals and then he returned to his home. Nine
months later Anna gave birth to Mary. She was a strong child,
and when she was only six months old she walked seven steps,
but her mother picked her up and vowed that she would not walk
on the ground until she had been presented in the temple. Anna
made a sanctuary in Mary's bedroom and engaged some virgin
Hebrew girls to carry the child so her feet would not touch the
ground. When Mary was a year old, her father gave a great
reception for the priests, scribes and elders. When she became two
years, old Joachim wanted to fulfill his promise and give Mary to
the temple, but Anna persuaded him to wait until she was three.
When she became three, Joachim hired virgin Hebrew girls to
hold burning lamps in their hands while they brought Mary into
the temple so that the child would not turn back when she was left
in the temple. So the priests received Mary with a kiss of greeting
and her parents rejoiced because the girl did not turn back after
them. And in the temple Mary was fed from the hand of an
angel.

When Mary reached the age of twelve, the priests met to discuss her status. They were afraid, that Mary, having reached the
age of puberty, would pollute the temple if they kept her there any
longer. They finally decided to give the high priest, Zacharias, a
free hand in the matter. Upon divine inspiration, he decided to
assemble the men of Israel. Each man gave a rod to the high priest
who then handed the rods back to them: when he gave the last rod
back to Joseph, a dove sprang forth from it and sat upon his head.
The high priest thereupon announced that Joseph should take
Mary into his care. Joseph was very embarrassed and protested
saying: "I am an old man and have sons, but she is a girl ..." But
the priest warned him that unless he wanted to suffer the same

fate as Dathan, Abiram, and Korah, who were swallowed up by
the earth, he had better take the girl.[2] So Joseph obeyed and took
Mary into his home while he went off to build his buildings.
Some time later the priests in the temple decided to make a veil for
the sanctuary. They assigned the job to virgin girls in Israel, and
Mary received the greatest honor: to make the scarlet and the true
purple.

While engaged at this task, Mary went to the well to draw
water. There she heard a voice saying: "Hail, thou favored one ..."
She looked about but did not see anything, and trembling with
fear she went back to the house to resume her work at the purple.
Suddenly an angel stood before her and announced that she
would conceive by the word of the Lord. But she questioned in
herself: "Shall I conceive and bring forth like other women?" The
angel answered: "Not so Mary; a power of the Lord shall over-
shadow you ..." Mary then finished the scarlet and the purple and
delivered it to the priests. After that she went to visit her kins-
woman, Elizabeth, who greeted her respectfully as "the mother of
my Lord." But Mary forgot the mysteries that Gabriel the
archangel had told her, and she said: "Who am I, that all women
of the earth shall praise me?" She stayed three months with
Elizabeth and her womb grew larger day by day. Then she went
home and hid herself in her house. She was sixteen years old
when all this happened. In the sixth month of Mary's pregnancy,
Joseph came home. He was very bitter. At first he accused himself
of not having taken proper care of Mary, but then he turned
against her and asked from where the baby came. She answered:
"As the Lord my God lives, I don't know ..." At that, Joseph stopped
talking to her, and after some thought he decided to send her
away quietly. That night, however, the angel appeared to him and
revealed that the child was from the Holy Spirit. Then Joseph
magnified the Lord and continued to take care of Mary, but one
day the scribe came to inquire why Joseph had not come to the
assembly and discovered that Mary was pregnant. He ran to break
the news to the high priest, who sent officers to bring both Mary
and Joseph before him. They both denied that they had had
intercourse with each other, but the high priest did not believe
them and he ordered them to undergo the water-test, i.e., they had
to drink of the "water of the conviction of the Lord." But neither
came to any harm so the high priest released them.

The decree for the census went out from Augustus, and Joseph
was uncertain how to enroll Mary, as his wife or as his daughter.
He was ashamed to do the first, and everyone knew Mary was not
his daughter. "I will enroll my sons," Joseph said, "but what shall
I do with this child?" He decided to leave the solution up to the
Lord, saddled a she ass, put Mary upon it, and they set out for
Bethlehem. One of his sons led the ass while Joseph followed.

---

[2] Numbers 16.1, 31-33.

Three miles from Jerusalem Joseph noticed that Mary was making a sad face at one moment and laughing the next. When Joseph asked her about this she explained that she saw two people: one weeping, the other rejoicing. Soon Mary asked to be taken down from the ass because she was in labor and the baby was about to be born. Finding a cave, Joseph left his sons to stay with Mary while he himself went in search of a midwife. (At this point the narrative changes from the third person to the first person: Joseph is speaking.) As Joseph was walking he suddenly realized that nature stood still; the birds stopped in flight, people stopped moving, even the river stopped flowing. After awhile everything resumed its normal course. A midwife came along and she went with Joseph to the cave. (The narrative then returns to third person.) A bright cloud overshadowed the cave, after which a great light was seen, and when, little by little, the light withdrew, the child Jesus appeared and he went immediately to Mary's breasts.

The midwife was amazed at what she had seen, and as she went out of the cave she met Salome and told her that a virgin has brought forth a child. Salome expressed doubts, but the midwife took her to the cave and told Mary: "Make yourself ready because no small controversy has arisen concerning you!" Salome then inserted her fingers to examine the condition of Mary's hymen and her hand immediately dried up. She prayed and an angel told her to touch the child with her hand, and when she did so her hand was immediately healed.

The wise men came to Bethlehem looking for the king of the Jews. When Herod heard of this he was troubled and sent officers to seek out the wise men. He ordered them to inform him when they found the child, but the wise men, having presented their gifts to Jesus, returned to their country by another way. Herod, then, ordered the "slaughter of the innocents." Meanwhile, Mary hid Jesus by wrapping him in swaddling cloths and laying him in an ox-manger. Elizabeth took John into the mountains where a mountain opened and hid them. Herod's soldiers came and asked Zacharias where his son was, and when he could not give an answer, he was killed. The priests found his blood turned to stone, but his body had disappeared. The people observed three days of mourning for Zacharias, after which they elected Simeon as his successor. It was Simeon of whom the Holy Spirit had said he would not see death until he saw Christ in the flesh. The *Protoevangelium* ends with the statement by "James" declaring that he had written this book in Jerusalem and that, when Herod died and a tumult had arisen in Jerusalem, he withdrew himself into the wilderness until the tumult ceased.[3]

---

[3] E. Hennecke, W. Schneemelcher, *New Testament Apocrypha*. Philadelphia: Westminster Press, 1963, Vol.I, pp. 370-388; W. Michaelis, *Die Apokryphen Schriften zum Neuen Testament*. Bremen: Carl Schunemann Verlag, 1958,

If the apocryphal gospels and acts were the Sunday supplement literature of the early Christians, the *Protoevangelium of James* is a superb example of the genre. But apocryphal stories were more; they often expressed popular beliefs which tended to become parts of the body of faith. Undoubtedly, this pseudo-Jamesian tract was written in honor of the mother of Jesus, and it is worth noting that even at such an early date, before other major doctrines of the church were fully developed and even before the canon of the New Testament was fully established, faith in the "virgin mother" of the Savior found such powerful expression. This must have happened in the eastern provinces of the Roman world where the "mother goddess" image was more intense and where Christians were more under the influence of female divinities than in the west. In fact, the Christian church in the west, at this time meaning, for the most part, Rome, initially rejected this sort of popular piety; later the decree of Pope Gelasius (492-496) condemned the *Protoevangelium*.[4]

Neither the place of composition nor the authorship of the *Protoevangelium of James* can be identified any closer. Attempts to identify Palestine as the place of origin and a Jewish Christian[5] as the author failed because the work betrays serious ignorance of Palestinian geography and Jewish customs. It is quite impossible, to mention only a few examples, that Mary, as a child, was at the "third step of the altar" in the temple,[6] and even more impossible that she had access to the Holy of Holies[7] where only the high priest could enter, and even he only once a year.[8] Furthermore, there are many incidents in the book which betray pagan rather than Jewish influence. Bringing a woman into such close relation to priestly functions is not Jewish but pagan. In Greco-Roman

---

pp. 62-95. M. R. James, *The Apocryphal New Testament*. Oxford: Clarendon 1955, pp. 38-49. English translation also in *ANF* 8.361-367.

[4] See Schneelmecher, *op. cit.* vol. 1, p. 47; according to B. Altaner – A. Stuiber, *Patrologie*, Freiburg: Herder, 1966, p. 463, the *Decretum Gelasianum de libris recipiendis et non recipiendis* was composed in the sixth century in southern Gaul; see also H. Denzinger – A. Schönmetzer, *Enchiridion Symbolorum*. Freiburg: Herder, 1965, p. 122.

[5] See e.g. Jacques Hervieux, *What are Apocryphal Gospels?* London: Burns & Oates, 1960.

[6] 7.3; 8.1.

[7] 13.2: "... you were brought up in the Holy of Holies and received food from the hand of an angel." Also 15.3.

[8] Hebrews 9.3 and 7.

religions, priestesses and other female religious officials, such as
the Vestal Virgins in Rome, were known, but in Judaism they
were not. Another curious reference is to the midwife, Salome,
whose name recalls the name of Semele, mother of Dionysus,
who was also born in a cave, deep in the "womb" of mother earth.
The cult of Dionysus, a fertility god whose retinue included the
female *maenads*, originated in Phrygia, where religion and fertility were closely associated.[9] The name Semele came from the
Phrygian "Zemelo", i.e., the Anatolian earth-mother. If indeed
the author of the *Protoevangelium of James* did borrow the name
Salome from Semele, a connection with near-Eastern mother goddess ideas is more than likely. In this case we find ourselves
again in the distinguished company of Cybele, Dionysus, Apollo,
the Montanists, Paul, Melito, and others, including the Muslim
mystics. Of course, it is also possible that the name Salome is
nothing more than a borrowing from the New Testament,[10] but
the context of a divine birth in a cave at least suggests Semele. We
observe also that according to *Protoevangelium* 7.3, when the child
Mary was placed upon the altar, "the Lord God put grace upon the
child, and she danced for joy with her feet ... " Dancing, rhythmic bodily movement often accompanied by music, is an expression of joy, an expression that was part of ancient Near Eastern
religious services up to the time of early Christianity.[11] It is
impossible to think that Mary actually danced on the steps of the
altar, but the author may very well have meant that Mary was
filled with the spirit of joy in the presence of God. This was the
case with the female followers of Dionysus, the *maenads*, who,
when they felt themselves filled by the god, broke out in uncontrollable dancing. As we have seen, worshippers of Cybele, the
Great Mother, were famous for their singing, dancing, and the
use of musical instruments. Of course, this is not an exclusively

---

[9] See above, Chapter II pp. 65ff., also R. Graves, *The Greek Myths*. Baltimore, Md,: Penguin, 1955, vol. pps. 56-57; 103-111; H.J. Rose, *Religion in Greece
and Rome*. New York; Harper, 1959, pps. 61f. On caves see Guthrie, *The Greeks*.
op. cit. p. 211; H. J. Rose "Caves" *Oxford Classical Dictionary*, *op.cit*. p. 218.

[10] E.g. Mark 15. 40; 16.1.

[11] Lillian B. Lawler, "Dancing" *Oxford Classical Dictionary*, p. 312, C.
Kerényi, *The Religion of the Greeks and Romans* , New York: E.D. Dutton, 1962,
p. 58; G. H. Davis, "Dancing" *Interpreters Dictionary of the Bible*, vol. 1 p. 760;
W.O.E. Oesterley, *The Sacred Dance* . Cambridge: Univ. Press, 1923. See also
p. 68.

pagan phenomenon; it was part of Hebrew religion and even of early Christianity.[12] But around the middle of the second century, religious dancing is reported mostly of pagans; after a double devastation of their country[13] not many Jews danced for joy. We conclude that the inspiration of the *Protoevangelium*'s author came from pagan experiences. We assume that he was a Christian of pagan cultural background with only a superficial knowledge of Jewish religion and history. Perhaps it is not be too much to suggest that the author was deeply influenced by the practices of Cybele's worship, which he or she may have known intimately.

Apparently the author's aim was to elevate Mary to the level of the great virgin-mother goddesses of the Greco-Roman world. Thus he should perhaps be placed in the distinguished group of second century Christian apologists who, in other areas of theology, tried to reconcile Christianity with the world in which it lived. The *Protoevangelium* presents Mary as a virgin prior to her conception of Jesus and affirms that she remained so after his birth. Why is Mary's physical condition so important in the history of salvation? Why would any one make her virginity a matter of such concern? For the Christian claim of salvation, the death and resurrection of Jesus were central issues, not the condition of Mary's hymen. But for minds accustomed to thinking in the categories of the prevalent pagan culture, the mother of the Son of God could have no lesser dignity than the Great Mother of the gods, the favorite subject of popular piety in the East. So the author lifted Mary out of the ordinary and elevated her to a goddess-like figure: her feet did not touch the ground until she was taken to the temple, her bedchamber was made into a sanctuary, and the "undefiled daughters of the Hebrews" attended her. Even after her marriage to Joseph she labored in the company of "pure virgins" at making a veil for the temple, much the same way that the girls of Athens worked at making the new *peplos* for the statue of the Virgin Athene.

The *Protoevangelium* was, in the long run, a very successful book. The ideas it promulgated gradually became universally accepted, and eventually even the resistance of Rome disappeared.

---

[12] See *Acts of John* 94-96.
[13] 70 and 135 A. D.

The Lateran Council of 469 under Pope Martin I declared: "If anyone does not confess in harmony with the holy Fathers that the holy and ever virgin and immaculate Mary is really and truly the mother of God, inasmuch as she in the last times and without semen by the Holy Spirit conceived God the Word himself specially and truthfully, who was born from God the Father before all ages, and she bore him uncorrupted, and after his birth her virginity remaining indissoluble, let him be condemned."[14] The perpetual virginiy of Mary thus became an official teaching of the church: Mary was a virgin before, during, and after the birth of Jesus.[15] In 1555, the Council of Trent confirmed this dogma in the Constitution of Pope Paul IV known as "*Cum Quorundam.*" Here the pope warns against teaching that "the same blessed Virgin Mary is not truly the Mother of God, and did not remain always in the integrity of virginity, i. e., before birth, in birth, and perpetually after birth."[16] Yet, despite the fact that these official formulations are of a rather late date, this dogma is by no means an innovation but belongs to a very early deposit of the Christian faith. Assuming, then, that the author of the *Protoevangelium* did not originate these ideas but found them already in some form, perhaps in an oral tradition circulated by popular piety, the roots of the dogma reach back to the first half, perhaps even to the first third, of the second century.[17]

The image of the "woman clothed with the sun" was the first expression of popular emotional piety centered on Mary; the contemplation of Mary as the new, more perfect Cybele, the mother of God, was next. In the development of Christian doctrines, popular piety precedes and points the way to the crystallization of an article of faith. "*Legem credendi lex statuat supplicandi.*" "The law

---

14 Canon 3. Denzinger, *op. cit.* p.172.
15 *Ante partum, In partu, Post partum.*
16 Denzinger, *op. cit.* p. 427.
17 The expression "semper virgo"="always virgin" was constantly used even by the Protestant reformers of the sixteenth century, who never really worried about the precise implications of the words, in spite of their often harsh criticism of Medieval mariolatry. The expression is very early, too, and comes from the Greek "*aeiparthenos.*" According to G. W. H. Lampe, *A Patristic Greek Lexicon.* Oxford: Clarendon, 1964, p. 38, it was already used by Athanasius (295-373), Didymus the Blind (313-398) and Epiphanius (315-403). See also Walter J. Burghardt, "Mary in Eastern Patristic Thought" in Juniper B. Carol, *Mariology.* Milwaukee: The Bruce Publishing Co., 1955-1961, vol. 2, p. 107.

of faith is determined by the law of prayer."[18] The *Protoevangelium* shows how Christians who were formerly pagans could find a place in their daily devotional life for the mother goddess. But this is only the beginning; pious practice eventually became a part of the faith of the church, which, in turn, gave rise to further clarifications and specifications of the role of Mary in the divine economy. Faith in the perpetual virginity of Mary and her divine motherhood led directly to the development of faith in her immaculate conception, total sinlessness, and fullness of grace, i.e., her gradual assimilation into the divine nature.

"Immaculate conception" means that the Virgin Mary "in the first instance of her conception, by a singular grace and privilege granted by Almighty God, in view of the merits of Jesus Christ, the savior oF the human race, was preserved free from all stain of original sin."[19] "Original sin" is the sin committed by Adam and Eve as described in Genesis 3, and by virtue of the fact that all human beings are descendants of Adam and Eve, all are subject to this sin which is inherited by birth. The Virgin Mary was exempted from this sin because she was destined to become the mother of God; had she been subject to sin even to such a nominal degree, she could not have conceived and borne Jesus. Such thoughts began to circulate in the Christian church very early. Nestorius (ca. 381-ca.451) and Pelagius (died after 418) made references to it.[20] But the full development came only during the Middle Ages, after much, often bitter discussion. There was an early proclamation of the dogma by the reform council of Basel in 1438, but this was condemned by Pope Eugenius IV (1431-1447) until the act of 1854 settled the issue as a "doctrine revealed by God."[21] This dogma was unanimously rejected by Protestants and

---

[18] *Capitula psuedo-Caelistina*, also called *Indiculus*; composed between 435-442. H. Denzinger, *Enchiridion Symbolorum* Edition XXXIII. Freiburg: Herder, 1965, #241, page 89.

[19] Bull *Ineffabilis Deus* issued by Pope Pius IX in 1854. See William J. Doheny, and Joseph P Kelly, *Papal Documents on Mary*. Milwaukee: Bruce, 1954. There is a very large body of literature on this topic, among the best is Edward D. O'Connor, ed. *The Dogma of the Immaculate Conception: History and Significance*. Notre Dame, Ind.: University of Notre Dame, 1958. Good summaries also in Carol, *Mariology*, vol. 1, 328-394; Scheeben, *Mariology*, vol. 2, 32-139. Roschini, *op. cit.*, vol. 3, pp. 9-336.

[20] Unfortunately, both of them were heretics; see references in Miegge, *op. cit.* p. 111.

[21] It was this statement of the Bull which prompted Adolf Harnack to

it is still a subject of scholarly criticism, yet it fits eminently in
the system of salvation as understood by Roman Catholics. The
aim of the Christian religion is to assist men to attain everlasting
life in the presence of God; this is made possible by salvation from
sin, the overcoming of mortality, and the bestowal of divine
nature upon men by union with the incarnate and immortal Son
of God. He became man in order that man might become God[22]
and, by his death and resurrection, already accomplished this
work of salvation. Incarnation took place by the miraculous conception in and birth through the Virgin Mary. How could a
human being tainted by original sin be a vehicle for such a
privilege? Restoration of the human race to its condition prior to
the Fall means the restoration of the image of God,[23] and that
could be done only by elevating Mary above a fallen, sinful state.
By thinking of Mary as free of all sin, including original sin,
Christian theology developed the concept of a human being
restored to Paradise, prior to the Fall. She is Eve before she was
corrupted, the female *par excellence* who alone is capable of the
hieros gamos, impregnation by the Spirit of God. As we have seen,
the Eve-Mary parallel is nearly as early as Christian theology
itself. The basic concern of this theology of salvation is, however,
that communication between God and man is impossible if they
are totally alienated from each other, if there is no point where
divine and human can connect. The *Immaculata,* representing
earthly humanity in its unspoiled state, is the one with whom
communion with God was restored. It follows logically from this
line of thought that Mary would come to be thought of as the
symbol of the church, the spotless bride whose marriage will be
the eschatological consummation of divine and human, the
union of all that was divided.

The fact that these doctrines are rooted in popular piety that was
motivated by pagan precedents, more precisely, by the worship of
Cybele, means only that Christianity is firmly anchored in the
historical process; it does not mean that Christianity reverted to an
earlier, primitive state of paganism. The fact that popular piety
developed the ideas of the "perpetual virginity" and "immaculate

---

make the sarcastic remark, "When and to whom was it revealed?" *History of
Dogma*, vol. 7, p. 100, New York: Dover, 1961 (reprint of the 1900 edition.)
[22] Irenaeus, *Adv. Haer.* Book 5, *prooem.*
[23] *Imago dei*, Gen. 1.26-27.

conception" was a positive contribution to the life of the church because it rescued a crucial part of religion which Christianity nearly lost, namely, the feminine aspect of the divine. The entire development may be looked upon as the response of the Christian genius to a challenge posed by paganism.[24] Paganism had its own elaborate system of thought to account for the divisions and opposites that people experience in the world and in their lives. By positing the existence of goddesses as well as gods, the pagans acknowledged male and female as having equal dignity because only the two together are "one," separately they are halves. By raising Mary to the level of goddess, Christianity provided a cosmic framework for its theory of salvation: salvation is universal, it is vastly more than the bestowal of eternal life on isolated souls. Salvation involves the cosmos, as Paul declared in Romans 5. But where there is a second Adam, there is also a second Eve. And when the two become one, that is the final redemption.

B. Mary as Earth-Goddess

For ancient people, the earth itself revealed the divine female. Observing the fecundity of the earth, they recognized the same mystery that is repeated by every woman in childbirth. The similarity is clear: the earth is like a mysterious womb, receiving the seed, nurturing it, and in due time bringing forth the fruit. Thus Earth, capitalized, became personified as the Mother *par excellence*. This was also the basis of the cosmogonic myth that a sexual union between sky and earth was the primordial cause through which everything was brought into being.[25]

---

[24] The doctrine of the "Immaculate Conception" rests largely upon the historicity of the stories recorded in Gen. 3. However, if Adam was not a historical person, then the doctrine faces a very serious challenge of interpretation. See further Edward D. O'Connor, "Modern Theories on Original Sin and the Immaculate Conception." *Marian Studies* 20 (1969) 112-136. This article deals with, among others, the theories of Teilhard de Chardin. See also George Soll, *Mariologie.* Freiburg: Herder, 1978, pp. 246-248. On "original sin" see: Oscar Hardmann, *The Christian Doctrine of Grace.* London: Geoffrey Bles: The Centenary Press, 1937; Carolo Boyer, S. J. *Tractatus De Gratia Divina.* Rome: Gregorian University, 1938; Henri Rondet, *The Grace of Christ. A Brief History of the Theology of Grace.* Westminster, Md.: Newman Press, 1966; Otto Hermann Pesch, Albrecht Peters, *Einführung in die Lehre von Gnade und Rechtfertigung.* Darmstadt: Wissenschaftliche Buchgesellschaft, 1981, M. Schmaus, etc., editors, *Handbuch der Dogmengeschichte* II/3. "Urstand, Fall, Erbsünde." Freiburg: Herder, 1982.

[25] Two excellent books deal with this topic: Albrecht Dieterich, *Mutter*

Ancient literature amply testifies to the divine awe and respect with which the Earth was treated. Already in Homer, sacrifices, prayers, and oaths were directed to Sun and Earth.[26] Later, more precise statements were made, such as the famous fragment of Xenophanes: "everything comes from earth and everything returns to earth."[27] Or, Aeschylus who put these words into the mouth of Electra: "... Earth herself, that bringeth all things to birth and having nurtured them receiveth their increase in turn ..."[28] The examples could be multiplied,[29] but we must turn to the important point of how the mystery of creation observed in the functioning of Earth was transferred to women. A good starting point may be Plato, who hypothesized that begetting and bringing forth children was not always done as it is today. Originally men did the act of impregnation *on earth* "like the crickets," but later Zeus moved their genitals to the front, so that a woman could be impregnated.[30] Here the image of a farmer sowing the seed on his field comes immediately to mind. And so we find that many ancient authors expressed the belief that there was a profound similarity between what the farmer did to earth when he ploughed it and what he did to his wife when he had intercourse with her and impregnated her. This thought goes back to Sumerian times, as

---

Erde. Leipzig, Berlin: Teubner, 1905 and Franz Altheim, *Terra Mater. Untersuchungen zur altitalienischen Religionsgeschichte.* Giessen: Töpelmann, 1931. Both are indispensable. See also W. K. C. Guthrie, *In the Beginning.* pp. 11-45.

[26] *Iliad*, 3.104; 3.276; 19.258. See A. T. Murray, *Homer. The Iliad*, vol. I, pp. 125; 137; vol. 2, p. 355. *LCL.* London: Heinemann, 1978.

[27] Fragment 27, Diels, *op. cit.* p. 135: ἐκ γαίης γὰρ πάντα καὶ εἰς γῆν πάντα τελευτᾶι.

[28] *The Libation Bearers.* 126-127; *LCL.* H. W. Smyth, ed. London: Heinemann, 1971, vol. 2, p. 171; see also p. 148.

[29] Aeschylus, *Seven Against Thebes*, 16-17, *op. cit.* p. 323; 69, *op. cit.* p. 237; *Prometheus* 88: παμμήτωρ γῆ *op. cit.* vol. 3, pp. 224-255; Pindar, *Pythian Ode* 9.98-103; *LCL* J. Sandys, ed. p. 283. For an extensive collection of pre-Socratic references to Earth see Diels, *Die Fragmente der Vorsokratiker.* Berlin: Weidmann, 1954, vol. 3, Wortindex by Walther Kranz, pp. 101-104. According to Hesiod, *Works and Days* 61, Pandora was the first woman, made of earth and water. Ovid, *Metamorphoses* 1.368-410 describes how, after the devastating flood, Deucalion and Pyrrha were told by the oracle to "throw behind you the bones of your great mother." Deucalion eventually came to the solution: "Our great mother is the earth and by her bones I think the oracle means the stones in the body of the earth." They threw stones behind them and these turned into men and women. ET.: by Mary M. Innes, *The Metamorphoses of Ovid.* New York: Penguin, 1982, p. 39.

[30] *Symposium* 191C; *LCL* W. R.M. Lamb, editor, London: Heinemann, 1967, vol. 3, p. 141.

was demonstrated by professor Samuel N. Kramer in his translation of the "sacred marriage" between the god Dumuzi (=Tam-
muz) and the goddess Inanna. In this dialogue the queen speaks
first:

> "As for me, my vulva, For me the piled-high billock, Me — the
> maid, who will plow it for me? My vulva, the water ground — for
> me, Me, the Queen, who will station the ox there?" The answer to
> her question is: "Oh Lordly Lady, the king will plow it for you,
> Dumuzi, the king, will plow it for you." Then she joyfully
> responds: "Plow my vulva, man of my heart."

They have intercourse, after which vegetation grows all around
them.[31] Similarly, in the Greek language the verb ἀρόω can
mean to plow the field but also to beget children; in the passive
voice it can express the idea of being begotten.[32]

Not only is the work of the farmer a sexual ritual, but human
intercourse can be viewed as a microcosmic version of earthly
fecundity. The sexual act has a "cosmic structure"; in it the primordial act of creation is repeated, and thus it is a constant reminder that the "cosmos is a living organism which renews itself."[33]
This close relationship between the work of the farmer and the
activity of the husband has been adopted even into Christian
theology. The great Alexandrian, Clemens, explained that the
purpose of sexual intercourse is the generation of children just as
the farmer's act of cultivating the earth and sowing the seeds has
the end of producing food. The farmer who gives his seed to an
animated soil is concerned for the life of the universe, and so is
on a much higher level than the simple farmer who produces

---

[31] Samuel Noah Kramer, *The Sacred Marriage Rite*. Bloomington,
Indiana: Indiana University Press, 1969, p. 148. Baumann, *op. cit.*, p. 382
quotes a Babylonian saying: "Ein Acker der nicht bestellt wird, ist gleich
einer Frau, die ohne Gatten is." I could not verify this saying. But compare
Lucian, *Lexiphanes* 19, *LCL* 5, 319: Cleinas does not have intercourse with his
wife any longer; she is "unapproachable and uncultivated." (ἄβατος καὶ
ἀνήροτός ἐστιν). Also see Robert Graves and Raphae Patai, *Hebrew Myths : The
Book of Genesis*, New York McGraw-Hill, 1966, pp.241–242: "Hebrew myths
treat women as fields to be ploughed and sown ..."
[32] Liddell and Scott, *op. cit.*, p. 245. Impregnating a woman is to "sow the
female soil" wrote Lucretius, *De rerum natura* 4.1107, *op. cit.*, p. 219. See also
C. C. Van Essen, *"Venus Cloacina"* Mnemosyne 9 (1956) 137-144. For more
examples see U. Winter, *op. cit.*, p. 322.
[33] Mircea Eliade, *The Sacred and the Profane. The Nature of Religion.* New
York: Harcourt, Brace & World, 1959, p. 148. See also Kees W. Bolle,
"Hieros Gamos." *ER* 6.317-321.

only perishable food. One cares only for himself, the other cares for God and obeys God, who said: "Be fruitful and multiply!" (Gen.1.28.)[34] Hippolytus preserved a sentence from the followers of the heretic Simon, who justified their promiscuous behavior with this argument: "All earth is earth, and there is no difference where any one sows, provided he does sow."[35]

The original mother is, of course, Earth, said Plato. She not only brought forth men but also food for nourishment, and thus it is not "earth that imitates the woman in the matter of conception and birth, but the woman the earth."[36] And so the poets sang the praises of "Earth, the mother of us all ... Well-formed Earth, oldest of all who nourishes all things living on land ... On you it depends to give life or take it away from mortal men."[37] "Divine Earth, mother of men and of the blessed gods, you nourish all, you give all, you bring all to fruition, and you destroy all."[38] In Athens there was a sanctuary to Earth "surnamed Olympian"[39] and an image of Earth "beseeching Zeus to rain upon her."[40] For the Athenians, the concept of "mother" was identical with "Earth,"[41] and this concept shines through in Latin literature, too. The fragment of Xenophanes, quoted above, appears in Latin in a fragment of Ennius.[42] Lucretius wrote that "Earth has won the name of Mother, since from earth have all things sprung."[43]

---

[34] *Paedagogus* 2.10.83; *ANF* 2.259. *Athenagoras, A Plea* ... uses the symbolism of "the husbandman throwing the seed" and the procreation of children. *ANF* 2.146.

[35] *Refutation* 6.14; *ANF* 5.80.

[36] *Menexenus* 238A, *LCL*, R. G. Bury, ed. London: Heinemann, 152, vol. 7, p. 345.

[37] *Homeric Hymn to Earth* 1.7; Apostolos Athannasakis, *The Homeric Hymns.* Baltimore and London: Johns Hopkins University Press, 1976, p. 67; Charles Boer, *The Homeric Hymns.* Chicago: The Swallow Press, 1970, p. 5. See also Aeschylus, *Libation Bearers,* quoted above.

[38] Apostolos N. Athannasakis, *The Orphic Hymns.* Missoula, Mont. Scholars Press, 1977, p. 37; see also Hesiod, *Theogony,* 5.126 ff. and for further examples Mircea Eliade, *Patterns in Comparative Religion.* London and New York: Sheed and Ward, 1958, pp. 239-264.

[39] Pausanias, *Description of Greece* 1.18.7 *LCL*, W. H. S. Jones, editor, London: Heinemann, 1918, v. l.p. 91: here was the opening in the floor where the flood waters disappeared.

[40] Pausanias, *op. cit.,* 1.24.3; *LCL, op. cit.,* p. 123.

[41] U. von Wilamowitz-Mollendorf, "Excurse zu Euripides Herakliden," *Hermes* 17 (1882) 357-358.

[42] *Epicharmus,* frg. 52, Diels, *op. cit.* p. 206-207: *"terris gentis omnis peperit et resumit denuo."*

[43] *On the Nature of Things* 5.790; Charles E. Bennet, ed. New York: W. J.

Many times we read about the important role the Romans assigned to Earth in marriage relations and the birth of children. At the wedding of Aeneas and Dido "Primal Earth and Nuptial Juno" gave the sign, and later we read that "Mother Earth was provoked to anger."[44] Newborn children were placed on the earth, from which the father picked them up in the presence of the goddess Levana, acknowledging the child as his own.[45] Consequently, in Italy little children who died were not cremated, but buried: it was believed that they still belonged to their "mother."[46]

Now, the best fertile soil is black in color and the blacker it is the more suited it is for agriculture. And so we hear that the Greek corn- goddess, Demeter, whose name already in ancient times was derived from Ge-meter = Earth mother, was in historical times still worshipped in Arcadia as an ancient earth-goddess. Pausanias knew that in Phygaleia, in Arcadia, there was a statue of the Black Demeter (Δημήτηρ Μέλαινα) which was eventually consumed by fire. He also says that a statue worshipped by the Phygaleans in a cave was dressed in black, because that is how the goddess mourned for her lost daughter.[47] Aristotle quotes a poem by Solon in which he says: "... before the judgment-seat of Time, the mighty mother of the Olympian gods, Black earth, would best bear witness ... "[48] Several other goddesses were pictured as black, among them the many-breasted Artemis of Ephesus, Isis, Ceres, and others. The meteorite stone at Pessinus,

---

Black, 1946, p. 268; see also 5.820-823, p. 269-270.

[44] Vergil, *Aeneis* 4.166, *LCL* H.R. Fairclough, ed. London: Heinemann, 1916, vol. 1, p. 407 and 4.178, *loc. cit.*; to which Servius in his commentary observed: *"Quidam sane etiam Tellurem praeesse muptiis tradunt; nam et in auspiciis nuptiarum invocatur."* G. Thilo et H. Hagen, *Servii Grammatici Qui Feruntur in Vergilii Carmina Commentarii*. Leipzig and Berlin: Teubner, 1923, p. 492.

[45] Augustine, *De civ. Dei* 4.11; it is in this chapter that Augustine fulminates against the idea that Jupiter and Juno, heaven and earth, would have relations with each other.

[46] Pliny, *Naturalis Historia* 7.72: "It is a universal custom not to cremate a person who dies before cutting his teeth." *LCL*. H. Rackham, editor, London: Heinemann, 1969, v. 2, p. 553; see also Juvenal, *Satire* 15, 1140 *LCL*, G.G. Ramsey, ed., London, Heinemann, 1950, p. 299.

[47] *Guide to Greece* 8.5.8 and 8.42; ET.: Peter Levi, *Pausanias. Guide to Greece.* Baltimore, Md.: Penguin, 1971, vol. 2, pp. 381 and 476. See also article "Demeter" in Pauly-Wissowa-Krol, *op.cit.* 4/2, 2713-2764, and article "Melaina", *op. cit.* 15/1, 384-386; Euripides, *Bacchae* 275-276 "... divine Demeter, Earth is she ..." *op. cit.* p. 25.

[48] *Athenian Constitution* 12.4; *LCL*, H. Rackham, ed. London: Heinemann, 1952, p. 39.

belonging to the Great Mother Cybele, was also black, which indicates that all these goddesses represented telluric fecundity and were worshipped as fertility goddesses.

In Christian tradition the role of earth as *genetrix* was based on Genesis 2.7: God formed the first man, Adam, from the earth. In Genesis 3:19 it is said that that is where men will again return: "You are dust and to dust you shall return." Although there is no indication in the Bible of any worship of earth, the idea of "Mother Earth" is there. It appears in texts like Job 1:21: "Naked I came from my mother's womb, and naked shall I return ...," or Isaiah 62.3-5, where the fruitful land is compared to a married woman. "Returning to dust" is a common expression of death[49] and the eschatological resurrection is described as coming back from the earth.[50] In 1 Corinthians 15, Paul uses the imagery of a farmer sowing seeds when he develops his thesis of the resurrection, and that, of course, is the classic text, used even today in Christian funeral services. On such occasions the idea of earth-mother sometimes still shines through. In the funeral oration of his father, Gregory Nazianzen said, "Life...takes its rise from the corruption which is our mother..."[51] When the apostle John prepared to die, according to an apocryphal story, he stood in his grave and told his followers to "throw my mother earth upon me and cover me up."[52]

The concept of earth as *genetrix* gained importance when the first Christian theologians established a parallelism between the primeval creation and the new creation brought about by Christ. Adam was made from earth without a father, and Jesus Christ, conceived without father, was born from Mary "as yet virgin."[53] In this text, Irenaeus already thought of Mary as representing earth. He was careful to emphasize her virginity at the time of conception because only so is the parallelism perfect. Thus in the *Martyrdom of S. Andrew* we read: "Since the first man, who brought death into the world through the transgression of the tree, had been produced from the spotless earth, it was necessary that the

---

[49] Psalm 90.3; 104.29.
[50] Ezechiel 37.1-28.
[51] *Oration* 18.42, *NPNF*, Series 2, vol. 7, p. 268.
[52] See Richard A. Lipsus, *Die Apokryphen Apostelgeschichten und Apostellegenden*. Braunschweig: C.A. Schwetschke und Sohn, 1883, vol. 1, p. 397.
[53] Irenaeus, *Adv. Haer* 3.21.10; 3.22.1. *ANF* 1. p. 454.

Son of God should be begotten a perfect man from the spotless virgin..."[54] Later, S. Ambrose spelled it out: *ex terra virgine Adam, Christus ex virgine.*[55] So Mary is presented as the virgin soil into which the creative word of God fell at the Annunciation when, through the Word, the conception of Jesus took place. Observe the parallelism: God created by his word both times. Earth brings forth when it is cultivated, woman conceives when her body is "cultivated" by a male. But it was not so in the case of the Virgin Mary; she was the *"terra non arabilis quae fructum parterit,"*[56] i.e., she conceived without her body being "violated" by a male. For Christians who thought in terms of a "first" and "second" creation, Mary more and more emerged as the sublime female, the earth-goddess who gives life. But, incorporated into the Christian history of salvation, Mary is thought of not as just another earth-goddess, but as an integral part of a "new creation" made by God. In the divine act of generation she is Earth with whom Heaven unites and thus she is the female component of the divine. But she is also a part of created humanity, representing earthbound mankind in its relation to heaven, her Son and God's Son is the first person of the new humanity. Thus the earth-goddess became a thoroughly Christian figure; Mary is not Cybele or Isis, she is the Mother of God, Jesus.

In addition to Cybele, the Great Mother, there were many other divine females whose worshippers could transfer their devotion to Mary when they came to identify themselves with the new faith. Statues and statuettes of pagan goddesses, some of them holding a child, are very close to, one could say identical with, representations of Mary and the child Jesus. A Celtic votive statue, reprinted by Jacques Huynen,[57] is very similar to the statue of the venerated Virgin of Marsat, reprinted on the opposite page in Huynen's book. It is well known that the iconography of Isis and Horus was basically adopted by Christians when they started to portray Mary and Jesus as Mother and Child.[58] It is entirely possible that in

---

[54] *MPG* 2.1225; *ANF* 8.512.
[55] *In Lucam* 4.7.8; *CChL* 14, 108, followed by Augustine, *De genesi contra Manichaeos* 2. 37, *MPL* 34, 21. See also Epiphanius, *Panarion* 79.7.2: "He re-creates himself out of the Virgin as an artist and Lord, as if from earth."
[56] Medieval hymn quoted by M. Eliade, *Patterns...* p. 259.
[57] *L'enigme des vierges noires.* Paris: Editions Robert Laffant, 1972, between pp. 1-129.
[58] R. E. Witt, *op. cit.* pp. 216-217; plates 3 and 69.

some cases pagan statues may have been "baptized" and rededicated as objects of veneration of Mary. It is a well known fact that sanctuaries dedicated to Mary were often built on sites that were originally used for the veneration of pagan goddesses. The same development could have happened in regard to statues, particularly when the statue of the Virgin is black in color. Shrines of earth-goddesses were scattered all over Europe, as are venerated statues of the "Black Madonna," which can be found in great numbers from Great Britain to Hungary and Poland. In none of them with which I am familiar can negroid features be detected; therefore, they are not black because of their race. In some cases the material from which they are made is black; in other cases, it is claimed that accumulated dirt and soot may account for their color. This explanation, usually given by Roman Catholic scholars,[59] does not explain why the whole body of the statue turned black, even under the clothing, and not just the face and hands. And what about those to which none of these arguments apply? One answer lies at hand: they are black because they represent earth, the mother of all. That Christians could so easily think of Mary as black should not be surprising. Not only was the relationship between Mary and the virgin earth long established, from quite early the Song of Songs was interpreted in the church in a Marian way. This love song was explained as referring to the relationship between Christ and the church, his bride; since the church was identified with Mary, the song could be also be applied to the love of God and Mary; and the female lover in the Song of Songs is black: "I am black but beautiful, O daughters of Jeruselem."[60]

Thus nothing stands in the way of seeing in the veneration of the Black Madonnas a continuation of the popular piety with which the great mystery of earth was honored. In some areas of Europe the roots of this piety, such as that of the Celts,[61] may go back to pre-Roman times. It may have been Artemis or Isis who inspired the cult. In Tindari, Sicily, the *Madonna Nera* is in a

---

[59] M. R. Brown, "Black Madonna." *Encyclopaedic Dictionary of Religion.* Washington, D.C.: Corpus Publications, 1979, vol. 1, p. 465; Bruguera, Justino, *Montserrat.* Barcelona: Editoril Planete, 1964. (a Spanish travelers guide to the shrine of Montserrat).

[60] Song of Songs 1.5; see the commentary by Marion H. Pope, *Song of Songs.* Garden City, N.Y.: Doubleday & Co., 1977.

[61] See Footnote 57.

church erected on the site of a former sanctuary of Cybele.[62]
Lyons, France, was also a city of Cybele where a huge temple was
built in her honor, only to be replaced later by a Christian church
in which the black virgin is venerated; it is assumed to be the
replica of an ancient image.[63] In Italy, Monte Vergine near
Naples was in Roman times a place of pilgrimage for worshippers
of Cybele. Here again her sanctuary was transformed into a
church. Many stones from the pagan structure were used to build
the new one in which the *Madonna Bruna* (brown Madonna) is
now honored.[64] In Marseilles, which was formerly the Greek
colony of Massilia, the most popular goddess was Artemis, whom
the Phocaeans, founders of Massilia, brought from Ephesus. The
statue of Artemis from Ephesus is black, and so is the Virgin
venerated in the Notre Dame de la Confession.[65] In Paris, a center
of the worship of Isis, a black statue of Isis was actually venerated
as the Virgin until the sixteenth century.[66] The French sometimes affectionately call Mary "la Bonne Mère," the good mother,
which was the name of an obscure Roman goddess, *Bona Dea*,
who was worshipped exclusively by women in secret nocturnal
ceremonies.[67] It was probably that version of the Great Mother
which the Hungarians brought from Asia, and which, re-inter-
preted as Mary, is still included in the church calendar there
under its ancient name. The two feast days assigned to this celebration, called the "Greater" and "Lesser,"[68] are the most popular
Marian holidays in Hungary. But regardless of place or origin, it
was the desire to worship the mother goddess that eventually
restored these images, in which people found expressed reverence
for the fertility of the earth, for childbirth, and for the feminine
aspect of God. The same idea was transplanted to the new world.
Soon after the conquest of Mexico by Cortez, the native mother of

---

[62] See article "Tyndaros" in Pauly, *op. cit.* Zweite Reihe, vol. 4, pp. 1776-
1796; on the Black Madonna, p. 1783.
[63] Ean Begg, *The Cult of the Black Virgin.* London: Arkana, 1985, pp. 58,
195.
[64] Begg, *op. cit.* p. 244. Th. Trede, *Das Heidentum in der römischen Kirche.*
Gotha: I.A. Perthes, 1889, II, 88-93.
[65] Begg, *op. cit.* p. 197.
[66] Begg, *op. cit.* p. 64-64; he also mentions the possible derivation of the
word Paris from Par-Isis = "grove of Isis."
[67] *The Oxford Classical Dictionary*, p. 172.
[68] Nagy Boldog Asszony; Kis Boldog Asszony.

life in Guadelupe was replaced by the Virgin Mary. Her image, dark like that of an Indian, is said to have been imprinted miraculously on the mantle of an Indian convert.[69]

There are more than four hundred Black Madonnas all over the world. Not all of them are native creations. Some of the most famous are attributed to the workmanship of St. Luke and are believed to have been brought to Europe one way or another. The Black Madonna of Czestochowa was, according to tradition, painted by St. Luke on a table made by Jesus and discovered by St. Helena, Mother of Constantine. Other Madonnas also claim such distinguished origins, and pious tradition keeps alive the faith that many of them were brought back by the crusaders when they returned from the Holy Land. Yet the origin of the cult of the Black Virgin is shrouded in mystery. It began to flower during the Middle Ages, but clearly it was there much before. Many attempts were made to account for the origin of the cult: it was connected with medieval initiation rites, spiritual traditions, even the Holy Grail and the Ark of the Covenant. Historical methods, psychological techniques, even astrology have been used to explain the phenomenon. Yet the solution seems to be simple: the Black Madonna is the ancient earth-goddess converted to Christianity.[70]

Earth, however, is not only the source of fertility and new life. It is also an agent of death. Franz Altheim and Albrecht Dieterich collected much material demonstrating that in Greek and Roman religion the cult of the earth also included the cult of the dead.[71] We have seen above how often Greeks and Romans expressed the idea that "everything comes from earth and everything returns to it." This is ultimately what lies behind the saying of Paul, "What you sow does not come to life unless it dies."[72] Terra Mater

---

[69] Marina Warner, *Alone of All Her Sex*. New York: Alfred A. Knopf, 1976, p. 302-303; Ena Campbell, "The Virgin of Guadelupe and the Female Self-Image: A Mexican Case History." in J. J. Preston, *Mother Worship*. pp. 5-24; Alan R. Sandstrom, "The Tonantsi Cult of the Eastern Nahua." J. J. Preston; *op. cit.* pp. 25-50; Begg, *op. cit.* pp. 247-248, and Marie Durand-Lefebvre, *Étude sur l'origine des vierges noires*. Paris: G. Durassie and Cie., 1937.

[70] See the works by Huynen and Begg, quoted above. In addition to these and the other works quoted above, there are many other publications dealing with the general topic and also with individual, local "Black Virgins."

[71] See footnote 25.

[72] 1 Cor. 15.32.

controls the fate of seeds and of the dead; she is the great womb in which seeds grow and in which the dead wait for the renewal of their life. In ancient Greece not only the harvested seeds were placed in earthen jars, but also the bodies of the dead. In many ancient cults, rites for the dead and rites for fertility coincided.[73] For these are the two overwhelmingly important issues of human existence: birth and death, the beginning and the end of life, which the earth goddess unites in herself. She is indeed the "Great Mother" and that is why the pious pray to the Madonna in the "Hail Mary": "Holy Mary, Mother of God, pray for us sinners now and at the hour of our death. Amen."

C. THE QUEEN IS CROWNED

As Mary gradually became identified with the great goddesses of the ancient Greco-Roman world, pious believers began to accord to her the same honorary titles that were accorded to other goddesses. Among these the most exalted was that of "Queen," a name by which Juno, Isis, and many others were called. Revelation 12 already presented Mary in a queenly role, and by the time the Council of Ephesus met in 431, the people on the streets of the city freely hailed her with the same titles with which they previously had hailed their Artemis. Exegesis of Genesis 3.15 also pointed in this direction, for if Mary is so closely associated with Christ in the work of salvation, and if Christ is indeed King,[74] then Mary could rightly be called Queen. Christian iconography, as we have seen, adopted the theme of Isis and Horus in the representation of Mary and Christ, thus further popularizing Mary's queenship. Nor could the fact that so many Christian churches were built on the sites of the sanctuaries of pagan goddesses fail to make an impact on public piety. Mosaics of these churches bear witness to the same popular belief: In the S. Maria Maggiore (on the site of Juno Lucina's temple) Mary is presented enthroned and dressed in the robes of a Byzantine princess. This theme became quite common. In the S. Maria in Trastevere Mary and Christ sit

---

[73] M. Eliade, *Patterns* ... pp. 345-358.
[74] Rev. 17:14, "King of Kings and Lord of Lords," also 19:16. The title of Jesus as "Lord" applies here, too, because that name was associated with supreme authority, e.g., Eph. 5:20; Col. 3:17; see also the use of the "name which is above every name." Phil. 2:9.

next to each other on thrones, like king and queen. During the Middle Ages and later, when the title "Queen" was freely used in reference to Mary, many of her statues and paintings show her with a crown on her head.

The "official" enthronement of Mary, however, occurred only in 1954, when the pope, Pius XII, issued his Encyclical *Ad Coeli Reginam* (To the Queen of Heaven), establishing a liturgical feast in honor of Mary.[75] While this is not a dogmatic constitution defining Mary's queenship as a "revealed truth," it does sanction the use of the title, for encyclicals are papal letters to which the people are expected to show respect and obedience. The letter came as no surprise to anyone because already a year before the pope announced a "Marian year" to commemorate the one hundredth anniversary of the proclamation of the dogma of the "Immaculate Conception." This encyclical, known as the *Fulgens Corona Gloriae* , begins with these words: "The radiant crown of glory, with which the most pure brow of the Virgin Mother was encircled by God, seems to us to shine more brilliantly, as we recall to mind the day...etc."[76] Thus, the pope made a clear reference not only to Revelation 12, but also to the widely held belief in Mary's queenship. This pope, who was noted for his singular devotion to Mary, also used the occasion of the promulgation of the dogma of the bodily Assumption of Mary to stress this point. In this Bull he said:

> "Hence the revered Mother of God, from all eternity joined in a hidden way with Jesus Christ in one and the same decree of predestination, immaculate in her conception, a most perfect virgin in her divine motherhood, the noble associate of the divine Redeemer who has won a complete triumph over sin and its consequences, was finally granted, as the supreme culmination of her privileges .. that she might be taken up body and soul to the glory of heaven where, as Queen, she sits in splendor at the right hand of her Son, the immortal King of the Ages."[77]

In 1943, when the pope issued the encyclical *Mystici Corporis*, in which he dealt extensively with the role of Mary in redemption, he had already referred to her with these words: "... her body and

---

[75] The official text is in the *Acta Apostalicae Sedis* 46 (1954) 625-640.

[76] *Acta Apostolicae Sedis* 45 (1953) 590; ET: Dahony and Kelly, *op. cit.* 252-268.

[77] *Munificentissimus Deus. AAS* 42 (1950) 768-769; *ET* Doheny and Kelly, *op. cit.* p. 236.

soul refulgent with the glory of heaven, where she reigns with her Son ..."[78] It would take too much space to review all the honors that Pius XII paid to Mary. In various other pronouncements he called her "Queen of the Family," "Queen of Saints," "Queen of Mothers," and so forth, thus giving expression to a belief that was widely held in the church at least since the Middle Ages.

With these pronouncements a development of nearly two thousand years reached its climax: Mary has been officially enthroned as Queen of Heaven where she reigns jointly with Jesus. In this book we have followed this line of development. Now we will take a brief look at the actual content of this faith, for clearly Mary is a Christian phenomenon. While the evolutionary process started from paganism and developed through pagans converted to Christianity, it gradually shed all pagan associations. How, then, does Christian theology explain, support, and justify faith in the queenship of Mary?

To understand this point clearly we must know how the minds of Christians work when they talk about articles of faith. The basic point is that nothing can be an object of faith that does not rest on divine revelation. Divine revelation is found in the Bible, which is *The Word* of God; therefore, what is in the Bible (Old and New Testaments) is revealed truth.[79] So far most Christians would agree, but at this point differences arise. Some, mostly those whose roots go back to the sixteenth-century Reformation, say that the Bible contains the apostolic tradition which was closed when the canon, i.e., the list of authoritive books in the Bible, was established. Others, mostly Roman Catholics, say that "... it is not from sacred Scripture alone that the Church draws her certainty about everything which has been revealed. Therefore, both sacred tradition and sacred Scripture are to be accepted and venerated with the same sense of devotion and reverence."[80] Scripture and tradition, however, should not be considered two sources, but one, because "both of them, flowing from the same divine wellspring,

---

[78] *AAS* 35 (1943) 248.
[79] I must omit any discussion of such questions as "verbal inspiration" and related matters.
[80] *The Documents of Vatican II.* W.l. Abbott, S.J., General Editor, New York: The American Press, 1966, p. 117: Dogmatic Constitution on Divine Revelation. Ch. II. 9. The statement reflects the position of the Council of Trent (1546- 1563) that the church *"pari pietatis affectu ac venerentia suscipit et veneratur"* both Scripture and Tradition. See Denzinger, *op. cit.* 1501.

in a certain way merge into a unity and tend toward the same end.''[81] The Bible has a chronological primacy because it was committed to writing before tradition began to develop. However, when the apostles appointed bishops as their successors, they also transmitted to them the teaching authority. Tradition, therefore, means apostolic teaching as it "develops in the church with the help of the Holy Spirit."[82] The difference between scripture and tradition is merely the fact that one is contained in a book and the other is transmitted without writing.[83] Thus, divine revelation is contained in both written tradition and "living" tradition.

But this is not all. Scripture and tradition need to be interpreted and the privilege of interpretation "has been entrusted exclusively to the living teaching office of the church."[84] An object of faith must be supported by all three of these elements, because, "... sacred tradition, sacred scripture, and the teaching authority of the church, in accord with God's most wise design, are so linked and joined together that one cannot stand without the others, and that all together and each in its own way under the action of the Holy Spirit contribute effectively to the salvation of souls."[85] The teaching authority of the church is called the *Magisterium* and any discussion of a matter pertaining to an article of faith, in our case, the queenship of Mary, must begin with an exploration of what the *Magisterium* teaches; only after that can scripture and tradition be examined. Pope Pius XII laid down the following general rule: the task of the theologian is "to show how that which is taught by the living *Magisterium* is contained explicitly or implicitly in scripture and in divine tradition."[86] The starting point is, therefore, the mind of the *Magisterium*, because compared with that scripture and tradition are "remote" sources.[87] The teaching authority of the church culminates in the pope and since the pope is infallible when he makes a solemn declaration in matters of faith and

---

81 *The Documents of Vatican II*, p. 117.
82 *Op cit.* p. 116.
83 *The Council of Trent* is echoed here too, see Denzinger, 1501.
84 *The Documents of Vatican II*, pp. 117-118.
85 *Op. cit.* p. 118.
86 Encyclical *Humani Generis*, AAS 42 (1950) 568.
87 Cyril Vollert, "The Scientific Structure of Mariology." Carol, *op. cit.* vol. 2, p. 12. The *Magisterium*, however, does not have to support its teachings from Scripture and Tradition, because "the actual unanimity of the teaching church is a sufficient criterion." Vollert, *loc. cit.*

morals, he can declare an article of faith to be dogma on his own authority, i.e., *motu proprio*. This was the case with the promulgation of the dogma of Mary's bodily assumption into heaven.[88] Let us see how these principles are applied to the thesis of Mary's queenship.

The queenship of Mary is clearly a part of the teaching of the *Magisterium,* as the encyclicals *Fulgens Corona* and *Ad Coeli Reginam* show. The earliest magisteral references go back to the early Middle Ages and then gradually become more frequent as popular devotion to Mary becomes more widespread. The process, as we have seen, culminated under Pius XII. This teaching is supported by reference to Scripture. Two texts are especially quoted. One is Genesis 3:15, "I will put enmity between you and the woman ..." Here the prophecy, called protoevangelium, foretells the crushing of the serpent's head. Mary was so closely associated with this conquest that she is said to be truly foreshadowed in this text as queen. The other text is Revelation 12. This, as we have seen, has long been explained in a Marian sense. This is now the official exegesis of the church, since Pope Pius X declared: "Everyone knows that this woman signified the Virgin Mary..."[89] Mary is depicted in this text in a royal robe and with a royal crown, a clear reference to her queenship. A further biblical text quoted in this context is Luke 1:26-38. In this story of the annunciation, interpreters stress the fact that Mary responded to the angel, "Let it be to me according to your word." With this statement, they argue, she actively cooperated in the work of salvation because her answer constitutes an active consent to the conception of Jesus. Without her *Fiat* ("let it be"), conception could not have taken place; by giving her consent, Mary became intimately associated with Jesus, his redeeming work, and his kingly rule. Ancillary texts which are given a Marian interpretation include: Psalm 45, which is considered a "messianic" psalm, verse 9: "At your hand stands the queen." 1 Kings 2:19: Solomon "had a seat

---

[88]   *Ineffabilis Deus* (1854) was the Bull which declared the doctrine of papal infallibility, and *Munificentissiumus Deus* (1950) was the Bull in which Pius XII promulgated the dogma of Mary's bodily assumption "by the authority of our Lord Jesus Chirst, of the blessed Apostles Peter and Paul, and by our own authority." Doheny and Kelly, *op. cit.* p. 239.

[89]   *Ad diem Illum.* Doheny and Kelly, p. 146. Since then, this interpretation is routinely used in papal documents.

brought for the king's mother; and she sat on his right." Esther 2:17: "The king loved Esther ... and ... he set the royal crown on her head and made her queen ..."[90] Luke 1:39-56: Elizabeth greeted Mary with the title, "The mother of my Lord." Matthew 2:1-12, where the magis are thought to give royal honors to Mary. The scholars who quote these texts, however, know that only in retrospect, i.e., only when the queenship of Mary is already known, do they yield this interpretation.

Tradition can be ascertained from the works of the church fathers and other ecclesiastical authors and from the liturgy, the official form of public worship in which the church gives expression to what it believes. Neither of these goes back much beyond the Middle Ages as far as the queenship of Mary is concerned, which means only that this truth, which was *implicitly* always in the apostolic deposit of faith, became *explicit* gradually. Thus, *magisterium*, scripture, and tradition are all utilized to support the thesis, which thus can be viewed as a truth revealed by God.[91]

What is the function of Mary in her capacity as queen? The Greek and Roman goddesses were in charge of all female functions, presiding over marriage, childbirth, and similar issues. But what is Mary doing as a queen and what is the extent of her authority? In popular piety simple believers still turn to her with the same problems our pagan ancestors brought to their goddesses, and it is a common homiletic device, even among Protestants, to refer to Mary as the paragon of wife and mother. Officially, however, her queenship has not yet been completely defined and scholars still disagree among themselves concerning some issues. Everybody seems to agree that the kingdom of Mary is the kingdom of Jesus Christ and that she jointly rules with him. Authority is not divided between them because they rule in complete agreement and unity. Mary is not vice-regent, so to speak, neither does she have independent spheres of influence. She is so closely united with Christ that the two act as one. It is conceivable, therefore, that a definition of Mary's rule with Christ

---

90   See also Esther 5.3.

91   Once again we must remember that no such dogma has yet been promulgated.For the understanding of this problem I have used the papal documents and the massive Mariologies of Roschini, Scheeben, Carol and Soll. I do not know of any Protestant work dealing specifically with this issue.

may eventually conclude that in this association the words of
Paul receive their fulfillment, "there is neither male nor female";[92] masculine and feminine are reunited in the image of
the Godhead. The kingdom of Christ is a spiritual kingdom, the
unique nature of which is the salvation of mankind. The rulers'
function is directed toward this end and they exercise it in full
harmony with grace and mercy.

Three conclusions can be made from this view of Mary's
unique association with Jesus: First, she has a share in the work of
redemption which Christ accomplished. This means that Mary is
Co-redemptrix with Jesus, who is the Redeemer. Secondly, Mary is
a *Mediatrix* between mankind and Jesus, and thirdly, she is the
Dispensatrix of all graces. These are not offical articles of faith but
theses, which are very often used by Mariologists when they try
to define Mary's role in the economy of salvation. Of these three,
the *Co-redemptrix* role of Mary has been almost fully developed by
theologians and under favorable conditions it could be defined as
a dogma by the *magisterium*. The same principles that were used in
the definition of the "immaculate conception" could apply in this
case, too: the *magisterium* unanimously agrees with it; scripture
and tradition do not oppose it; the belief is universal among the
faithful; and it is a fitting doctrine.[93] The first pope to refer to Mary
with this title in an encyclical was Leo XIII in 1894. After him
many others used it and now it is a common designation of
Mary.[94] The biblical arguments in this case, too, rest upon the
interpretation of Genesis 3:15 and Luke 1:38: Mary cooperated
with Jesus in the work of redemption by assenting to be impregnated by the Holy Spirit of God. In the words of a famous Dutch
scholar:

---

[92] Gal. 3.28; see also Mt. 12.25.

[93] Again, I must refer the reader to the Mariologies listed above. A
Protestant work critical of this thesis and gravely concerned about the possi-
bility that it may be the next doctrine to be defined is Roland H. Seboldt,
*Christ or Mary? The Coredemption Role of Mary in Contemporary Roman Catholic
Theology.* St. Louis: Concordia Publishing House, 1963. Also, Cornelius A. de
Ridder, Maria als Miterlöserin. Göttingen: Vanderhoek, 1965. Critical is
Miegge, *op. cit.* pp. 155-177.

[94] Leo XIII: *Iucunda Semper* (1894); Pius X: *Ad diem Illum* (1904); Benedict
XV: *Inter Sodalicia* (1918); Pius XII: *Munificentissimus Deus* (1950) and *Fulgens
Corona Gloriae* (1953) referred to the work of redemption as "common to the
Blessed Virgin and her Divine Son."

Mary is "the receiving and co-operating principle of our redemption. By this we mean, in the first place, that Mary was, in her active conception and receptivity, the co-operating principle in 'objective redemption,' in that she was personally involved in the objective reality of *our* redemption in the man Jesus, and shared in the objective fact of the state of redemption of the whole of mankind brought about in principle in *Christ.*"[95]

Mary as "the receiving and cooperating principle" is as subtle and beautiful a definition as any pagan could have given of the nature of the divine female: it recalls the idea of *Terra Mater,* Caelestis, and all other goddesses, who in their own way expressed the same idea, namely that life is the result of an active cooperation between male and female. The *Co- redemptrix* idea, which is a horrendous thought to many Protestants,[96] could be the basis of a new definition of the concept of God in which womanhood will receive its equal share.

Mediatrix and *Dispensatrix of all Graces* are expressions of Mary's queenly function. The first means that the prayers and requests of the faithful go to Jesus through Mary and because of her mediation will receive a favorable response. According to the second, all good things and spiritual blessings that come to human beings are dispensed by Mary. These titles are outgrowths of Mary's role as *Co-redemptrix* and are supported by the same arguments that were used to support that thesis. Generally, the same popes who favored Mary's role as Co-redemptrix also promoted her as *Mediatrix* and *Dispensatrix of all Graces.* A few examples will suffice. Pope Leo XIII made this statement: "As no man goes to the Father but by the Son, so no one goes to Christ except through his Mother."[97] She is, therefore, "Mediatrix to the Mediator."[98] Pius IX: "God has committed to Mary the treasury of all good things, in order that everyone may know that through her we obtained every hope, every grace, and all salvation. For this is his will, that we obtain

---

95 E. Schillebeeckx, *Mary Mother of Redemption.* New York: Sheed and Ward, 1964, pp. 85, 87.
96 They use Acts 4:12: "There is salvation in no one else, for there is no other name under heaven given among men by which we must be saved." and 1 Timothy 2:5: "For there is one God, and there is one mediator between God and men, the man Christ Jesus." as biblical counter arguments.
97 *Octobri Mense* (1891), Doheny and Kelly, p. 56.
98 Leo XIII, *Fidentem Piumque* (1896), *op. cit.* p. 117. See also *Adiutricem Populi* (1895), *op. cit.* p. 103.

everything through Mary."[99] The quotes could be multiplied but the thrust of the argument is clear. It has been pointed out many times that these theses rest on an uncertain foundation, namely on the incorrect Latin translation of Genesis 3:15 in the Vulgate, which reads, "... she shall bruise your head ..." The Hebrew text, and all modern translations, have the masculine gender, "... he shall bruise your head..." So in several Marian treatises it is stated, "*Her* foot has crushed the head of Satan,"[100] while it should read "*His* foot ..." However, Mary belongs to the Adam-Christ, Eve-Mary parallelism even without this error. More significant is the fact that in the use of these titles there is a subtle shift of the enlightening and mediating role of the Holy Spirit, which is silently being assigned to Mary. Consciously or unconsciously, Marian theology is moving toward a significant reinterpretation of the original Christian concept of the Godhead as consisting of Father, Son, and Holy Spirit. The role of the Holy Spirit will be taken over by Mary, as is shown in a painting located in the Vatican's Galleria Pia. Mary is depicted here between God the Father and Jesus Christ; all three have the same height and appear to be equal. This is the image of the new Trinity in which the feminine has regained its proper place.[101]

The queenship of Mary has been confirmed by the Vatican Council II in the *Dogmatic Constitution on the Church*. Here it is stated that, "She was exalted by the Lord as Queen of All, in order that she might be the more thoroughly conformed to her Son ..."[102] However, this statement appears as a chapter in the larger *Constitution on the Church*. That the theme was not given independent treatment was understood by many as an attempt to tone down "fruitless and passing emotion ..." and "vain credulity," i.e., excessive Marian piety.[103] If this indeed was the desire of the council fathers, their success was partial. While no new doctrines on Mary were defined, popular piety is as strong as ever; new apparitions of the Virgin are reported periodically, such as the

---

[99] *Ubi Primum* (1849), *op. cit.* p. 3.

[100] *Ubi Primum, loc. cit.* For a brief review see Marina Warner, *op. cit.* pp. 245-246.

[101] I have not seen this picture personally and rely on the description of Trede, *op. cit. II.* 341. My efforts to obtain pictures of art work from Italy were very frustrating and unsuccessful.

[102] *Documents of Vatican II*, p. 90.

[103] *Documents of Vatican II*, p. 95.

recent one in Medjugorje in the former southern Yugoslavia.[104]
The presently reigning pope, John Paul II, is devoted to the patron
of Poland, the Black Virgin of Czestochowa. In June 1979, he
visited this image, prayed before it, and delivered a moving message to "all God's people throughout the world who are particularly aware of the presence of Our Lady of Jasna Gora."[105] For the
occasion the image was dressed as a queen, with a crown bearing
magnificent jewels, and a robe also richly bejeweled. The baby
Jesus on her arm is similarly attired.[106] The crown is, of course, a
symbol of queenly dignity. Since earliest Christian times, countless images have depicted Mary like that, and it is a particularly
favorite popular feast when a local statue of the Virgin is crowned.
The processions and ceremonies surrounding such crownings
are strongly reminiscent of ancient processions honoring statues
of goddesses, such as Athene, with a new *peplos*.[107] The abundance of gold and jewelry that constantly surrounds the image in
Czestochowa is breathtaking and would put to shame Lacinian
Juno or Caelestis in Carthage.[108] This seems to be the way devoted
followers of the goddess, from pagan to modern times, can best
express their love for the one they sense to be alive behind her
material likeness. A queen, after all, must have wealth.[109]

---

[104] Other modern apparations include one in Bayside, N.Y. in 1970, one
in Necedah, Wisconsin in 1950, another in Zeitoun, Egypt, between 1968-
1971 which was supposedly witnessed by many thousands. The list is very
long, few of these, however, received ecclesiastical approval.

[105] Devotion to Our Lady of Czestochowa. By the Daughters of St. Paul, St.
Paul Editions. No place or date given.

[106] The Black Virgin of Czestochowa (or Jasna Gora, which is the name
of the monastery in the village of Czestochowa) is a painting and not a
statue. Therefore, to dress the image flat pieces of decorations were prepared
with holes for the heads and hands of Mary and Jesus. Thus the decoration
can be simply superimposed over the painting to give it the impression of a
different dress. The Black Virgin of Czestochow has several dresses. One
shows her with a solid gold halo around her head, another one bedecked
with diamonds, one with pearls, one with rubies and, of course, one with
crown. See Zbigniew Bania and Stanislaw Kobielus, *Jasna Gora*. Warsaw:
Instytut Wydawniczy Pax, 1983. In Polish, with English summary. This
book has very good color pictures showing among others details of the
jewelry and votive offerings of the faithful.

[107] Trede described several of these from southern Italy, *op. cit.* I. 104; II.
345-358, 395; III. 154; IV. 245-250.

[108] See Chapter 2.

[109] Many images of the virgin possess great treasuries which prompted
M. Warner, *op. cit.* p. 117, to comment: "It would be difficult to concoct a
greater perversion of the Sermon on the Mount than the sovereignty of

The queen reigns again. In a recent encyclical the pope
solemnly announced a "Marian Year," a year-long celebration of
Mary. The encyclical, called *Redemptoris Mater*,[110] starts out by
affirming Mary's "precise place in the plan of salvation" but
stresses especially the mysterious relationship between Mary and
the church. It reviews all the biblical passages to which Marian
interpretations are given, from Genesis 3 to Revelation 12, and
reiterates the Marian doctrines and theses, her divine motherhood, her role as *mediatrix*, and others. Considering next the post-
apostolic period, it, interestingly, emphasizes that Mary did not
receive an apostolic mission on the day of Pentecost.[111] Church
councils, liturgical texts, and ecclesiastical authors are quoted in
this letter, which is really a Mariology in a nutshell, drawing on
all the well-known arguments and interpretations that support the
privileges of Mary. Noteworthy in this letter, however, is a
renewed emphasis upon what the pope calls "the Marian dimension of the life of Christ's disciples." A passage from this section
deserves to be more fully quoted:[112]

> This Marian dimension of Christian life takes on special impor-
> tance in relation to women and their status. In fact, femininity has
> a unique relationship with the Mother of the Redeemer, a subject
> which can be studied in greater depth elsewhere. Here I simply
> wish to note that the figure of Mary of Nazareth sheds light on
> womanhood as such by the very fact hat God, in the sublime
> event of the Incarnation of his Son, entrusted himself to the
> ministry of a woman. It can thus be said that women, by looking

---

Mary and its cult ... and equally difficult to imagine a greater distortion of
Christ's idealism than this identification of the rich and powerful with the
good." This is certainly true, but if the learned author had placed the
overflowing generosity of the faithful within the context of Mark 14.3-9, her
judgment may have been milder. Jesus, the author of the Sermon on the
Mountain, rebuked those who called it a waste when a woman poured very
expensive ointment on his head.

[110]   March 25, 1987. I used the English translation prepared by the Office
of Publishing and Promotion Services of the U.S. Catholic Conference. The
Marian Year was to begin June 7, 1987. The last Marian Year was ordered
by Pius XII in 1954 .

[111]   See *op. cit.* p. 57. This is an argument against the ordination of
women as priests. The same position was reiterated by the pope in the letter
Mulieris Dignitatem, issued in September 1988. In this "meditation" once
again, the pope holds up Mary as a model for women but does not grant
them the privilege of priestly service. According to this letter, a second,
more detailed analysis of the role of women in the church and society will
be issued later.

[112]   *Op. cit.* p. 101.

to Mary, find in her the secret of living their femininity with dignity and of achieving their own true advancement. In the light of Mary, the Church sees in the face of women the reflection of a beauty which mirrors the loftiest sentiments of which the human heart is capable: the self-offering totality of love; the strength that is capable of bearing the greatest sorrows; limitless fidelity and tireless devotion to work; the ability to combine penetrating intuition with words of support and encouragement.

A pagan who felt the need to explain why there were goddesses could have written this statement with very little change. For indeed, life does have a feminine dimension, indeed a goddess "sheds light on womanhood as such," and indeed, it is in the goddess that women find "the secret of living their femininity with dignity ..." Even with respect to God the "ministry of women" is indispensable, for femininity is part of the cosmic order. And had this imaginary pagan theologian been asked why the statues of the goddesses look so beautiful and dignified, he/she could have answered: Because we see "in the face of woman the reflection of a beauty which mirrors the loftiest sentiments of which the human heart is capable ..."

The elevation of Mary to queen of heaven completes a long process of clarifying her role in salvation history. Nothing more can be added to her honors. Still unclear, however, is a definition of her image as the feminine aspect of the divine. How this will come about is at present uncertain. I would suggest that in the future greater emphasis will be placed upon the role of the Holy Spirit in the life of the church. Since the Spirit is often identified with Wisdom, with *Sophia* or *Sapientia*, this will invite greater concentration on the feminine aspect of the Godhead. Leonardo Boff, a Roman Catholic scholar, provided the most perceptive analysis in this area of Mariology.[113] He stated his view as follows:

> We maintain the hypothesis that the Virgin Mary, Mother of God and of all men and women, realizes the feminine absolutely and eschatologically, inasmuch as the Holy Spirit has made her his temple, sanctuary and tabernacle in so real and genuine a way that she is to be regarded as hypostatically united to the Third Person of the Blessed Trinity. (p. 93)

---

[113] Leonardo Boff, *The Maternal Face of God. The Feminine and Its Religious Expressions.* San Francisco: Harper and Row, 1987.

"Hypostatic" means absolutely real union. The Greek word ὑπόστασις is used in philosophy almost like the word οὐσία = substance. In Christian theology this expression was used first in Trinitarian discussions to describe the relationships of the three divine persons, and later in Christological debates to discuss the human and divine natures in Christ.[114] By adopting this technical term, Boff affirms the divinity of Mary: "Mary's union with the divinity is of a hypostatic order." (p. 96). She was united with the Holy Spirit, the third person of the Trinity, because she received not only "the effects of the Holy Spirit's intervention in her life ... but ... specifically received the very person and godhead of the Third Person of the Holy Trinity." (p. 97) Thus Boff sees in Mary the "divinization of the female" as the male was divinized in Jesus, arguing that: "... it was *fitting* that God divinize the feminine, because of the equal dignity of masculine and feminine, both of which have the same mission ... therefore, God did so assume the feminine, directly, and the masculine, indirectly, in Mary. *Potuit, Decuit, Ergo Fecit!* God could, it was fitting that he should, and so he did." (p. 95)

The expression *"Potuit, Decuit, Ergo Fecit"* as a theological argument can be traced back to William of Ware (second half of the thirteenth century) but is generally attributed to Duns Scotus (died ca.1308) who used similar logic to promote the thesis of Mary's immaculate conception. Thus in Boff's theology Mary is part of the Trinity, but does not make it into a "Quaternity" as Jung proposed[115] because she is identical with the Holy Spirit. Indeed, to expand the trinitarian view of God into a "quaternity" by adding Mary to it would be disastrous for Christianity. On the other hand, to re-emphasize the role of the Holy Spirit in feminine terms would be, to paraphrase St. Bernard of Clairvaux, quite consistent with "Scripture, tradition and common sense."[116]

---

114   See H. Ringgren, "Hypostasen" *RGG*³ 3.504-506.
115   See Boff's discussion of Jung, pp. 227-241, esp. pp. 239-240.
116   Bernard (died 1153) argued against the Immaculate Conception with the words that it was a novelty "of which the rites of the church knew nothing, that reason does not approve, and ancient tradition does not recommend." *Epistola 174 (172) and Canones Lugdunenses.* Most of this letter was translated in Miegge, *op. cit.* p. 110.

CHAPTER SEVEN

MARY AND THE HISTORY OF SALVATION

How did the first Christian theologians deal with the question of the feminine aspect of the divine? The fact that the New Testament all but ignores the Mother of God suggests that its authors avoided the term, probably because of its pagan connotations. However, the early identification of the "woman clothed with the sun" (Rev. 12) with the church led to further explorations of the similarity between the church and Mary and the parallelism between Eve and Mary. Just as the last book of the Bible, dealing with the final consummation, begs for comparison with the first, which deals with the beginnings, so the woman of Revelation 12 begs for comparison with the first woman, Eve. We shall investigate how Christian thinkers dealt with this theme and, in the second part of this chapter, sketch the process and the theological discussions that led finally to the establishment of the term "Mary, Mother of God."

A. Eve, Mary and the Church

Thinking of the church as feminine has a long history in Christian tradition. The first written evidence goes back to the time of the Apostolic Fathers, that is, the group of writings which chronologically follow the books of the New Testament. In his treatise called *The Shepherd*, Hermas (around 150 AD) describes an experience as he walked one day toward Cumae: an old lady appeared to him and gave him a book to copy. At first, he believed the old woman was the Sibyl since it was in Cumae that the famous oracle of the Sibyl was located.[1] Later, however, it was

---

[1] Cumae, or Cuma today, was founded around 750 B.C. by Greek colonizers from Chalcis. Its favorable location near Napeles on the coast made it a desirable place to visit and many country villas were erected nearby. The Cumaean Sybil was always thought of as a very old woman. Legend had it that she lived for a thousand years and eventually shriveled up so that she just floated in her cave as a whisper. A good example of contemporary beliefs about the Cumaean Sibyl and her manner of prophesying is the description by Virgil in the sixth book of the *Aeneid*. According to tradition preserved by

revealed to him that she was the church, old because she is the first of creation and "it was because of her that the world was formed."[2] So great was his respect for the Sibyl that Hermas did not hesitate to refer to her to convey a Christian message.[3] Moreover, he gave the church cosmic attributes comparable to those with which the woman in Revelation 12 is described. As the "woman clothed with the sun" reflects back upon Eve in Genesis, so the "church" of Hermas reaches back to the very beginning of creation.[4]

Dionysius of Halicarnassus 4.62.1-6; Pliny, *Naturalis Historia* 13.88, and others, she sold her prophecies to Tarquinius Priscus (fifth king of Rome, 616-579 B.C.). This collection was put under the care of the *Quindecemviri Sacris Faciundis*, a priestly college which alone could consult the books at the order of the Senate. These books burned in a fire in 83 B.C. and were replaced with a new collection. Such was the authority of the oracles that Christians began to imitate them and interpolate the original ones with Christian themes. This gave rise to the Christian Sibyllines which were often highly regarded by the church fathers. The Sibylline oracles were last consulted in 363 (Ammianus Marcellinus 23.1.7) and then the whole collection was destroyed under Stilicho, the ruler of the Western Empire from 395 to 408 under the emperior Honorius. See Dionysius of Halicarnassus, *The Roman Antiquities* 4.62.1-6. The Loeb Lassical Library. Cambridge, Mass., Harvard U. Press, 1953, pp. 465-469 (Editor: Earnest Cary.); Pliny, *Naturalis Historia* 13.27.88. The Loeb Classical Library. Cambridge, Mass., Harvard U. Press, 1960, p. 151(Editor: H. Rackham); Ammianus Marcellinus, *History* 23.1.7. The Loeb Classical Library. Cambridge, Mass., Harvard U. Press, 1950, p. 315 (Editor: John C. Rolfe) and others. For a good Bibliography see Edgar Hennecke, *New Testament Apocrypha.* Edited by Wilhelm Schneemelcher, English translation edited by R. McL. Wilson. Vol. 2. Philadelphia; The Westminster Press, 1964, p. 703.

    [2] Visions 1.1.3; 2.1.1-4; 2.4.1-3; 3.1.1 ff.

    [3] He was not alone in this attitude toward the Sibyl. About the same time the following Christian apologists also made references to the Sibyl: Justin Martyr, *Apologia* 1.20.1; 1.44.12; Tatian, *Oratio* 4.1.1; Athenagoras *Supplicatio* 30.1. Respect for the Sibyl never declined in the early church but rather grew, no doubt due to the influence of Virgil's *Fourth Eclogue*. This exalted poem, composed in 40 B.C., begins with a reference to the "last age of the Cumaean song" and then foretells the birth of a boy who will establish the golden age. The poem was early interpreted by Christians as a pagan prophecy of the birth of Christ. St. Augustine (354-430) referred to the Sibyl and the *Fourth Eclogue* numerous times and through him the respectability and popularity of the Sibyl was established all through the Middle Ages. For a detailed discussion and complete Bibliography, see Stephen Benko, "Virgil's Fourth Eclogue in Christian Interpretation." *Aufstieg und Niedergang der römischen Welt.* Ed. by Hildegard Temporini and Wolfgang Haase. Berlin, New York: Walter de Gruyter, 1980. II/31. pp. 646-705.

    [4] For commentary see Martin Dibelius, *Der Hirt des Hermas.* Tübingen: J. C. B. Mohr (Paul Siebeck), 1923, p. 452. The statement of Hermas about the prominence of the church is similar to that voiced by the apostle Paul in

A short time after Hermas composed the *Shepherd*, an anonymous sermon, now called *The Second Letter of Clement*, also affirmed the pre-existence of the church: the original, spiritual church was created before the sun and the moon; it "existed from the beginning."[5] With a reference to Genesis 1.27, ("God made man male and female") the author continues: "the male is Christ, the female is the Church." In addition to calling the church female, the sermon also suggests (but does not expressly state) the spiritual motherhood of the church. Isaiah 54.1 (Gal. 4.27), "Sing, o barren one who did not bear ..." is said to refer to Christians, "for our Church was barren before children were given to her." (2.1)[6]

The great bishop of Lyon, Irenaeus (c.130-202) came close to identifying Mary with the church when he wrote in *Adversus Haereses*, "And Mary, exulting because of this, cried out, prophesying on behalf of the Church, 'My soul doth magnify the Lord...'"[7] He did not elaborate on this statement and thus we cannot draw further conclusions from it. While the sentence may simply mean that Mary spoke as an agent or spokesperson of the church, it seems certain, at least, that Irenaeus, too, thought of the church as female and as the mother of Christians. "It behooves us," he wrote,[8] " ... to flee to the Church, and be brought up in her bosom, and be nourished with the Lord's Scriptures." The image of a mother suckling her children is also used by Clement of Alexandria (died before 215) in his encomium to the church: "O mystic marvel! The universal Father is one, and one the universal Word: and the Holy Spirit is one and the same everywhere, and one is the only virgin mother. I love to call her the Church ... She is once virgin and mother pure as a virgin, loving as a mother. And calling her children to her, she nurses them with holy milk, viz. with the Word for childhood."[9] These hesitating

---

Eph. 3.9-11 where the church is presented with these words: " ... that through the church the manifold wisdom of God might now be made known to the principalities and powers in the heavenly places. This was according to the eternal purpose which he has realized in Christ Jesus our Lord ..."

[5] 14.1-2.

[6] 2. Clement 2.1. An English translation of both *The Shepherd* of Hermas and *The Second Letter of Clement* is available in Cyril C. Richardson, *Early Christian Fathers*. Philadelphia: Westminster, 1953.

[7] 3.10.2, *ANF* 1.424.

[8] *Adv. haer.* 5.20.2. ET: *ANF* 1.548.

[9] *Paedagogus* 1.6. *GCS* 12.115; ET.: *ANF* s.220. See also *Paedagogus* 1.5: "the

and probing allusions of the fathers finally led to the definite, no uncertain statement of Tertullian (c. 160-c.220): "Domina mater ecclesia."[10] Tertullian, with the clear and precise mind of a lawyer (which was probably his profession), liked to call things by their name. He came to the conclusion that the presence of a "Father" and a "Son" require the reality of a "Mother." When in the Lord's Prayer we say "Our Father," we include the Son, because the Father and the Son are one.[11] "Nor is even our mother the Church passed by, if, that is, in the Father and the Son is recognized the mother, from whom arises the name both of Father and of Son."[12] He told new church members that the church where they were baptized and where they pray is "the house of your mother."[13] In discussing the salutary effects of sleep, Tertullian used the example of Adam, "the fountain of the human race." Adam was made to sleep by God and during this sleep God formed Eve.[14] Now, sleep is an image of death, and since Adam was a figure of Christ, the sleep of Adam prefigured the death of Christ. Just as from the side of Adam Eve was formed, so from the wounded side of Jesus the church, "the true mother of all living," arose.[15]

Tertullian's definition of the motherhood of the church was

---

mother draws the children to herself; and we seek our mother the Church." *ANF* 2.214; ibid. 3.12: "Let us complete the fair face of the Church; and let us run as children to our good mother." *ANF* s.295.

[10] *Ad martyras* 1: "Blessed martyrs designate, — along with the provisions which our lady mother the Church from her bountiful breasts, and each brother out of his private means, makes for your bodily wants in prison, accept also from me some contribution to your spiritual sustenance ..." *ANF* 3.693.

[11] John 10.30.

[12] *De oratione* 2, *ANF* 3.682.

[13] *De baptismo* 20; *ANF* 3.679.

[14] Gen. 2.21-22.

[15] *De anima* 43; *ANF* 3.222. The Latin text is more complex: "Si enim Adam de Christo figuram dabat, somnus Adae mors erat Christi dormituri in mortem, ut de injuria perinde lateris ejus vera mater viventium figuraretur Ecclesia." *MPL* 2.723. Tertullian is thinking here of Gen. 3.20: "The man called his wife's name Eve, because she was the mother of all living." This is based on the assumption that the word "Eve" is derived from the Hebrew root Ch-Y- H=life, alive, living. In this case Tertullian's parallelism is correct: from Eve was born mankind in a physical way, from the Church the new creation of God. This would be the "feminist" side of the Adam-Christ theology that Paul developed in Romans 5. — There is also a brief reference to "the mother" whom the sinners invoke in *De pudicitia* 5, *ANF* 4.78; here again the Church is meant.

universally accepted. His pupil and follower, Cyprian (c. 200/10-258), could say without hesitation: *"Habere non potest deum patrem qui ecclesiam non habet matrem."* (He cannot have God as father who does not have the Church as mother.)[16] To fully appreciate Cyprian's categorical statement we must remember that the unity of the church was an overriding concern for him. Faced with severe persecutions, many Christians were denying their faith (these were called the *lapsi)*; faced also with the schismatic movements of Novatus in Carthage and Novatianus in Rome, Cyprian stressed that to be a Christian means to be in the church,[17] a statement which he subsequently amplified to the famous sentence: "Outside the Church there is no salvation!"[18] The image of the mother[19] served Cyprian's intentions well: as the mother holds a family together, so the church holds together the family of God.

The parallelism Adam-Christ/Eve-Church used by Tertullian returned in the theology of Methodius (died 311). As Adam was the husband of Eve, so Christ, the Word, came down to be joined to his wife, the church. He cleansed the church for the receiving of his spiritual seed which he implants in the mind.[20] There conception takes place "by the church as by a woman," resulting in birth. In this way the command given to the first man and woman, "increase and multiply,"[21] is fulfilled by the church increasing daily "in greatness, beauty and multitude." In a somewhat obscure way Methodius also applied Genesis 2.18; i.e., the statement that Eve is a helper of Adam, to the church and Jesus: the more perfect believers are the church and helpmate of Christ; to him they are betrothed and given in marriage as a virgin;[22] they receive the "pure and genuine seed of his doctrine" and cooperate with him in preaching salvation.[23] Methodius applies

---

[16] *De unitate ecclesiae* 6, *CSEL* 3. 1.214; *ANF* 5.423.

[17] *"Christianus non est qui in Christi ecclesia non est," Epistula* 55.24.

[18] *"Salus extra ecclesiam non est." Ep.* 73.21.

[19] It occurs more than thirty times in his writings, according to Johannes Quasten, *Patrology* . Utrecht/Antwerp: Spectrum, 1953, vol. 2, p. 374. It is interesting that around the same time in Rome Hippolytus (died 235) never used the word "Mother" with reference to the Church, in spite of his exegesis of Apoc.12.1-6.

[20] Eph. 5.31; 5.25-27.

[21] Gen. 1.28.

[22] 2 Cor. 11.2.

[23] *Symposium* or *The Banquet of the Ten Virgins* 3.8; *ANF* 319-320.

the image of the sexual relationship of Adam and Eve for the purpose of producing children to the relation of Christ and the church. However, while the seed of Adam was material and impregnated Eve who thus gave birth to humankind, the seed of Christ is the Word which impregnates the mind and so produces new Christians. This same line of thought was repeated by Zeno, bishop of Verona (362-372), in one of his sermons: the devil had corrupted Eve by the ear,[24] so when Christ entered into Mary by the ear[25] and was born of the virgin he cured "the wound of the woman;" thus *"Adam per Christum, Eva per Ecclesiam renovaretur."* (Adam should be renewed through Christ, Eve through the church.)[26] Methodius and Zeno saw the motherhood of the church in the fact that it was the renewed Eve, the spouse of Christ, who is the second Adam. Yet Zeno's conclusion is surprising: if Christ entered into Mary, why is not Mary the spiritual mother? What then is the relationship between Mary and the church?

The bishop of Milan, Ambrose (333/4?-397), offered an answer to this question by declaring that Mary is "the type of the Church" = *Ecclesiae typos*.[27] The church is immaculate yet married, so is Mary. The virgin church conceives Christians by the Spirit and bears them without pain. Mary is married to Joseph but filled with another,[28] so the individual churches are joined to a priest but are filled with the Holy Spirit. Ambrose was the first to define this relationship between Mary and the church and he mentioned it often, as in his reference to the words of Jesus from the cross: when Christ said: "Behold your mother!" — he then said to the church: "Behold your son!"[29] Ambrose, who spoke of Mary in the most exalted terms, transmitted this devotion to his spiritual son, Augustine (354-430). No wonder, therefore, that the motherhood of the church as exemplified in Mary is also a part of Augustine's

---

[24] Gen. 3: the serpent seduced Eve by speaking to her.
[25] Luke 2.28.
[26] *Tractatus Liber* 1;13.10. *MPL* 11.352.
[27] *Expositio Evang. Sec. Luc.* 2.7; *MPL* 15.1555B; *CSEL* 32.45.
[28] The reference is to Mary having been filled with the Holy Spirit, Luke 1.35.
[29] John 19.26-27; See Ambrose ... *Exp. Ev. Luc.* 7.5 *MPL* 15.1700; *CSEL* 32.284: *"Dicat et Ecclesiae: Ecce filius tuus."* In the gospel account, of course, Jesus says these words to his mother, Mary. See also *De Institutione Virginis* 14.88-89; *De Obitu Theodosii Oratio* 47; among others.

theology, as a few examples will suffice to illustrate: "Let us love the Lord our God, let us love his Church: him as a father, her as a mother; him as Lord and her as his servant, because we are children of his servant ... hold fast, beloved, hold fast to God the Father and mother church."[30] "The Church ... is at the same time virgin and gives birth. It resembles Mary who bore the Lord. Was not the holy Mary a virgin and gave birth, and remained virgin? So also the Church ... [31] "Mary bore your head, the Church gave birth to you ... "[32] "Honor the holy Church, your Mother."[33] Let us mention finally Quodvultdeus (died about 455), a friend and pupil of Augustine. In his sermon to the catechumens, he echoes not only his master, but also the great Tertullian: *"Non habebit Deum Patrem qui Ecclesiam noluit habere matrem."* (He who will not have the Church as mother will not have God as father.)[34]

By this time the idea was fully developed. Later fathers, including the medieval authors, could not add more to it. They faithfully repeated the tradition which they received: the church is female, Mary is the type of the church, and the church is now doing in a spiritual sense what Mary did physically. Thus there is a mysterious relationship between Mary and the church. But this mystery has not been explored. If anything, the relationship between Mary and the church was neglected during the Middle Ages in favor of the development of other privileges of Mary. Indeed, it is only in modern times that Mary and the church have again become the focus of attention, especially since the second Vatican Council included the teaching on Mary in the Dogmatic Constitution on the Church, called *Lumen Gentium.*[35]

However, simultaneously with the development of the Mary-church parallelism, there also developed the parallelism between Eve and Mary.[36] As interest in Mary grew, it was natural to

---

[30] *In Psalm 88. Sermon* 2.14. *MPL* 36.1140-41.

[31] *Sermon* 213.7; *MPL* 38.1063-64; also *Sermon* 195.2; *MPL* 38.1018.

[32] *Sermon* 192.2.2; *MPL* 38.1012-13.

[33] *Sermon* 214.11; MPL 38.1071; see also *De Symbolo Sermon ad Catechumenos* 1.1; *MPL* 40 . 62.

[34] *De Symbolo ad Catechumenos* 3.13 13; *MPL* 40 668.

[35] Walter M. Abbott, *The Documents of Vatican II.* New York: Guild Press, 1966, pp. 14- 96.

[36] The literature on this topic, as in every aspect of Mariology is without end. The following titles, however, are specifically helpful: Walter Delius, *Geschichte der Marienverehrung.* München/Basel: Ernst Reinhardt Verlag, 1963. Hilda Graef, *Mary: A History of Doctrine and Devotion.* New York: Sheed

compare Eve, "the cause of sin" (Gen. 3) with Mary, who by her birth of the Savior could be called "the cause of salvation." Justin Martyr (d. 165) was the first Christian author to make such a statement: "For Eve, who was a virgin and undefiled, having conceived the word of the serpent, brought forth disobedience and death. But the Virgin Mary received faith and joy when the angel Gabriel announced the good tidings to her that the Spirit of the Lord would come upon her ... and she replied 'Be it unto me according to thy word.' And by her He has been born ... by whom God destroys both the serpent and those angels and men who are like him ... "[37] An in-depth theological explanation of this thesis was given by Irenaeus (c. 130-202) in the *Adversus Haereses.* According to Irenaeus, the economy of salvation demanded that Adam be recapitulated in Jesus.[38] The means of this was Mary from whom Jesus received actual flesh "which had been derived from the earth, which He had recapitulated in Himself."[39] This was according to the eternally predestined will of God who decreed that the first man should be of an animal nature and be saved by one of a spiritual nature. It was also in accordance with this design that Mary was found obedient and answered to the angel who announced to her the conception of Jesus: "Behold the handmaid of the Lord; be it unto me according to thy word."[40] Eve was disobedient and thus she became the cause of death, "both to herself and to the entire human race." Mary, on the other hand, by yielding obedience, became "the cause of salvation, both to

---

and Ward, vol . 1, 1963, vol . 2, 1965. Hugo Koch, *Adhuc Virgo: Mariens Jungfrauschaft und Ehe in der altkirchlichen Überlieferung bis zum Ende des 4. Jahrhunderts.* Tübingen: Mohr (Siebeck), 1929. Hugo Koch, *Virgo Eva - Virgo Maria: Neue Untersuchungen über die Lehre von der Jungfrauschaft und der Ehe Mariens in her ältesten Kirche.* Berlin/Leipzig: Walter de Gruyter, 1937. Walter J. Burghardt, "Mary in Western Patristic Thought." In Juniper B. Carol, Editor, *Mariology.* Milwaukee: Bruce, 1955, Vol. 1, pp. 109-155. Walter J. Burghardt, "Mary in Eastern Patristic Thought." In Carol, *op.cit.* vol. 2 (1957), pp. 88-153. Stephen Benko, *Protestants, Catholics and Mary.* Valley Forge: Judson Press, 1968. R. E. Brown, K. P. Donfried, J. A. Fitzmyer, J. Reumann, Editors, *Mary in the New Testament. A Collaborative Assessment by Protestant and Roman Catholic Scholars.* Philadelphia: Fortess, 1978.

[37] *Dialogue with Trypho* 100; *ANF* 1.249.
[38] "For He would not have been one truly possessing flesh and blood, by which he redeemed us, unless He had summed up in Himself the ancient formation of Adam." *Op.cit.* 5.1.2; *ANF* 1.527.
[39] 3.21.10 and 3.22.2. *ANF* 1.454.
[40] Luke 1.38.

herself and the whole human race ... And thus also it was that the knot of Eve's disobedience was loosed by the obedience of Mary. For what the virgin Eve had bound fast through unbelief, this did the Virgin Mary set free through faith."[41]

Irenaeus based his theology of recapitulation on S. Paul's philosophy of history, presented in Romans 5 and to a lesser degree in 1. Corinthians 15. In chapter 5 of Romans Paul starts out by affirming the hope with which mankind in the present can look toward the future, because of the reconciling death of Christ and the love of God which, through the Holy Spirit, is already active in us.[42] He then goes on to examine the significance of the past for the present and the future. In so doing he puts the whole of human history under the light of the gospel by demonstrating that there is a real relationship between Adam and Christ. From Adam came sin and death over the entire human race, from Christ came justification and life for all who are united with Christ through faith.[43] Adam is the first, the physical, the earthly; Christ is the second, the spiritual, the heavenly. As Adam is the representative of a sinful, physical, earth-bound mankind, so is Christ representative of a justified, spiritual, heavenly mankind. World history for Paul is determined by the relationship of Adam and Christ: only these two persons had a lasting, decisive and general impact upon the fate of humanity, Adam having been the cause of the fall and Christ, the cause of redemption. Adam determined the fate of mankind with respect to sin, Christ with respect to salvation, therefore, Christ is the second Adam. We do not understand Christ unless we see him in the light of Adam, and *vice*

---

[41] 3.22.3-4; *ANF* 1.455. Irenaeus summarized again his views in the final book of the *Adv. Haer.* 5.19.1. He repeats here what he said before and then adds: "For just as the former was led astray by the word of an angel, so that she fled from God when she had transgressed His word; so did the latter, by an angelic communication, receive the glad tidings that she should sustain God, being obedient to His word. And if the former did disobey God, yet the latter was persuaded to be obedient to God, in order that the Virgin Mary might become the patroness of the Virgin Eve. And thus, as the human race fell into bondage to death by means of a virgin, so is it rescued by a virgin; virginal disobedience having been balanced in the opposite scale by virginal obedience. For in the same way the sin of the first created man receives amendment by the correction of the First-begotten, and the coming of the serpent is conquered by the harmlessness of the dove, those bonds being unloosed by which we had been fast bound to death."

[42] Verses 1-11.

[43] See also 1.Cor. 15.22, 45 ff.

versa, Adam is the "type" of Christ and only through Christ can Adam be understood. Sin, which came into the life of mankind through Adam, i.e., original sin, can be eliminated only by the absolute and complete universal redemption in Christ, and *vice versa*, an absolute and complete universal redemption by Christ is impossible without the original sin brought about by Adam. For the work of salvation such a unity of the individual with the human race is essential, because without this a "once-for-all" redemption is impossible. If the sin of Adam is an isolated case, without further consequences, if every individual sinner is independent, then every sinner needs his or her individual savior. But salvation is universal, so Paul teaches. Christ does not meet us as Jew or Greek but as members of the human race, because the ultimate aim of God in history is the reconstruction of the universe, "to unite (in Christ) all things in heaven and things on earth."[44] This is what Irenaeus calls "recapitulation", i.e., the restoration of all creation under one head. "Being in Christ," another favorite expression of Paul, is thus parallel to the unity of all in Adam.[45]

This thesis of Paul became immensely popular and determined the Christian view of history and salvation for centuries to come. It was soon to become a central part of the Christian message. Already the earliest Christian manual reports that during the Eucharist the following prayer was said over the bread: "As this piece of bread was scattered over the hills and then was brought together and made one, so let your Church be brought together from the ends of the earth into your kingdom ... "[46] Augustine, in his interpretation of Mark 13.27 ("He shall gather together his elect from the four winds,") comments as follows: "He gathered all his elect from the four winds: therefore, from the

---

[44] Eph. 1.1-14 = Col. 1.20.

[45] See Karl Barth, *Christ and Adam, Man and Humanity in Romans 5*. New York: Harper and Brothers, 1957. Originally published as *Christus und Adam nach Römer 5*, Zollikon-Zürich: Evangelisher Verlag, 1952. John G. Gibbs, *Creation and Redemption. A Study in Pauline Theology*. Leiden: E.J. Brill, 1971, surveyed most of the literature dealing with the theological issue of creation and redemption. (On K. Barth's *Christ and Adam* and his critics, see pp. 4-5; Gibbs however, maintiains that "Karl Barth's understanding of the Pauline Adam-Christ typology is basically correct." p. 50.) See also John A. Phillips, *Eve. The History of an Idea*. San Francisco: Harper & Row, 19 4.

[46] *Didache* 9.4; ET: C. C. Richardson, *op. cit.* p. 175.

whole world. For Adam himself (this I had said before) signifieth in Greek the whole world; for there are four letters A, D, A and M. But as the Greeks speak, the four quarters of the world have these initial letters, Ἀνατολή they call East; Δύσις, the West; Ἄρκτος the North; Μεσημβρία, the South: thou hast the word ADAM. Adam therefore has been scattered over the whole world. He was in one place and fell, and as in a manner broken small, he filled the whole world: but the mercy of God gathered together the fragments from every side, and forged them by the fire of love, and made one that which was broken. The Artist knew how to do this; let no one despair; it is indeed a great thing, but reflect who that Artist was. He who made restored: He who formed reformed. What are righteousness and truth? He will gather together His elect with him ..."[47]

In the theology of Irenaeus the universal character of Christ's work means that it includes not only present and future but in a retroactive way the past as well. He argues that Abraham, too, will inherit the kingdom of God through Jesus Christ[48] and this complete redemption, encompassing past, present, and future, is truly the "*communio dei et hominis.*"[49] It is in this context that his parallelism of Eve and Mary is to be understood: since the event of Christ is the perfect counterbalance to the event of Adam, the role played by Eve also must be counterbalanced; here Mary was an excellent choice. We note that while Paul did not see a need to counterbalance Eve, the conclusions of Irenaeus are in harmony with Pauline thought.

Tertullian (c. 160 - c. 120) also mentioned the Eve-Mary parallel within the framework of the recapitulation theory, taking his

---

[47] In *Ps.* 96.15; *NPNF* 8.474 f. See also *In.Joh.Tract.* 10.12 and *Tract.* 9.14. Compare *Didache* 10.4: "Remember, Lord, your church, to save it from all evil and to make it perfect in your love, and gather it together in its holiness from the four winds, into your kingdom ... " Libertine Gnostics used the same Pauline principles to practice immorality, see S. Benko, "The Libertine Gnostic Sect of the Phibionites according to Epiphanius." *Vigiliae Christianae* 21 (1927) 103-119.

[48] *Op. cit.* 4.8.1. Irenaeus refers to Matthew 8.11: "I tell you, many will come from east and west and sit at table with Abraham, Isaac and Jacob in the kingdom of heaven." The same idea also occurs in Ignatius, *Philadelphians* 5.2: "And the Prophets, let us love them too, because they anticipated the gospel in their preaching and hoped for and awaited Him, and were saved by believing on him. Thus they were in Jesus Christ's unity." C. C. Richardson, *op. cit.* p. 109.

[49] *Op. cit.* 5.1.1.

point of departure also from Paul. The words are familiar: "As Eve had believed the serpent, so Mary believed the angel." But Tertullian introduced a new element to the story which was later adopted by Methodius and Zeno:[50] both women conceived by *words*. For Eve, even though she was not directly impregnated, "the devil's words afterwards became as seed to her that she should conceive as an outcast, and bring forth in sorrow. Indeed, she gave birth to a patricidal devil..." — i.e., Cain. Mary, of course, conceived by the Word of God directly. Here Tertullian found yet another parallelism, namely between Cain and Abel, the "evil brother" and the "good brother." Jesus is the "good brother" "who should blot out the memory of the evil brother."[51]

Firmicus Maternus wrote (ca. 346-348) an aggressive book to the emperors Constantius and Constans demanding the abolishment of paganism. In his arguments he used the Eve-Mary parallelism as he learned it from Irenaeus and Tertullian.[52] By this time the theme was commonplace. The Syrian Ephraem (c. 306-73) used it often in his hymns,[53] and it flowed through the words and works of preachers, exegetes, and systematic theologians. Epiphanius of Salamis (315-403) said that as Eve was the cause of death, so Mary became the cause of life.[54] Gregory of Nyssa (335-392) elaborated the same point,[55] but the emphasis was slowly changing: Mary appeared more and more in the center, as one who played a role in the redemptive process and was somehow a touchstone of Christological orthodoxy. Central issues now will be the definition of her title as Theotokos = Mother of God, her perpetual virginity, her sanctity,[56] and even her assumption into heaven,

---

[50] See above p. 233f.

[51] *De carne Christi* 17: ANF 3.536. See also *Adv. Marcionem* 2.4: God in his goodness provided a helpmate to Adam, so he may not be alone. "He knew full well what a blessing to him would be the sex of Mary, and also of the Church." ANF 3.300.

[52] *De errore profanorum religionum* 25; German translation in Bibliothek der Kirchenväter. Kempten and München: Kösel Verlag, 1913. Vol. 14, p. 69.

[53] For quotations see Walter J. Burghardt. "Mary in Eastern Patristic Thought" in Juniper B. Carol, editor, *Mariology*. Milwaukee: The Bruce Publishing Co. 1957. Vol. 2, pp. 88-153.

[54] *Panarion*, Heresy 78.18, Against the Antidikomarionites. GCS 37. 468-469.

[55] *In diem natalem Christi*. MPS 46.1140.

[56] Hippolytus (died 235) attached the adjective "holy" to her name, in *Contra Noetum* 17: "God the Word came down from heaven into the holy

the earliest written reference to which dates around 377[57]: issues more germaine to the "woman clothed with the sun" than to "a virgin betrothed to a man whose name was Joseph."[58]

According to yet another line of thought in the early church, Mary was not a representative of the church but a symbol of the synagogue, not a type of the new covenant but a type of the old. This view appeared first in Tertullian, in his comments on those passages of the gospels which refer to the unbelief of his mother and brothers.[59]

> ... there is some ground for thinking that Christ's answer denies His mother and brethren for the present ... 'The Lord's brethren had not yet believed in Him.' So it is contained in the Gospel which was published before Marcion's time; whilst there is at the same time a want of evidence of His mother's adherence to Him, although the Marthas and the other Marys were in constant attendance on Him. In this very passage indeed, their unbelief is evident. Jesus was teaching the way of life, preaching the kingdom of God and actively engaged in healing infirmities of body and soul; but all the while, whilst strangers were intent on Him, His very nearest relatives were absent. By and by they turn up, and keep outside; but they do not go in, because, forsooth, they set small store on that which was doing within; nor do they even wait, as if they had something which they could contribute more necessary than that which He was so earnestly doing; but they prefer to interrupt Him and wish to call Him away from His great work ... He denied His parents, then, in the sense in which He has taught us to deny ours — for God's work.[60] But there is also another view of the case: in the abjured mother there is a figure of the synagogue, as well as of the Jews in the unbelieving brethren. In their person Israel remained outside, whilst the new disciples who kept close to Christ within, hearing and believing, represented the Church, which He called mother in a preferable sense

Virgin Mary." ANF 5.230; MPG 10.825.

[57] Epiphanius, Panarion, Heresy 78. 10, 11, 23. GCS 37. 461, 462, 374.

[58] Luke 1.26.

[59] The main texts are Matthew 12.46-49: his mother and brothers stood outside and when told about it he stretched out his hand toward his disciples and said, "Here are my Mother and my brothers! For whoever does the will of my Father in heaven is my brother, and sister, and mother." John 7.5: "For even his brothers did not believe in him." Luke 11.27-28: A woman in the crowd cried to him, "Blessed is the womb that bore you, and the breasts that you sucked." — and Jesus replied: "Blessed rather are those who hear the word of God and keep it."

[60] The reference is to Matthew 10.37: "He who loves father or mother more than me is not worthy of me." Cf. Luke 14.26: "If anyone comes to me and does not hate his own father and mother and wife and children and brothers and sisters, yes, and even his own life, he cannot be my disciple."

and a worthier brotherhood, with the repudiation of the carnal relationship. It was in just the same sense, indeed, that He also replied to that exclamation (of a certain woman), not denying His mother's 'womb and paps,' but designating those as more 'blessed who hear the word of God.'[61]

This theory is consistent with Tertullian's view that the new Eve is the Christian church, as the new Adam is Jesus. If this is so, then the Pauline idea that the church is the "bride" of Christ falls easily in the pattern and the "motherhood" of the church also makes good sense. The parallelism in this case looks like this: Adam and Eve = sinful mankind; Jesus and the church = redeemed mankind. In this scheme, however, there is no place for Mary and Tertullian solved the problem by introducing in the image of the synagogue and the community of those who did not believe. This conclusion was not difficult to reach: since the physical body of Jesus was born of Mary's humanity,[62] Tertullian could identify that with the old dispensation, "according to the law, according to the flesh," as opposed to the new, "according to the Spirit."

Hilary of Poitiers (315-367) echoed Tertullian in his commentary on the Gospel of Matthew:

> ... when the man came and announced that his mother and his brothers were waiting for him outside, he stretched out his hand toward his disciples and answered that they were his brothers and his mother, and whoever obeys his father's will, he is his brother, sister and mother. Thus, by retaining the right and the name of all relationships no longer for the condition of birth but for the communion of the church, he constituted a model of general activity and thinking. However, he should not be regarded as thinking contemptuously of his mother for whom he devoted the affection of greatest care in his passion.[63] There is also a typical sense in the fact that his mother and his brothers remained outside because they had the opportunity to come in to him just as

---

61 *De carne Christi* 7; *CSEL* 70.211 f; *ANF* 3.527-528. In *Adversus Marcionem* 4.19. Tertullian also stressed the point that the mother and the brethren of Jesus were outside, while others listened to him inside. "He transferred the names of blood relationship to others, whom He judged to be more closely related to Him by reason of their faith ... He substituted the others, not as being truer relatives, but worthier ones." *CSEL* 47.483; *ANF* 3.378. The thrust of the argument here is anti-Gnostic: Jesus did have a mother and brothers otherwise He could not have transferred this designation to others.

62 Gal. 4.4.

63 John 19.26-27.

the others did. But because he came to his own and his own did not receive him, in his mother and brothers the synagogue and the Jews are prefigured abstaining from going in to and approaching him."[64]

"The Athanasius of the West" and champion of orthodoxy, as Hilary is often called,[65] wrote this book on the basis of homilies which he delivered for the instruction of his congregation. His aim was to find the "deeper" meaning of the text and not to write a dogmatic treatise.[66] Yet together with Tertullian he does represent a thought pattern which, alongside the others we have seen, goes back to the earliest periods of ecclesiastical history. This concept, however, was not widely accepted. The suggestion that Mary's motherhood paralleled the motherhood of the church was much easier to understand and thus it remained the tacitly approved and accepted view.[67]

In the Old Testament, God's chosen people, Israel, is commonly refered to as female and sometimes also as virgin. A few examples will suffice to illustrate this point:

2 Kings 19.21: "... the virgin daughter of Zion ..."
Isaiah 37.22: "... the virgin daughter of Zion ..."
Isaiah 52.2: "... O captive daughter of Zion ..."
Isaiah 62.11- "... Say to the daughter of Zion ..."
Jeremiah 6.23: "... O daughter of Zion ..."
Jeremiah 14.17: "... the daughter of my people ..."
Jeremiah 1813: "... the virgin Israel ..." (also 31.04, 81.21)
Lamentations 1.15: "... the virgin daughter of Judah ..."
Lamentations 2.13: "... virgin daughter of Zion ..."[68]

---

64 *In Evangelium Matthaei Commentarius* 12.24. *MPL* 9.993.

65 He was an ardent opponent of Arianism and a promoter of the trinitarian faith in the defense of which he wrote two books, *De synodis* and *De Trinitate*. He was a native of Gaul. In 1851 the honorary title *"Doctor Ecclesiace"* was bestowed on him by the Roman Catholic Church and thus Hilary is one of the select group of theologians whose teachings constitute a basis for Roman Catholic teaching.

66 Similarly to the Gospel of John in which there is also a sharp contrast between light and darkness, flesh and spirit, the synagogue and the followers of Jesus, etc. See 1.5,11,13; 3.6,19; 9.34.

67 John 19.26-27 is interpreted this way, too.

68 For the Revised Standard Version of the bible *Nelson's Complete Concordance*, New York: Thomas Nelson & Sons, 1957, pp. 390-394 offers many more examples.

In these and many similar passages a female symbolizes the totality of the people of God. The image may have come from two preconceptions, one, the idea of God as male and second, the concept of the covenant, that is, the idea of a unique relationship between God and Israel as a people chosen for his unique service. This covenant relationship is like a marriage and thus "Israel" was naturally imagined as the female counterpart of God. The message of the prophet Hosea is built on this concept.[69] Thus the image of Israel as female, virgin, and wife was familiar to readers of the Old Testament.[70] Israel as bride is a natural analogy to the church as bride[71] and God as "husband of Israel" is paralleled in Jesus as "husband" of the church. This analogy raises human marriage to cosmic levels: not only is it a reflection of Yahweh's relation to Israel, it is a proleptic realization of the eschatological consummation in which the primordial *henosis* of male and female (i.e. the condition before the sexes were separated) is restored.[72] This is another aspect of the recapitulation theory of Irenaeus and Paul and thus brings us back to the Adam = Christ/Eve = Mary parallelism.

Implicit in these speculations about Mary is the idea that she

---

[69] See also Jeremiah 2.1f; 3.1ff; Ezekiel 16; 23; Isaiah 50.1 and Isaiah 62.5: "... as the bridegroom rejoices over the bride, so shall your God rejoice over you." Zion as bride: Isaiah 49.18.

[70] See Walter Eichrodt, *Theology of the Old Testament*. Philadelphia: Westminster Press 1961, vol.1 which is centered around the idea of the covenant. J. Hempel, "Bund" *Die Religion in Geschichte und Gegenwart*.[3] Tübingen: J. C. B. Mahr, 1957, vol. 1, pp. 1511-1515. E. Stauffer, Article γαμέω, γάμος in G. Kittel, *Theologisches Wörterbuch zum Neuen Testament*. Stuttgart: Kohlhammer, 1933, vol. 1, pp. 646-655. H. Strack und P. Billerback, *Kommentar zum Neuen Testament aus Talmud und Midrasch*. München: C. H. Beck, 1922 (reprinted 1956), from which the following rabbinic parallels are particularly interessant: Pirque Rabbi Eliezer 41: The day when God gave the Law was like a wedding day. God was the bridegroom, Israel the bride and Moses led the bride to meet the groom. Meckhiltha, Ex. 1917: "God came from Sinai" (Deut. 33.21) like a bridegroom to receive his bride. *Op.cit.* vol. 1, pp. 970 and 969.

[71] Eph. 5.25-33; John 3.29: John the Baptist calls himself "friend of the bridegroom", Jesus is the groom "who has the bride." 2 Cor.11.2: "I betrothed you to Christ to present you as a pure bride to her one husband." Rev. 19.7: the marriage of the Lamb and his Bride; 21.2 "... the holy city, new Jerusalem, coming down out of heaven from God, prepared as a bride adorned for her husband." Also 21.9 and 22.17. Compare Matthew 9.15; 25.1-13; parabole of the virgins who waited to meet the bridegroom. See Joach. Jeremias, Article νύμφγ, νυμφίος in Kittel, *op.cit.* 4.1092-1099.

[72] Gen. 2.24.

plays a necessary part in the economy of salvation: without her, incarnation is impossible and the whole redemptive process cannot take place. The word "implicit" needs to be underlined, because no church father spelled this out. Explicitly, they placed Mary into the context of Romans 5 by enlarging the Adam-Christ parallel to include Eve-Mary. This did not quite work because the biblical references point to the church, not Mary, as the bride and spiritual wife of Christ. Consequently, with an unerring instinct, they began to draw the parallel between Mary and the church. When this mystical identity was sufficiently common, the expanded recapitulation theory of Romans 5 posed no difficulties. It was easy to think of the church as female, the Old Testament having paved the way by calling the chosen people of God "daughter," "virgin," and "wife." The church as the new Israel could easily adopt these names, and the universal role assigned to Eve supplied the vehicle for transforming Mary into a collective personality.

B. MARY, THE MOTHER OF GOD

How did the scattered thoughts of the early Christian Fathers about Eve, Mary, the church and their mystical interrelation eventually come together in the theological definition of Mary as the "Mother of God"? Let us now trace this development, at the end of which the Christian goddess emerged in all her glory.[73]

Christian theology started with Christology. By this we mean that the first concern of the primitive church was a definition of the person and the work of Christ Jesus.[74] At its simplest level this took the form of identifying Jesus of Nazareth with the Messiah, as appears in New Testament texts such as Mark 8:29, "You are the Christ." Similarly, Christian confessions of faith started with the Christologial article and in their simplest form were statements concerning Christ Jesus and his redemptive work.[75] Christology

---

[73] The following is part of an essay first published in *Oikonomia. Heilsgeschichte als Thema der Theologie*. Ed. Felix Christ. Hamburg: Reich, 1967, pp. 261-272.

[74] For a definition of Christology see O. Cullmann, *The Christology of the New Testament*. Philadelphia: Westminster, 1959, pp. 1ff.

[75] J. N. D. Kelly, *Early Christian Creeds*, London: Longmans, 1960 (second ed.) pp. 13 ff. presents another theory but he himself admits that so far as explicityly formulated credal confessions are concerned, those of the single

was thus alive in the church from the earliest times, but the problem of the birth of Jesus was seldom included in it. For the primitive church the focal point of faith was the resurrection. Only gradually did Christians turn their attention to the birth of Jesus, and even then only in a rather limited way.[76] This limited interest is clearly reflected in the gospels. The earliest gospel has no birth-narrative; Matthew and Luke each have two chapters concerning the birth, whereas the passion-narratives receive considerably more attention. In the fourth gospel there is no nativity narrative; rather, the prologue speaks of the incarnation of the eternal Word. Paul's lack of interest in the birth of Jesus is well known,[77] and this is also true of the other New Testament books. Indeed, the primitive church did not even have a Christmas festival. Sunday was celebrated as the day of the resurrection, and the only yearly Christian festivals were the Easter holidays in memory of Christ's death and resurrection.[78]

This lack of interest, however, was limited to the manner of the incarnation, i.e., the way in which Jesus Christ came into the world. The incarnation itself was always an integral part of the faith of the early Christians. That is to say, the uniqueness of Jesus was beyond doubt for them. The assumption of a supernatural relationship between Jesus and God shines through the gospel of

---

clause, Christological pattern seem to have been far and away the most popular in the apostolic age. (p. 25) For our position see O. Cullmann, *The Earliest Christian Confessions.* (E. T. by J. K. S. Reid) London, 1949.

[76] In this matter, therefore, the mind of the early Christians worked in a way different from ours. When we treat Christology in a systematic way the first question we raise is that of the incarnation. This seems natural for us because the birth of Jesus stands at the beginning of his human life and work. However, this method is correct only if we approach Christology with the idea of proceeding along chronological lines, starting with the birth and ending with the resurrection and the ascension. After which, in systematic theology, the doctrine of the church, Ecclesiology, begins. But this, as we see, was not the method of the early Christians. They were looking at the events surrounding Jesus backwards and they discovered as the last what was chronologically the first, i.e., the birth of Jesus.

[77] Phil. 2:5 ff. mentions the incarnation with respect to Christ's death; Gal. 4:4 says that Jesus was born of a woman. But these instances only underline our statement that Paul was not interested in the birth of Jesus and refers to it only at the periphery of his theology.

[78] See O. Cullmann, "The Origin of Christmas" in *The Early Church*, pp. 21-36. Philadelphia: Westminster, 1961. For additional literature see J. Beckman, "Weihnachten," RGG 3, vol. VI. p. 1564. For the infancy narratives in Matthew and Luke, see Raymond E. Brown, *The Birth of the Messiah.* New York: Doubleday, 1977.

Mark, in which at the Baptism, a heavenly voice calls Jesus "my beloved Son."[79] The Fourth Gospel presents the locus classicus of all later Christologies in John 1:14, the Latin version of which (*"verbum caro"*) is the source of the technical term "in-carnation". The birth-stories of Matthew and Luke belong to a later stratum of each gospel, and can best be understood if considered within the scope of the development of Christology in the primitive church. The ultimate question in both of them is the relationship of the divine and human in the person of Jesus Christ. This is essentially what the Fourth Gospel seeks to express with the words "ὁ λόγος σάρξ ἐγένετο" and this is also the theme of the hymn in Philippians 2:5–11, to which we shall return. Is not this also the starting point of Mariology? That Jesus Christ was not only "conceived by the Holy Spirit" but also "born of woman" makes it essential that a Christology based upon the New Testament concern itself with the mother of Jesus. This concern could safely be called "maternology," the doctrine of the mother of Jesus, had not the gospel narratives preserved for us the name of this mother, which happened to be Mary.[80]

The early church did not elaborate on this latter point, but the problem of the relation between the divine and the human in Christ is present in the New Testament. Besides the birth narratives, the gospels are full of various Christological titles which are applied to Jesus and which contain in themselves answers to particular questions that arose concerning Jesus Christ. In the other books Christological definitions appear. Romans 1.2-4, for example, characterizes Jesus as the one "who was descended from David according to the flesh and designated Son of God in power according to the Spirit of holiness by his resurrection from the dead, Jesus Christ our Lord ..." The post-apostolic church then

---

[79] Mark 1:11.

[80] J. Brinktrine gave this appropriate title to his Mariology published in Paderborn, 1959: "Die Lehre von der Mutter des Erlösers." This is also the title of the latest papal encyclical letter: *Redemptoris Mater* (March 25, 1987) by John Paul II. Indeed, the New Testament attaches no special significance to the name of the mother of Jesus. She is mentioned by name only in the following passages: Matthew 1.:16, 18, 20; 2:11; 13:55. Mark 6.3. Luke 1:27, 30, 34, 38, 39, 41, 46, 56; 2:5, 16, 19, 34. Acts 1:14. Her name is not mentioned at all in the fourth gospel, by Paul or the rest of the New Testament literature. Concerning the meaning of the name see Walter Delius, *Geschichte der Marienverehrung*. München/Basel: Reinhardt, 1963. p. 9 f.

began to speculate on the person of Christ and the prevailing emphasis of the following centuries was upon the definition of the nature of Christ within himself, i.e., the relation of his divine and human nature, or the relation between Jesus the Son and God the Father. Immediately after the New Testament period there were two radical attempts to resolve the Christological dilemma. They are diametrically opposed to each other in that the one denied the divinity of Jesus and the other denied his humanity. The first of these is associated with the sect of the Ebionites, although similar views persisted in the church long after this group disappeared from the scene. The Ebionites were originally the Jewish Christian group beside the Gentile Christian faction. In addition to their insistence upon keeping the Jewish laws, the Ebionites also denied the virgin birth and looked upon Jesus as the natural son of Joseph and Mary. Nevertheless, they accepted Jesus as the Messiah and waited for his return. A few years before the destruction of Jerusalem in 70 A.D. the Jewish Christian group immigrated to Pella in Transjordan. This immigration took the group out of the flow of the main historical events and it soon shrank to an insignificant sect.

The other solution is known as Docetism. We must remember, however, that Docetism was not a sect but a way of thinking which was employed particularly by the Gnostic theologians. Docetism (from *dokein* = to appear) held that Christ had no real body, but only appeared to be in flesh, only appeared to suffer on the cross; in fact he was completely spiritual. Naturally, then, his birth was not real; his body came through Mary's as water flows through a tube, without taking with it anything of the substance of the tube. Docetism must have existed as early as New Testament times. Several passages in the Johannine letters are interpreted as combatting this kind of teaching. Ignatius, the bishop of Antioch, must have had Docetism in mind when he went to great lengths to emphasize that Jesus Christ was actually born and that he actually went through various human experiences. In this connection, Ignatius often referred to Mary as the mother of Jesus as proof of the reality of his flesh and humanity.

These early attempts served only as preludes to the later Christological debates, which laid the basis and, so to speak, created the possibility of subsequent Mariological speculations. Thus far the interest in Mary as a Christological subject was negligible. Even in the struggle against Docetism, the church made very little use of her. In the same breath with Mary, Herod the Tetrarch or Pontius Pilate the governor could be mentioned in support of the claim that Jesus was indeed a real, historical person. That is basically the conviction held by Paul of Samosata, who however, injected a new emphasis into the debate. Paul, who was bishop of Antioch around 260, is sometimes called the forerunner of Nestorius because, as Eusebius says,[81] "he held, contrary to the teaching of the church, low and degraded views of Christ, namely that in his nature he was a common man ..." He used the word *"homoousios"* (consubstantial) in describing the relation between Father and Son but, curiously enough, the Synod which condemned him at Antioch in 268 rejected the term. He was an Adoptianist, i.e., he held that Jesus Christ was a human being upon whom the Holy Spirit descended. There was no room in his theology for a real incarnation because only Jesus, not the Logos, was born of Mary. "Mary did not bear the Word, for Mary did not exist before the ages. Mary is not older than the Word; what she bore was a man equal to us, but superior in all things as a result of holy spirit."[82] Paul of Samosata was the first theologian to hold to an Adoptianist Christology,[83] but he touched on a relationship in Christology which thus far had been largely neglected, namely the *divinity* of Jesus Christ in relation to his mother. That Jesus Christ was a real human being and Mary was his mother is easy to understand. Nobody could quarrel with the statement that if a person had a human mother, he was a human being, too. But what about the divine nature of Christ? What was Mary's relation to that? If the Logos and Jesus Christ were one, then Mary, who certainly bore Jesus, bore the Logos. Paul rejected this concept and in so doing he focused attention on the problem of what did take place in the incarnation. Did Mary bear God or man? Paul's answer was that she bore a man, but while he gave this answer, Mary was already being called *"theotokos,"* "God bearer".

It was, as we see, Christological speculations in the post-apostolic church that gradually led to a clarification of Mary's role in

---

[81] Church History 7, 27. *The Nicene and Post-Nicene Fathers*, Series Two, Vol. I. 312.

[82] F. Loofs, *Paulus von Samosata.* Leipzig, 1924, pp.70 and 242 ff. Also J.N. D. Kelly, *Early Christian Doctrines.* New York: Harpers, 1958. p. 140.

[83] Kelly, *Early Christian Doctrines*, p. 115 ff. give a good survey.

the incarnation. Let us now further explore this line of thought with special attention to the term *theotokos*, because the development of this term will shed light upon the basic characteristics of Mariology in its formative period.

As far as we know the word *theotokos* was first used by Origen (†253/54). At least this is what we gather from Socrates' *Church History*. [84] But the expression did not become popular until the time of the Arian controversies when Athanasius (295—373) frequently employed it. The Arian controversy centered on the problem of the relation between God the Father and the Logos; the problem of the mother of Jesus did not enter it. The Creed which was accepted at the Synod of Nicea in 325 contains no reference at all to Mary, but it made a significant statement which inevitably led toward further questioning. It sanctioned the use of the term *homoousios* (the Son is consubstantial with the Father) and this firmly established the divinity of Jesus Christ. Indeed, the position taken by Arius was so devoted to the *monarchia* of God that Jesus was reduced to a demi-god, which is not really the Christian concept. As it was, the Nicene fathers were no less monarchistic in their theology than was Arius, and we can easily understand that the term *homoousios* was not congenial to many of them. After all, if the Son is consubstantial with the Father, how are we to safeguard the unity and oneness of God? Moreover, how are we to explain the incarnation? The theologically uninitiated could logically draw the conclusion that since Jesus is of the same substance as God, and since Mary bore Jesus, therefore, Mary bore God. But how could a creature give birth to her own creator? With respect to the divine and human natures of Christ, Nicea answered the question of divinity beyond any doubt, but concerning the humanity it left a great deal of confusion.

It is no surprise that the first great heresy after Nicea was inaugurated by a devotee of the term *homoousios* and an ardent fighter against Arianism, Apollinarius of Laodicea (about 310–390). He

---

[84] VII, 32. *NPNF*, Ser. Two, Vol. II, 171. (Quasten in his *Patrology* vol. II, p. 81 wrongly attributes the passage to the historian Sozomen.) For the history of the term "theotokos" see John Henry Cardinal Newman, *Select Treatises of St. Athanasius in Controversy with the Arians*. Volume II. London: Longmans, Green and Co. Fifth ed. 1890. pp. 210-215. Also J. Brinktrine, *op. cit.* pp. 15 f. Compare with this Delius, *op. cit.* pp. 78 ff. and note that Hippolytus' use of the word is debatable, see G. W. H. Lampe, *A Patristic Greek Lexicon*. Oxford: Clarendon, 1964. pp. 639-641.

was also a friend of Athanasius and consequently he began to develop his ideas as a defender of orthodoxy against the surviving influence of Paul of Samosata. But whereas Paul reduced Jesus Christ to a mere man, Apollinarius exalted him to such a degree that the humanity of Jesus all but disappeared. He rejected the idea that there could be a distinction between the Son of God and the Son of Mary because Christ is one person, and insofar as he is consubstantially united with God, even his body, which he received from the Virgin Mary, is divine.[85] The vocabulary of Apollinarius is strangely reminiscent of the word *theotokos*, "God-bearer." He speaks of Jesus not only as "God incarnate" but also as the "flesh-bearing God," "θεός σαρκοφόρος," and "God born of woman." These are expressions which today are widely applied to Mary, only the order of words is reversed: "The woman of whom God was born," "the flesh which carried God," "σάρξ θεοφόρος" if we want to twist Apollinarius' words, are among the many honorary expressions used in reference to Mary. Be that as it may, the heresy underlying Apollinarius' subtle theology soon became apparent, for he acknowledged only one nature in Jesus Christ and in doing so overthrew the delicate balance between Christ's divine and human natures. He de-emphasized the humanity of Jesus to such a degree that ultimately his Christology would have ended in Docetism. In 381 the Council of Constantinople condemned him and several laws were enacted against his followers by Emperor Theodosius.[86]

Now the Christological debate swung back to the other pole. As a natural reaction against Apollinarianism the interest centered on the humanity of Jesus. Gregory Nazianzen (c. 329/30 - c. 390) gives us an excellent example of this in his second letter to Cledonius (*Epistle* 102) in which he writes: "And since a questions has also been mooted concerning the divine assumption of humanity, or incarnation, state this also clearly to all concerning me, that I join in One the Son, who was begotten of the Father, and afterward of the Virgin Mary , and that I do not call him two sons but worship him as one and the same in undivided Godhead and honor."[87] The question in Gregory's mind, as we see from

---

[85] Kelly, *op. cit.* pp. 289 ff.

[86] See N Q. King, *The Emperor Theodosius and the Establishment of Christianity.* Philadelphia: Westminister, 1961, pp.36 ff.

[87] E.R. Hardy and C.C. Richardson, *Christology of the Later Fathers,* (The

this quotation, was not whether Jesus Christ was divine or not; this he held without any doubt, and apparently so did others. The question that called for an answer was how the divine could assume humanity, i.e., the incarnation. Gregory points here to the birth of Jesus from the Virgin Mary as an undeniable proof of his humanity. In his first letter to Cledonius against Apollinarius (*Epistle* 101) he writes: "For we do not sever the man from the God-head, but we lay down as a dogma the unity and identity (of person), who of old was not man but God and the only Son before all ages, unmingled with body or anything corporeal; but who in these last days has assumed manhood also for our salvation ... that by one and the same (Person), who was perfect man and also God, the entire humanity fallen through sin might be created anew. If anyone does not believe that holy Mary is the Mother of God, he is severed from the God-head. If anyone should assert that he passed through the Virgin as through a channel, and was not at once divinely and humanly formed in her (divinely, because without the intervention of a man; humanly because in accordance with the laws of gestation), he is in like manner godless."[88]

We have quoted this passage more fully so that the clarity of Gregory's thought may not be obscured. Unfortunately, sometimes the sentence: "If anyone does not believe that holy Mary is the Mother of God, he is severed from the God-head," is quoted out of context as if it were a "Mariological statement as a test of orthodoxy."[89] As it is, however, the statement is not Mariological but Christological, and its purpose is to emphasize the fact of the incarnation, or, in other words, the fact that God really became man. Gregory employs here the word *theotokos*, and for him this means only one thing, that God really assumed humanity through a human birth. That Mary is *theotokos* expresses the Christological idea that he who was born of her is real God and real man. In this sense the term *theotokos* means exactly the opposite of what it later came to mean.[90] Later, when the term was

---

Library of Christian Classics, vol III.) Philadelphia: Westminister, 1954. p. 225. *MPG*, 37.196.

[88] Ibid. p. 216 f. *MPG* 37, 177.

[89] Hilda Graef, *Mary: A History of Doctrine and Devotion.* Vol.I New York: Sheed and Ward, 1963, p. 64. See also Juniper B. Carol (editor), *Mariology.* vol. 2. Milwaukee: Bruce, 1957, p. 120.

[90] Hardy and Richardson, *Christology*...p. 31: "For this connection the term 'theotokos' 'God-bearer', is first formally employed with a reverse

used, everybody understood it as a kind of royal title underscoring Mary's privileged position and honor. However, when these fathers used the term, they did not think of Mary; they thought of Christ.

The other Gregory, the Bishop of Nyssa (†394) used the word *theotokos* five times in his works in a similar meaning. In his struggle against Apollinarius he was also anxious to emphasize that "Christ really was present in the human compound, and so to leave no room for their surmise who propound that a phantom or form in human outline and not a real Divine Manifestation, was there."[91] For this reason he emphatically rejected the term *anthropotokos*, "man-bearer," and declared that Mary indeed was *theotokos*, because "Christ is the power of God and the wisdom of God, always changeless, always imperishable, though He comes in the changeable and the perishable ..."[92]

The Christological debate with respect to the human side of the incarnation continued in the works of the contemporary theologians, especially Theodore of Mopsuestia (†428). For our purpose, however, it is sufficient to know the precise meaning of the term *theotokos* on the eve the Council of Ephesus. It is important to remember that the meaning was Christologial and not Mariological.

The council of Ephesus (431) was convened by Emperior Theodosius II to resolve the dispute which arose between Nestorius (348–451) and Cyril of Alexandria (d. 444). The dispute itself started over Nestorius' definition of the two natures of Christ and his insistence that the divine nature in Christ cannot really have a human mother. Nestorius was forced to give a definition of his Christology when he became bishop of Constantinople in 428 and discovered that public opinion was sharply divided on the issue.[93]

---

emphasis from that which it carries later."

[91] *Letter* 17 to Eustathia, Ambrosia and Basilissa. *NPNF*, Series Two. Vol.5.pp.542 ff. *MPG* 46, 1015-1024.

[92] Ibid.

[93] Ch. J. Hefele, *A History of the Councils of the Church.* Vol. 3, English Translation: Edinburgh: T. & T. Clark, 1883. A good concise description of the historical background and of the proceedings at the Council is given by Giovanni Miegge, *The Virgin Mary.* Philadelphia: Westminister, 1955. pp.53 ff. Relevant works of Nestorius are available in the edition Friedrich Loofs, *Nestoriana. Die Fragmente des Nestorius.* Halle: Max Niemeyer, 1905, especially the following statements: *Sed et virginem christotocon ausi sunt cum codo quodam deo tactare divinam.* Letter "Ad Caelestinum I. Loofs, *op. cit.* p. 164, lines 4 - 5;

In his sermons he made clear that the union of the two natures must be kept intact but without confusion; therefore, the incarnation should be described by calling Mary "Christbearer," *Christotokos*, i.e., neither *anthropotokos*, "man-bearer" nor *theotokos*, "God-bearer." Because of this position he soon found himself under attack by Cyril. When he discovered that Cyril was in communication with Bishop Celestine of Rome on this issue, Nestorius also wrote to Celestine. In his first letter he proposed that the term *theotokos* leads to a corruption of Christology similar to Apollinarius' and Arius' "blending together the Lord's appearance as man into a kind of confused combination."[94] What he meant by this statement is that if we employ the term *theotokos* then we can mean only one of two things. Either the Son is a creature, which is Arianism, or the humanity of Christ is imperfect, which is exactly what Apollinarius taught. Some of his own clergy, Nestorius continued, "openly blasphemed God the Word consubstantial with the Father, as if he took his beginning from the Christ-bearing Virgin ... they refer the Godhead of the Only-begotten to the same origin as the flesh joined (with it), and kill it with the flesh, and blasphemously say that the flesh joined with the Godhead was turned into deity by the deifying Word which is nothing more nor less than to corrupt both. They even have to treat the Christ-bearing Virgin in a way as along with God (or: include the Virgin in the topic of *theologia*),[95] for they do not scruple to call her *theotokos*, when the holy and beyond-all-praise Fathers at Nicaea said no more of the holy Virgin than that our Lord Jesus Christ was incarnate of the Holy Spirit and the Virgin Mary, not to mention the Scriptures, which everywhere, both by angels and apostles, speak of the Virgin as mother of Christ, not of God the Word." The term *theotokos* is not appropriate for Mary, Nestorius argues, because a mother is of the same essence as what is born of her, and Mary could not give birth to God the Word who was older than she herself. Therefore, *Theotokos* may be used in reference to the humanity of Christ, that is, only in the

---

see Hardy and Richardson, *op. cit.*, 348; τὴν θεοδόχον τῷ θεῷ λόγῳ συνθευλογῶμεν μορφήν First Sermon against the θεοτόκος Loofs, *op. cit.* p. 263, lines 12-13; τὴν θεοδόχον τῷ θεῷ μὴ συνθεολογῶμεν μορφήν Sermon τὰς (μὲν εἰς ἐμὲ) παρὰ Loofs, *op. cit.* p. 276, lines 4-5-6.
  [94] Hardy and Richardson, *op. cit.* p.347.
  [95] *Ibid.* p.348, n. 6.

sense that what was born of the Virgin was the "inseparable temple of God the Word," but not to imply that Mary is the mother of God the Word.

It is impossible not to sympathize with Nestorius' concern for a healthy Christology because so much that he dreaded from a vague and uncontrolled use of *theotokos* was realized in later Mariological speculations. Yet Nestorius was wrong, but not because he recognized the dangers latent in the term *theotokos;* in this he was all too right. The orthodoxy of his intentions cannot be doubted either. But he was unable to resolve the relationship of the two natures in Christ in a way that would guarantee the unity of Christ. As he presented it, his Christology was open to attack, and his enemies took full advantage of this fact.

Cyril of Alexandria attacked Nestorius on the grounds that the union of the two natures which Nestorius proposed was not a real union at all. If the person of Christ is not understood correctly, Cyril maintained, then Christ's work of redemption is in danger, too, for this must be understood as the work of God incarnate. From this viewpoint one could only conclude that when Nestorius, even in a limited sense, rejected the use of the term *theotokos,* he became guilty of a great heresy. Cyril presented his opinions in sermons and in various letters. When Bishop Celestine sided with him in 430, Cyril composed a long letter to Nestorius to which were added twelve anathemas. He called upon Nestorius to subscribe to these. In the course of the letter he declared: "Since the holy Virgin gave birth after the flesh to God who was united by hypostasis with flesh, therefore we say that she is *theotokos*, not as though the nature of the Word had the beginning of its existence from flesh ... (nor that the Word needed human birth, but that by accepting it he blessed the beginning of our existence, and removed the curse from it) ... " Consequently, the first of the twelve anathemas reads: "If anyone does not confess that Emmanuel is God in truth, and therefore the holy Virgin is theotokos - for she bore in the flesh the Word of God become flesh – let him be anathema."[96] The Antiochene theologians did not like this formulation and in 432 Cyril was seriously charged with Apollinarianism, a charge from which he had to clear himself by explaining his position. However, the Council which met in

---

[96] *Ibid.* pp. 352-353.

Ephesus in 431 officially approved Cyril's position and Nestorius was excommunicated. The term *theotokos* was subsequently included in the "Formula of Union of 433" which was intended to bring together the Antiochene theologians who leaned toward Nestorius, and the Alexandrian group, which was represented by Cyril.[97]

After the case of Eutyches (born around 378), who was excommunicated because of monophysitism in 448, the Christological debate was finally settled by the Council of Chalcedon in 451. In this council the fathers referred to the incarnation in the following way: "... begotten before ages of the Father in Godhead, the same in the last days for us; and for our salvation (born) of Mary, the virgin *theotokos*, in manhood, one and the same Christ."[98] Thus the term *theotokos* was firmly established.

We are accustomed to think of the council of Ephesus as having made a major Mariological declaration. One theologian states: "A bishop had questioned Mary's most precious prerogative, and his brother bishops had banned him from their fellowship."[99] Another says: "The controversy was at an end. Mary had solemnly been affirmed to be *Theotokos*."[100] This view must undergo some revision. First of all, the circumstances under which the Council met and approved the term *theotokos* were such that no true Christian could recount them without embarrassment.[101] Yet the fact that Mary was officially declared to be *theotokos* in Ephesus, where "the temple of the great goddess Artemis" stood, must not be set aside as insignificant. The people of Ephesus reacted to the Council in much the same way their ancestors had almost 400 years before when they thought that the honor of Artemis was at stake (Acts 19). Although they probably had little understanding for the Christological issue, they demonstrated in the streets and shouted "Praised be the *Theotokos!*" just as their ancestors had shouted "Great is Artemis of the Ephesians." This

---

97   Text in Hardy and Richardson, *op. cit.*, pp.356 ff.
98   *Ibid.* p. 373.
99   Carol, *Mariology*, vol.2.p.123
100   Graef, *Mary* ..., p.111. However, see a more realistic appraisal by Rene Laurentin, *Queen of Heaven. A Short Treatise on Marian Theology.* (E.T. by Gordon Smith.) Dublin and London, 1956.pp 48 ff.
101   See the material in a condensed form in Philip Hughes, *The Church in Crisis: A History of the General Councils 325-1870.* New York: Doubleday, 1961.pp. 46-47, or Hefele, *op.cit.*

display of popular pious use of the term *theotokos* should have been sufficient warning to Cyril and the other Council fathers of where the real source of the problem lay, but they did not, or could not, face that problem. The fact is that even today "Mother of God" is a very subtle theological term, a popular and careless use of which is likely to result in the conclusions indicated by the Ephesian populace. In their minds, there was probably little or no difference between Artemis and Mary.

But the council of Ephesus was not interested in Mary and that is the point to keep in mind. It approved of the term *theotokos* not as a prerogative of Mary, but as an expression of the doctrine of the two natures of Christ. *"Theo-tokos"* unites the idea of God (*"theo"*) with the ideal of human birth (*"-tokos"*) and thus presents the Christian idea of the incarnation in a well balanced way. This balance between the two natures had been scrupulously observed by Cyril, especially in the later debate that led to Chalcedon. The references in this debate to the human side of the incarnation make it clear beyond the shadow of a doubt that the fathers were not interested in conferring privileges upon Mary; their only concern was to give adequate expression to their faith about the person of Jesus Christ. However, in their struggles for a correct formulation of their faith, they referred more and more to Mary. Thus, to use Nestorius' words, Mary was included "in the topic of *theologia.*" Once this happened, the way was opened for a shift in emphasis. Even in Ephesus, the fathers who said *"theotokos"* were concerned about him who was born. But it is very easy, indeed, to place the emphasis on her who bore him, and when this happens a Christological statement immediately becomes a Mariological title.

As soon as Mary was included as a theological argument in the Christological debates, Mariology became a theological discipline. Now let us investigate the outstanding characteristics of this early Mariology.

The Christological debates were centered on the problem of the natures of Jesus Christ. While the New Testament is basically concerned with the question of what God has done in Christ, and not who Christ was, the fathers of the church were forced to discuss the issue because the incarnation was not easy to accept or to explain. The statement "God became man" contains a contradiction to which Celsus logically objected that if God were to come down to men he would have to "undergo a change, a change from good to evil, from virtue to vice, from happiness to misery, and from best to worst."[102] In the face of such criticism Christian theologians had no alternative but to defend what Origen called "the condescension *(katabasis)* of God to human affairs." The issue had to be clarified for the benefit of the church as well, for questions similiar to those Celsus raised were also asked within the church. The union of the human and the divine in Jesus had to be explained in some way. In this endeavor the fathers made extensive use of Philippians 2:5 -11: "Have this mind among yourselves, which you have in Christ Jesus, who, though he was in the form of God, did not count equality with God a thing to be grasped but emptied himself taking the form of a servant, being born in the likeness of man. And being found in human form he humbled himself and became obedient unto death, even death on a cross. Therefore God has highly exalted him and bestowed on him the name which is above every name, that at the name of Jesus every knee should bow, in heaven and on earth and under the earth, and every tongue confess that Jesus Christ is Lord, to the glory of God the Father."[103]

The means by which the self-emptying takes place is the birth from the virgin's womb. The second century fathers referred to Mary in this way.[104] In the later controversies Mary was again represented as the means of the *kenosis*. This motif played an important role in the Arian controversy and afterwards even Apollinarius used it when he wrote, "Incarnation is self-empty-ing."[105] According to Gregory of Nazianzen, the *kenosis* was God's way of liberating mankind from the bondage of sin. "For in truth he was in servitude to flesh and to birth and to the conditions of our life with a view to our liberation, and to that of all those whom

---

[102] Origen, *Against Celsus* 4, 14. *ANF* IV, 502.

[103] See the exegesis of this passage in Cullmann, *Christology*...pp.174 ff. Also Donald G. Dawe, *The Form of a Servant/A Historical Analysis of the Kenotic Motif.* Philadelphia: Westminister, 1964.

[104] See S. Benko, "Second Century References to the Mother of Jesus." *Religion in Life*, Vol. XXVI, No. 1. 1956-57 Winter Issue, pp. 98 ff. The thesis of this article is that references to Mary in the second century are always in connection with the humanity of Jesus. See also H. v. Campenhausen, *The Virgin Birth in the Theology of the Ancient Church.* Studies in Historical Theology, No. 2. London: S.C.M. Press, 1964.

[105] Dawe, *op.cit.*, p.60.

he has saved who were in bondage under sin. What greater destiny can befall man's humility than that he should be intermingled with God, and by this intermingling should be deified, and that we should be so visited by the day-spring from on high that even that holy thing that should be born should be called the Son of the Highest and that there should be bestowed upon him a name which is above every name? And what else can this be than God — and that every knee should bow to him that was made of no reputation for us, and that mingled the form of God with the form of a servant, and that all the house of Israel should know that God has made him both Lord and Christ? For all this was done by the action of the begotten, and by the good pleasure of Him that begot him.''[106]

A similar position was also taken by Cyril of Alexandria who made extensive use of the kenotic motif in his writings against the Antiochean theologians.[107] In his letter to John of Antioch, accepting the so called "Formula of Union of 433" which sought to reconcile the two groups separated at Ephesus, Cyril wrote: "For you must surely clearly understand that almost all our fight for the faith was connected with our declaring that the holy Virgin is *theotokos*. But if we say that the holy body of Christ the Savior of us all was from heaven and not of her, how could she be thought of as *theotokos* ? For whom indeed did she bear, if it was not true that she bore Emmanuel after the flesh ...? But since God the Word, who descended from above and from heaven, emptied himself, taking the form of a servant and is styled Son of Man, while remaining what he is, that is, God, there is one Lord Jesus Christ, although the difference of the natures is not ignored, out of which we say that the ineffable union was effected."[108]

In the West, Hilary of Poitiers (ca. 315-367) used the kenotic-

---

[106] *The Fourth Theological Oration*, 3. Hardy and Richardson, *op. cit.*, p. 178 *MPG* 36, 105-108. Other interesting passages from Gregory include *Oration* II, 23 (*NPNF* Series Two, Vol . 7, 209); *Oration* 12, 4 (*ibid.*, p. 246); *Oration* 37 2 (*ibid.*, p. 338) *Oration* 37, 3 (*ibid.*, p. 339) which explains the reason of kenosis with the following words: "But inasmuch as He strips Himself for us, inasmuch as He comes down (and I speak of an exinanition, as it were, a laying aside and a diminution of His glory), He becomes by this comprehensible." See also his *Second Letter to Cledonius Against Apollinaris*, Hardy and Richardson, *op . cit.*, p. 227.

[107] This is well summarized by Dawe, *op. cit.*, pp.58 ff.

[108] Hardy and Richardson, *op.cit.*, p. 357.

motif: "Christ abode in the form of God when He assumed the form of a servant, not being subjected to change, but emptying Himself; His unbounded might contracted itself, until it could fulfil the duty of obedience even to the endurance of the body to which it was yoked. But since He was self-contained even when He emptied Himself, His authority suffered no diminution, for in the humiliation of the emptying He exercised within Himself the power of that authority which was emptied."[109] Similar notions are also found in the works of Ambrose (339-397), who used the words *exinanire* (emptying) and *celare* (hiding) concerning the divinity of Christ in the incarnation. "For of a truth He died in that which He took of the Virgin, not in that which He had of the Father ... For He took on Him that which He was not that He might hide that which He was."[110] It is possible that these two men influenced Leo, bishop of Rome between 440-461, in the formation of his own Christology. Becoming involved in the Christological controversies through the Eutychian heresy, Leo composed a letter, the so called "Tome of Leo," which was intended to end the controversy at the Council of Ephesus of 449.[111] The letter, however, was suppressed. It was not officially approved until the Council of Chalcedon in 451, although not as the official document of the Council. Nevertheless, the letter is significant because it is respresentative of Western thinking on the Christological issue. In it, Leo made several references to the kenotic-motif. It seems that his mind constantly returned to the formulation of Philippians 2:5 ff.: "He took on him the form of a servant without the defilement of sins, augmenting what was human, not diminishing what was divine; because the 'emptying of himself,' whereby the Invisible made himself visible, and the Creator and Lord of all things willed to be one among mortals, was a stooping-down of compassion, not a failure of power. Accordingly, the same who, remaining in the form of God, made man, was *made Man in the form of a servant.*" [112] Leo is clear that the *kenosis*, the

---

[109] *On the Trinity*, II 48. *NPFN* 9, 217 *MPL* 10, 431 f. See also in the same book 8.45; 9.14; 10.25; 12.16.

[110] *On the Holy Spirit*, Book I, Chapter 9, 107 *NPNF* 10 107, MPL 16, 759. See also *De Incarnationis Sacramento* 5, 41. mpl 16, 804.

[111] Contemptuously, Leo called this synod "Latrocinium," i .e., "Synod of Robbers."

[112] Hardy and Richardson, *op.cit.* pp.363 f. See Also Hefele, *op.cit.*pp. 225 ff., or *NPNF* Series Two, 12, 38 ff. and in the same series among the acts of

humiliation of Christ, lies in his being "made of a woman, made under the law,"[113] i.e., being born of Mary. The Son of God descended from heaven and entered this lower world: the Lord of the universe allowed his infinite majesty to be overshadowed and took upon him the form of a servant.[114] The Virgin supplied the matter of Christ's flesh; the divine power is manifested by the new mode of birth in which the incarnation took place. That is the true significance of the Virgin birth of Christ, since to deny his true flesh is also to deny his bodily sufferings.[115]

What, then, were the outstanding characteristics of Mariology as it first emerged from the Christological controversies? It is characterized by the words "condescension" (*katabasis*) and "self-emptying" (*kenosis*). Mary supplied the means by which this condescension and self-emptying took place. Incarnation, being born of Mary, was a humiliation for Christ which made him of no reputation. What he received from her was "the form of a servant" and thus we see that the fathers spoke of Mary in closest connection with *Heilsgeschichte*, that is, with Christ's obedience in condescending to human affairs. For them, to speak about Mary was meaningful only in view of God's revelatory actions.[116] Her significance lay not in her *being*, but in her involvement in a particular πλήρωμα τοῦ χρόνου ("fullness of time") in redemptive history, when God sent forth his Son, born of woman.[117]

This is the crucial point, the point at which the Council fathers failed. Ephesus was a victory for the theologians and priests, who successfully defended orthodoxy from pagan influences, especially from the dreaded idea of polytheism. In the process, however, they failed to recognize the rapid progress of an already deeply rooted popular religion which adopted and baptized innumerable pagan practices. The veneration of martyrs, saints, statues, relics and amulets became accepted expressions of pious devotion. All of these, however, faded in comparison with the devotion accorded to the Virgin Mary. The excellent fathers of orthodoxy did their

---

the Council of Chalcedon (451), vol. 14.254. The Latin text is available in Migne, *PL* 54, 756 ff.

[113] Hardy and Richardson, *op.cit.* p. 365.

[114] *Ibid.*, p.364.

[115] *Ibid.*, p.367.

[116] O. Cullman, *Christology. op.cit.* p.293.

[117] Gal. 4.4.

best to secure the full humanity and full divinity of Jesus Christ. But they did not adequately deal with Mariology. Only if Mary is part of sinful mankind could she supply to Christ the "form of a servant." But the questions raised by such a union were so great that the most specious reasoning could not answer them all. The solution came when the concept of Mary's "immaculate conception," i.e., complete sinlessness, including freedom from original sin, was fully developed. Then *incarnation* could be understood as a true cosmic event paralleling the primeval "*communio dei et hominis.*" In Mary, the Immaculate, the divine united himself with mankind *prior to sin* and thus the new creation could take place. The adoption of the title *theotokos* paved the way toward this development, but it was, as a theological definition, several steps behind popular piety, which already depicted Mary clothed with the sun and accorded her all the honor that pagans gave to their Queen of Heaven.

Thus the theological definition of Mary's role in the incarnation and consequently in the history of salvation came about in a remarkably absurd way. In their attempt to avoid polytheism, theologians included Mary in their Christological debates as an argument for the humanity of Jesus. The results, however, were exactly the opposite of what they intended, for once having included the mother of Jesus in the "topic of *theologica,*" the wheels were set in motion that would lead to the declaration of the *theotokos* title. But a *theotokos* who is human is a contradiction, and so the church entered upon the long and arduous journey toward the final conclusion: the Mother of God must be the Queen of Heaven.

MARIOLOGY: PAST AND FUTURE
A SUMMARY

In this study we have traced the roots of Mariology back into classical Mediterranean devotion to the goddesses of fertility and motherhood. Hopefully our thesis, that there exists a direct line between the pagan goddesses and Mary and that Mariology is a continuation of the veneration accorded to fertility goddesses, is now substantiated.

We have seen that pagan fertility goddesses were conceived of as fulfilling the feminine role in the divine act of creation, and that therefore they represented the female principle in the divine as well as everything that femininity means on a human level. As such, goddesses filled a cosmic role, participating in the creation, maintenance, and nurture of the universe and every living thing in it. Because the central concept in their veneration was motherhood, they were commonly called mother goddesses; one of their honorary titles was "Mother of the gods."

The veneration of Mary strictly adheres to these principles, from which it is derived. She is the female agent in the "new creation." Her participation in the divine act of redemption is of a cosmic character, for as the mother of the new generation she stands with the father. In the figure of Mary femininity is divinized and motherhood is raised to the same level as the fatherhood of God.

Classical Mediterranean spirituality conceived of the present condition of the universe, in which divisions exist that did not exist "in the beginning," as "unnatural." These divisions and separations will disappear when the original conditions return. One aspect of this separation is the forceful disjunction of heaven and earth, which is similar to the division of male and female. The separation, however, is not absolute; heaven and earth still intermingle and earth is fertilized by the moisture of the sky. Male and female similarly unite, albeit temporarily, in sexual intercourse, which is an anticipation of the final consummation.

In acknowledgement of this, the *hieros gamos* was practiced in many ancient cults.

Christianity adopted, purified, and crystallized these ideas by developing the theology of the recapitulation (or, as Irenaeus said ἀνακεφαλαίωσις) of all things in Christ. In this theology, sexual imagery was widely used and the union of all things was demonstrated by reference to marriage. In this *hieros gamos* Mary received the role of the bride, as the "virgin earth" who was impregnated by the word of God, as the symbol of the church, the bride of Christ, and as Queen of Heaven.

Thus in a theological perspective, Mary is the direct continuation of the pagan goddesses and unites in herself the basic principles that in Mediterranean piety underlay and determined the worship of mother goddesses.

Historically the divinity of Mary is first indicated in the book of Revelation and later in the piety of Asia Minor where Christians were more sensitive toward the female aspect of God due to the influence of Cybele and the age old religious history of Asia Minor in which the union of the divine and human was prominent. In this general geographic area the first Mariological impulses appeared in popular piety, leading the way to later theological speculation. The motherhood of Mary, which is the basic principle of Mariology, came from the pagan *"Magna Mater"* and "Mother of the Gods" designations of certain goddesses. Here, too, the influence of Cybele was crucial, because of all Greek and Roman goddesses she alone could be called a "virgin mother"; thus she offered the only possible connection with the Christian image of the virgin mother of God.[1]

This does not mean that other goddesses had no impact on the Christian cult. We have seen that popular piety easily identified local goddesses with Mary. The rapid spread of the cult of Mary is due in no small measure to the fact that people could so easily transfer to it the worship they had offered to their pagan goddess. This development continued even in the New World, one example of which is the cult of the Virgin of Guadelupe. However, the influence of these goddesses, including Isis, was secondary:

---

[1] This has been pointed out by Lewis R.Farnell, *The Cults of the Greek States*. Oxford: Clarendon,1907, vol. 3, pp. 305-306 and M. P. Carroll, *op. cit.*, p.10. Carroll also argues against deriving the Mary cult from the cult of Isis, see *op. cit.*, pp. 111-112.

for the origin of the cult, all evidence points to Asia Minor and to Greco-Roman pagan piety. Other aspects of Mariology, such as Gnosticism and the "Wisdom" (Sophia) concept, also enriched Mariology but did not originate it. Mariology is firmly rooted in a cosmic view of redemption and only in this context can it be understood.

The veneration of Mary cannot be viewed in isolation and it is wrong to see it as a uniquely Christian phenomenon which grew out of Christianity without any outside influence, as it is sometimes claimed by Mariologists. But it would be equally wrong to claim that the introduction of Mary into Christian thinking was a relatively late phenomenon and therefore does not belong to the original stratum of Christian theology. This position has often been taken by opponents of Marian piety who also point out that the cult of Mary began to flourish only after the Council of Ephesus in 431. While it is certainly true that after 431 Mariolatry spread rapidly, it is equally true that in an implicit way the cosmic role of Mary in salvation can already be detected in the nativity stories of Matthew and Luke, in Revelation 12, and then, from the middle of the second century on, in numerous investigations of the Eve-Mary parallel.

What is the future of Mariology? This depends on the work of Christian scholars and theologians. This study suggests that Mariology offers a way to deal with a major deficiency of Christian theology in which the feminine image of God has all but disappeared.

BIBLIOGRAPHY

CHAPTER ONE

Alastruey, Gregory, *The Blessed Virgin Mary*, St. Louis, Mo.: B. Herder, 1964.

Barnhouse, Ruth, Tiffany, and Holmes, Urban T. (ed.), *Male and Female. Christian Approaches to Sexuality*. New York: Seabury Press, 1976.

Baumann, Hermann, *Das Doppelte Geschlecht*. Berlin: E. Reimer, 1955.

Benko, Stephen, "The Libertine Gnostic Sect of the Phibionites." *Vigiliae Christianae* 21 (1967) 103–19.

——, *Pagan Rome and the Early Christians*. Bloomington: Indiana U. Press, 1984.

——, *Protestants, Catholics and Mary*. Philadelphia: Judson Press, 1969.

Benz, Ernst, *Adam. Der Mythus von Urmenschen*. München-Planegg: Otto-Wilhelm-Barth Verlag, 1955.

Bertholet, Alfred, *Das Geschlecht der Gottheit*. Tübingen: J.C.B. Mohr (Paul Siebeck), 1934.

Boettcher, Helmuth M., *Die Grosse Mutter. Zeugungsmythen der Frühgeschichte*. Düsseldorf/Wien: Econ Verlag, 1968.

Boff, Leonardo, *The Maternal Face of God. The Feminine and Its Religious Expressions*. San Francisco: Harper & Rowe, 1979.

Brown, Peter, "The Notion of Virginity in the Early Church" in Bernard McGinn, etc. (edd.) *World Spirituality*. Vol. 6: *Christian Spirituality* ... pp. 427–443. New York: Crossroad, 1985.

Buckley, Jorunn, Jacobsen, *Female Fault and Fulfillment in Gnosticism*. Chapel Hill, N.C./London: University of N.C. Press, 1986.

Burnett, John, *Early Greek Philosophy*. New York: Macmillan, 1892.

Bynum, Caroline, Walker, *Jesus as Mother. Studies in the Spirituality of the High Middle Ages*. Berkely, Los Angeles, London: U.C. Press, 1982.

Campbell, Joseph and Musès, Charles, *In All Her Names. Four Explorations of the Feminine in Divinity*. San Francisco: Harper, 1991.

Carol, Juniper, B., *Mariology*. Milwaukee: Bruce, 1955–1961.

Castelli, Elizabeth, "Virginity and Its Meaning for Women's Sexuality in Early Christianity." *Journal of Feminist Studies in Religion* 2 (1986) 61–88.

Christ, Carol, P., *Daughter of Aphrodite. Reflections on a Journey to the Goddess*. San Francisco: Harper & Row, 1987.

Danielou, Jean, "Le Culte Marial et le Paganisme." in: *Maria*. P. Du Manoir (ed.) Paris: Beauchesne, 1949, vol. 1, 159–181.

Dieterich, Ernst Ludwig, "Der Urmensch als Androgyn." *Zeitschrift für Kirchengeschichte* 58 (1939) 297–345.

Delius, Walter, *Geschichte der Marienverehrung*. München/Basel: Reinhardt, 1963.

Downing, Christine, *The Goddess. Mythological Images of the Feminine*. New York: Crossroad, 1984.

——, *Psyche's Sister. Re-imagining the Meaning of Sisterhood*. San Francisco: Harper & Row, 1988.

Drijver, J. W. "Virginity." *ER* 15, 179–281.

Eliade, M. and O'Flaherty, W. D. "Androgunes." *ER* 1, 276–281.

Eliade, Mircea, *Patterns in Comparative Religion*. New York: Sheed and Ward, 1958.

——, *The Two and the One*. London: Harvill Press, 1965.

Fendt, Leonard, *Gnostische Mysterien*. München: Kaiser Verlag, 1922.
Goodspeed, E. J., *The Apostolic Fathers*. New York: Harper and Brothers, 1950.
Grant, Robert M., *The Secret Sayings of Jesus*. Garden City, N.Y.: Doubleday & Co., 1960.
Greely, Andrew, M. *The Mary Myth. On the Feminity of God*. New York: Seabury Press, 1977.
Gryson, R., *The Ministry of Women in the Early Church*. Collegeville, Minn. Liturgical Press, 1976.
Guillemont, A. (ed.) *The Gospel According to Thomas*. Leiden: E. J. Brill; New York: Harper and Brothers, 1959.
Hase, Karl von, *Handbuch der Protestantischen Polemik gegen die Römisch Katholische Kirche*. Leipzig: Breitkopf und Härtel, 1862; sixth edition 1894.
Hedrick, Charles W., Hodgson, Robert, Jr., *Nag Hammadi, Gnosticism and Early Christianity*. Peabody, MA.: Hendrickson Publishers, 1988.
Heiler, Friedrich, *Die Frau in den Religionen der Menschheit*. Berlin: De Gruyter, 1977.
Hennecke, E. and Schneemelcher, W., *New Testamnet Apocrypha*. Philadelphia: Westminister, 1963.
Hurtado, Larry, (ed.) *Images of the Feminine in Gnosticism*. Philadelphia: Fortress Press, 1988.
Kee, Howard C. "'Becoming a Child' in the Gospel of Thomas". *Journal of Biblical Literature* 82 (1963) 307–314.
King, Karen, L. (ed.) *Images of the Feminine in Gnosticiam*. Philadelphia; Fortress Press, 1988.
Knopf, Rudolf, *Lehre der zwölf Apostel. Zwei Clemensbriefe*. Tübingen: J.C.B. Mohr (Paul Siebeck), 1920.
Koepgen, George, *Die Gnosis des Christentusmus*. Salzburg: Otto Muller Verlag, 1939.
Leeming, D. A., "Virgin Birth". *ER* 15, 272–276.
Leenhard, Franz J., *Der Protestantismus im Urteil der römisch katholischen Kirche*. Zürich: Zwingli Verlag, 1943.
Lubac, Henri de, *The Eternal Feminine*. London: Collins, 1970.
MacDonald, Dennis R., *There is no Male and Female: The Fate of a Dominical Saying in Paul and Gnosticism*. Philadelphia: Fortress, 1987.
Matthews, Caitlin, *Sophia: Goddess of Wisdom. The Divine Feminine From Black Goddess to World Soul*. San Francisco: Harper, 1991.
Meeks, Wayne A., "The Image of the Androgyne. Some Uses of a Symbol in Earliest Christianity." *History of Religions* 13 (1974).
Miegge, Giovanni, *The Virgin Mary*. Philadelphia: Westminster, 1956.
Mollenkott, Virginia Ramey, *The Divine Feminine*. New York: Crossroad, 1983.
Neuman, Erich, *The Great Mother. An analysis of the Archetype*. New York: Pantheon Books, 1955.
Ochshorn, Judith, *The Female Experience and the Nature of the Divine*. Bloomington: Indiana University Press, 1981.
O'Flaherty, Wendy, D., *Women, Androgynes, and Other Mythical Beasts*. Chicago: University of Chicago, 1980.
Olson, Carl, *The Book of the Goddess. Past and Present*. New York: Crossroad, 1938.
Patai, Raphael, *The Hebrew Goddess*. New York: Ktav Publishing House, 1967.
Pestalozza, Uberto, *Eterno Femminino Mediterraneo*, Venice: Neri Pozza, 1954. French translation, *L'éternal féminine dans la religion méditerranéenne*. Bruxelles: Latomus, 1965. (Collection Latomus, Vol. LXXIX).
Pirani, Alis, *The Absent Mother. Restoring the Goddess to Judaism and Christianity*.

San Francisco. Harper, 1991
Preston, James J. "Goddess Worship". *ER* 6 35–39.
Prümm, Karl, *Der Christliche Glaube und die altheidnische Welt*. Leipzig: Jakob Hegner, 1935.
Richardson, C. C., *Early Christian Fathers*. Philadelphia: Westminster, 1953.
Roschini, P. B. M., *Maria Santissina Nella Storia Della Salvezza*. Isola Del Liri: Editrice M. Pisani, 1969 (4 volumes).
Ruether, Rosemary and McLaughlin, Eleanor, *Women of Spirit. Female Leadership in the Jewish and Christian Traditions*. New York: Simon and Shuster, 1979.
Ruether, Rosemary Redford., *Mary — The Feminine Face of the Church*. Philadelphia: Westminster, 1977.
Sjoo, Monica and Moor, Barbara, *The Great Cosmic Mother. Rediscovering the Religion of the Earth*. San Francisco: Harper& Row, 1987.
Smith, Jonathan Z., "The Garment of Shame." *History of Religions* 5, 1966.
Stone, Merlin, *When God was a Woman*. New York: The Dial Press, 1976.
Swidler, Leonard, *Biblical Affirmations of Woman*. Philadelphia: Westminster, 1979.
Trible, Phyllis, *God and the Rhetoric of Sexuality*. Philadelphia: Fortress, 1978.
Ulanov, Ann Belford, *The Feminine in Jungian Psychology and in Christian Theology*. Evanston: Northwestern U. Press, 1971.
Watts, A. W., *The Two Hands of God. The Myths of Polarity*. New York: George Braziller, 1963.
Werblowsky, R. J. Zwi, "Synkretismus in der Religionsgeschichte." in: *Syncretismus in den Religionen Zentralasiens*. Wiesbaden: O. Harrassowitz, 1987, p. 2.
West, M. L., *The Orphic Poems*. Oxford: Clarendon, 1983.
Witt, R. E., *Isis in the Graeco-Roman World*. Ithaca, N.Yl: Cornell U. Press, 1971.

CHAPTER TWO

Attridge, Harold W., and Oden, Robert R., (edd.) *De Dea Syria*, Missoula, Mont.: Scholars Press, 1976 (Society of Biblical Literature, Texts and Translations 9).
Audollent, Auguste, *Carthage Romaine*. Paris: Ancienne Libraire Thorin et Fils, 1901.
Baramki, Dimitri, *Phoenicia and the Phoenicians*. Beirut: Khayats, 1961.
Baudissin, Wolf, "Atargatis" in A. Hauck, (ed.) *Realenchklopädie für Protestantische Theologie and Kirche* Leipzig: J. C. Hinrichs, 1896–1913, vol. 2, pp. 171–177.
Berger, Philippe M., "Tanit Pene Baal." *Journal Asiatique*. Septieme Serie, 9 (1877) 147–160.
Bernstein, Alvin H., (ed.) *Polybius on Roman Imperialism*. South Bend, Indiana: Regnery Gateway, Inc., 1980.
Bickerman, E. J., "Hannibal's Covenant" in the *American Journal of Philology* 73 (1952) 1–23.
——, "An Oath of Hannibal." *Transactions of the American Philological Association* 75 (1944) 87–102.
Borgeaud, Willy, "Le Deluge, Delphes, et les Anthesteries." *Museum Helveticum* 4 (1947) 205–250.
Charles-Picard, G., *Les Religions de l'Afrique antique*. Paris: Plon, 1954.
Charles-Picard, Gilbert and Colette, *Daily Life in Carthage*. London: Allen and Unwin, 1961.

——, *The Life and Death of Carthage*, London: Sidgwick & Jackson, 1968.

Charles-Picard, Gilbert, *Carthage*. London: Elek Books, 1956.

——, *La Civilization de L'Afrique Romain*. Paris: Plon, 1959.

——, *Les Religions De L'Afrique Antique*. Paris: Plon, 1954.

Clemen, Carl C., *Die Phönikische Religion nach Philo von Byblos*. Leipzig: J. C. Hinrichs, 1939.

——, *Lukian's Schrift über die Syrische Göttin*. Leipzig: J. C. Hinrichs, 1938.

Cross, F. M., "Yahweh and the God of the Patriarchs." *Harvard Theological Review* 55 (1962) 225–259.

——, *Canaanite Myth and Hebrew Epic*. Cambridge, Mass.: Harvard, 1973.

Cross, Frank Moore Jr., "The Origin and Early Evolution of the Alphabet." *Eretz Israel* 8 (1967) 8–24.

Cumont, F., "Caelestis" in *Pauly's Realencyclopädie, op. cit.* vol. 3:1; pp. 1247–1250.

Dalman, Gustav, *Neue Petra Forschungen und der Heilige Felsen von Jerusalem*. Leipzig: Hinrichs, 1912.

——, *Sacred Sites and Ways*. London: SPCK, 1935.

Davis, N., *Carthage and her Remains*. New York: Harper, 1861.

Deubner, Ludwig, *Attische Feste*, Berlin: Keller, 1932.

Dölger, Joseph, *IXΘYC das Fischsymbol in frühchristlicher Zeit*. München: Aschendorf, 1928.

——, "Die Himmelskönigin von Carthago. Ein religionsgeschichtlicher Beitrag zu den Schriften Tertullians." *Antike und Christentum* 1 (1929) 92-106.

Domaszewski, Alfred von, *Abhandlungen zur römischen Religion*. Leipzig-Berlin: Teubner, 1909.

——, *Die Religion des römischen Heeres*. Trier: Fr. Lintz, 1895.

Drijvers, H. J. W., *Cults and Beliefs at Edessa*. Leiden: E. J. Brill, 1980. (Etudes Preliminaries aux Religious Orientales Dans L'empire Romain. Vol. 82).

——, "Die Dea Syria und andere syrische Gottheiten im Imperium Romanum." in: Maarten J. Vermaseren, *Die orientalische Religionen im Römerreich*. Leiden: E. J. Brill, 1981, pp. 241–263.

Eliade, Mircea, *Cosmos and History. The Myth of the Eternal Return*. New York: Harper, 1959.

Foerster, W., "δαίμων δαιμόνιον" *Theologisches Wörterbuch zum Neuen Testament*. G. Kittel, (ed.) Stuttgart: Kohlhammer, 1935, vol. 2, pp. 1–21.

Furtwängler, A., "Aphrodite" W. H. Roscher, *op. cit.* vol. 1, pp. 390–419.

Gabba, Emilio and Smith, Morton, (edd.) *Religions and Politics in the Hellenistic and Roman Periods*. Como: Edizioni New Press, 1985.

Griffith, John Pedley (ed.) *New Light on Ancient Carthage*. Ann Arbor: University of Michigan Press, 1980.

Halsberghe, G. H., "Le Culte de Dea Caelestis." *Aufstieg und Niedergang der römischen Welt*. Berlin New York: Walter de Gruyter, 1984. Series II (Prinzipat) vol. 17 4, pp. 2204–2223.

Harden, Donald, *The Phoenicians*. London: Thames and Hudson, 1962.

Herm, Gerhard, *The Phoenicians*. New York: William Morrow, 1975.

Hopfner, Th. H., "Mageia" in Pauly-Wissowa-Krol, *Realencyclopädie der Classischen Altertumswissenschaft* vol. 28. Stuttghart: Druckenmüller Verlag, 1928, pp. 301–394.

——, *Griechisch-Ägyptischer Offenbarungszauber*. 2 vols. Studien zur Palaeographie und Papyruskunde, 21 and 23. Leipzig: H. Haessel, 1921–1924.

Hörig, Monika, "Dea Syria-Atargatis" *ANRW* II. Prinzipat. 17.3, Berlin New York: Walter de Gruyter, 1984, pp. 1536–1581.

Huss, Werner, *Geschichte der Karthager*, München: C. H. Beck, 1985.

Judeich, Walter, *Topographie von Athen*. München: Beck, 1931.

Kerenyi, Carl, *Dionysus. Archetypal Image of Indestructible Life.* (Bollingen Series, LXV. 2) Princeton: Princeton U. Press, 1976.

Labarre, Franz, *Die römische Kolonie Karthago.* Potsdam: Kraemer-Brandt, 1882.

Latte, Kurt, *Römische Religionsgeschichte.* München: Beck, 1967.

Lewis, Naphtali, and Reinhold, Meyer, *Roman Civilisation* vol. 1. NewYork: Harper, 1966.

Lipinski, E., "Syro-Fenicische Wortels Van De Karthaagse Religie." *Phoenix* 28 (1982) 51–84.

Marsh, F. B., *A History of the Roman World 146–30 B.C.* Revised by H. H. Scullard. London: Methuen, 1971.

Meltzer, Otto, *Geschichte der Karthager.* Two volumes. Berlin: Weidmann, 1879.

Meyer, E., "Astarte" in W. H. Roscher, *Ausführliches Lexikon der Griechischen and Römischen Mythologie.* Leipzig: Teubner, 1884–1886, vol. 1, pp. 645–655.

Mommsen, August, *Feste der Stadt Athen.* Leipzig: Teubner, 1898.

Mommsen, Th., *The History of Rome.* Cleveland NewYork: World, 1967.

Moscati, Sabatino, *The World of the Phoenicians.* New York: Praeter, 1968.

Movers, F. C. *Die Phönizier.* Two volumes. (Vol. 2 has three parts). Bonn: Weber, 1841 and Berlin: Dummler, 1849.

Mundle, Ilsemarie, "Dea Caelestis in der Religionspolitik des Septimius Severus und der Julia Domna." *Historia* 10 (1960) 228–237.

Munter, Friedrich Ch., *Die Religion der Karthager.* Kopenhagen: Schubothe, 1821.

Nilsson, Martin P., *Geschichte der Griechischen Religion.* München: Beck, 1955.

——, *Greek Piety.* New York: W. W. Norton, 1969.

——, "Die Anthesterion und die Aiora." *Eranos* 15 (1915) 181–200.

Oden, R. A., *Studies in Lucian's De Dea Syria.* Missoula, Mon.: Scholars Press, 1977.

Pisciculi. Studien zur Religion and Kultur des Altertums. (F. J. Dölger Festschrift) ed. Theodor Klauser und Adolf Rucker. München: Aschendarff, 1939.

Preisendanz, K., "Tanit' *Pauly's Realencyclopädie der Classischen Altertumswissenschaft.* Stuttgart: Druckenmüller Verlag, 1932. 2. Reihe, S. Halbband (IV A 2) pp. 2178–2215.

Rohde, Erwin, *Psyche. Seelencult und Unsterblichbeitsglaube der Griechen.* Tübingen: J.C.B. Mohr, 1925.

Ronzevalle, P., "Trace de Cult de Tanit en Phenicie." *Melanges de la Faculte Orientale Universite Saint Joseph* 5 (1912) 75–83.

Roscher, W. H., "Iuno Caelestis" in *Roscher's Lexikon, op. cit.* pp. 612–615.

Rose H. J., "Juno" in the *Oxford Classical Dictionary, op. cit.* pp. 568–569.

——, *Religion in Greece and Rome.* New York: Harper& Row, 1959.

Sabatino Moscati, *The World of the Phoenicians.* (Praeger History of World Civilization) New York Washington: Praeger, 1968.

Scott-Kilvert, Ian, *Polybius, The Rise of the Roman Empire.* New York: Penguin, 1979.

Scullard, H. H., "Caelestis" *The Oxford Classical Dictionary*[2]. Oxford: Clarendon, 1970, pp. 187–188.

——, "Caelestis" *The Oxford Classical Dictionary, 2nd ed.* pp. 187–188.

Smith, R. Bosworth, *Carthage and the Carthaginians.* London: Longmans, Green & Co. 1849.

Stocks, H., "Studien zu Lukian's 'De Dea Syria'". *Berytus* 4 (1937) 1–40.

Usener, Herman, *Die Sintfluthsagen*. Bonn: Cohen, 1899. (Religionsge-schichtliche Untersuchungen, dritter theil.)

Vogel, Iul., "Iuno" in Roscher, W. H. *Ausführliches Lexikon der Griechischen und Römischen Mythologie*. Leipzig: Teubner, 1890–1897, vol. 2, pp. 574–611; also W. H. Roscher "Iuno Caelestis", *op. cit.* pp. 612–615.

Warmington, B. H., *Carthage*. New York: Praeger, 1969.

Zwi Werblowsky, R. J. "Synkretismus in der Religionsgeschichte" in W. Heissig and H. J. Klimkeit (edd.) *Synkretismus in den Religionen Zentralasiens*. Wiesbaden: Otto Harrassowitz, 1987.

CHAPTER THREE

Anthes, Rudolf, "Mythology in Ancient Egypt." in *Mythologies of the Ancient World*. Samuel Noah Kramer, (ed.) New York: Doubleday, 1961, pp. 15-92.

Benko, Stephen, "Virgil's Fourth Eclogue in Christian Interpretation." *Aufstieg und Niedergang der römischen Welt*. Hildegard Temporini und Wolfgang Haase, (edd.). Berlin: Walter de Gruyter, 1980. I. 311 p. 657.

Bertholet, Alfred, *Das Geschlecht der Gottheit*. Tubingen: J.C.B. Mohr, 1934, p. 22.

Boll, Franz and Bundel, W., "Sternbilder." Roscher, *Lexikon op. cit.* vol. 6, pp. 867–1070.

Boll, Franz, *Aus der Offenbarung Johannis. Hellenistische Studien zum Weltbild der Apokalypse*. Leipzig Berlin: Teubner, 1914.

———, "Der Stern der Weisen." *Zeitschrift für die neutestamentliche Wissenschaft*. 18 (1917 18) 41–48.

———, *Sphaera. Neue griechische Texte und Untersuchungen zur Geschichte der Sternbilder*. Leipzig: Teubner, 1903.

———, *Sternglaube und Sterndeutung. Die Geschichte und Wesen der Astrologie*. Leipzig und Berlin: Teubner, 1931 (First edition 1919).

Bolle, Kees W., "Cosmology: An Overview." *ER* 4.100-107.

Bonnett, Hans, *Reallexikon der Ägyptischen Religionsgeschichte*. Berlin: Walter de Gruyter, 1952

Bousset, Wilhelm, *Die Offenbarung Johannis Kritisich-Exegetischer Kommentar über das Neue Testament*. Begründet von Heinr. Aug. Wilh. Meyer, vol. 16. Göttingen: Vandenhoeck and Ruprecht, 1906.

Brandon, S. G. F., *Creation Legends of the Ancient Near East*. London: Hodder and Stoughton, 1963.

Bratton, F. G., *The First Heretic. The Life and Times of Ikhnaton the King*. Boston: Beacon Press, 1962.

Brown, R. E. *et al.* (edd.), *Mary in the Church*. Philadelphia: Fortress Press, 1978.

Budge, E. A., *From Fetish to God in Ancient Egypt*. New York: Benjamin Bloom, 1972.

Bue, Francesco Lo, *The Turin Fragments of Tyconius' Commentary on Revelation*. Cambridge: University Press, 1963.

Bulfinch, Thomas, *Mythology*. New York: Dell Publishing Co., 1979.

Butler, H. E., *The Odes of Horace*. London: G. Bell, 1929.

Chemerey, Peter, "Sky. Myths and Symbolism." *ER* 13. 345-353.

Clemen, Carl, *Religionsgeschichtliche Erklärung des Neuen Testaments. Die Abhängigkeit des ältesten Christentums von den nichtjüdischen Religionen und philosophischen Systemen*. Giessen: A. Töpelmann, 1909.

Collins, Adele Yarbro, *Crisis and Catharsis: The Power of the Apocalypse*. Philadelphia: Westminster Press, 1984.

272 BIBLIOGRAPHY

——, *The Combat Myth in the Book of Revelation*. Missoula, Mont.: Scholars Press, 1976.

Coomaraswamy, Alexander Coburn, "The Symbolism of the Dome" can be found in Roger Lipsey, *Coomaraswamy*. Princeton: University Press, 1977 (Bollingen Series 89).

Cornford, F. M., *Principium Sapientiae. The Origins of Greek Philosphical Thought*. Cambridge: Univ. Press, 1952.

Crawley, Ernest, *Dress, Drinks and Drums*. London: Methuen, 1931.

Culianu, Ian Petru, "Sky. The Heavens as Hierophany." *ER* 13, 343–345.

Day, John, *God's Conflict with the Dragon and the Sea. Echoes of a Canaanite Myth in the Old Testament*. New York: Cambridge University Press, 1985.

Dieterich, Albrecht, *Abraxas. Studien zur Religionsgeschichte des späteren Altertums*. Leipzig: Teubner, 1891.

——, *Mutter Erde*. Leipzig Berlin: Teubner, 1905.

Diobouniotis, Constantin and Harnack, Adolf, *Der Scholien-Kommentar des Origenes zur Apokalypse Johannis*. (Texte und Untersuchungen zur Geschichte der Christlichen Literatur. Vol. 38.3). Leipzig: J. C. Hinrichs, 1911.

Dölger, F. J., "Esietus. Der Ertrunkenen oder zu einem Osiris Geworden." *Antike und Christentum 1* (1929) 174–183.

——, "Nilwasser und Taufwasser." *Antike und Christentum 5* (1939) 153–82.

Doresse, J., *The Secret Books of the Egyptian Gnostics*. New York: Viking, 1958.

Eisler, Robert, *Weltmantel und Himmelszelt. Religionsgeschichtliche Untersuchungen zur Urgeschichte des antiken Weltbildes*. München: C. H. Beck, 1910.

Eissfeldt, Otto, "Gott und das Meer in der Bibel." *Studia Orientalia Ioanni Pedersen Dedicata*. Hauniae: Einar Munksgaard, MCMLIII.

Eliade, Mircea, *The Sacred and the Profane*. New York: Harcourt, Brace & World, 1958.

Erman, Adolf, *Die Religion der Ägypter*. Berlin and Liepzig: Walter de Gruyter, 1934.

Flugel, J. C., *The Psychology of Clothes*. New York: International Universities Press, 1971.

Foerster, Werner, ἀστήρ ἄστρον *TWNT* 1.501502.

Fontenrose, Joseph, *Python. A study of Delphic Myth and Its Origins*. Berkeley and Los Angeles: University of California Press, 1959.

Frankfort, Henri, *Ancient Egyptian Religion*. New York: Columbia University Press, 1948.

Frazer, James G., *The Worship of Nature*. New York: Macmillan, 1926.

Frazer, F. M., *The Poems of Hesiod*. Norman: University of Oklahoma, 1983.

Frost, Frank J., *Greek Society*. Lexington, Mass.: D. C. Heath, 1971.

Gaster, Theodor H., "Cosmogony." *The Interpreter's Dictionary of the Bible*. Nashville: Abingdon, 1962, v. 1,,pp. 702–709.

——, "Leviathan," *The Interpreter's Dictionary of the Bible*. Nashville: Abingdon, 1962, v.3, p. 316.

——, *Thespis. Ritual, Myth and Drama in the Ancient Near East*. New York: Henry Schuman, 1950.

Giles, F. J., *Ikhnaton, Legend and History*, London: Hutchinson, 1970.

Girandot, N. J., "Chaos" *ER* 3.213–218.

Gisinger, F., "Okeanos" *Pauly, op. cit.* 17 2 (34 Halbband) 2308–2349.

Glotz, Gustave, *Ancient Greece at Work*. An Economic History of Greece from the Homeric Period to the Roman Conquest. New York: Norton, 1967.

Göllinger, Hildegard, *Das "Grosse Zeichen" von Apokalypse 12*. Würzburg: Echter Verlag, 1971.

Gordon, Cyrus H., "Canaanite Mythology", *Mythologies of the Ancient World*

(S. N. Kramer, ed.) pp. 184–201.

Graef, Hilda, *Mary. A History of Doctrine and Devotion.* New York: Sheed and Ward, 1963.

Grant, Michael, *Myths of the Greek and Romans.* New York: New American Library, 1962.

——, *The World of Rome.* Cleveland and New York: World, 1960.

Graves, Robert and Patai, Raphael, *Hebrew Myths: The Book of Genesis.* New York: McGraw Hill 1964.

Green, Peter, *Ovid. The Erotic Poems.* Harmondsworth, England: Penguin Books, 1982.

Griffith, F. L., "Herodotus II. 90–Apotheosis by Drowning." *Zeitschrift für Ägyptische Sprache und Altertumskunde.* 46 (1910) 132–134.

Griffiths, J. Gwyn, *Apuleius of Madauros. The Isis Book. (Metamorphoses, Book XI).* Leiden: E. J. Brill, 1975.

——, *Plutarch's De Iside et Osiride.* Cardiff: University of Wales Press, 1970.

——, *The Conflict of Horus and Seth.* Liverpool: Liverpool University Press, 1960.

——, *The Origin of Osiris and His Cult.* Leiden: E. J. Brill, 1980.

Gunkel, Hermann, *Genesis.* Göttingen: Vandenhoeck& Ruprecht 1922[5].

——, *Schöpfung und Chaos in Urzeit und Endzeit.* Göttingen: Vandenhoeck and Ruprecht 1895.

——, *Zum religionsgeschichtlichen Verständnis des Neuen Testaments.* Göttingen: Vandenhoeck and Ruprecht, 1910, p.1.

Guthrie, W. K. C., *In the Beginning. Some Greek Views on the Origins of Life and the State of Man.* London: Methuen, 1957.

Halsberghe, Gaston H., *The Cult of Sol Invictus.* Leiden: Brill, 1977.

Heath, Thomas L. and Neugebauer, Otto E., "Constellations" *Oxford Classical Dictionary, op. cit.* pp. 282–285.

Heil, John Paul, *Jesus Walking on the Sea: Meaning and Gospel Functions of Matt. 14.22–23, Mark 6.45–52 and John 6.15b–21.* Rome: Biblical Institute, 1981.

Henze, Helen R., *The Odes of Horace.* Norman: University of Oklahoma Press, 1961.

Hermann, A., "Ertrinken" *Reallexikon für Antike und Christentum* Stuttgart: Anton Hiersman, 1966, v. 6, pp. 370–410.

Hopfner, Theodor, *Plutarch über Isis and Osiris.* Hildesheim: Georg Olms, 1974.

Horn, Marilyn J. and Gurel, Lois M., *The Second Skin. An Interdisciplinary Study of Clothing.* Boston: Houghton Mifflin, 1975.

Hornung, Erich, "Chaotische Bereiche in der geordneten Welt." *Aeitschrift für Aegyptische Sprache und Altertumskunde* 81 (1956) 23–32.

Hoskier, H. C., *The Complete Commentary of Oecumenius on the Apocalypse.* Ann Arbor: University of Michigan Press, 1928.

Innes, Mary M., *The Metamorphoses of Ovid.* New York: Penguin Books, 1982.

Jaeger, Werner, *Paideia.* New York: Oxford University Press, 1965.

Jager, F., *Das Antike Propemptikon und das 17. Gedicht des Paulinus von Nola.* Rosenheim, 1913.

James, E. O., et al., "Water, Watergods." *Encyclopaedia of Religion and Ethics.* James Hastings (ed.). New York: Charles Scribner's Sons, 1925, vol. 12, pp. 104–719.

James, E. O. *The Ancient Gods.* New York: Putnam, 1960.

Jeremias, Alfred, "Sterne. (Bei den Babyloniern)" Roscher, *op. cit.* vol. 4.1427–1500.

——, *Das alte Testament im Lichte des alten Orients.* Leipzig: J. C. Hinrich'sche Buchhardlung 1905; Third ed. 1916.

——, *Die Pambabylonisten* Leipzig: J. C. Hinrichs 1907.

Kaiser, I. O., *Die Mythische Bedeutung des Meers in Ägypten, Ugarit, und Israel.* (Beihäfte zur Zeitschrift für die Alttestamentliche Wissenschaft #78). Berlin: Töpelmann, 1962.

Kees, Hermann, "Apotheosis by Drowning." *Studies Presented to F. L. E. Griffith.* Egypt Exploration Society, London: Oxford University Press, 1932, pp. 402–405.

——, "Seth." *Pauly's Realencyclopädie der Classischen Altertumswissenschraft.* (edd.) G. Wissowa, W. Kroll, K. Witte. Stuttgart: Alfred Druckernmüller, 1923. Vol. II. A1. 2. p. 1896–1922.

——, *Horus und Seth als Götterpaar.* (Vorderasiatisch-Aegyptische Gesellschaft. Mitteilungen, Vol. 28 and 29.) Leipzig: J. C. Hinrichs'sche Buchhandlung, 1923-1924.

Kerenyi, Karl, "Vater Helios" *Eranos Jahrbuch* 10 (1943) 81–124.

——, *Tochter der Sonne.* Zürich: Rascher Verlag, 1944.

Kirk, G. S. and Raven, J. E., *The Presocratic Philosophers.* Cambridge: University Press, 1957.

Kloos, Carola, *Yhwh's Combat with the Sea. A Canaanite Tradition in the Religion of Ancient Israel.* Leiden: E. J. Brill, 1986.

Kramer, Samuel, Noah (ed.), *Mythologies of the Ancient World.* Garden City, N.Y.: Doubleday, 1961.

——, *History Begins at Sumer.* New York: Doubleday, 1958.

——, *Sumerian Mythology. A Study of Spiritual and Literary Achievement in the Third Millenium B.C.* Philadelphia: University of Pa. Press, 1972, pp. 68-75.

Krause, W., *Die Stellung der frühchristlichen Autoren zur heidnischen Literatur.* Wien: Herder, 1958.

Kretschmar, Georg, *Die Offenbarung des Johannes. Die Geschichte Ihrer Auslegung im 1. Jahrtausend.* Stuttgart: Calwer Verlag, 1985.

Kroll, Joseph, "Das Gottesbild aus dem Wasser." *Märchen, Mythos, Dichtung.* Festschrift zum 90. Geburtstag Friedich von der Leyens. Herausgegeben von Hugo Kuhn und Kurt Schier, München: Beck, 1963.

LeFrois, Bernard T., *The Woman Clothed With the Sun (Ap. 12): Individual or Collective?* Rome: Orbis Catholicus, 1954.

Lehman, Karl, "The Dome of Heaven." *Art Bulletin* 27 (1945) 1–27.

Lloyd, G. E. R., *Early Greek Science: Thales to Aristotle.* New York: Norton, 1970.

Long, Charles H., "Cosmogony" *ER* 4.94–100.

——, *Alpha. The Myths of Creation.* New York: Modern Library, 1950.

Mackail, J. W., *Virgil's Works.* New York: Modern Library, 1950.

Malbon, Elizabeth Struthers, "The Jesus of Mark and the sea of Galilee." *Journal of Biblical Literature* 103 (1984) 363–377.

Marton, Paolo, *Rome, Mirror of the Centuries.* Udine: Magnus, 1983.

Masson, Georgina, *Rome.* New York: McKay, 1971.

May, H. G., "Some Cosmic Connotations of 'Mayim Rabbim', Many Waters." *Journal of Biblical Literature* 74 (1955) 9–21.

McDannell and Lang, Bernhard, *Heaven: A History.* New Haven: Yale University Press, 1988.

Merkelbach, R., "Drache" *Reallexikon für Antike und Christentum.* Stuttgart: Anton Hiersemann, 1954. vol. 4, pp. 226–250.

Meyer, E., *Seth-Typhon. Eine religionsgeschichtliche Studie.* Leipzig: W. Englemann, 1875.

Miller, Frank Justin, *Ovid. Metamorphoses.* The Loeb Classical Library. London; Heinemann, 1929 pp./ 2–7.

Morenz, Siegfried, *Ägyptische Religion*. Stuttghart: Kohlhammer Verlag, 1960.

Nauck, August, *Tragicorum Graecorum Fragmenta*. Hildesheim: Georg Olms, 1964 (reprint with additions of Bruno Snell).

Niditch, Susan, *Chaos to Cosmos: Studies in Biblical Patterns of Creation*. Chico, CA: Scholar's Press, 1985.

Nilsson, Martin P., *Geschichte der Griechischen Religion*. München: Beck, 1961.

Ninck, M., *Die Bedeutung des Wassers im Kult und Leben der Alten*. (Philologus, Supplementum 14.2) Leipzig: Diterich'sche Verlagsbuchhandlung, 1921. (Reprint; Darmstadt: Wissenschaftliche Buchgesellschaft, 1960).

Nisbet, R. G. M. and Hubbard, Margaret, *A Commentary on Horace: Odes, Book 1*. Oxford: Clarendon Press, 1970.

Oberhummer, E., "Urania." Pauly, *op. cit.* Zweite Reihe, 9 1 (17. Halbband) 931–942.

Pope, Marvin H., *Job*. (The Anchor Bible, vol. 15). Garden City, N.Y.: Doubleday, 1965.

Prigent, Pierre, *Apocalypse 12. Histoire De l'Exegese*. Tübingen: J.C.B. Mohr. 1959. (Beitrage zur Geschichte der Biblischen Exegese, #2).

Pritchard, J. B., *Ancient Near Eastern Texts Relating to the Old Testament*. Princeton: University Press, 1950.

Rapp, A., "Helios", Roscher, *op. cit.* pp. 1993–2026.

Ray, J., "Baal" *The Interpreter's Dictionary of the Bible*, 1.328–329.

Roeder, G., *Urkunden zur Religion des Alten Aegyptens*. Jena: E Diederichs, 1923.

Roscher, W. H., "Mondgöttin." Roscher, *op. cit.* 2. 3119–3200.

——, *Ausführliches Lexicon der Griechischen und Römischen Mythologie*. 6 volumes. Leipzig: Teubner, 1937–1984.

Rose, H. J., "Andromede: *The Oxford Classical Dictionary²*, pp. 6364.

Rose, H. J., *et. al.* "Cadmus" in *The Oxford Classical Dictionary.²* Oxford: Clarendon Press, 1970, p. 186–187.

Scarborough, John, *Facets of Hellenic Life*. Boston: Houghton Mifflin, 1976.

Schafer, Heinrich, "Das Gewand der Isis." Festschrift zu C. F. Lehmann-Haupt's sechzigstem geburtstage. Herausgegeben von K. Regling und H. Reich. Wien und Leipzig: Wilhelm Braumüller, 1921.

Sethe, Kurt Heinrich, *Die Altägyptischen Pyramidentexte*. Leipzig: J. C. Hinrichs, 1908.

——, *Übersetzung und Kommentar zu den altägyptischen Pyramidentexten*. Glückstadt, Hamburg: J. J. Augustin, 1936–62.

——, *Urgeschichte und Älteste Religion der Ägypter*. Leipzig: Deutsche Morgenländische Gesellschaft, 1930.

Simon, Ulrich, *Heaven in Christian Tradition*. New York: Harper& Brothers, 1958.

Simpson, Cuthbert A., *The Book of Genesis*. The Interpreter's Bible, volume 1. New York/Nashville: Abingdon Cokesbury Press, 1952.

Sjoo, Monica and Mar, Barbara, *The Great Cosmic Mother*. San Francisco: Harper and Row, 1987.

Skinner, John, *A Critical and Exegetical Commentary on Genesis*. New York: Charles Scribner's Sons, 1925.

Soper, Alexander Coburn, "The 'Dome of Heaven' in Asia." *Art Bulletin* 29 (1947) 225–248.

Sproul, Barbara C., *Primal Myths. Creating the World*. San Francisco: Harper and Row, 1979.

Staudacher, Willibald, *Die Trennung von Himmel und Erde*. Darmstadt; Wissenschaftliche Buchgesellschaft, 1968.

Taber, Linda and Lusby, Stanley F., "Heaven and Hell." *ER* 6. 237–243.

Thiele, George, *Antike Himmelsbilder*. Berlin: Weidmann, 1898.

Unger, D., "Did St. John See the Virgin Mary in Glory? (Apoc. 12.1)" *Catholic Biblical Quarterly* 11 (1949) 248–262, 392–405; 12 (1950) 74–83, 155–161, 292–300, 405–415.

Vega, P. A. C., *Apringii Pacensis Episcopi Tractatus in Apocalypsin*. Escurial, 1940.

Velde, H. te, *Seth, God of Confusion*. Leiden: E. J. Brill, 1977.

Vischer, Eberhard, *Die Offenbarung Johannis eine jüdische Apokalypse in Christlicher Bearbeitung, mit einem Vorwort von A. Harnack. (Texte und Untersuchungen II.3)* Leipzig: J. C. Hinrichs, 1886.

Wallace, Howard, "Leviathan and the Beast in Revelation", *The Biblical Archeologist* (1948) 61–68.

Warmington, B. H., "Thirty Tyrants" *Oxford Classical Dictionary op. cit.* pp. 1064–1065.

Wendland, Paul, *Die hellenistisch-römische Kultur in ihren Beziehungen zu Judentum und Christentum*. Tübingen: J.C.B. Mohr, 1907.

Wensinck, A. J., *The Ocean in the Literature of the Western Semites*. Wiesbaden: Dr. Martin Sandig, OHG., 1968.

West, M. L., *The Orphic Poems*. Oxford: Clarendon Press, 1983.

White, Leslie A., "Ikhnaton: The Great Man vs. the Cultural Process." *Journal of the American Oriental Society* 68 (1949) 91–103.

Wild, Robert A., *Water in the Cultic Worship of Isis and Sarapis*. Leiden: E. J. Brill, 1981.

Wust, Ernst, "Uranos" in Pauly, *op. cit.* Zweite Reihe, 9 1 (17. Halbband) 966–980.

Ziegler, Konrat, "Menschen und Weltwerden." *Neue Jahrbücher für das klassische Altertum*. 16 (1913) 529ff.

——, "Orphische Dichtung" Pauly, *op. cit.* 18 2 (36. Halbband) 1322–1417.

CHAPTER FOUR

Aland, K., "Montanus' and "Montanism". *The Encyclopedia of Religion*. 10.81–83.

——, *Kirchengeschichtliche Entwürfe*. Gütersloh: Gütersloher Verlagshaus, 1960.

Albright, William F., *From Stone Age to Christianity*. New York: Doubleday Anchor, 1957.

Andresen, *Die Kirchen der Alten Christenheit*. Stuttgart: Kohlhammer, 1971, pp. 110–115.

Austin, R. G., *P. Vergili Maronis Aeneiidos Liber Sixtus With a Commentary*. Oxford: Clarendon Press, 1977.

Bailey, D. S., *Sexual Relation in Christian Thought*. New York: Harper and Brothers, 1959.

Barnes, Timothy D., "The Chronology of Montanism." *Journal of Theological Studies* N.S. 20 (1970).

Batey, Richard A., *New Testament Nuptial Imagery*. Leiden: E. J. Brill, 1971.

Belck, Waldemar, *Geschichte des Montanismus*. Leipzig: Dorffling und Franke, 1883.

Betz, H. D., *The Greek Magical Papri*. Chicago: University of Chicago Press, 1986.

Bonwetch, G. Nathanael, *Geschichte des Montanismus* Erlangen: Andreas Deichert, 1881.

——, *Texte zur Geschichte des Montanismus*. Bonn: A. Marcus und E. Weber's Verlag, 1914. (Kleine Texte, #129.)

Brown, Peter, *The Body and Society. Men, Women and Sexual Renunciation in Early Christianity.* New York: Columbia University Press, 1988.

Calder, W. M., "Philadelphia and Montanism." *Bulletin of the John Rylands Library* 7 (1922–23) 309–354.

Danielou, Jean, *The Ministry of Women in the Early Church.* London: The Faith Press, 1961.

Deubner, Ludwig, *Attische Feste,* Berlin: Akademie Verlag, 1966.

Dodds, E. R., *Euripides Bacchae.* Oxford: Clarendon, 1960.

———, *The Greeks and the Irrational.* Boston: Beacon Press, 1957.

Drexel, W., "Meter" in Roscher, *op. cit.* 2.2848–2931.

Duthoy, Robert, *The Taurobolium: Its Evolution and Terminology.* Leiden: E. J. Brill, 1969.

Esposito, John L., *Islam. The Straight Path.* New York: Oxford U. Press, 1988.

Evans-Pritchard, E. E., "Some Collective Expressions of Obscenity in Africa." *Journal of the Royal Anthropological Institute of Great Britain and Ireland.* 49 (1929) 311331.

Fehrle, Eugen, *Die Kultische Keuschheit in Altertum.* Gieszen: Töpelmann, 1910.

Ficker, Gerhard, "Wiederlegung eines Montanisten." *Zeitschrift für Kirchengeschichte* 26 (1905) 447–463.

Ford, J. Messingberd, "Was Montanism a Jewish Christian Heresy?" *Journal of Ecclesiastical History.* 17 (1966) 145–158.

Frend, W. H. C., *Martyrdom and Persecution in the Early Church.* New York: University Press, 1967.

———, *The Rise of Christianity.* Philadelphia. Fortress, 1984.

Friedrich, Johannes, "Phrygia" in Pauly, *op. cit.* 20 1, 883.

Gero, Stephen, "Montanus and Montanism according to a Medieval Syriac Source." *Journal of Theological Studies.* N.S. 28 (1977) 520–524.

Goree, William B. Jr., *The Cultural Bases of Montanism.* Ph.D. Thesis, Baylor University, 1980.

Graves, Robert, *The Greek Myths.* Baltimore, MD.: Penguin, 1955.

Guthrie, W. K. C., *The Greeks and their Gods.* Boston: Beacon Press, 1955.

Hanna, Judith Lynn, "Dance" *The Encyclopedia of Religion.* 4.203 and 206.

Harnack, A., *History of Dogma.* New York: Dover, 1961 (reprint of the 1900 edition).

Heine, Susanne, *Women and Early Christianity. A Reappraisal.* Minneapolis Augsburg Publishing House, 1988.

Hoffman, R. Joseph, *Celsus on the True Doctrine.* New York and Oxford; Oxford U. Press, 1987.

Hyde, Walter W., *Paganism to Christianity.* New York: Octagon Books, 1970 (originally published 1946).

Julicher, Adolf, "Ein Gallisches Bischofsschreiben des 6. Jahrhunderts als Zeuge für die Verfassung der Montanistenkirche," *Zeitschrift für Kirchengeschichte* 16 (1896) 664–671.

Kelsey, Morton T., *Tongue Speaking. The History and Meaning of Charismatic Experience.* New York: Crossroad, 1981.

Kerényi, Karl, *Apollon und Niobe.* Wien: Albert Langen, 1980, pp. 420–426.

———, *Dionysos; Archetypal Image of Indestructible Life.* Princeton: Princeton University Press, 1976.

Klinz, Albert, *Hieros Gamos.* Halle: E. Klinz, 1933.

Knox, R. A., *Enthusiasm. A Chapter in the History of Religion.* Oxford: Clarendon Press, 1950.

Kraemer, Ross Shepard, *Ecstatics and Ascetics: Studies in the Functions of Religious Activities for Women in the Greco-Roman World.* Ph.D. Thesis,

Princeton University, 1976.

Kraft, Heinrich, "Die altkirchliche Prophetie und die Entstehung des Montanismus." *Theologische Zeitschrift* 11 (1955) 249–271.

Kramer, Samuel N., *The Sacred Marriage Rite*. Bloomington: Indiana University Press, 1969.

Labriolle, P. de, *La Crise Montanist,* Paris: E. Leroux 1913.

——, *Les Sources de L'Histoire du Montanisme.* Fribourg, Switzerland: Universite de Fribourg 1913.

Meeks, Wayne A., "The Image of the Androgyne: Some Uses of a Symbol in Earliest Christianity." *History of Religions* 13 (1974) 165–208.

Messingberd Ford, J., "Was Montanism a Jewish Christian Heresy?" *Journal of Ecclesiastical History* 17 (1966) 145–158.

Meyer, Marion W., *The Ancient Mysteries. A Sourcebook*. San Francisco: Harper and Row, 1987.

Miegge, Giovanni, *The Virgin Mary*. Philadelphia: Westminster Press, 1956.

Momigliano, A., "Cybele" *The Encyclopedia of Religion* (Mircea Eliade, ed.) New York: Macmillan, 1984, 4.185-187. München: Beck, 1955.

Nilsson, M. P., "Dionysus" *Oxford Classical Dictionary,*[2] pp. 352–353.

——, *Geschichte der Griechischen Religion* I 2.

——, *The Dionysiac Mysteries of the Hellenistic and Roman Age*. Lund: C.W.K. Gleerup, 1957.

Nock, A. D., "Eunuchs in ancient Religion." *Archiv für Religionswissenschaft*. 23 (1952) 25–33.

Norden, E., "Vergilstudien." *Hermes* 28 (1893) 501–521.

Otto, W., *Dionysos, Myth and Cult*. Bloomington: Indiana U. Press, 1965.

Padel, Ruth, "Women: Model for Possession by Greek Demons." In: A. Cameron and A. Kuhrt, *Images of Women in Late Antiquity*, pp. 3–19. Detroit, Mich.: Wayne State U. Press, 1983.

Pagels, Elaine, *The Gnostic Gospels*. New York: Random House, 1979.

Pope, M. H., *Song of Songs*. Garden City, N.Y.: Doubleday, 1977.

Powell, Douglass, "Tertullianists and Cataphrygians." *Vigiliae Christianae* 29 (1975) 33–54.

Reuther, Rosemary and McLaughin, Eleanor, *Women of Spirit. Female Leadership in the Jewish and Christian Traditions*. New York: Simon and Schuster, 1979.

Rohde, Erwin, *Psyche*. London: Rutledge and Kegan, 1925 (original German edition was in 1893).

Rose, H. J., *Religion in Greece and Rome*. New York: Harper, 1959.

Rupp, A., *Die Beziehungen des Dionysus-kultes zu Thrakien und zur Kleinasien*. Stuttgart, 1882.

Sanders, G. M., "Gallos" *RAC* 8, 983–1034.

Schepelern, Wilhelm, *Der Montanismus und die Phrygischen Kulte*. Tübingen: J. C. B. Mohr, 1929.

Schimmel, Annemarie, "Rumi, Jalal Al-din" *ER* 12, 482–486.

Seeburg, R., *Lehrbuch der Dogmengeschichte*. Graz: Akademische Druck und Verlagsanstalt, 1953.

Showerman, Grant, *The Great Mother of the Gods*. Chicago: Argonaut, 1969 (Reprint of the 1902 edition).

Smith, Z., "The Garment of Shame." *History of Religions* 5 (1966) 217–238.

Stauffer, E., "Antike Madonnenreligionen." *ANRW* 2.17.3. pp.1425–1499.

Taylor, Henry Osborn, *The Medieval Mind*, Cambridge, Mass.: Harvard U. Press, 1951.

Tentori, Tullio, "An Italian Religious Feast: The *Fujenti* Rites of the Madonna dell-Arco, Naples." J. J. Preston, *op. cit.* pp. 95–122.

Thomas, Garth, "Magna Mater and Attis." *ANRW* 2.17.3, pp. 1500–1535.

Vermaseren, Maarten J., *Cybele and Attis. The Myth and the Cult.* London: Thames and Hudson, 1977.

Vogt, Joseph, "Ecce Ancilla Domini" in *Ancient Slavery and the Ideal of Man.* Cambridge, Massachusetts: Harvard University Press, 1955, pp. 146–169.

Warmington, E. H., "Albania" *The Oxford Classical Dictionary, op. cit.* p. 34.

Wilhelm, Schepelern, *Der Montanismus und die Phrygischen Kulte.* Tübingen: J.C.B. Mohr, 1929.

Willoughby, Harold, *Pagan Regeneration.* Chicago: U. of Chicago Press, 1929.

CHAPTER FIVE

Article, "Altar" by various authors in *Die Religion in Geschichte and Gegenwart.* Tübingen: Mohr, 1957, pp. 251–266.

Bangerter, Otto, *Frauen im Aufbruch.* Neukirchen: Neukirchner Verlag, 1971.

Bayer, F. W., "Augensalbe" *RAC* 1.972–975.

Beck, H. F., "Bread of the Presence," *Interpreter's Dictionary of the Bible,* vol. 1. p. 464.

Behm. Johannes, "ἄρτος" *Theologisches Wörterbuch zum Neuen Testament* Stuttgart: Kolhammer, 1933, vol. 1, pp. 475–476.

Benko, S., "Virgil's Fourth Eclogue in Christian Interpretation." *Aufstieg und Niedergang der römischen Welt.* H. Temporini and W. Haase, edl Berlin: de Gruyter, 1980. II 1, pp. 646–705.

——, *The Meaning of Sanctorum Communio.* London: SCM Press, 1964.

Blome, Friedrich, *Die Opfermaterie in Babylonien und Israel* (Sacra Scriptura Antiquitatibus Orientalibus Illustrata Rome: Pontifical Biblical Institute, 1934.

Cunningham, I. C. *Herodas. Miniambi.* Oxford: Clarendon, 1971.

Dautzenber, Gerhard, et al. (edd.), *Die Frau im Urchristentum.* Freiburg: Herder, 1983.

Dölger, F. J., "Heidnische und Christliche Brotstempel mit religiösen Zeichen." *Antike und Christentum.* Münster: Aeschendorffsche Verlagsbuchhandlung, 1929. vol. 1, pp. 1–46.

——, "Die eigenartige Marienverehrung der Philomarianiten oder Kollyridianer in Arabia." *Antike und Christentum* 1 (1929) pp. 107–140.

Eissfeldt, Otto, *Einleitung in das Alte Testament.* Tübingen: J. C. B. Mohr, 1956.

Epiphanius, Panarion, in K. Holl, *Die Griechischen-Christlichen Schriftsteller der ersten Jahrhunderte.* Akademie der Wissenschaften, Berlin. Leipzig: J. C. Hinrichs, 1933 vol. 37, pp. 475–484.

Farnell, Lewis R., *The Cults of the Greek States.* Oxford; Clarendon Press, 1907.

Fauth, W., "Baubo," *Der kleine Pauly.* Stuttgart: Druckenmüller, 1964.

Frazer, James G., *The Golden Bough.* Part V. "Spirits of the Corn and of the Wild." London: MacMillan, 1955.

Goodenough, Erwin R., "An Early Christian Bread Stamp." *Harvard Theological Review* 57 (1964) 133–137. Reprinted in: *Goodenough on the Beginnings of Christianity* (ed.) A. T. Kraabel, Atlanta, BA: Scholars Press, 1990.

Graves, R., *The Greek Myths.* Baltimore, Md.: Penguin, 1955.

Gryson, Roger, *Le Ministère Des Femmes Dans L'Eglise Ancienne.* Gembloux: Duculot, 1972.

Guthrie, W. K. C., *The Greeks and Their Gods.* Boston: Beacon Press, 1955.

Haase, Felix, *Altchristliche Kirchengeschichte nach Orientalischen Quellen.* Leipzig: Otto Harrassowitz, 1925.

Harnack, A. von, *History of Dogma*. New York: Dover (reprint) 1961.
Heine, Susanne, *Frauen der Frühen Christenheit*. Göttingen: Vandenhoeck & Ruprecht, 1986.
Herter, "Priapus," Pauly-Wissowa-Kroll, *op. cit.* 20.1.2 (24 Halbband) pp. 1914–1942.
Hopfner, Th., "Mageia" In Pauly-Wissowa-Kroll, *op. cit.* ppl 305, 321, 373.
Humphrey, W. L., "Esther" in *Harper's Bible Dictionary*. San Francisco: Harper & Row, 1985, pp. 2380–282.
Innes, Mary M., *The Metamorphoses of Ovid*. New York: Penguin, 1982.
Iuniani, M., Iustini Epitoma Historiarum Philippicarum Pompeii Trogi. Otto Seel (ed.). Stuttgart, Teubner, 1985.
Jackson, S. M. "Collyridians." *The New Schaff-Herzog Encyclopedia of Religious Knowledge*. Grand Rapids, Mich. Baker, 1950. vol. 3, p. 162.
James, E. O., *The Ancient gods*. New York: Putnam, 1960.
Jeremias, A., *Das Alte Testament im Lichte des Alten Orients*. Leipzig: J. C. Hinrichs'sche Suchhandllung, 1916.
Kelly, J. N. D., *Early Christian Doctrines*. New York: Harper, 1958.
Kind, A., "κολλύριον" Pauly, *op. cit.* XI.I, pp. 1100-1106.
Kirsch, J. P., and Klauser, Th., "Altar" *RAC* 1, 310-354.
Knox, A. D., *Herodes, Cercidas and the Greek Choliambic Poets. LCL*. London: Heinemann, 1929.
Kraemer, Ross S. (ed.), *Maenads, Martyrs, Matrons, Monastics: A Sourcebook on Women's Religions of the Greco-Roman World*. Philadelphia: Fortress, 1988.
Laing, Gordon J., *Survivals of Roman religion*. New York: Cooper Square, 1963.
Man, A., "Bäckerei" Pauly-Wissowa-Kroll, *op. cit.* II.2, pp. 2734–2743.
Mischkowski, Herbert, *Die heiligen Tische im Götterkultus der Griechen und Römer*. Königsberg: Otto Kummel, 1917 (Diss. Königsberg.)
Mommsen, August, *Feste der Stadt Athen im Altertum*. Leipzig: Teubner, 1898.
Mylonas, G. E., *Eleusis and the Eleusinian Mysteries*. Princeton: Princeton University Press, 1961.
Pfeiffer, R. H., *Introduction to the Old Testament*. New York: Harper, 1948, pp. 732–747.
Pope, Marvin H., *Song of Songs*. Garden City, N.Y.: Doubleday, 1977.
Rose, H. J., "Lectisternium: *Oxford Classical Dictionary, op. cit.* p. 590.
——, "Priapus," *Oxford Classical Dictionary, op. cit.* p. 876.
——, *Religion in Greece and Rome*. New York: Harper & Row, 1959.
Seeberg, Reinhold, *Lehrbuch der Dogmengeschichte*. Graz: Akademische Verlagsanstalt, 1953.
Sexti Pompei Festi, *De Verborum Significatu quae supersunt cum pauli Epitome*. Wallace M. Lindsay, editor. Leipzig: Teubner, 1913.
Stuiber, A., "Brot." *Reallexikon für Antike und Christentum* (ed. Theodor Klauser). Stuttgart: A. Hiersemann, 1954, pp. 611–619.
Wassou, R. Gordon, *et al.*, *The Road to Eleusis*. New York and London: Harcourt Brace Jovanovich, 1978.
Wehr, Lothar, *Arznei der Unsterblichkeit* München: Aschendorff, 1987.
Wieland, F., *Altar and Altargrab der christlichen Kirchen im 4. Jahrhundert*. Leipzig: J. C. Hinrichs, 1912.
Willoughby, H. R., *Pagan Regeneration*. Chicago, Ill.: University of Chicago, 1929.
Wunsch, R., "Amuletum" *Glotta* 2 (1910) 219–230.
Wunsch, Richard, "Ein Dankopfer an Asklepios." *Archiv für Religionswissenschaft* 7 (1904) 95–116.

CHAPTER SIX

Abbott, W. M., S. J., (general editor), *The Documents of Vatican II.* New York: The American Press, 1966.

Altaner, B. – Stuiber, A., *Patrologie.* Freiburg: Herder, 1966.

Altheim, Franz, *Terra Mater. Untersuchungen zur altitalienischen Religionsgeschichte.* Giessen: Töpelmann, 1931.

Athannasakis, Apostalos N., *The Orphic Hymns.* Missoula, Mont. Scholars Press, 1977.

——, *The Homeric Hymns.* Baltimore and London: Johns Hopkins University Press, 1976.

Bania, Zbigniew and Kobielus, Stanislaw, *Jasna Gora.* Warsaw: Instytut Wydawniczy Pax, 1983.

Begg, Ean, *The Cult of the Black Virgin.* London: Arkana, 1985.

Boer, Charles, *The Homeric Hymns.* Chicago: The Swallow Press, 1970.

Bolle,. Kees W., "Hieros Gamos." *ER 6.317–321.*

Boyer, Carolo, S. J., *Tractatus De Gratia Divina.* Rome: Gregorian University, 1938.

Brown, M. R., "Black Madonna." *Encyclopaedic Dictionary of Religion.* Washington, D.C.: Corpus Publications, 1979, vol. 1, p. 456.

Bruguera, Justino, *Montserrat.* Barcelona: Editoril Planete, 1964.

Campbell, Ena, "The Virgin of Guadelupe and the Female Self-Image: A Mexican Case History." in J. J. Preston, *Mother Worship,* pp. 5–24.

Carol, Juniper B., *Mariology.* Milwaukee: The Bruce Publishing Co., 1955–1961.

Daughters of St. Paul, *Devotion to Our Lady of Czestochowa,* St. Paul Editions. No place or date given.

Davis, G. H., "Dancing" *Interpreters Dictionary of the Bible,* vol. 1 p. 760.

"Demeter," PaulyWissowa-Krol, *op. cit.* 4.2, 2713–2764.

Denzinger, H. – Schönmetzer, A., *Enchiridion Symbolorum.* Freiburg: Herder, 1965.

Diels, H., *Die Fragmente der Vorsokratiker.* Berlin: Weidmann, 1954, vol. 3, Wortindex by Walther Kranz.

Dieterich, Albrecht, *Mutter Erde.* Leipzig, Berlin: Teubner, 1905.

Doheny, William J. and Kelly, Joseph P., *Papal Documents on Mary,* Milwaukee: Bruce, 1954.

Durand-Lefebvre, Marie, *Etude sur l'origine des vierges noires.* Paris: G. Durassie and Cie., 1937.

Eliade, Mircea, *Patterns in Comparative Religion.* London and New York: Sheed and Ward, 1958.

——, *The Sacred and the Profane. The Nature of Religion.* New York: Harcourt, Brace & World, 1959.

Graves, R., *The Greek Myths.* Baltimore, Md.: Penguin, 1955.

Hardmann, Oscar, *The Christian Doctrine of Grace.* London: Geoffrey Bles: The Centenary Press, 1937.

Harnack, Adolf, *History of Dogma,* Vol. 7, p. 100, New York: Dover, 1961 (reprint of the 1900 edition).

Hennecke, E., *New Testament Apocrypha.* Philadelphia: Westminster Press, 1963.

Hervieux, Jacques, *What are Apocryphal Gospels.* London: Burns & Oates, 1960.

Huynen, Jacques,, *L'enigme des vierges noires.* Paris: Editions Robert Laffant, 1972.

Innes, Mary M., *The Metamorphoses of Ovid.* New York: Penguin, 1982.

James, M. R., *The Apocryphal New Testament.* Oxford: Clarendon 1955.

Kerenyi, C., *The Religion of the Greeks and Romans*, New York: E. D. Dutton, 1962.

Kramer, Samuel Noah, *The Sacred Marriage Rite.* Bloomington, Indiana: Indiana University Press, 1969.

Lawler, Lillian B., "Dancing" *Oxford Classical Dictionary*, p. 312.

Levi, Peter, *Pausanias. Guide to Greece.* Baltimore, Md.: Penguin, 1971.

Lipsus, Richard A., *Die Apokryphen Apostelgeschichten und Apostellegenden.* Braunschweig: C. A. Schwetschke und Sohn, 1883.

"Melaina" Pauly-Wissowa-Krol, *op. cit.* 15 1, 384–386.

Michaelis, W. *Die Apokryphen Schriften zum Neuen Testament.* Bremen: Carl Schunemann Verlag, 1958.

O'Connor, Edward D., "Modern Theories on Original Sin and the Immaculate Conception." *Marian Studies* 20 (1969) 112–136.

——, *The Dogma of the Immaculate Conception: History and Significance.* Notre Dame, Ind.: University of Notre Dame, 1958.

Oesterley, W. O. E., *The Sacred Dance.* Cambridge: University Press, 1923.

Pesch, Otto Hermann, and Peters, Albrecht, *Einführung in die Lehre von Gnade und Rechtfertigung.* Darmstadt: Wissenschaftliche Buchgesellschaft, 1981.

Ridder, Cornelius A., *Maria als Miterlöserin.* Göttingen: Vanderhoek, 1965.

Rondet, Henri, *The Grace of Christ. A Brief History of the Theology of Grace.* Westminster, Md.: Newman Press, 1966.

Rose, H. J., "Caves" *Oxford Classical Dictionary, op. cit.* p. 218.

——, *Religion in Greece and Rome.* New York: Harper, 1959.

Sandstrom, Alan R., "The Tonantsi Cult of the Eastern Nahua." J. J. Preston, *op. cit.* pp. 25–50.

Schillebeeckx, E., *Mary Mother of Redemption.* New York: Sheed and Ward, 1964.

Schmaus, M., etc., (edd.) *Handbuch der Dogmengeschichte* II 3. "Urstand, Fall, Erbsünde." Freiburg: Herder, 1982.

Seboldt, Roland H., *Christ or Mary? The Coredemption Role of Mary in Contemporary Roman Catholic Theology.* St. Louis: Concordia Publishing House, 1963.

Soll, George, *Mariologie.* Freiburg: Herder, 1978.

Thilo, G. et Hagen, H., *Servii Grammatici Qui Feruntur in Vergilii Carmina Commentarii.* Leipzig and Berlin: Teubner, 1923.

Trede, Th., *Das Heidentum in der römischen Kirche.* Gotha: I. A. Perthes, 1889.

"Tyndaros" in Pauly, *op. cit.* Zweite Reihe, vol. 4, pp. 1776–1796.

Van Essen, C. C., "*Venus Cloacina*" *Mnemosyne* 9 (1956) 137–144.

Vollert, Cyril, "The Scientific Structure of Mariology." Carol, *op. cit.* vol. 2, p. 12.

Wilamowitz-Mollendorf, von, "Excurse zu Euripides Herakliden," *Hermes* 17 (1882) 357–358.

Warner, Marina, *Alone of All Her Sex.* New York: Alfred A. Knopf, 1976.

CHAPTER SEVEN

Abbott, Walter M., *The Documents of Vatican II.* New York: Guild Press, 1966.

Barth, Karl, *Christ and Adam, Man and Humanity in Romans 5.* New York: Harper and Brothers, 1957. Originally published as *Christus und Adam nach Römer 5*, Zollikon-Zürich: Evangelischer Verlag, 1952.

Beckman, J., "Weihnachten", *RGG* 3, vol. VI p. 1564.

Benko, S., "Second Century References to the Mother of Jesus." *Religion in Life*, Vol. XXVI, No. 1. 1956–57 Winter Issue, pp. 98ff.

——, "Virgil's Fourth Eclogue in Christian Interpretation." *Aufstieg und Niedergang der römischen Welt.* (edd.) Hildegard Temporini und Wolfgang Haase. Berlin, New York: Walter de Gruyter, 1980. II 31. pp. 646–705.

——, *Protestants, Catholics and Mary.* Valley Forge: Judson Press, 1968.

Brown, Peter, R. L., *The Cult of the Saints.* Chicago: University of Chicago Press, 1981.

Brown, R. E., Donfried K. P., Fitsmyer J. A., Reumann, J., (edd.), *Mary in the New Testament. A Collaborative Assessment by Protestant and Roman Catholic Scholars.* Philadelphia: Fortress, 1978.

Burghardt, Walter J., "Mary in Eastern Patristic Thought" in Juniper B. Carol, (ed.) *Mariology.* Milwaukee: The Bruce Publishing Co., 1957. Vol. 2, pp. 88–153.

——, "Mary in Eastern Patristic Thought." In Carol, *op. cit.* vol. 2 (1957) pp. 88–153.

——, "Mary in Western Patristic Thought." In Juniper B. Carol (ed.) *Mariology.* Milwaukee: Bruce, 1955, Vol. 1, pp. 109–155.

Campenhausen, H. V., *The Virgin Birth in the Theology of the Ancient Church.* Studies in Historical Theology. No. 2. London: S.C.M. Press, 1964.

Christ, Felix (ed.) *Oikonomia. Heilsgeschichte als Thema der Theologie.* Hamburg: Reich, 1967, pp. 261–272.

Congar, J., "Marie et L'Eglise Dans La Pensee Patristique." *Revue des Sciences Philosophiques et Theologiques.* 38 (1954) 3–38.

Cullmann, O., "The Origin of Christmas" in *The Early Church,* pp. 21–36. Philadelphia: Westminster, 1961.

——, *The Christology of the New Testament.* Philadelphia: Westminster, 1959.

——, *The Earliest Christian Confessions.* (English translation by J. K. S. Reid) London, 1949.

Dawe, Donald G., *The Form of a Servant. A Historical Analysis of the Kenotic Motif.* Philadelphia: Westminster, 1964.

Delius, Walter, *Geschichte der Marienverehrung.* München/Basel: Reinhardt, 1963.

Dibelius, Martin, *Der Hirt des Hermas.* Tübingen: J.C.B. Mohr (Paul Siebeck), 1923.

Eichrodt, Walter, *Theology of the Old Testament.* Philadelphia: Westminster Press, 1961.

Filson, F. V., *A New Testament History.* Philadelphia: Westminster Press, 1964.

Gibbs, John G., *Creation and Redemption. A Study in Pauline Theology.* Leiden: E. J. Brill, 1971.

Graef, Hilda, *Mary: A History of Doctrine and Devotion.* New York: Sheed and Ward, vol. 1, 1963, vol. 2, 1965.

——, *Mary, A History of Doctrine and Devotion.* Vol. 1. New York: Sheed and Ward, 1963, p. 64.

Hardy, E. R., and Richardson C. C., *Christology of the Later Fathers,* (The Library of Christian Classics, vol. III.) Philadelphia: Westminster, 1954.

Hefele, Ch. J., *A History of the Councils of the Church.* Vol. 3, English translation: Edinburgh: T. & T. Clark, 1883.

Hempel, J., "Bund" *Die Religion in Geschichte und Gegenwart.*[3] Tübingen: J.C.B. Mohr, 1957, vol. 1, pp. 1511–1515.

Holstein, S. J., R. P. H., "Marie et L'Église chez les Peres ante-niceens." in *Marie et L'église.* Études Mariales. Bulletin de la Societe Francaise D'Études Mariales. Bulletin de la Societe Francaise D'Études Mariales.

Paris: P. Lethieleux, 1951, pp. 11–25.

Hughes, Philip, *The Church in Crisis: A History of the General Councils 325–1870.* New York: Doubleday, 1961.

Jeremias, Joach, Article νύμφη νυμφίος in Kittel, *op. cit.* 4.1092–1099.

Kelly, J. N. D., *Early Christian Creeds*, London: Longmans, 1960 (second ed.)

——, *Early Christian Doctrines.* New York: Harpers, 1958.

King, N. Q., *The Emperor Theodosius and the Establishment of Christianity.* Philadelphia: Westminster, 1961.

Koch, Hugo, *Adhuc Virgo: Mariens Jungfrauschaft und Ehe in her altkirchlichen Überlieferung bis zum Ende des 4. Jahrhunderts.* Tübingen: Mohr (Siebeck), 1929.

——, *Virgo Eva — Virgo Maria: Neue Untersuchungen über die Lehre von der Jungfrauschaft und der Ehe Mariens in der ältesten Kirche.* Berlin Leipzig: Walter de Gruyter, 1937.

Laurentin, Rene, *Queen of Heaven. A Short Treatise on Marian Theology.* (English translation by Gordon Smith.) Dublin and London, 1956.

Loofs, F., *Paulus von Samosata.* Leipzig, 1924.

——, Friedrich, *Nestoriana. Die Fragmente des Nestorius.* Halle: Max Niemeyer, 1905.

Miegge, Giovanni, *The Virgin Mary.* Philadelphia: Westminster, 1955.

Newman, John Henry Cardinal, *Select Treatises of St. Athanasius in Controversy with the Arians.* Volume II. London: Longmans, Green and Co. Fifth ed. 1890.

Pernveden, Lage, *The Concept of the Church in the Shepherd of Hermas.* Lund: CWK Gleerup, 1966.

Philipps, John A., *Eve. The History of an Idea.* San Francisco: Harper and Row, 1984.

Quasten, Johannes, *Patrology.* Utrecht Antwerp: Spectrum, 1953.

Richardson, Cyril C., *Early Christian Fathers.* Philadelphia: Westminster, 1953.

Rissi, Matthias, "Die Hochzeit in Kana (John. 2.1–11)." *Oikonomia.* Heilsgeschichte als Theme der Theologie. Festschrift Oscar Cullmann. Ed. by Felix Christ. Hamburg-Bergstedt: Herbert Reich, 1967, pp. 76–92.

Stauffer, E., Article γαμέω γάμος in G. Kittel, *Theologisches Wörterbuch zum Neuen Testament.* Stuttgart: Kohlhammer, 1933, vol. 1, pp. 646–655.

Strack, H. and P. Billerback, *Kommentar zum Neuen Testament aus Talmud und Midrasch.* München: C. H. Beck, 1922 (reprinted 1956).

GENERAL INDEX

ILLUSTRATIONS

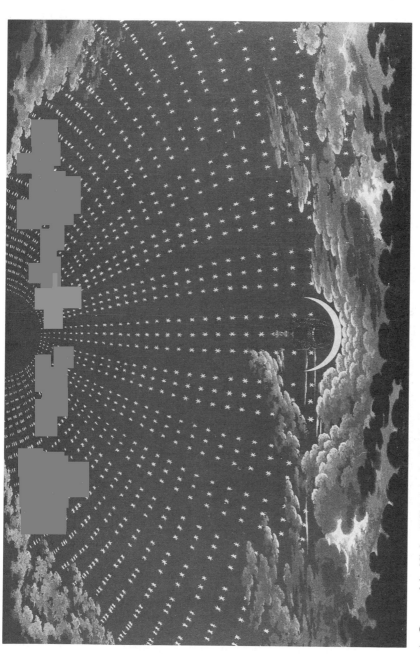

1. Queen of the Night. ("Königin der Nacht," surrounded by the starry sky as a robe. Stage design for Mozart's Zauberflöte, Berlin, 1823. Reprinted by permission of the Deutsches Theatermuseum, München.)

2. Mary "clothed with the sun with the moon under her feet." Albert Glockendon
(Nürnberg, 1545) Gebetbuch des Herzogs Wilhelm IV v. Bayern (Reprinted by
permission of the Österreichische Nationalbibliothek, Wien.)

3. Black Madonna of Czestochowa. (Reprinted by permission of the Kunst-verlag Maria Laach.)

4. Dressed statue of the Virgin with crown. Lindenholz, ca. 1150. Benediktiner Priorat, Mariazell. (Reprinted by permission of Foto Kuss, Mariazell.)

5. Cake mould from the palace of Mari (Mesopotamia) for making cakes in the form of Ishtar. (Reprinted by permission of the Réunion des musées nationaux, Paris.)

6. Stamp of a physician with the imprint YΓEIA. (Reprinted by permission of the Historisches Museum, Basel.)

7. Modern roman catholic eucharistic host with the chi-rho motiv.

8. Hungarian roman catholic church Csiksomlyo, Transsylvania: Madonna crowned with twelve stars – on her right S. Peter, left S. Paul, at her feet S. Francis and S. Dominic.